DISPLACEMENT AND REHABILITATION

DISPLACEMENT AND REHABILITATION

Solutions for the Future

Editors
Nihar Ranjan Mishra
Kamal K. Misra

Indira Gandhi Rashtriya Manav Sangrahalaya
(National Museum of Mankind)
Bhopal

GYAN PUBLISHING HOUSE

ISBN : 978-81-212-1160-4

Published by
Indira Gandhi Rashtriya Manav Sangrahalaya
Shamla Hills, Bhopal-462013 (Madhya Pradesh)
E-mail: directorigrms@gmail.com

Gyan Publishing House
23, Main Ansari Road, Daryaganj,
New Delhi - 110002
Phones : 23282060, 23261060
Fax : (011) 23285914
E-mail: books@gyanbooks.com
website: gyanbooks.com

Laser Type Setting : Rajender Vashist, Delhi
Printed at : Salasar Imaging System, Delhi

Contents

List of Tables

Preface

Displacement has become a sine qua non of modern developmental process worldwide. In the present era of globalization all most all the countries have given emphasis on industrialization which have raised lots of controversies over development-induced displacement. Forced displacement results from the need to build infrastructure for new industries, irrigation, transportation highways, power generation, and for urban development have raised major issues of social justice and equity. While these projects were considered as symbols of national progress, the irony behind it is the displacement of large number of people from their original habitats and occupations in the name of development. The livelihood of displaced communities has not been restored. In fact, the vast majority of the displaced have become impoverished and refugee in their own land. The issue of conflict between the refugee and original habitats further problematize the whole condition. It cumulates physical exclusion from a geographic territory with economic and social exclusion out of a set of functioning social networks. The uprooting of millions of people to new unknown places is a matter that is now becoming increasingly a contentious issue. Such displacement results not only in profound socio-economic and cultural disruption but also the disturbance of social fabric of local communities. Displacement also brings a great loss to women and tribal communities (adivasis) and creates a high risk of chronic impoverishment. The effect of displacement is more disastrous in the case of tribal people. They happen to be amongst the most underprivileged and vulnerable position, even after decades, they still remain outside the preview of any change.

Over the years, we have been standing at the crossroad and are looking for better solutions. To normalize, however, we may state development is indisputably needed; but should it be at the cost of others? The repeated instances of resettlement without rehabilitation have habitual defects in the current domestic policies of many countries and not just in the planning procedures. Till recently the government has not paid adequate attention to the problems of rehabilitation of the oustees. The project authorities so far considered rehabilitation problem primarily as an administrative problem and feel that their responsibility ends with payment of compensation and transfer of people from project to other location.

Again lack of accountability on the part of the state for promised entitlements has led to poor implementation of resettlement measures. However, resettlement of the affected population has been widely considered to be a failure. The trauma is more severe when displacement is attended by niggardly compensation. Hence the only factor that plays a crucial role in this kind of development process is an "effective compensation package". Due to lack of co-ordination among various stakeholders, project affected people are not getting justice. The welfare government fails to bring development, either due to its faulty strategy or due to petty politics by the opponents. This gives an opportunity for peoples' movement for which most of the development projects have not come up into existence. And in some cases it costs human lives as well.

Throwing light on unexplored and little explored aspects of displacement and rehabilitation would certainly help in formulating better policies and providing alternative livelihood opportunities to the poor and marginal communities.

In order to take a stand on current research on development, displacement and rehabilitation issues, an international conference was convened at the department of Humanities and Social Sciences, NIT Rourkela on 13 and 14 November, 2010 in collaboration with Indira Gandhi Rashtriya Manav Sangrahalaya, Bhopal; supported by Socio-economic Research division, Planning Commission, Government of India, New Delhi. The Present volume is the outcome of that conference. The volume is thematically divided into two sections that include Issues on Displacement and Livelihood and Rehabilitation Policy and Implementation Issues and People's Responses. The contributors to this volume come from different academic backgrounds and different professions. Anthropologists, sociologists, economists, political scientists, and NGOs have contributed to this volume. Therefore, we sincerely hope that it would be immensely help to the researchers, policy planners and scholars working in the field of environment, displacement and rehabilitation.

The writing of this volume was made possible by a number of institutional and individual forms of support. We wish to convey our sincere gratitude to all of them.

We are grateful to the Secretary and Director, Socio Economic Research Division, Planning Commission, Govt. of India; Prof. Sunil Kr. Sarangi, Director, NIT Rourkela; all the faculty colleagues and staff members at the Department of Humanities and Social Sciences, NIT Rourkela and IGRMS, Bhopal; Team Orissa, IPICOL, MCL and many others for their support and encouragement. A special word goes to all research scholars and students of the Department of Humanities and Social Sciences, NIT Rourkela, for their spirited cooperation. We thank Prof. Siva Prasad, Head, Department of Anthropology, University of Hyderabad, Prof. Premananda Panda, Sambalpur University, Dr. Nilakantha Panigrahi, Social Anthropologist, NCDS, Bhubaneswar, for their help and valuable feedback. We also thank the following individuals and friends for their continuous support during this journey: Sujit Mishra, Bibhuti Dash and Ajaya Pradhan, Shahida and Sharada. We thank Dhananjay Kumar and Sudhir Shrivastava for their fine work in helping to prepare this manuscript. All the contributors have also rendered timely support. We acknowledge that without the cooperation of all the people mentioned, it was indeed too difficult task to a complete this volume.

Finally, we thank our publishers IGRMS, Bhopal, and Gyan Publishing House, New Delhi, for their extended support to bring out this volume. Needless to say, any mistake or omission is exclusively ours.

Nihar Ranjan Mishra
Kamal K. Misra

1

Displacement and Rehabilitation: Some Contemporary Issues

Nihar Ranjan Mishra

In the era of globalization, the issues of development, displacement and rehabilitation vis-à-vis local communities have acquired a special significance. The post-colonial model of development adopted by most of the third world nations has no doubt brought lots of development. Development projects such as industrialization, irrigation, power, mining etc., have contributed to the economic growth and human well-being. These infrastructure projects have created employment opportunities and triggered growth in agricultural, industrial, and other allied sectors. However, these projects also paved the way for social exclusion and deprivation – they cause displacement of native population. Dube writes, "Even in India, which proudly claims to be the tenth most industrialized nation of the world, number of those living in absolute poverty has remained stationary" (1988). The development projects that most of the countries in the world witnessed after post-colonial period have led to alienation and deprivation of large sections of population through the process of displacement.

According to an estimate by the World Bank, on an average, 300 large dams get constructed every year that displace 4 million people. The urban development and transportation programmes that get framed each year in developing countries are estimated to displace an additional 6 million people (World Bank, 1994). Due to scarcity of land and high density of population, India and China together account for 74% of the people to be displaced under the current active portfolio.

The impact of dam construction on the people and the livelihood of the people below the dams have been particularly devastating in Asia, Africa and Latin America, where the existing river systems supported local economies, and the cultural lifestyle of a large population containing diverse communities has been on the receiving end. The overall global level of physical displacement could range from 40 to 80 million. According to official statistics, dams have displaced 10.2 million people in China between 1950 and 1990 (WCD Report, 2000). In Nepal, indigenous groups displaced by a dam on the Kaligandaki River have lost their land and livelihood and have reportedly been inadequately compensated. The livelihood of an estimated 35,000 indigenous Ibaloi people is threatened by the construction of the San Roque Dam in the Philippines. Mon, Karen and Tavoyans in Burma are probably among the worst off, displaced by large infrastructure projects and subjected to forced labour and abuses by the military.

In the contemporary days, the magnitude and frequency of development-related displacements have brought about involuntary resettlement as a problem of worldwide relevance (Cernea, 1993), because involuntary resettlement is a consequence of planned change generated by major development projects or programmes (Cernea, 1996). Presently, the involuntary displacements caused by development programs have created major impositions on large population segments. They restrict that population's rights by state-power intervention and are often carried out in ways that cause the affected populations to end up worse off (Cernea and Mathur, 2008). Corporate interests backed by state governments are trampling on indigenous livelihoods and threatening ecological reach areas (Sahu, 2008). Impoverishment begins with landlessness, joblessness and ends with lower access to work. Most of the PAPs come from the backward areas and for these reasons, their access to education becomes very low, and declines further after displacement as child labour grows among them because of "new poverty" resulting from loss of land and forests that are their sustenance. Children suffer more than adults mainly because the mother is unable to attend to her duties as the caretaker of the family. When the project alienates the land which serves as the foundation of the tribal woman's relatively high status, it declines the status of women more than that of man (Fernandes, 2007). In India, the record of rehabilitation of victims due to varieties of development projects has drawn the attention of the activists, researchers and human rights institutes. The problems that arise from the displacement and forced relocation of people due to various reasons have increasingly come to receive the attention of journalists, jurists, planners, social activists, and other concerned individuals during the last few years (Mankodi, 1989).

Studies conducted by Walter Fernandes and others revealed that between 1947 and 2000, around 47,64,000 acres of land has been acquired because of these so-called development projects and 70 lakh persons have been displaced in India (2007). The displacement of people generally gives rise to severe economic, social and environmental problems; production systems are dismantled; productive assets and income sources are lost; people are relocated to environments where their productive skills may be less applicable and the competition for resources is high; kin groups are dispersed; and cultural identity, traditional authority and the potential for mutual help are diminished (World Bank, 1990).

Singh (1982) has discussed the impact of the Patratu Project in terms of the disintegration of traditional culture, rehabilitation of uprooted villagers and new trends in the emergence of the industrial society. Rapid development of open cast coal mining in the North Karanpura Valley in Hazaribagh and Chatra Districts of Jharkhand, in India is destroying the livelihood source of Adivasis. The region has extremely fertile land which is now being converted into a mining site, taking away vital farming land and forests, and polluting the Damodar River, which is the lifeline of the area (Indigenous Portal, 2009). With the increasing pressures on land due to urbanization, rapid economic development, increasing infrastructure requirements, etc., especially in a fast growing economy like India, the acquisition of land by the Government has increased. The Indian Government, under the doctrine of "Eminent Domain" for "Greater Good" and "development" purposes has acquired massive lands of villagers. As a result of this millions of people have been displaced and have lost their habitat as well as productive assets. For example, most of the development projects in Orissa have brought adverse effects in the form of displacement of people from their traditional homeland and way of life, denying them their basic rights of livelihood (Velath, 2009).

Displacement triggered by violence and conflict is not only a humanitarian crisis; it is also likely to affect political stability if left unattended, or inappropriately/poorly governed, or unresolved politically through peace-building. Particularly in fragile and conflict-affected countries, the presence of displaced persons adds a serious strain on very weak national and local institutions, as well as potentially causing or exacerbating strained relations between the displaced and the host community. Highlighting the pain of refugees due to displacement, Alvares and Billorey (1987) have pointed out that the distribution of a part of the village pasture as land compensation to those displaced by the Sardar-Sarovar Project led to a clash between the ousters and the local population. The studies of Barnbas (1985) and Singh (1988) have mentioned the absence of any provision for alternative land or jobs to those who are cultivating forest areas and agricultural lands without legal titles. Such cultivating families are not entitled for compensation and thus left to agonizing misery. Viegas and Menon (1985), and Rao (1986) have also cited instances of displaced persons left without rehabilitation under various projects in Bihar, West Bengal, Orissa and Madhya Pradesh. Sharma (1986) has pointed out that due to lack of appropriate rehabilitation measures, the persons displaced by major dams in India are unable to meet their requirements. That raises doubts about the sincerity of the promise of rehabilitation made by the State. Even if the promise of rehabilitation is kept, skewed land laws will ensure that its benefits do not reach many DPs/PAPs. Where there was no agitation or World Bank pressure, rehabilitation is weak. It is ironical that we celebrate our independence every August 15, but the World Bank has to tell us to rehabilitate our citizens deprived of their livelihood in the name of national development! (Fernandes, 2007).

Every state is acquiring land in order to encourage corporate investment but fails to face the issues of people's impoverishment, food security and the right to a life with dignity. Appeasing multinational companies and acquiring private profit seems to have become the sole criterion. No doubt, economic growth is required, but not by impoverishing people. That is what is happening because most PAPs who lack the skills required for industrial jobs and other benefits are impoverished to the benefit of another class (*ibid.*). If anybody raises the question against the Governments' monopoly decision becomes a victim of the police force.

Studies by Alvares and Billorey (1988) have mentioned cases of inadequate compensation, disparities in fixation of compensation, scandals in payment, especially to tribals, and many instances of exploitation by land owners, money lenders and lawyers. The consequences of displacement are particularly dire for the tribal people, as they are deeply attached to their ancestral lands and find it virtually impossible to readjust in resettlement colonies, which is planned with no regard to the their culture and emotions (Somayaji, 2008). In most of the projects, jobs go to the outsiders because those who lose their livelihood lack the skills required for the jobs. Very few industries make efforts to provide training to those affected communities so that they can be rehabilitated later; and the few who have taken such initiation are have mostly done so under pressure or agitations by activists.

The study group of CSD in 1999 found that there is no evidence of consultation through Gram Sabha by the State related to land acquisition and R&R package. The local administration in the region in league with the company does not seem to have any respect for and commitment towards the rule of law, which it is supposed to uphold (Bandopadhya, 2004; Sahoo, 2005). In most of the cases, the violation of provisions of the Panchayats Extension to the Scheduled Areas (PESA) Act, 1996, is observed. The trauma is greater when displacement is attended by lack of information, uncertainty, long waiting, very little compensation, social dislocation and the cultural shock that accompanies any diaspora when cohesive rural, especially tribal, communities are scattered and resettled away from their kinship and linguistic group (Varghese, 1990). The ousted, being the "victims" of development, through the loss of their livelihood and sustenance economy, are forced to depend on the market economy for survival. Their entry into direct market relations, without the necessary capital or skills, places them at a disadvantage from the very beginning. Displacement, thus usually leads to their pauperization and increased marginalization (Singh, 1997).

The displaced people have thus been pushed to lower levels of economic status compared to their predisplacement situation (Mishra, 2002; Ota, 1996). Historically all projects have caused displacement and it has been a saga of marginalization, yet, given the growing needs of modern society, all projects cannot be stopped. What is required is to consider the larger implications of displacement while assessing the viability, social, environment and economic values of a project as a pre-emptive measure to tackle the problems. Though cost-benefit analysis is also undertaken presently, the credibility of the methods adopted is questionable as the authorities fail to evaluate the social and environmental costs. In spite of the tremendous amount of benefits generated by such projects, the rural people residing in the vicinity of dams have experienced very little economic gains (Reddy, 1989). The greatest sufferers are the villagers displaced by construction of the reservoirs (Paranjpye, 1987). The social costs of these displacements are often underestimated and paid least attention. In many projects, benefits are inflated and social costs are deflated in order to justify the viability. Proper Resettlement and Rehabilitation (R&R) of these Project-Affected People (PAP) has been a grossly neglected aspect so far in almost all countries including India. Often, rehabilitation aspects of these projects receive little attention in the mass media while the project construction and benefits, which are inflated and untrue, receive the limelight.

It is observed in almost all developing projects that the needs of the local populations and their problems were never considered in designing and implementing such projects. In other words, ideally speaking, these programmes had different target groups which did not favour the Scheduled Tribes and Other Backward Communities of the locality (Patnaik, 1996). The development planners, national and local politicians, and bureaucrats have no worries about the price the uprooted natives are paying for the so-called development (Mehta, 2002). Giving a justification to their work, they argue that individuals can be sacrificed in the larger interests of the nation. It is again argued that the material gain would outweigh the overall loss of the concerned people.

Development cannot be used as an argument to disguise discrimination or any other human rights violation. In the words of Mahapatra (1991), there is a crying need for world assistance to the displaced persons for their proper rehabilitation and adequate compensation for the "social cost" and "human cost" involved. Over the years, many policies in relation to R&R aspects are being formulated and various models are developed by prominent academicians globally. However, the repeated instances of resettlement without rehabilitation have habitual defects in the current domestic policies of many countries and not just in the planning procedures. Again, lack of accountability on the part of the State for promised entitlements has led to poor implementation of resettlement measures. However, resettlement of the affected population has been widely considered to be a failure. The trauma is more severe when displacement is attended by niggardly compensation. Hence, the only factor that plays a crucial role in this kind of development process is an "effective humanitarian compensation package".

Due to lack of co-ordination among various stakeholders, the PAP are not getting justice. Over the years, people have started visualizing the development projects of the Government with suspicion. This leads to resentment, which in turn leads to resistance. The welfare Government fails to bring development, either due to its faulty strategy or due to petty politics by the opponents. This gives opportunity for people's movement for which most of the development projects have not been realized.

However, the issue of displacement and rehabilitation has remained unsolved over the century. It is no more confined to any boundary. Lots of questions have arisen in the minds of different individuals working in this area. How are the above described trends changing rehabilitation management practices? The fact, however, is that the issue of involuntary resettlement has never received the attention it deserves. If displacements are inevitable, they must be carried out in a way that would not only protect but also improve the livelihood of the displaced people. How can the livelihoods of the displaced be reconstructed and be prevented from impoverishment? How can we ensure justice to all PAP irrespective of ethnicity, landholding and gender with adequate compensation? What roles have international and multilateral institutions / companies played in influencing the direction and content of R&R policies and reform processes? What should be the role of various civil societies and corporate sectors? Can the technological institutes or the Department of Science and Technology help those displaced people in finding an alternative livelihood through certain training and easy software in recording the data process? How can we protect the tribal rights and provide justice to them? How can we develop a meaningful rehabilitation policy and implementation procedure so that, there would be "less" to lament and "more" to rejoice in the progressive nature of human development? With all these questions in mind, academicians, NGO personals and Government officials have tried to have a fresh look at this issue and to find a better solution to the above mentioned problems. This volume is a modest attempt in this direction.

The contributors to this volume come from different academic backgrounds and different professions. Anthropologists, sociologists, economists, political scientists, law and reprehensive from administration, and NGOs have contributed to this volume. The contributors have seen the whole issue from the prism of their own discipline, which is an added advantage as the phenomena of displacement, is seen from every possible angle to explore and bring in the voices of the victims as well as issues for advocacy for further developmental activities. The following account is a brief of the contributions.

The volume is thematically divided into two sections that include Issues on Displacement and Livelihood and Rehabilitation Policy and Implementation Issues and People's Responses. Section 1 consists of 12 chapters (2-13) and largely deals with the socio-economic consequences of displacement and emerging issues on rehabilitation and sustainable livelihoods.

In chapter 2 of this volume, Ratikanta has tried to elaborate some macro and micro scenarios of displacement and rehabilitation issues in Orissa. According to him, the rise in the number of developmental projects not only creates a fear in the minds of people, rather in the absence of a sustainable R&R policy, but also turns the displaced and unemployed people into refugees and urban proletariats. This may give birth to lumpenisation throughout the country. The state's favouritism towards industrialists and capitalists gave birth to people's movements and a great loss for the marginal communities. The introduction of Export Promotion Zone (EPZ) or the Special Economic Zone (SEZ) has no doubt contributed to the state's economic growth and employment, but the state has also incurred a huge social cost by directly displacing people and by destroying the common property resources on which people were directly relying upon for their livelihood. Showing his concern towards marginal communities, Ratikanta claims that the political economy aspects of displacement have shown that the SCs/STs have been the most affected victims of displacement as most of the projects undertaken are found largely in SC/ST populated areas. Further, as the development projects destroyed forests (the major and perhaps the only source of livelihood for the poor and the tribals); the ultimate burden of displacement threatened the food security and has pushed these disadvantaged groups into hunger and deprivation.

There was no proper Rehabilitation and Resettlement Policy for the displaced people of the state until a revised R&R Policy was introduced during 1994. The new R&R Policy has some effects in ensuring some amount of compensation for the displaced people; however, it has failed to provide a sustainable compensation for the displaced people and hence, has added to the existing hunger and deprivation in the state.

Reflecting on economic degeneration as a by-product of the process of development, Narendra Kumar Behera, in Chapter 3, has tried to highlight the cases from Orissa. All the mega projects implemented in Orissa have left an imprint of untold misery upon a section of population through displacement which has resulted in loss of land, home, livelihood, and many more for the affected people of the region. The concept of inclusive growth is of little importance for these displaced people who have sacrificed a lot for the cause of the country's economic development. The violation of human rights by the corporate bodies in connivance with the political parties in power is rising. In addition to this, there is large-scale depletion and degradation of natural resources and environment of the project areas, which appears to be irreparable. Putting his reservation over the land allocation, he has argued that the private corporate units should allot share or lease the require land rather than acquiring the land and making poor villagers landless and marginalized in the face of development.

Displacement caused by development projects leads to serious economic, social and cultural disruption of the lives of those affected in the process. People who are historically marginalized get even more marginalized due to such projects. In this context, Panda in his paper in chapter 4 has described the impact of mining and development projects in backward states. He argued that the mining industries have contributed the most towards altering the physical geography that hitherto remained as the major sources of livelihood of the people at the grassroots. In the process of displacement, the state assumes the status of acquiring body in favour of the requiring bodies. The result is protest by the losers against the forces applied by the acquiring bodies that offer the compensation and rehabilitation package to the displaced. With the onset of macroeconomic reforms in 1990s, state-led development seems to have been negotiated with outside agencies at the cost of the natives. While technology-based export-oriented economy is flourishing, dwarfing agricultural economy as a result, the peasants associated with land and forest remain preoccupied with daily struggle to ensure their livelihood. He suggested that any form of development has to be viewed through an integral approach where income, growth and distribution are integral to the process of development from the people's perspective.

However, in the case of involuntary resettlement the people's voice is ignored. Involuntary resettlement under development projects, if unmitigated, often germinates into severe economic, social and environmental risks: productive systems are dismantled; people face impoverishment when their productive assets or income sources are lost; people are relocated to environments where their productive skills may be less applicable and the competition for resources may be more; community institutions and social networks are weakened; kin groups are dispersed; and cultural identity, traditional authority, and the potential for mutual help are either diminished or lost. Linking the above aspects, Tripathy has tried to reflect on mining and displacement problems in Orissa in Chapter 5. The tribes evicted by the industrial houses had been pushed to starvation in Koraput District and other parts of the state. Certain groups—especially indigenous people, the elderly and women—have been found to be more vulnerable to displacement-induced impoverishment risks.

Reflecting on the agony of displacement in Jammu and Kashmir due to violent armed conflicts on Children, Falendra Kumar Sudan in Chapter 6 has said that it inevitably takes its toll on children's education and increases the pressures on the young children to work, possibly at the expense of their schooling; it also leads to under-nourishment and malnutrition, which results in poor physical growth, inability to learn and poor work performance. Numerous distressed marriages took place to save the young girl children from sexual abuse and exploitation from the members of their own community as well as the host community; a large number of them left their studies mid-way. Most of the displaced persons are suffering from psychological disorders. The 'care and maintenance' assistance and aid received by displaced non-Kashmiri migrant families were completely undependable, erratic and inadequate. The displaced non-Kashmiri children have special vulnerabilities.

In another case study of Development-Induced Displacement in Moolampilly of Kerala, Swamy in Chapter 7 has discussed the dilemma of development-induced displacement. He has made an attempt to view the development context from the position of poor people, who actually bear the cost of development and also touch ahead its legal and social ramifications.

From the Moolampilly experience, he states that the colonial model with its anti-people character will not bring any success to a project. The major conflict starts with the conflict over interests of various stakeholders. Any understanding on land acquisition should start with an inquiry – who is the stakeholder in the development and what their interests are. Here, while one stakeholder, the state, is supporting to the other stakeholder that is the construction company, the primary stakeholders, the villagers, are victimized. There were violations of human rights by both revenue and police officials on account of which the residents including ladies and children suffered. The said eviction process was carried out by violating all the directions of the Court and the Government has not given any rehabilitation facilities to the evictees. The provisions of the National Rehabilitation and Resettlement Scheme were not formulated and no package scheme was published apart from a statement by the District Collector in the newspapers.

Reflecting on the impact of displacement on forest and other resources and the impact of rehabilitation programs on livelihoods of the Chenchus, Venkata Sivaiah in Chapter 8 has claimed that the Chenchus who were traditionally hunting and food-gathering nomadic groups have now turned to different activities such as migration labour and agricultural wage labour. The Chenchus are struggling to survive, and choose the available alternative options which are suitable to their perception. The introduction of agriculture brought many changes in the division of labour between men and women. The women feel that their work load has increased to the extent that it has become burden for them. The intervention of outsiders stands as a major threat to forest resources on which the Chenchus are dependent; and private contractors are taking advantage of the ignorance of the Chenchu tribe to lure them towards migrational works and exploit their labour.

Taking Mandira Dam Project in the Sundargarh District of Orissa into consideration Kar and Jena in Chapter 9 analyzed the issue of tribal marginalization in the context of development-induced displacement, throwing light on the effectiveness of the R&R measures in facilitating the process of mainstreaming the affected tribal communities. Displacement has not only forced them out of their age-old habitat, and livelihood system, but has also posed a threat to their distinct culture and identity. Instead of bringing them to the mainstream, the very process of development has resulted in further marginalization of the tribals. The poor tribals were displaced from their villages without adequate information, and were made to sacrifice all their resources. The resettlement and rehabilitation of the affected tribal communities of the Mandira Dam Project, has been piecemeal in approach, haphazard, and grossly ineffective. There were many loopholes, which have made the process more time taking and stressful for the poor tribals. The rehabilitation measures have been taken as only one-time phenomenon, without any further investigation into its effectiveness.

The social inequalities that arise due to displacement pose a different set of problems for rehabilitation. They involve injustice to the tribal community and total violation of their constitutional rights. In Chapter 10, Biswas and Banerjee attempted to highlight the pain of some primitive tribals due to displacement in Andaman Islands.

The aborigines of these islands set the unique example of original culture of human pre-civilization. But the Great Andamanese, the Jarawas, and the Onges have failed to sustain their Palaeolithic cultural heritage like the hostile aborigines, i.e. the Sentinels of these Islands. The new resettlement policy of the authorities has forced them to modify their primitive culture and tradition. The rehabilitation programme that was operationalised has shown adverse effects on the socio-economic conditions of the tribes as well as on their ecology. A serious lapse was seen on the part of the administration under the pressure of resettlement of Bengali refugees in Andaman Islands – no attention was given to these unfortunate tribes. Moreover, the rehabilitation of Bengali families was carried out in the heart areas of the Jarawa territories. Their movements were thus restricted. The on-going development activities, sudden exposure to the outsiders, import of alien economy and technology, and continuous depopulation, along with disordered socio-cultural conditions, are considered to be the factors which account for the present pattern of social organization of these tribal communities. The size, structure and marital status of the respective tribal families have thus been affected. Women feel helpless and they are often exploited, physically and mentally, by the unscrupulous outsiders. Financial misery has forced the women of the Great Andamanese tribal society to have sexual relations with outsiders which resulted in various diseases. The once socially coherent and unified tribal people are now suffering from distrust and disintegration in their family as well as in their society.

In Chapter 11 of this volume, Aparajita has tried to explore the impact of establishment of various private industries on the livelihoods and culture of the Ho tribe in Kalinganagar Industrial Complex (KNIC), in Jajapur District, Orissa. In her entire description, she has given much importance towards tribal culture and community participation in the R&R process. She has highlighted the plight of the displaced living in transit camps and temporary arrangements. The community is in a limbo state as neither it is part of their original settlement nor has been shifted to a permanent rehabilitation colony. While planning and executing rehabilitation and resettlement programmes, officials have ignored the socio-economic, cultural and livelihood aspects of the displaced. The programmes, before implementation, should ensure the participation of the displaced people and their concerns. The author has strongly criticized the role of Government in the entire R&R process.

In Chapter 12, Saswat Kishore tests the hypothesis that displacement and subsequent resettlement of people at the Tata Steel Parivar Colony in Jajapur District of Orissa (a resettlement colony) due to TISCO Project has brought structural changes in their consumption expenditure pattern. He has used a two variable linear regression model to test the significance of the relationship between pre-settlement and post-settlement monthly household income and expenditure. The model was also used to analyze and find out to what degree the compensation amount predicted the total expenses on building of house in the resettlement colony. It was found that structural changes occurred in the post-resettlement period as a result of increase in the marginal propensity to consume.

The problem of displacement seems to be a contagious disease of the modern State, which many a time, affects the social, economic and political fabric of a state. The welfare commitments of the state for the displaced for a long time have been ignored and to a greater extent shifted to corporate sectors during last couple of years. These are compared with the time bound special packages as interpreted by the state and corporate agencies from time to time. The Governments' favouritism has lost people's faith. Nilakantha recounts these issues in case of Orissa in Chapter 13. He has given an overview of the R&R policies so far implemented by different stakeholders in the State of Orissa and provides a comparative assessment of the State and National R&R policies of the day. He has added the plight of villagers displaced due to NALCO project in Angul. Criticizing the R&R Act 2006 of Orissa, he stated that it is inadequate to safeguard the economic, cultural and social interests and identities of the displaced. This has strongly affected the mindset of the potential displaced. This calls for a revival of the relationship between the people and the State from a contractual type to a symbiotic type.

The second section of this volume consists of 9 chapters, which mainly reflect on various policies of R&R and people's responses towards these policies and implementation procedures. The geographical spread of the chapters is from Arunachal Pradesh and Arunachal Pradesh in the North East to Andhra Pradesh in South, and includes Uttar Pradesh, Orissa and Madhya Pradesh.

State-led acquisition of agricultural land for setting up new industries or extending the existing industries is an emerging issue in the contemporary period. Throughout the globe this issue has kept the State in cross roads. In most of the areas, the State's apathy towards the corporate in the name of development has stirred up lots of violence, as seen in case of Singur in West Bengal, POSCO in Orissa and Jamuna Corridor in UP. Reflecting on these aspects, Majumder in Chapter 14 has described the role of the State in the entire process of industrialization and displacement. He has drawn some of the examples from the states of UP and Orissa in India. Criticizing the entire process of displacement and rehabilitation, he claimed that in all most all cases there is violation of human rights. The State has ignored the people's voice. The process displaces people from the land that has sustained their livelihood without taking the 'prior informed consent' of the displaced.

The Land Acquisition (Amendment) Bill, 2007 is nothing but a further amendment of the Land Acquisition Act, 1894. It has never given any scope to people's rights. According to the act, land can be acquired for public purpose, and the State has an upper hand in this regard. The State is strengthened internally by imposition of laws. It formulates for non-or-restricted access of the original settlers to forests and on land that is the initial insiders to the resources. The State is strengthened in the name of protection of forests and land. The tribals and dalits who protected these resources since time immemorial, not backed by any state laws but as a natural practice in life because it was not only considered to be their life-support system but also their deity, are now evicted. By State reservation and acquisition of land, collective social ownership-cum-use is surrendered – what gets supreme is State authority.

In present days, people's movement has stood as a major threat in any kind of development project. Mishra *et al.* in Chapter 15 reflected in detail the causes of agitation against the proposed Ultra Mega Power Plant in Sundargarh District of Orissa. They emphasized that consensual decision between the planners and the affected people regarding adequate and just compensation is the only remedy to any kind of resettlement plan. The term 'public purpose' that figured in the Land Acquisition Act (LAA) 1894 is not defined properly. In fact, the absence of an explicit and proper guideline, which defines the term 'public purpose', makes the application of the whole act an arbitrary one. Taking the history of displacement into account, they claim that mere passing of laws does not help the people directly in distress situations. Hence, in this context, a system has to be created where both the parties, i.e., the project authorities and the affected get to decide the different components of adequate compensation. Emphasizing on total process, they said that it will be achieved through a process of sensitizing the people regarding the real cost and benefits of the project in a slow and steady process.

Paradoxically, the ongoing process of development in Orissa has not only deepened but also widened deprivation and caused large-scale displacement. Sahu in Chapter 16 has criticized the entire development process from the human rights perspective. The large-scale development projects are basically designed to enhance the power of the state and private capital; but they are incapable of representing or serving the interests of the vast majority of the people. This centralization has a bias in favour of large landholders, rich farmers, engineers, bureaucrats, and politicians. He emphasized that what needs to be addressed today is the right to development, in which all their fundamental rights and freedom are realised. In conclusion, it is said that though infrastructure development is necessary, it has to be implemented with a human face so that the effect of displacement is minimized and the goal of inclusive development is achieved.

While on one side we are looking for preservation of human rights, on the other hand, the introduction of various development approaches are throwing people in crossroads. In order to enhance the industrial production and growth, the concept of Special Economic Zones (SEZs) is being introduced throughout India. The corporate owners and business tycoons have been supporting the concept and the policy and currently it is considered a panacea for development by enhanced exports. However, it became synonymous with protests by the farmers, social activists, environmentalists, and some intellectuals too. In the light of above aspect, Vinita Pandey has discussed the emerging issues in the context of SEZs in Chapter 17. The increasing role of the state as the promoter of corporate-led economic growth is underlined by the acquisition of land for SEZs and the transfer of ownership of land to "developers". Here the State is withdrawing its role as welfare state. Displacement thus gets pushed to a private arena with compensation potentially negotiated by the market and without the state's responsibility for rehabilitation. The author is not anti-SEZs, and opines that SEZs definitely have a positive role to play in enhancing exports, investments, creating employment, and economic growth. But the author is much concerned about the entire process of SEZs in India that has become synonymous with displacement of people and livelihoods with severe socio-economic, environmental, psychological and cultural impacts.

A comprehensive policy framework is inevitable if impoverishment risks have to be avoided in the case of displacement. The role of various agents like the state and NGOs should be very clear in all stages. When interactions among the three important agents — the state, the civil society, and the community — are insignificant, judicial activism tries to fill the vacuum. In absence of help from state as well as the NGOs, the excluded community copes with the emerging situation. In Chapter 18, D.C. Sah has tried to raise a debate over the issue of Sardar Sarovar Project. The super-interaction between State and the civil society post-1987 undermined the existence of PAPs. This has led to the exclusion of the community in the rehabilitation process. In the absence of help from State as well as the NGOs, the excluded community is forced to initiate its own coping mechanisms. Claiming the existing policy as inappropriate, the randomness of relocation and absence of the traditional arrangements at the new sites could make the oustees vulnerable to exploitation.

All present 'development' seems hell-bent on impoverishing people and strengthening the hands of the rich sections of the society. Forced displacement is not just confined to rural or tribal areas. In the present era of globalization, it has become a major issue in urban areas too. Forced displacements have remained to date as relatively silent companions of urban growth. Yet the frequency and magnitude of compulsory displacement are likely to increase in the developing world as the trend towards urbanization grows stronger. Rooted in this topicality, Nanda Kishore describes the displacement effects of a mega project, an international airport that is located on the periphery of Hyderabad, Andhra Pradesh, in Chapter 19. The government's anti-people attitude was reflected in the process of displacement. A short notice of 15 days to vacate the area petrified the people and they were unable to decide if they were to move or stay back and protest. The politics of divide and rule principle gave an upper hand to the Government. The politics of caste and political affiliation stood as a hurdle in uniting the PAPs to fight for their cause. The amount of compensation was very low. The vulnerability level at the resettlement colony is the worst part of the whole process. The people were staying in huts without even a proper roof. The decline of status from land owners to wage labourer brought a great loss and points at the lacunae existing in the project formulation. The gamut of unethical development contrasts the very component of inclusive development and egalitarian principles, and this case stands as one such towering example.

In recent years, coal mining and displacement of marginal communities have become a serious issue in the State of Orissa. Taking this issue into account, Kabita Kumari has reflected on the extent of justice given to the displaced communities in coal mining areas in Talcher, Orissa, in Chapter 20. Mining in Talcher area has resulted in large-scale displacement of the people. The entire rehabilitation process is an injustice to the marginal communities. Even the married sons who are having separate family are not given compensation. Women are highly victimized in terms of loss of their traditional forest-based livelihoods. Rehabilitation programmes taken up so far have been entirely insensitive to gender concerns in terms of providing land, housing, jobs or cash. Rehabilitation colonies provide no space for women for basic needs like privacy, toilets, washing, domestic, health, recreation or educational facilities. She has highlighted the infiltration of migrant labourers and non-tribal populations into Adivasi regions and their roles in placing women in more vulnerable situations.

Displacement, rehabilitation and refugees are emerging issues throughout the globe. In the context of India, most of the border states are suffering from the issue of refugees. India is the largest nation experiencing refugeehood. It has been hosting refugees for a long time. Chunnu Prasad in Chapter 21 provides the case of Chakma refugees and their settlement in Arunachal Pradesh. It is believed that the Chakmas migrated from the Champa Kingdom in Cambodia and the Lushai's called them Tui-Chek, which means the people who lived near water. The author has given a brief history of the Chakmas' movement to remain in India and the historical injustice towards them.There was no discrimination towards the Chakmas when Arunachal Pradesh was a Union Territory. The problem started after it was made a full-fledged State. The political appeasement towards other communities encouraged the State Government to withdraw all facilities given to the Chakmas. It resulted in hunger among the community. All the schools were closed in their regions. Their students were not allowed to take admission into any school. Their ration cards were withdrawn. This was not only a crime against the helpless Chakmas but also a crime against humanity. They were denied the citizenship and nationality though they fall within the ambit of the citizenship rights acts of the Constitution of India. The lack of legal mechanisms and policies on refugees is one of the fundamental flaws of refugee protection in India. The Chakma problem is nothing but a political and policy problem in Arunachal Pradesh in particular and the North-East in general.

In the twenty first century, the entire globe has given emphasis on inclusive growth. But in reality, this issue has become more and more complex. Today the marginal communities that were historically excluded are facing more complex problems emanating from various issues like globalization, apathy of state apparatus, inactive civil society and lastly, faulty policy formulation which has created bottlenecks to achieve inclusive development. Rudra Prasad in Chapter 22 has discussed this issue taking the case of UP. Throughout his discussion, he questions the very structure of the development policy. He argues that the popular paradigm of development has created a madness which is coterminous with the discourse of development of rationality with advancement of science and technology, irrespective of cultural, social and political ideologies of the nations. The so-called growth led development policy adopted by the government not only brings misery to the life of the tribal communities but also has handicaps them. Their aspiration to lead a life goes unnoticed. They are not only physically excluded from their land but also denied to live like human beings.

References

Alvares, C. and R. Billorey (1987) The Deemed, *The Illustrated Weekly of India*, *I*, November 8:17.

Alvares, C. and R. Billorey (1988) *Damming the Narmada*, Penang: Third World Network/APPEN.

Bandopadhya, D. (2004) Rayagada Story Retold: Destitute of Development, *Economic and Political Weakly*, 39 (5):408-411.

Barnabas, A.P. (1985) Development Policies and Human Deprivation, *Indian Journal of Public Administration*, 31(4):1269-77.

Cernea, M.M. (1993) *Socio-Economic and Cultural Approaches to Involuntary Resettlement*, Reprint Series No. 486, Washington DC: The World Bank.

Cernea, M.M. (1996) Public Policy Responses to Development-Induced Population Displacements, *Economic and Political Weekly*, 31(24):1515-1523.

Cernea, M.M. and H.M. Mathur, (ed.) (2008) *Can Compensation Prevent Impoverishment? Reforming Resettlement through Investments and Benefit-Sharing*, New Delhi: Oxford University Press.

Dube, S.C. (1988) *Modernization and Development: The Search for Alternative Paradigm*, New Delhi: Vistar Publications.

Fernandes, Walter (2007) Singur and Displacement Scenario, *Economic and Political Weekly*, 42(3): 203-206.

Indigenous Portal (2009) India: Open-cast Coal Mining Destroys the Livelihood of Indigenous People in Jharkhand, Wednesday, 11, November.

Mahapatra, L.K. (1991) Development for Whom? Depriving the Dispossessed Tribals, *Social Action*, 41 (3):271-288.

Mankodi, K. (1989) Displacement and Relocation: Problems and Prospects in Development, In W. Fernandes and E.G. Thukral (ed.) *Displacement and Rehabilitation*, New Delhi: ISI.

Mehta, S. (2002) Derailed Development: Review of Development and Rehabilitation Models for Tribal India, *Anthropologist, Special Issue No. 1*: 213-226.

Mishra, S.K. (2005) Impact of Rehabilitation Policy and Low Crop Yield: Rengali Dam in Orissa, *Economic and Political Weekly*, 40 (26): 2688-2691.

Ota, A.B. (1996) Counting the Impoverishment Risks: The Case of Rengali Dam Project, In A.B.Ota and A. Agnihotri (ed.) *Involuntary Displacement in Dam Projects*, New Delhi: Prachi Prakasan.

Paranjpye, V. (1987) Dams and Their Dangers, *Seminar*, 33 (3):40-43.

Patnaik, S.M. (1996) *Displacement Rehabilitation and Social Change*, Tribal Studies of India Series, New Delhi: Inter India Publications.

Rao, N. (1986) Driven to Starvation: Thousands Rendered Destitute by Dam Project, *The Week*, 4 (36): 36-37.

Reddy, I.U.B. (1989) Cost of River Valley Projects in India, *Indian Journal of Public Administration*, 35(3).

Sahoo, S. (2005) Tribal Displacement and Human Rights Violations in Orissa, *Social Action: A Quarterly Review of Social Trends*, 55(2): 153-166.

Sahu, G. (2008) Mining in the Niyamgiri Hills and Tribal Rights, *Economic and Political Weekly*, 43(15):19-21.

Sharma, N.K. (1986) Large Dams: A Necessary Developmental Choice, *Bhagirathi*, 33(2): 55-65.

Singh, K. (1988) Narmada Issue: An Overview, *Mainstream*, 26 (23):19-22.

Singh, N. (1982) Studies on Urban and Industrial Centres in Bihar, In A.K. Haldar and L.P. Vidyarthi and V.S. Upadhyay (ed.), *Development of Researches in Anthropology in India*, New Delhi: Concept Publishing Company.

Singh S. (1997) *Taming the Waters: The Political Economy of Large Dams in India*, New Delhi: Oxford University Press.

Somayaji, S. (2008) Man-made Disasters: Displacement, Resettlement and Rehabilitation in Orissa — Reflections from the Field, *Social Change, 38(4): 689-704.*

Varghese, B.G. (1990) *Waters of Hope*, New Delhi: Oxford & IBH Publishing Co.

Velath, P.M. (2009) Development and Displacement: Rights-based Theoretical Analysis, In Renu Modi (ed.), *Beyond Relocation: The Imperative of Sustainable Resettlement*, New Delhi: Sage Publication.

Viegas, P. and G. Menon (1985) The Social Costs of Deforestation, *Social Action*, 35(4): 326-350.

World Bank (1990) *Involuntary Resettlement*, Operational Directive 4.30, Washington, DC: The World Bank.

World Bank (1994) *Resettlement and Rehabilitation in India*, Vols. 1 and 2, Washington DC: The World Bank.

World Commission on Dams (2000) *Dams and Development — The Report of the World Commission on Dams*, London and Sterling, VA: Earthscan Publications Limited.

Section I: Issues on Displacement and Livelihood

2

Structural Inequality and Displacement: The Multiple Burdens among the SCs/STs of Orissa*

R.K. Kumbhar

Introduction

Land is the only source of livelihood in most agrarian economies. Given the structural specificity of Orissa, the SCs/STs who mostly live in the forest areas depend to a large extent on land and forest for their livelihood. For the poorer sections, including the SCs/STs, land is more than a livelihood as it serves the purpose of collateral, fallback resources, and economic and social power to claim citizen rights in various circumstances. But in a neoliberal strategy, in the name of development, industrialisation and modernisation, these lands have been taken away by the profit-seeker capitalist, and the forests were destroyed to extract iron ore for business. In this process, the State also works like an agent to collect the land to handover to the capitalist. In the process, the poor, mainly the SCs/STs, among whom the incidence of hunger and deprivation is already high, have suffered the most, due to loss of habitat and source of livelihood, compared to others who do not depend directly on forest for their livelihood.

Although this is a common phenomenon in many states in India, the forced displacement makes the situation worse in Orissa, since it already faces high incidence of hunger and deprivation. Displacement not only affects the current agrarian situation by reducing output and increasing unemployment, but also reduces the potential capacity of future industrial

*The paper is part of my Ph.D. thesis. I am thankful to my supervisors Prof. K.P. Kannan and Dr. P.K. Panda.

growth in the state as the raw materials, which can help industrialisation, are being drained away. So far, there are not many instances in Orissa that the already settled mine companies might have established manufacturing firms with vertical integration. Rather, the main motive of these companies is limited to extraction of iron ore or coal, which is then drained to other countries to develop the manufacturing sector like tractors, automobiles, and so on. In the absence of such vertical integration, the state becomes the victim, and the displaced unemployed also move towards lumpenisation.

This paper examines how displacement in the name of development, is producing hunger and deprivation in Orissa. The benefits of development do not often reach the displaced people. In the process of development, the local inhabitants become victims of irrigation projects, and hydro and thermal electricity projects, mineral-based industrial projects, etc. Yet there is also a long list of projects, which may displace more people, if approved. In the absence of a sustainable Rehabilitation and Resettlement (R&R) Policy, the displaced people fall into the net of hunger and deprivation.

The paper also examines the issue of displacement and its association with hunger and deprivation, and its disproportionate impacts on the SCs/STs. The paper is organised into three sections: Section one presents the macro-picture of the magnitude of development-induced and disaster-induced displacement, and their contributions to existing hunger and deprivation in Orissa. Section two explores the magnitude of hunger and deprivation among the displaced households and relates it to structural inequality. This section is primarily a result of the field survey data from Lanjigarh Block in Kalahandi District of Orissa. It also presents some observations from the displacement due to POSCO. Section three concludes the paper.

Development and Disaster-Induced Displacement: A Macro-Picture

Displacement or forced displacement implies the forced dislocation of people from their home or home region due to their own government's order or due to occurrences of different disasters in the region. The forced displacement of population not only leads to break up of living patterns and social continuity, but also dismantles the existing modes of production, disrupts social networks, causes the impoverishment of many of those uprooted, threatens their cultural identity, and increases the risk of epidemics and health problems (Cernea, 1995; Parasuraman, 1999; Chatterjee, 2004). Before we elaborate on the consequences of displacement, we have narrated below the distinction between the development and disaster-induced displacements.

(i) Development-Induced Displacement

Development-induced displacement relates to the dominant view of development, i.e., the modernisation theory. During the 1950s and 1960s, it was pointed out that the less developed countries are underdeveloped, because of their traditional form of development and hence,were encouraged to transform from simple traditional form of production process to a modern complex, westernised production process. Many big dams and reservoirs for irrigation, mining industries, power plants, urban infrastructures, and transportation (roads, highways and canals) have become inevitable. Though such efforts facilitated development for the whole economy, they also brought poverty among those few who were forcefully displaced and left out from the rehabilitation process. Such displacement leads to vulnerability of the people to various dimensions and is known as development-induced displacement. In Orissa, the Hirakud, Balimela, Machhkund, Salandi, Rengali, Kolab and Indravati dams have displaced large numbers of people in the name of development. Similarly, the industries, especially the mine-led industries, such as, Rourkela and Daitari Steel Plants, NALCO, POSCO, Lanjigarh bauxite mining, etc., have also led to development-induced displacement.

(ii) Disaster-Induced Displacement

The United Nations has defined disaster as "a serious disruption of the functioning of a society, causing widespread human, material, or environmental losses which exceed the ability of the affected society to cope with using its own resources". When such disaster leads to displacement, it is considered as disaster-induced displacement. For example, in the cyclone of 1999 in Orissa, the'tragedy of living' was compounded with damages amounting to over Rs. 7,000 crores. About 13,50,000 homes were destroyed; 10,000 km of roads were damaged; 30,00,000 people were unemployed; and 24,00,000 hectares of farm land was inundated (Suri, 2000). Such incident is also included in disaster-induced displacement. However, as per the above definition, fire, earthquake, drought, epidemic, or industrial accidents, are also called disasters, for which the society needs external support to cope with.

Disaster-induced displacement may be of two forms: natural and man-made. Natural disasters, further, may be broken down into two sub-categories : sudden impact and slow onset. Similarly, man-made disasters include two sub-categories, namely industrial/technological disasters and complex emergencies. The sudden impact disasters include floods, earthquakes, tidal waves, tropical storms, volcanic eruptions and landslides. All these disasters may affect the habitat and livelihood of the people and force them to migrate away from their own habitat. The slow-onset disasters include droughts, famine, environmental degradation, deforestation, pest infestation, and desertification (conversion of arable lands to deserts), which are usually the result of adverse weather conditions combined with poor land use.

In Orissa, there are a number of cases, where due to drought conditions, people leave their original villages and migrate to wet areas and settle down there. Though these people are not registered in government records as displaced persons, they form a part of disaster-induced displacement.

The industrial/technological disasters are a result of the society's industrial and technological activities leading to pollution, spillage of hazardous materials, explosions, and fires. Such disasters may occur due to poor planning and construction facilities or from neglect of safety procedures.

In Orissa, the main disaster-induced displacement may include droughts in south-western Orissa, and floods and cyclone in coastal Orissa. However, development-induced displacement is better known in the state than the disaster-induced displacement. Given the brief discussion on various kinds of displacement, the following sections examine in details the impact of these displacements in Orissa.

(iii) Impacts of Displacements in Orissa

Orissa is endowed with plenty of natural resources such as forests, inland water, mineral deposits, and raw materials, which are the most essential elements required for pursuing the goal of modern development. It has a long coastline, combined with potentially viable ports that are suitable for developing Special Economic Zones (SEZs). Orissa is now developing into an industrial hub. Paradoxically, Orissa is generally known as a poor, traditional, backward and non-industrialised state in India with the highest incidence of poverty; and it is observed that although rapid industrialisation has taken place, the traditional industrial base has been eroded, leading to a number of people being displaced and out of work. The history of development and displacement in the state is presented in the following sections.

There are, mainly, two kinds of development-induced displacement that have occurred in Orissa: The construction of dams for irrigation and power purposes, which led to the displacement of a large number of people[2], and industrialisation through mining and land acquisition, which also displaced a large number of people. Both kinds of displacement are examined here:

River Dam Project and Displacement

Table 2.1 Major and Medium Irrigation Projects in Orissa till 2004

Major Irrigation Projects in Orissa			
Completed Projects		*Ongoing Projects*	
1	Baitarani System	1	Rengali Irrigation Project
2	Hirakud System	2	Subarnarekha Irrigation Project
3	Mahanadi Delta System	3	Upper Indravati Irrigation Project
4	Rusikulya System	4	Kanupur Irrigation Project
5	Salandi System	5	Upper Kolab Irrigation Project
6	Potteru	6	Lower Indira Project
7	Anandapur Barrage	7	Lower Suktel Project
8	Machhkund	8	M.C.I.I. Projects
Medium Irrigation Projects in Orissa			
	Completed Projects	33	Remal
1	Aunli	34	Saipal
2	Bagh Barrage	35	Salia
3	Baghalati	36	Salki
4	Baghua	37	Sarafgarh
5	Bahuda	38	Satiguda
6	Balidiha	39	Sundar
7	Bankabahal	40	Sunei
8	Bhaskel	41	Talsara
9	Badnalla	42	Titilagarh
10	Budhabudhiani	43	Upper Suktel
11	Dabaraghati	44	Uttei
12	Daha	45	Gobardhanpur Barrage
13	Dahuka	46	Upper Jonk
14	Derjang	47	Harabhangi
15	Dhanei	48	Hariharjore
16	Dumerbaha	49	Birupa Genguti
17	Ghodahada		*Ongoing Projects*
18	Gohira	1	Baghua Dhanei Doab
19	Hiradharbati	2	Chheligarh

20	Jayamangal	3	Deo
21	Jharabandha	4	Manjore
22	Kalo	5	Rajua D/W
23	Kanjhari	6	Ret
24	Kansbahal	7	Rukura
25	Khadkhai	8	Telengir
26	Kuanria	9	Upper Jonk (Kharkhara)
27	Nessa	10	Sapua-Badjore
28	Ong		*Extension Projects*
29	Pillasalki	1	Bagh Barrage
30	Pitamahal	2	Baghlati
31	Ramnadi	3	Titilagarh
32	Ramial		

Source: www.orissagov.nic.in

The river dam projects in Orissa are meant to facilitate irrigation and hydro-electricity. Table 2.1 presents some of the large and medium dams in the state. Table 2.2 presents the capacity of these large dams in power supply and irrigation. Some of the major water-related projects (which are meant for both irrigation and power generation) are Machhkund, Hirakud, Balimela, Rengali, Upper Kolab, Indravati, Potteru and Salandi. The major producers of power are Indravati (600 MW), Balimela (360 MW), Hirakud I & II (347.5 MW), and Rengali (250 MW). In terms of irrigation, Hirakud Dam is one of the major sources. However, these dams, which were producing power for the state and supplying water to many agricultural fields, have also been the major cause of displacement in the state (see Table 2.3).

Table 2.2 Power Generation Capacity of Major Projects

Station/Dam	*River*	*District*	*Year (foundation and inauguration)*	*Capacity*
Machhkund (Orissa shares)	Duduma	Koraput	1946-1955	34.5 MW
Hirakud I (Burla)	Mahanadi	Sambalpur	1948-1957	275.5 MW
Hirakud II (Chiplima)	Mahanadi	Sambalpur	1956-1963	72 MW

Station/Dam	*River*	*District*	*Year (foundation and inauguration)*	*Capacity*
Balimela	Sileru	Malkanagiri	1963-1973	360 MW
Rengali	Brahmani	Angul	1976-1986	250 MW
Upper Kolab	Kolab	Koraput	1976-1993	320 MW
Upper Indravati	Indravati and Hati	Bhawanipatana	1979-2001	600 MW
Potteru	Canals	Malkanagiri		6 MW

*Source:*http://www.ohpcltd.com

Table 2.3 Number of Families Displaced and Amount of Land Acquired due to Different Development Projects in Orissa, from 1950 to 1995

Types of Project	*Number of Villages Displaced or Affected*	*Number of Families Displaced or Affected*	*Total Land Acquired in hectares*	*Percentage of Displaced families*	*Percentage of Land Acquired*
Mines	79	3143	2427.03	3.87	0.39
Industries	113	10704	21963	13.19	3.52
Thermal Power	73	2426	3155.31	2.99	0.51
Irrigation and Hydel Power (Dams)	1181	64903	595918.6	79.95	95.58
Total	1446	81176	623463.9	100	100

Note: Parida (2006) gives another 142 and 4,792 families that were affected due to wildlife sanctuaries and urban slums. So the total number of displaced families increases to 86,110.

Sources: Dalua, 1993; Fernandes and Reddy, 1993; Parida, 2006.

Table 2.3 presents the number of families displaced[3] during 1950 to 1995 due to different types of development projects. These data however do not cover all kinds of displaced people, as development projects in Orissa were started prior to 1950 and have been continuing even after 1995. This implies that the magnitude of displacement in the state must be higher than whatever has been presented in the table. During these 45 years, there are as many as 81,176 families that have been displaced

Table 2.4 A Conservative Estimate of Persons and Tribals Displaced by Development Projects in India 1951-90 (in lakhs)

Type of Project	*All DPs (lakhs)*	*Percentage of DPs*	*DPs Resettled (lakhs)*	*Percentage of Resettled DPs*	*Backlog (lakhs)*	*Percentage of Backlog*	*Tribals Displaced (lakhs)*	*Percentage of All DPs*	*Tribal DPs Resettled (lakhs)*	*Percentage of Tribal DPs*	*Back log of Tribal DPs*	*Percentage of Backlog*
Dams	164.0	77.0	41.00	25.0	123.00	75.0	63.21	38.5	15.81	25.00	47.40	75
Mines	25.5	12.0	6.30	24.7	19.20	75.3	13.30	52.20	3.30	25.00	10.00	75
Industries	12.5	5.9	3.75	30.0	8.75	70.0	3.13	25.0	0.80	25.0	2.33	75
Wildlife	6.0	2.8	1.25	20.8	4.75	79.2	4.5	75.0	1.00	22.0	3.50	78
Others	5.0	2.3	1.50	30.0	3.50	70.0	1.25	25.0	0.25	20.2	1.00	80
Total	213	100	53.80	25.0	159.20	75.0	85.39	40.9	21.16	25.0	64.23	79

Source: Fernandes, 1994, pp. 22-32 in Pati, 2000.

or affected, of which most of them (79.95 per cent) have been displaced due to irrigation and hydro-power projects, followed by industrial projects (13.19 per cent). A similar pattern is seen, in case of land acquisitions. Most of the total acquired land (95.58 per cent) is due to irrigation and hydel projects.

However, incidence of such displacement is not equal for all social groups. Since, these dams are located in the high lands or hilly areas, where often the ST and SC people live, it is likely that more of these populations are displaced. In this regard, Pati (2005) presents a conservative estimate from Fernandes (1994). As Table 2.4 shows, the proportion of tribals displaced due to different types of projects is 40.9 per cent, which implies a higher magnitude of displacements among the tribals. Though the STs were materially better off than the SCs, they might have become resource-poor due to displacement. However, if a higher percentage of displaced tribals would have been rehabilitated, probably the possibility of poverty among them would have been checked to certain extent. But the proportion of displaced persons who were

Table 2.5 A Conservative Estimate of Families Displaced by Development Projects in Orissa across Social Groups (1951-95)

Station/ Dam	*Gen*	*SC*	*ST*	*Total No. Families Affected*	*Number of Families*
Machhkund	38	10	52	100	2938
Hirakud	NA	NA	NA	-	22144
Balimela	NA	NA	NA	-	2000
Salandi	NA	NA	NA	-	569
Rengali	73.55	15.69	10.76	100	10897
Upper Kolab	39.00	14.18	46.82	100	3067
Subarnarekha	30.29	5.14	64.58	100	3427
Upper Indravati	42.89	15.27	41.85	100	5568
Medium Projects	41.72	11.59	46.69	100	4892
Total	52.70	13.42	33.88	100	27851*

Note: * implies that the figure does not include the displaced families of Hirakud, Balimela and Salandi, for which data on social group-wise displacement is not obtainable.
Source: Record of Irrigations Department, Government of Orissa (Parida, 2006).

Table 2.6 Dam-wise and Region-wise Displaced Persons and Submerged Areas, and Some of the Notable Multipurpose Hydro-Electricity Projects in Orissa

Station/Dam	*River*	*District*	*Time Period*	*Submerged*		*No. of Families*		*Population Affected*
				V	*A*	*D*	*R*	
Machhkund	Duduma	Koraput	1946-1955	225	20794	2938	600	14690
Hirakud	Mahanadi	Sambalpur	1948-1957	285	182593	22144	1879	160000
Balimela	Sileru	Malkanagiri	1963-1973	89	48000	2000	NA	9600
Rengali	Brahmani	Angul	1976-1986	265	105905	10897	6639	54235
Upper Kolab	Kolab	Koraput	1976-1993	149	24794	13095	525	50771
Upper Indravati	Indravati & Hati	Bhawanipatana	1979-2001	99	32530	5568	3585	26505
Total				1112	414616	56642	13228	315801

(Contd...)

(Contd...)

				Percentages				
Station/Dam	*River*	*District*	*Time period*	*Submerged*		*Number of family*		*Population affected*
				V	***A***	***D***	***R***	
Machhkund	Duduma	Koraput	1946-1955	20.23	5.02	5.19	4.54	4.65
Hirakud	Mahanadi	Sambalpur	1948-1957	25.63	44.04	39.09	14.20	50.66
Balimela	Sileru	Malkanagiri	1963-1973	8.00	11.58	3.53	NA	3.04
Rengali	Brahmani	Angul	1976-1986	23.83	25.54	19.24	50.19	17.17
Upper Kolab	Kolab	Koraput	1976-1993	13.40	5.98	23.12	3.97	16.08
Upper Indravati	Indravati & Hati	Bhawanipatana	1979-2001	8.90	7.85	9.83	27.10	8.39
Total				100	100	100	100	100

Notes: V – Villages, A – Area in acres, D – Displaced, R – Rehabilitated. This table shows only some of the displaced families and not all due to paucity of data.

Source: Compiled from Tripathy (2003).

resettled remained almost similar in both cases. This may also imply that more of the benefits of rehabilitation have gone to non-tribal displaced persons. In the Orissa context, distribution of displaced persons, according to their social group is not available for all projects. Table 2.5 presents some of the figures available, which depict the incidence of displacement among different social groups. Though it differs from project to project, yet the incidence has remained higher among the STs, when compared to their proportion in total population and their proportion in the number of displaced families.

Table 2.6 provides the magnitude of displacement by different dams. The regional dimension of displacement is also revealed through this data.

The Machhkund hydro-project built on the Duduma River in Koraput District is the earliest development project of its kind. Though the project work had started during 1946, the displacement and rehabilitation aspects of the project are not much clear (Dalua, 1993). But as Mahapatra (1989:96) noted, out of the total 2,938 families that were displaced by the project, about 1,500 (51 %) belonged to STs; 300 (10.21 %) belonged to SCs, and the remaining were from other castes. Mahapatra (1989: 96) also pointed out that in the Machhkund Project, out of the 2,938 displaced families, only 600 families (450 tribal and 150 others) were rehabilitated. Stanley (1996:1533-1534) further pointed out that the displaced people were rehabilitated with "land for land" provision, and that there were two villages, where the villagers were not willing to leave their birth place and had given a memorandum to the Chief Minister and the local government officials. But ultimately, the villagers were forced to settle, but for a higher compensation and better rehabilitations than originally envisaged; and there is no further information available on the people's response towards the project.

Hirakud Dam was the first multipurpose project in independent India. It is situated in the Sambalpur District of Orissa. The scheme for the dam was conceived by Er. M. Visveswaraya in 1937[4]. Hence, it seems that the displacement might have occurred during this period, i.e., between 1949 and 1956. The second phase of the dam was the Chiplima Scheme, which was sanctioned during July 1956 and was inaugurated on 14.9.1963. Therefore, it seems that the displacement due to Hirakud I and Hirakud II might have continued from late 1940s to early 1960s. Therefore, if the displaced people might have joined as agricultural labour, then there might also be chances that the percentage of agricultural labour in the state or in the district of Sambalpur, might have increased during that period. The third phase expansion of the Hirakud Dam had taken place during 1982 to 1990. Therefore, here too the displacement effects may get reflected in the census data. However, as far as direct information is concerned, Hirakud Dam has displaced 22,144 families from 249 villages in Orissa (Dalua, 1993).

In the case of the people displaced by the Hirakud Dam also, there were no specific policy guidelines for rehabilitation, and the affected people were paid compensation only for the land property. It was pointed out that only 11 per cent of the land owners were settled with some land, since the land was located on a hilly slope and the forest area was not suitable for cultivation (Tripathy, 2003). The situation was worse for some people who have become the victims of multiple displacements due to mine project in the resettled place. For Hirakud Dam also, there was opposition by the local people and leaders, but the protest did not have much impact on the construction of the project.

The Balimela Project is the second largest hydro-electricity project in Koraput District. The project commenced on 1962-63 and was completed in 1977. The project has displaced 2,000 families (Dalua, 1991). The R&R Policy followed for the project was similar to that of Hirakud Dam.

The Rengali Dam Project started around mid-1970s and was completed by mid-1980s. It displaced as many as 10,847 families, and a similar R&R Policy was followed. The Indravati Hydro-project Dam was started in 1978-79. The four dams across the River Indravati and its tributaries Patogoda, Kapur and Muvan would form a single reservoir submerging 44 villages in Koraput District and 51 villages in Kalahandi District. Mahapatra (*ibid.*) pointed out that about 578 families have been displaced.

The Upper Kolab Hydro-electric Project located in the district of Koraput (Orissa) was initiated in 1976 by the Irrigation and Power Department, Government of Orissa, to produce power and supply irrigation. The project utilises the water potential of the River Kolab, a tributary of River Godavari. It generates 320 MW of power and provides irrigation facilities to 47,985 hectares by lift canal irrigation, and supplies drinking water to Damonjodi, Koraput, Sunabeda and Jeypore towns.

Table 2.6 was compiled from different sources, due to lack of proper records; the data do not include all displaced people. However, the table reveals that the share of displacement, that occurred due to Hirakud Dam in Sambalpur District, was the largest. It has displaced around 39 per cent of the total number of families displaced due to all projects. This is

23 per cent. In Koraput District, the total number of families displaced may increase as the 44 villages displaced by the Indravati Project were also from this district.

In terms of population displaced, these two dams hold the major share. However, the impact of displacement is not merely confined to these numbers: Many sociologists and anthropologists have also documented various qualitative consequences of the displacement in Orissa. Ota (1996) found that in the Rengali Irrigation Project, the percentage of landless families after relocation had doubled. Reddy (1997) found that in the coal mining displacement around Singrauli, the proportion of landless people skyrocketed from 20 percent before displacement, to 72 percent after displacement. Pandey (1998) studied seven projects causing displacement during 1950-94 in Orissa and found that there was a problem of Common Property Resources (CPRs) in the post-displacement period.

However, due to paucity of data, to measure the magnitude of hunger and deprivation, a popular method was used: collecting evidence from village surveys. However, these are micro evidences and have their own limitations, asthey may not throw much light on the conditions (especially human rights related, for which there is legal support) of the displaced persons. Therefore, a primary survey has been attempted. Though displacement occurred regularly in undivided Koraput, Kalahandi District was chosen for primary survey, due to the highest proportion of agricultural labour there. The following section examines the mines-led industrialisation and displacement.

Mine-led Industrialisation and Displacement

Most contemporary discussions, on the development in Orissa, give an impression that the state is really backward in terms of industrialisation, but the actual scenario shows that Orissa has been there in the industrial and mining map of the country, ever since the inception of mining and industry in India. The modern day mining in Orissa can be traced back to 1909, when coal was first excavated in the Rampur area of Ib valley. The TISCO mines for iron ore at Gorumohisani and manganese mines at Goriajhar were started during 1910. Followed by this, during 1914, dolomite and limestone mining was started at Panposh and Bisra respectively. In the pre-independent era, mining of chromites in Baula area was started during 1942. After independence, a number of initiatives were taken to establish public sector industries in Orissa. Industries like Rourkela Steel Plant, Hindustan Aeronautics Ltd. (HAL), and National

Aluminium Company (NALCO) came up in the state, expanding the mining sector significantly. Next, Bauxite mining was started at Panchpatmali Hills in Koraput in 1984. Even during 1985-2000, while the mineral development in the state was very slow, the production of bauxite by NALCO in Koraput and coal mining by MCL in Ib-valley and Talcher area were notable. Until late 1950s, the mines were small and mostly manual; hence, the industrial growth in the state was low, and so were the environmental impact, and the industry-led displacement. But post 1984, the mineral production has increased very rapidly and during this period, displacement has increased as well. During 2007-08, about 1,785.81 lakhs tons of minerals valued Rs.10,636.70 crores were produced in the state. In 1991-92, the mineral production was estimated at 3,72,00,000 tons, which reached to more than 7,49,00,000 tons by 2001-02, (Economic Survey of Orissa, 2008). However, this rapid increase in the mineral production cannot be taken as synonymous with industrialisation as the latter remained at low level. Moreover, despite the emphasis in the successive industrial policies of Orissa for large industries and mining sector, which resulted in an expansion of industries, their contribution in terms of poverty reduction has not been much, according to the data. Hence, the mine-led development has brought negative impacts on the native population, the local economy, as well as the state, in the form of displacement. Table 2.7 presents the reserve of ores and minerals in Orissa.

However, the nature of manufacturing activities in the state has been primarily concentrated on natural resource-based industries, particularly the mineral-based industries. As the Annual Survey of Industries (1997-98) pointed out, industries like electricity, basic metal and alloys, non-metallic minerals and food products accounted for about 75 percent of the total industrial employment and 80 per cent of the net value added. However, on the other hand, these industries also led to large-scale deforestation. The Economic Survey of Orissa reveals that mining and industrial sectors have accounted for nearly 39 per cent of total conversion of forest area to non-forest area, and it led to acquisition of 6,22,463.94 hectares of land (Vasundhara, 2005). Since the majority of the large industries and mineral resources are located in the northern and southern tribal-dominated regions, the incidence of displacement is more likely to happen among the tribals, who lose their major source of livelihood like forest products, forests, CPRs, revenue lands, etc. Therefore, though the tribal people constitute 22.21 per cent of the total population (2001 Census), the incidence of poverty among them in the southern and northern areas is 85.5 per cent and 79.1 per cent respectively. On the one hand, displacement for mining hardly helped the natives; and on the other hand, stagnation in agriculture has shrunk their base of employment.

Table 2.7 Data on Reserves of Ores and Minerals in Orissa (in Million Tons as on 1.1.2000)

Mineral	*Location/District*	*Resources*
Bauxite	Koraput, Rayagada, Kalahandi and Balangir and small deposits in Phulbani, Nuapada and Sundargarh	1733 (3075)
Beach Sand	Ganjam and Puri	82* (366)
China Clay	Mayurbhanj and small deposits in Malkanagiri	314 (2353)
Chromite	Keonjhar and Jajpur	183* (186*)
Coal	Sambalpur, Jharsuguda, Angul and Talcher	60987 (245692)**
Dolomite	Sundargarh and Koraput	882 (7349)
Fire Clay	Cuttack, Sambalpur and Jharsuguda	177 (706)
Graphite	Bargarh, Sambalpur, Balangir, Kalahandi, Phulbani and Rayagada	4.6 (16)
IronOre	Sundargarh, Keonjhar, Mayurbhanj, Jajpur	4177 (12317)
Limestone	Sundargarh, Bargarh, Koraput and Malkanagiri	2224 (169941)
Manganese	Sundargarh, Keonjhar and Rayagada	116 (406)
Nickel	Jajpur and Keonjhar	174 (188)

Notes and Sources: Figures in brackets are the reserves of India, * as per latest figures of Directorate of Geology, Orissa, ** as per latest figures of Ministry of Coal, and the rest of the data are from Indian Bureau of Mines.

In the post 1990s, Orissa adopted three successive industrial and mining policies (1992, 1996 and 2001). These policies envisage the growth of private investment in the sectors of infrastructure development, mineral-based industries and large industrial projects. What is the relevance of such industrialisation in producing hunger and deprivation? What are the consequences of these displacements that need to be addressed from the grass-root level data to find the Deviations in the land acquisition act and Rehabilitation and Resettlement policies?

Table 2.8 presents the number of persons displaced due to a few industry and mining projects in Orissa. The results show that around 44,000 people have been displaced due to the above-mentioned projects. Apart from this, there are many other projects, which might have displaced people in various parts of the state, for which there is not much information. In the absence of a proper Rehabilitation and Resettlement Policy, displacement may push the people into hunger and deprivation. Some of the evidences from the primary survey carried out at various levels are presented below:

Table 2.8 Displacement due to some Industry and Mining Projects in Orissa

Project	*Year*	*Land Acquired (acres)*	*No. of Villages*	*No. of Families Displaced*	*Population Displaced*
Hindustan Aeronautic Ltd. in Koraput	1962	7200	10	1200	6000
Bauxite mining in Koraput	1981	5936	41	788	3104
Bauxite mining in Sambalpur	1985	2379	24	1396	9111
Steel plant of Rourkela in Sundargarh	1962	19557	30	2467	12335
Steel plant of Gopalpur in Ganjam	1996	7598	11	2912	13892
Aluminium smelter plant at Angul	1985	3828	3	0	0
Total		46498	119	8763	44442

Source: Tripathy, 2003.

The survey carried out by Pandey (1996) among tribal households in five villages in Talcher found an increase in unemployment from 9 per cent to 43.6 per cent, accompanied by a large shift from primary to tertiary occupation, and reported reduction in the level of earning upto 50 to 80 per cent among the tribes and the Scheduled Castes. Further,

Downing (2002) pointed out that in some of the survey villages, the proportion of landlessness became almost twice due to displacement by some of the mining projects. As we would show the evidence below, the impact of displacement is more among the SCs/STs who lose their livelihood.

Structural Inequality and Displacement in Orissa

Structural inequality is one of the perennial features of Orissa economy. The SCs/STs are the most disadvantaged with respect to: access to education, health, better paid jobs, land, or even to food and other capabilities-enhancing facilities provided through public provisioning. Such precarious situation affects them directly by displacement and indirectly through destruction of the forest, which is the source of livelihood for most of them. Incidentally, it is observed that the projects undertaken, and hence the people displaced, are in those areas where SC/ST concentrations are high. Table 2.9 presents the sector-wise diversion of forest area to non-forest use. Out of the total forest area of 2,26,622 hectares in 2003, about 27,274 hectares were diverted for various development projects, particularly after the enactment of the Forest Conservation Act, 1980. Of the various development projects for which forest land has been diverted, mining (35 per cent) and irrigation (22 per cent) constitute the most. This has serious implications on hunger and deprivation, especially among the SCs/STs.

Table 2.9 Sector-wise Diversion of Forest Land to Non-Forest Use (under Forest Conversion Act, 1980)

Name of the Sector	*Number of Projects*	*Forest Area Diverted as on 31.03.2003*	*Percentage of Total Area Diverted*
Irrigation	59	6092.4829	22.34
Industry	5	2406.086	8.82
Mining	77	9469.4384	34.72
Transmission	44	2723.4265	9.99
Roads & Bridges	25	197.8122	0.73
Railways	5	1965.0287	7.20
Others	32	4420.179	16.21
Total	247	27274.45	100

Source: Vasundhara, 2005.

Table 2.10 Percentage Distribution of Displaced Social Groups in Orissa (1951-1955)

Project	*DPs*				*PAPs*				*Grand Total*
	Tribal	*Dalits*	*Others*	*Total*	*Tribals*	*Dalits*	*Others*	*Total*	
Water	153540	42335	214125	410000	154830	37986	197184	390000	800000
Percentage	37.45	10.33	52.22	100	39.7	9.74	50.56	100	54.57
Industries	25937	11045	34812	71794	14719	13286	58270	86275	158069
Percentage	36.13	15.38	48.49	100	17.06	15.5	67.54	100	10.78
Mines	50000	15000	35000	100000	100000	30000	70000	200000	300000
Percentage	50	15	35	100	50	15	35	100	20.47
Wildlife	840	Nil	Nil	840	80250	16050	10700	107000	107840
Percentage	100			100	75	15	10	100	7.36
Others	25000	5240	197699	50000	11000	7500	31500	50000	100000
Percentage	50	10.46	39.52	100	22	15	63	100	6.82
Total	255317	71620	303697	632634	360799	104822	367654	833275	1465909
Percentage	40.36	11.64	48.01	43.16	43.14	12.53	43.96	56.84	100

Source: Development-induced displacement and rehabilitation in Orissa (1951-1995; database on its extent and nature, by Fernandes and Asif, 1997).

Table 2.10 presents a conservative estimate of displaced and partially affected people due to displacement during 1951-55. It shows that the incidence of displacement is the highest among the SCs/STs. Out of the total number of displaced people, SCs/STs together account for 56 per cent (43 per cent for SCs and 13 per cent for SCs). Yet as the report by Vasundhara (2005) reveals, only 25 per cent of the displaced persons have been rehabilitated.

The Resettlement and Rehabilitation policies in Orissa have been discussed below in details with micro-evidences.

Employment and Output Growth in Mining and Quarrying

The Economic Survey of Orissa, 2010 reveals that since 2003-04, the mining sector has contributed about 7 per cent towards the state's GSDP. However, as the data depicts, the total employment in the mineral industry has decreased between 2001-02 and 2008-09, which is due to modernisation in this sector (see Table 2.11).

Table 2.11 Production of all Minerals/Ores and Number of Workers directly Employed in Mineral Sector from 2001 to 2008-09

Year	*Output (in lakh tons)*	*Value (Rs. in crores)*	*No. of Workers*
2000-01	689.24	2776.15	52937
2004-05	1270.48	6130.93	49837
2005-06	1396.78	6604.41	55764
2006-07	1614.45	7629.63	47376
2007-08	1785.81	10636.7	49176
2008-09	..	..	44173

Source: Economic Survey, 2010.

Rehabilitation and Resettlement Policy in Orissa

(i) A Macro Picture

Rehabilitation and Resettlement (R&R) is not a recent phenomenon in Orissa. The program can be traced back to the Land Acquisition Act of 1894. However, the extent of benefit from the R&R policy is very less. Table 2.12 presents the percentages of displaced people who are resettled in Orissa.

Table 2.12 Percentage of Displaced People who are Resettled (1954-1995)

Category	*Displaced*	*Resettled*	*Percentage Resettled*	*Backlog*	*Percentage Unsettled*
Water Resource	325000	90000	27.69	235000	72.31
Industries	71794	27300	38.03	44494	61.97
Mines	100000	60000	60.00	40000	40.00
Miscellaneous	546794	192840	35.27	353954	64.73
Total	546794	192840	35.27	353954	64.73

Source: Fernandes and Asif, 1997.

The table presents only the conservative method, while the actual figures might be higher than the figures presented here. This shows that during the period from 1954 to 1995, around 65 per cent of the displaced people are unsettled, and emphasises the necessity of an effective and sustainable R&R policy. It is also observed that only 35 per cent of the displaced people are resettled during 1954 and 1995, and the incidence of unsettled people is the lowest (40 per cent) among the people displaced by mines.

It is also explored from the Mining and Industrial Update, Orissa, 2006, that till 20th July 2005, there were already 593 mining projects working in the state of which around 100 are located in Kalahandi, Koraput, Rayagada, Malkanagiri, Nuapada and Kandhamal (the southern region), where there is higher concentration of tribal people. The same source also depicts that till November 2006, there are additional 78 projects pending for state approval. Such large-scale displacement produces more fear than a fatal disease.

However, after several public pressures, protests and resistance from communities, the Rehabilitation and Resettlement policies of 1994, 2005 and 2006 were evolved. The main features of the policies are presented below:

Features of Land Acquisition Act of 1894

The Land Acquisition Act (LAA) of 1894 authorises the Government to acquire land compulsorily for "public purposes", for which individual hardship can never outweigh the question of public demand. However, if the people affected object to such forceful acquisition, the District Collector (DC) may intervene, mainly to decide the compensations after which a notice would be given to the people concerned. Thereafter, the DC would take possession of the land. This may imply that though there is legal right for land acquisitions or displacement, there is no legal right for rehabilitations, and that might be the reason that the earlier LAA might have contributed to hunger and deprivation. However, there was provision for compensation in the LAA of 1894. The Act (Sections 23 and 24) suggests for the valuation of the land to be acquired and payment of adequate compensation to the legal owner of the property. The valuation may include: (i) the market value of the land; (2) the damage sustained by the person interested; and (3) if there is damage of standing crops, trees or if other types of damage are suffered by the individual aggrieved.

Therefore, the act suggests that the right of the state over land is superior to the right of the individual and hence, the former can take away the property of any individual at any time; of course, for public purposes. However, as the term "public purpose" has not been defined in the act, the applications of the whole act become arbitrary (Reddy, 1995). Anything put by the Government in the name of "public purpose" is eligible for acquisition of land. Further, it is the District Collector who has the absolute authority to determine what public purpose is and what is not, and the affected person cannot even question the decision of the collector on the element of public purpose though he can go to court questioning the amount of compensation. In brief, it may be said that though there was an act, in practice there was a lot of arbitrariness involved.

In 1973, Orissa came up with its first Resettlement and Rehabilitation Policy. The first mining sector and the revised resettlement policy were introduced in 1994.

The Resettlement and Rehabilitation Policies of 1994

During 1994, the Department of Water Resources of the Government of Orissa came out with the most comprehensive policy on Resettlement and Rehabilitation of the Project affected Persons (PAPs). As documented by Mahapatra (1995), the 1994 policy is the outcome of persistent agitations and political pressure. The new policy emphasised, "before 1994, the widows, divorcees, orphans, physically and mentally handicapped without independent means of livelihood, in addition to the landless, were recognised as displaced persons in the submergence zone. Cash in lieu of homestead land, house construction assistance, maintenance allowance for one year, and rehabilitation assistance (2 acres of irrigated land or 4 acres of unirrigated land), or cash grant in its lieu will now be paid jointly to husband and wife in the family concerned".

The new R&R Policy refers to the displaced persons including: (i) the landless labourers; (ii) persons who lose a proportion of their only holding in the village and thereby are compelled to lead an uneconomic living; and (iii) if in a village, more than 75 per cent of the total agricultural land is acquired, or it is found on due enquiry that partial acquisition of land property in the submergence zone may lead to a socially and economically unviable living, the entire village may be treated as fully submerged village, even if homestead land is not affected or is partially affected; and all the villagers (including those who do not have landed property) will be treated as equivalent to displaced persons.

Another special feature of this policy is the construction of compensatory afforestation, plantation and similar other uses. The displaced persons include not only the landless labourers in the submergence zone, but also the landless persons losing only their house due to acquisition for the project, and those located in the village but not displaced; they all will be entitled to only an equal area of the house site, subject to a maximum of 0.20 acres of land along with house building assistance as applicable. Similarly, "...If a landless person loses his house in the submerged zone because of the project, he should be considered in all senses to be a displaced person and entitled to all benefits : a displaced person is to receive rehabilitation and resettlement". The contradiction that has been pointed out is, "for the purpose of displacement, the village should be taken as the unit" so that everyone in village gets the benefits.

The Orissa Government further improved the Rehabilitation and Resettlement Policy in 2006, which is better than the National Rehabilitation and Resettlement Policy in many respects (Jena, 2006). But how effective the policy is in the field needs to be examined through a specially conducted survey: The objective of the survey is to examine the impacts of displacement: Does displacement result in hunger and deprivation and thereby in violation of human rights? If yes, how does it violate? Further, what are the effects of the recent policies of Orissa on the displaced people? To what extent the reduction of hunger and deprivation has been achieved due to new policy?

Micro Study

Here we have presented two case studies: (1) Displacement due to the Vedanta Alumina Limited and (2) Displacement due to POSCO. The primary survey for the former was conducted by us.

Displacement due to Vedanta Alumina Limited: The case study was carried out in Lanjigarh Block of Kalahandi District, where the Vedanta Alumina Limited, a subsidiary of M/s Sterile Industries (India) Limited (SIIL), plans to exploit the Niyamgiri bauxite (for commercial purposes) reserve located on the top of Niyamgiri Hill. The company is to mine the bauxite deposit from the hill jointly with the Orissa Mining Corporation (OMC) Limited as per the lease agreement signed between OMC and Vedanta Alumina Ltd. (VAL) in October 2004. Vedanta required 723.343 ha of land for setting up an Alumina Complex and another 721.323 ha of land for bauxite mining. Most of this land was categorised as Reserved Forest and Revenue Land. The forest land is composed of forest and grassland ecosystems of extremely high value, due to its wildlife habitat, while the Revenue Lands were the settlements of human beings and were used as agricultural fields.

VAL has evacuated three villages: Some of these displaced villagers had to leave the place and there is no account where they went, while some others are living in nearby villages or are resettled in the rehabilitated village provided by the Vedanta. We could meet the latter two categories of displaced people and conducted personal interviews.

Experiences of the displaced people living in nearby villages:

There are four categories of displaced people:

(a) People, who lost their land but not home and hence got negligible compensation, are not eligible to get a house in the rehabilitated colony. They had to find a place of living near Lanjigarh (main village), where the real estate price is much higher than the compensated value.

(b) People who lost their home and received some compensation but did not like to stay in the rehabilitated colony as it is located around 6 to 7 kilometres away from the main village, where all other facilities (health, education, police, postal, etc.) are available, and as there is a possibility that the rehabilitated colony may again be displaced.

(c) People who lost both land and home and received partial compensation but did not get a house in the rehabilitated colony.

(d) People were residing adjacent to the Alumina factory. They had to leave the place because of the negative externality of the factory and were not paid anything. This group also includes the landless labourers, who were completely dependent on the villagers as agricultural or non-agricultural labourers. Most of them are socially excluded SC population.

The loss of food security and livelihood, especially of the marginal farmers and landless agricultural labourers, is the key problem. These farmers, who have worked for generations together to convert the bush and forest cover land into agricultural land, were now forced to leave, and hence rendered landless. With the compensation money they received, they could not buy the same quality or amount of land they had possessed earlier, as the demand for land has increased. The case of landless labourers is even worse: they were working in the agricultural fields and were rendered jobless. As a result, some are migrating to distant places like Rajkot and Kerala to earn their livelihood. In the absence of regular livelihood, the common property resources would have supplemented to an extent, but these also got depleted by the company's work. As people have been displaced and there is no proper account of all the habitants, it has affected the already established community services and social integration.

Experiences of the displaced people living in the rehabilitated colony: For the company purposes, almost four villages were displaced (Barbhatta and Kinare villages were displaced completely and Sindhi Bahal and Kotdwar were displaced partially). There is also speculation by the local people that another five villages (Khajur Padar, Tangankana, Kasi Gadi, Goiputa and Bandguda) are going to be displaced as soon as the company discovers more mines storage in that region. The company started its survey during 2002 and the displacement began during 2003. At that time the people were hardly aware about the aim and objective of the company. However, they were given assurance by the company that the displaced people will get home for home, land for land; and job. However, these promises by the Company were only partially met.

Our enquiry revealed that around 300 households have been displaced so far, out of which around 150 households have been resettled. The resettlement started during 2006. Tables 2.13 and 2.14 provide some information about the resettled households in the rehabilitated colony. The results show that the cost of access to almost all the facilities, including health, education, and other civil rights, have increased after displacement. However, unlike the earlier category of case study, a positive thing is that almost all the rehabilitated households have received some amount of compensation. However, the beneficiaries themselves do not know how to use the money in a sustainable manner. Some of these beneficiaries have already spent their money and are now agitating frequently, before the company for a permanent job. However, the company is unable to accommodate all the displaced people into jobs. Moreover, the company also chooses its work force in such a manner that it would help the interest of the company rather than threaten it. Perhaps, therefore, even the daily workers were being brought from outside the state.

Table 2.13 Nearest Education and Health Institutes (in km)

Education	*Old Village*	*New Village*	*Health*	*Old Village*	*New Village*
LP School	1	1	PHC	2	7
UP School	2	7	Medical	2	7
High School	2	7	ICDS Centre	1	1

Source: Field survey.

Table 2.14 Nearest Civil Rights and other Institutions (in km)

Nearest	*Old Village*	*New Village*	*Nearest*	*Old Village*	*New Village*
Police Station	3	7	Electricity	No	Yes
Post Office	3	7	Main Road	2.5	3
Voting Booth	3	1	Drinking Water	1.5 (From River Banshi Dhara)	From tube-well which is polluted water
PDS Distribution Point	3	7	Bathing Water	Niyamgiri Stream	-
Bus Stop	3	7	Pond	2	0
Forest	1	2	River	Banshi Dhara	Getting polluted
Daily Market	2	7-8	Cultural Programs	2	7-8
Bank Services	2	7-8			

Source: Field survey.

Another thing that came out clearly during our investigation was, that almost all the displaced persons (including those who are living in the rehabilitated colony) are unhappy and agitating against the company. Our investigation reveals that the company received full support from the local politicians and police authorities. So it is not merely the interest of the company but the interest of the local politicians, bureaucrats and police authorities which together went against the displaced persons, and therefore, the company could sustain and function. As a result, despite the existence of a R&R policy, displacement is contributing to the existing hunger and deprivation in Orissa.

Displacement due to POSCO

On June 22nd 2005, the State Government of Orissa signed a Memorandum of Understanding (MoU) with the Korean steel giant, the Pohang Steel Company (POSCO). This is India's largest Foreign Direct Investment (FDI), which also involves a 12-million ton integrated steel plant, and over 4,500 acres of land for the construction of a new port. The steel plant is expected to affect seven villages in three Gram Panchayats, namely Dhinkia, Nuagaon and Gadakujang, and will allow POSCO to extract 600 million tons of iron ore over the next 30 years. As per the MoU, the State Government has agreed to provide almost all facilities required by the company including free encumbrances to POSCO, mining and prospecting licenses, clearances related to matters of forest and environment, and permits for drawing water from the Mahanadi River; defending the various recommendations made in favour of POSCO in the eventuality of litigation in the appropriate judicial and quasi-judicial areas, and extending similar facilitation of clearances by the State Government for all aspects of the project : the steel plant, mines, roads, railways and port. Finally, in 2006, the project was also granted "Special Economic Zone" (SEZ) status, and the Prime Minister issued a statement saying that land acquisition by POSCO must be expedited. However, the project has great impacts on the people of affected areas.

The Lives and Livelihood Issues

The report of the Government and POSCO stated that about 400 families will be displaced by the project, which will be around 2,000 people, assuming five members per household. But according to the 2001 Census, the three Panchayats have 3,350 households which add up to 22,000 people who will be affected and displaced. The difference may be due to anomalies in the Government records, which recognise only 438 acres out of the 4,000 acres as being privately owned. The other lands have been under betel, cashew and other cultivation by the ST communities for several generations, who may not be having legal entitlements for the land : this land is not only their living place but also their source of livelihood.

About 50% of the families are also involved in pisciculture (mostly prawns). There are also many landless families that depend on ancillary employment, such as, making baskets for packaging, paan leaves grown in the area and people living adjacent to the mines (Banspal Block) which may also suffer if their source of livelihood is curtailed; apart from this, they are also likely to face various health-related problems.

Negative Externality to Agricultural Growth

It is reported that the project will require 286 million litres of water per day, which will be supplied from the nearest Jobra and Naraj barrages of River Mahanadi, as a result of which the farmers who were using the irrigated water from the canals of Taldanda, Machhagaon, Birupa of Cuttack, Jagatsinghpur, and Kendrapada may suffer great loss and agricultural productivity may come down.

Impact on Environment

Orissa has some of the largest mass nesting areas in the world for the Olive Ridley Turtle, an endangered species. The proposed POSCO port site lies between the mass nesting beaches of Gahirmata and Devi River mouth, where the offshore waters house large numbers of turtles from November to April every year. In 2007, as many as 1,30,000 of these animals nested at the beaches along the Gahirmata Marine Sanctuary. The port lies just inland from beaches on which turtle nesting occurs, and less than 30 km from the mass nesting beaches of River Devi. Lighting, marine pollution, ship traffic, and ancillary development of what is currently a largely untouched coastline will pose a long-term threat to the species. Similarly, the proposed port will endanger several species of fish in the Jatadhari Estuary, additionally impacting the livelihoods of the fishing communities.

The project also involves the felling of over 2,80,000 trees which will directly affect the dense forest covers in the Gandhamardhan and Malangatoli areas. Furthermore, mining will affect the Kandadhar Waterfall, a famed tourist destination. The new port might entail erosion, thereby threatening the existing Government port in Paradeep. POSCO has applied for environmental clearance for different parts of the project separately rather than as a whole in the hope of expediting clearance.

Implications of SEZ Status

POSCO gets a 10-year tax-break as a result of its SEZ status, granted by the Central Government. Land will also be sold to POSCO at lower-than-market price. However, these impose significant costs to the exchequer. The SEZ status of this project also removes it from the purview of the local Panchayat governments, thus further decreasing the control of the villagers over their local environment. Further, the SEZ status also grants immunity to POSCO from adherence to hard-won labour and environmental laws designed to protect the employees.

The number of jobs created due to the steel plant is supposed to number 13,000, and it is claimed that another 48,000 indirect jobs are likely to be created. These numbers do not justify the subsidies granted to the project, including the discounted price of Rs. 2000 ($50) per ton of iron ore.

Relief and Rehabilitation

The Government records recognise only a small fraction of the total number of affected people for compensation, while most of the villagers have not received the compensation. Moreover, there was state-sponsored violence (through 15 platoons of armed paramilitary forces) against the villagers who opposed to the POSCO Steel Plant. However, the tussle between the local inhabitants and the State Police is on. It is unfortunate but not hard to imagine that the POSCO struggle may cost the lives of the poor and the disadvantaged people in the future as the evidence of many deaths of tribal people in police firing in Kashipur and Kalinganagar show.

Summary and Conclusion

The study attempted to enquire how displacement (especially, development-induced displacement) has contributed to the existing hunger and deprivation in Orissa. Development-induced displacement in Orissa, which started since the latter part of the 1940s, still continues. In fact, in almost all decades there have been displacements in the state, due to one or the other developmental project.

The Export Promotion Zone (EPZ) or the Special Economic Zone (SEZ) has primarily two objectives: economic growth and the employment expansion. In case of Orissa, there might be some contribution of the EPZ and SEZ to the state's economic growth and employment; but the state has also incurred a huge social cost by directly displacing people and by destroying the common property resources on which people were directly relying upon for their livelihood. There was no proper Rehabilitation and Resettlement Policy for the displaced people in the state until a revised R&R policy was introduced in 1994. The new policy to some extent ensured some amount of compensation for the displaced people, but failed to provide a sustainable compensation to the displaced people and hence, has added to the existing hunger and deprivation in the state, which is also reflected in the micro level case study.

The political and economical aspects of displacement have shown that the SCs/STs have been the most affected victims of displacement, as most of the projects undertaken are found largely in areas with maximum concentration of SC/ST population. Further, as the development project destroyed forests (the major and perhaps the only source of livelihood for the poor and the tribals), the ultimate burden of displacement threatens food security, and might be pushing these disadvantaged groups into hunger and deprivation.

The state, aligning with "capitalists", would like to extract the material resources from Orissa, which hits the poor most. The increasing number of developmental projects not only created a fear in the minds of the people, in the absence of a sustainable R&R policy, but also displaced and created unemployment among people who have also become refugees and urban proletariats. These may lead to lumpenisation in the state. In fact, whatever little was done to help the poor through public provisioning, is being snatched away by displacement.

Notes

1. In Orissa, since 1901, there have been as many as 149 medium and large dams, out of which 18 are under construction, ranging in height from 10 to 71 meters and length from 45 to 6245.85 meters (CWC, 1990:87-90).
2. The area displaced or the number of households/people displaced may slightly differ from study to study. However, such differences would not affect to elicit the larger picture of displacement.
3. The official processing took place till 1946, when the foundation laying ceremony of the dam was supposed to be held, but the foundation was laid by Sri Jawaharlal Nehru on 13.4.1948; and the construction of the project was commenced in February 1949. The first phase of the dam was completed in August 1956 and the project was inaugurated by Sri Jawaharlal Nehru on 13.1.1957.

References

Central Water Commission (1990): *National Register of Large Dams*, New Delhi: Government of India.

Cerena, M. (1995): "Understanding and Preventing Impoverishment from Displacement: Reflections on the State of Knowledge", *Refugee Studies*, 8(3), pp. 245-64.

Currie, B. (2000): *The Politics of Hunger in India: A Study of Democracy, Governance and Kalahandi's Poverty*, Chennai: Macmillan India Ltd.

Dalua, A.K. (1991): "Displacement and Rehabilitation of the Tribal People in the Event of Implementation of Irrigation Projects in Orissa", *Adivasi,* 31(2).

Dalua, A.K. (1993): *Environmental Impact of Large Reservoir Projects on Human Settlement*, New Delhi: Ashish Publishing House.

Das, K. (2002): "Social Mobilisations for Rehabilitations: Relief Work in Cyclone Affected Orissa", *Economic and Political Weekly*, 28(4), pp. 4784-88.

Dash, B. (2002): "Lessons from Orissa Super Cyclone: Need for Integrated Warning System", *Economic and Political Weekly*, 28(4), pp. 4270-71.

Downing, T.E. (2002): *Avoiding New Poverty: Mining-Induced Displacement and Resettlement*, Occasional Paper No. 58, London: International Institute for Environment and Development.

Fernandes, Walter (1994): *Development-Induced Displacement in the Tribal Areas of Eastern India,* New Delhi: Indian Social Institute.

Fernandes, Walter and Mohammed Asif (1997): *Development-Induced Displacement in Orissa. 1951 to 1995: A Database on Its Extent and Nature*, New Delhi: Indian Social Institute.

Fernandes Walter (1994): An Activist Process around the Draft National Rehabilitation Policy, *Social Action*, 45: July-September, pp. 277-98.

Government of Orissa (2006): "Orissa Resettlement and Rehabilitation Policy, Revenue Department", No. 18040/R, Bhubaneswar.

Jena, M. (2006): "Orissa: Draft Resettlement and Rehabilitation Policy", 2006, *Economic and Political Weekly*, 41(5), pp. 384-87.

Mahapatra, L.K. (1989): *Rehabilitation of Tribals affected by Major Dams and Other Projects in Orissa*, A Report on the Workshop on Rehabilitation of Persons Displaced by Development Projects, Institute for Social and Economic Change.

Mahapatra, L.K. (1995): "The Orissa Resettlement and Rehabilitation of Projects Affected Persons Policy, 1994: A Critique", *Social Action*, 45(3).

Ota, A.B. (1996): "Countering the Impoverishment Risk: The Case of Rengali Dam Project", In A.B. Ota and A. Agnihotri (eds.) *Involuntary Displacement in Dam Projects*, New Delhi: Prachi Prakasan.

Ota, A.B. (2001): *Orissa Drought 2001: Its Magnitude and Consequences*, Paper Presented at the Conference, Livelihoods and Poverty Reduction: Lessons from Eastern India, 25-27 September.

Stanley, W. (1996): "Machkund, Upper Kolab and NALCO Projects in Koraput District", Orissa, *Economic and Political Weekly*, 31(24), pp. 1533-38.

Tripathy, S.N. (2003): *Economic Development and Problem of Displacement*, New Delhi: Anmol Publications Pvt. Ltd.

3

Economic Development and Disparity: A Concern for the Displaced People

Narendra K. Behera

Introduction

In the age of new global order, all the countries, particularly developing countries, have come forward with new projects to accelerate the process of progress and to ensure their people a developed economy. But these developmental activities are never without a dark side : evils of suffering, misery, and socio-economic degeneration arising due to population displacement and large-scale damage to the environment. The extent of suffering and miseries of human beings, caused due to development projects, such as, dams, industries, defence establishments, linear projects, etc., is more serious in case of developing countries such as, India, where a sizable section of the affected population are farmers and tribal/indigenous people depending on agriculture and forest as their source of livelihood.

The era of liberalisation has coined development terminologies, such as sustainable development and inclusive growth, to focus on a broader framework of economic development. The concept of inclusive growth has become a popular terminology among the politicians and policy makers alike. It scored over the gains of development without an adequate touch to the cases of those people who had/have become the initial victims of the adverse consequences of development. They are termed as Internally Displaced People (IDP) or 'oustees' in their homeland. The poverty, inequality and discrimination, inflicted upon this section, have received the least attention over the past decades of post-independent India. Moreover, the aggressive 'development terrorism' of neo-liberalism for industrialisation is expected to create millions of IDPs and devastation of environment, leading to climate changes not known ever before. "The key question, however, is common to all involuntarily displaced persons. Given that industrial transformation is necessary to shift surplus workers from agriculture to industry, and that this involves dams, mines, factories, etc., all of which requires changes in land use, how can this be brought in an inclusive manner?" (Nathan, 2009:22). The denial of adequate jobs/ livelihood for the displaced people results in marginalisation

There is increasing pressure from corporate houses and government to acquire more and more land from the people. The vested groups are united to grab farming land and forest land by presenting a rosy picture of development through perpetuating the policy of industrialisation. There is also the operation of international forces to acquire land for multinational corporations. The governments at the centre and the states are guiding the interest of these forces to a larger extent, rather than the interest of the affected people.

While modernisation has been a force for well being in the third world and has brought in some of the expected economic, political and other advantages, it also has revealed its ugly side: It has failed to produce the much vaunted trickle down effect to reduce the vast economic and social inequalities and to empower the poor (Parekh, 1995:21) development projects are not 'space neutral', displacement is inevitable. Does this justify in all cases?

Approaches towards Displacement

Although the study of the basic problems of displacement lies with economists, it has largely been dominated by sociologists and social anthropologists. Despite the negative effects of displacement, the economic study relating to displacement and resettlement is inadequate basically, due to externalisation of social and economic costs of the affected people/area. "Basic research by professional economists on population displacement, to the best of my knowledge, currently is not carried out any where. Development economics still has to respond in full to the challenge of analysing not only the economic dimension of dislocation, but also the economic content of other social development ....population displacement is just another one of those 'social' costs; however, the economic book on displacements' costs is yet to be written" (Cernea, 1999:9). There is enough reason for the study of displacement due to dam projects, because it completely shattered the lives of the displaced people compared to any other projects, and tops the list of involuntary displacement.

In this context, it will be unjust if we fail to mention the displacement scenario of the Hirakud Dam, whose reservoir forms the largest artificial lake in Asia, spreading over 743 sq km at full level. Protection of Coastal Orissa from floods dominated the reasons for the construction of the dam. This project was built over the tears of 18,000 families who were displaced from the most fertile track of Western Orissa. A total of 22,144 families with a population of about 1.1 lakh to 1.6 lakhs, spread over 249 villages in the then Sambalpur District of Orissa, and 36 villages inRaigarhDistrict of Chhattishgarh, have been affected. However, displacement attracted least attention of the planners. On the altar of development, a large number of people have sacrificed their land, home, and lot more, and invited the misery of economic and social deprivation and degradation. Time and again, they have been treated badly by the politicians and bureaucrats: While laying the foundation stone, Nehru told the villagers, "if you are to suffer, you should suffer in the interest of the country" (Supakar, 2007; Viegas, 1992). The construction of IB Thermal Power Station, sponge iron plants, thermal power plants, aluminium industries and coal mining around the Hirakud Reservoir, in the 80s and 90s, again uprooted them for the second/third time.

Another post-independent altar for sacrifice was the construction of Bhakra Dam across the River Sutlej in Punjab. It displaced 7,206 families from 371 villages and affected 36,000 persons. Even today, 50 years after their displacement, they are still struggling to put their lives back on track. The entire economic and social structure of this population was completely disrupted, due to displacement. Long arduous years were spent trying to scrap up enough for minimum sustenance (Dharmadhikari *et al.*, 2005:209, 216).

The displaces of Bhakra Dam and Ranjit Sagar Dam at Pong on the River Beas are going to face a second displacement due to the construction of Special Economic Zones (SEZs) at Gagret in Una Districts of Himachal Pradesh. Here the state violates the basic concept that fertile agricultural land should not be diverted for non-agricultural purposes. It is also a fact that Una District has large plain areas while the rest of the State of Himachal Pradesh is covered with hilly tracks. This implies that to show favour and preference, the state attaches the least care to the former oustees, who have yet to regain their lost status, and farmers who will lose their land to the SEZs.

A few studies, on displacement arising out of industrial projects, have also set a mile stone in this regard. To mention a few, there is the study by B.K. Roy Burman on Rourkela Steel Plant (RSP), S. Parsuraman on

National Thermal Power Station (NTPC) in Korba, K.C. Samal on National Aluminium Company (NALCO), etc. The findings on RSP show that although the benefits accruing to the nation from the multiple benefits of RSP are immense, the locals are affected to a great extent by the 'backwash effects' of industrialisation. Most of the direct and organised sector jobs generated by the steel plant have been monopolised by outsiders, hailing from different parts of the country, and also by the people from the relatively more advanced coastal districts of Orissa, while the backward tribal people of the region and people from other depressed categories of adjacent tribal districts mostly landed up with informal and contractual category jobs of an exploitative nature (Meher, 2001:290).

Mohapatra, P. (1998), a prominent Indian Administrative Service personnel in Orissa and Member of Parliament, admits that little attention was given to the adverse effects of displaced people, over their social, economic and community disruption, although they sacrificed for the building of the nation. The bureaucracy or the civil servants obstruct the implementation of any beneficial schemes announced even by the Chief Minister of the state. In the case of RSP land acquisition, the displaced suffered as the land was allotted to outsiders and employees at a price 100-400 times more than what the government paid as compensation to the displaced people, who were deprived of land and commercial complexes by the authorities. The steel plant employed nearly 10,000 unskilled workers and never thought of accommodating members of the families of displaced persons.

"A cost-benefit analysis, of the major development projects implemented in the country, brings us to the stunning discovery that the Planning Commission criterion of 1:1.5 cost-benefit proportions has rarely been realised in any of them" (Murickan *et al*, 2003:346). The Environmental Impact Assessment (EIA) is hardly carried out properly to guard against the cause of global warming and climate change, which has become a threat to the human and other living species. Industrial waste adversely affects the productivity of the agricultural fields located near the industrial units, and the affected farmers are never compensated. The anti-pollution laws seldom operate in favour of the affected population. Lip service continues towards the issues of environmental, social and human concerns but development dominates these issues, and there is 'lack of human touch' towards the victims of the development projects in general. According to Lobo and Kumar (2009:290), "studies show that a very large number of projects do not fulfil the norms on which they are sanctioned". The misinformation campaigns that are usually launched by affluent developers, tend to exaggerate the benefits and mask the cost of the projects. Nagarjuna Construction Company's project near Sompeta (Andhra Pradesh) is one among many such merchant power projects (Sarma, 2010).

Thus, the studies on the major dams and industries show that the affected population have not become a part of development process, but have been marginalised in terms of employment and livelihood. The general conviction that these people get much through compensation is a fallacious one. On this count, they are again marginalised and are perceived as anti-development by the general public. This sentiment of the people is largely exploited by the politicians against those who face the wrath of displacement through the engine of economic development. The decision of fixing a timeline for availing compensation and R&R measures creates not only discriminations but also a sense of marginalisation amongst the affected population (Behera, 2009).

Estimate of Displacement

Asian countries record the highest incidence of displacement. In India around 21 million people were affected during the last four decades (Fernandes, 1991). Among the displacing agents like dams, industries and mines, dams occupy the top position. During the last two decades of the previous century, the magnitude of forced population displacement caused by development programmes was of the order of 10 million people each year or about 200 million people globally during that period (Cernea, 2000). An estimate in eight states of India, viz. Andhra Pradesh, Assam, Gujarat, Goa, Jharkhand, Kerala, Orissa and West Bengal, shows that about 19,781,109 people were displaced/project affected between 1947 and 2004. If other states of the country are to be added, the figure becomes more than double.

A significant number of the displaced people are the tribal and economically marginal rural populations that depend on natural resources, such as, forests and rivers for their livelihoods. The 29th Report of the Commissioner for Scheduled Castes and Scheduled Tribes (1990) makes a very interesting revelation: The report pointed out that till 1990, of the total displaced persons, 40 per cent were Scheduled Tribes. Their share in the total population of India, however, is only 7.5 per cent; The Scheduled Caste people, who constitute about 16 per cent of the country's population, form 20 per cent of the total displaced persons. But the tribal people can no longer be deceived or deprived of their *jal, jungle* and *jamin* (water, forest and land).

With the adoption of the New Economic Policy, 1991, the domestic private sector and multinationals have assumed the role of industrialising the state, mainly through mineral-based industries, rather than through any value added industries. The era of liberalisation is going to see more displacement in future. Presently, the displacement scenario arising due to POSCO Steel Plant near Paradip and Vedanta Aluminium Project of Niyamgiri has assumed a new dimension between the Government of Orissa and the Government of India. The process of land acquisition for the Vedanta University near Puri, has been questioned by the Hon'ble Lok Pal, and Hon'ble High Court of Odisha.

People's Voice

When a person is transferred from one place to another for a short period of one to three years, he/she-uses all possible means to either cancel or to change the place of transfer, in case the place is not of his/her choice. And when a person is forced to leave her/his birth place and is snatched away from all social and economic means, will he/she not raise a voice? This was the straight, simple truth told by a displaced person to the officials. Once they are out of their original habitations, they are marginalised and their grievances remain unresolved forever. The acquisition of land for various private sector projects, at a low price, has also an ulterior motive in the name of public purpose: The investment in land by the large corporate bodies is considered to be very lucrative and promises very high dividend in future. However, this clashes with the interest of the affected people, and their sources of livelihood; hence the increasing protests against land acquisition and displacement.

It has been an observed fact that the project authorities and the displaced people have no economic compulsion to 'work together'. The oustees organize public processions *rastarokos* (road block), gheraos and bandhs which are often brutally suppressed by force. The political leaders and media often act out of self interest and political directions without promoting the cause of the oustee. Once they are physically removed, whatever little attention was initially paid is also lost, and their grievances are completely isolated. The cases of Hirakud Dam and Rourkela Steel Plant substantiate the point of negligence and marginalisation of the displaced people even after 50 years.

A significant number of people have gradually refused to become silent sufferers of the ill effects of development and are now raising their voices collectively to counter development plans that they feel are against their interest and existence. In the process, they are profoundly influencing the emergence of an alternative development paradigm for India and the North East. (Hussain, 2008)

Medha Patkar and others, through the Narmada Bachao Andolan (NBA) against the construction of Sardar Sarovar Project, could internationalize the cause of the displaced people. The history of struggle against development projects has shown a small record of success, such as the Silent Valley Project, Tikarpara Dam, BALCO aluminium project at Gandhamardan, Baliapal Test Range, etc. The strong protest with a solid political backing forced Tata's Nano car project to move from Singur in West Bengal to Sananda in Gujarat. The long march in October 2007 by more than 25,000 displaced and landless dalits and tribals from Gwalior to New Delhi to pressurize the Central Government to form a national lands commission and formulate a national land reforms policy, was the culmination of many years' struggle, despair, and hope of thousands of landless people (Pai, 2007).

In the recent past, the cases of Kalinganagar, Singur, Nandigram and Kashipur are worth mentioning: The police firing in Kalinganagar killed 13 tribal people (January, 2006), who were protesting against Tata Steel, which is likely to displace 443 families. In 2001, about ten tribal people were killed in a police firing in the protest against the Koel Karo Hydro Power Project. Similarly on December 6, 2008, one person was killed and several were injured in a police firing near Dumka in Jharkhand. A recent release of the people's tribunal on Nandigram has described the police firing and killings of March 14 in Nandigram, as nothing less than a 'state sponsored massacre'. The report of the people's tribunal, headed by Justice S.N. Bhargava finds, "there was unprovoked, indiscriminate firing without sufficient warning and without following the established procedure in accordance with law against a peaceful and lawful gathering of mostly women and children from Nandigram". The report names 14 people, including two women, who were killed by police, and one person who is missing. Further, it describes the unsavoury collusion between the government agencies and the ruling CPI(M) party. Thus, the motive behind this massacre seems to be the ruling party's wish 'to teach a lesson' to the poor villagers in Nandigram, by terrorising them for opposing the proposed Special Economic Zone (SEZ) project (Chaudhuri and Sivaraman, 2007).

On the role of Indian Judiciary, Colin Gonsalves, a senior advocate of the Supreme Court of India says, "there were mass protests against displacement everywhere but the superior judiciary remained unmoved, doggedly anchored to their notions of 'development' unresponsive to the distress of farmers, tenants, and agricultural labourers and the decline of agriculture. During the period of globalisation from 1990 onwards, the Union Government withdrew credits from agriculture and followed conscious anti-farmer policies, rendering agricultural production non-remunerative. In this context, the compulsory acquisition of lands using this (LAA) draconian statute, was the cruellest blow of them all" (Gonsalves, 2010).

The growing euphoria on the part of the state, to create more mineral-based industries, is going to witness the ugly face of development-induced displacement along with serious consequences to the environment in the days to come. In the name of economic development, the developed countries have successfully transferred the most polluting industries to the developing countries, while the brunt of pollution has to be faced by the people of these developing countries.

Brunt of Displacement

Once displacement takes place, whatever may be the policy of R&R, displaced people are marginalised ; their voice remains unheard, they become rootless, and get suppressed ruthlessly. They also face economic and social exclusion. The displaced people of Hirakud Dam, Salandi Irrigation, and many more development projects were not allotted land in the command area of the concerned project. The health and mental status of the affected people was totally ignored in these projects. Based on the issues of resettlement, Prof. Michel M. Cernea evolved eight major impoverishment risk factors, arising out of displacement. These are: (i) landlessness, (ii) joblessness, (iii) homelessness, (iv) marginalisation, (v) food insecurity, (vi) increase in morbidity and mortality, (vii) loss of access to common property, and (viii) social disarticulation. Other risks like the risk of education, shifting of occupation, and risk of loss of livestock may also be added to the above list. The consequence of the insufficient and poorly-conceived compensation, and the resultant failure to recreate livelihoods is impoverishment (Cernea, 2003).

"Expropriation of land removes the main foundation upon which people's productive systems, commercial activities and livelihoods are constructed. This is the principal form of decapitalisation and pauperisation for most rural and many urban displaces, who lose this way both natural and man-made capital" (Cernea, 1999:17). The draft National Tribal Policy (NTP), 2006, also admits that alienation of tribal land is the single most important cause of pauparisation of tribals. The differed investment, in the affected areas and the non-access to the collateral assets, adversely affects their economic and social fabric for a long time. The unsatisfactory and unsettled cases of displacement have led to the growth of depeasantisation and Malthusian refugees.

Further, the women in the society of a displaced community bear a greater burden of displacement, and there also arises the problem of health and life in the process of industrialisation. "Deterioration of air, water and soil becomes obvious and this affects agricultural production, which again deteriorates the condition of the peasant community. Depletion of mineral resources, deforestation, dumping of industrial waste, pollution, haphazard and unplanned human settlement.............This is the stark evidence of the peril of mining and industrialisation" (Dhagamwar, 2003). Various studies have marked out that all cases of involuntary displacement, due to sub-serving development projects are inequitable in which the displacees are not the targeted beneficiaries (Mahapatra, 2006). In the race of development and prosperity, we are leaving behind our environment, which is quite irreversible.

The issue of tribal land or specially that of tribal land alienation has always been a matter of great concern to planners, policy-makers, academicians and activists. This is because, despite progressive and protective legislations, tribal people all over the country are perpetually threatened over their land rights. "......At present, the threat has become more compounded than ever, due to the onslaught of industrialisation, urbanisation, commercialisation and infrastructure development. The traditional mode of securing their livelihood is seriously threatened without any appropriate alternatives in sight" (Ambagudia, 2010).

Although there is no systematic data on the migration of people due to development projects, this is observed largely in the case of dam projects. For example, the displaced people of Hirakud Dam have settled in various parts of Western Orissa and neighbouring Chhattisgarh without availing the irrigation of Hirakud's water, the influx of farmers from Andhra Pradesh dominated the command area. This is also the case with the displaced people of Bhakra, SSP, and other dam projects in the country. No measures have been taken to prevent migration of displaced people of various development projects. This creates a subaltern economy.

Legal and Policy Aspect on Displacement

To carryout the process of expropriation and alienation from landholding rights, the state is well-equipped with a set of colonial laws under the Land Acquisition Act (LAA), amended in 1984. The British were all set to modernize the then capital city, Calcutta, but they were ill equipped, without acquiring the state rights over individual land. The first All India Act VI of 1857 was passed, where land owners were required by the legislature to surrender some of their rights they possessed over their land for a purpose of public utility. A comprehensive LAA covering the whole of British India came as the Act 1 on March 1, 1894. Under the clause of 'Eminent Domain' and 'Public Purpose' the state acquires private land. The Central LAA enables acquisition of land. On the other hand, the matter of state's provision for compensation and R&R measures differ from state to state. In addition to LAA, the Coal-Bearing Areas Act, 1957, occupies a prominent place, in land acquisition and displacement.

It is pointed out that no statute, in colonial India or independent India, has been used against the interests of the poor in such a systematic and widespread manner, causing misery, as the Land Acquisition Act, 1894. Since independence and up to 1995, millions of people were forcibly displaced from their lands, due to a variety of reasons including public projects. The judiciary played a significant role in executing this statute without caring for its effects, on the small and medium landholders and agricultural labourers (Gonsalves, 2010). In the age of globalisation, the state governments have come under the grip of the corporate sector and are eager to spend large public funds to assist private corporate bodies in the acquisition of lands using the Act. But it is a matter of concern that there has been no proper R&R measure for a long time in the country. Maharashtra formulated a policy in 1976, which was followed by other states after a lot of struggle by the affected communities.

In Japan, in order to ease tension and conflict due to land expropriation and relocation, land acquisition has been substituted by leasing of the lands required for reservoirs. In Canada, the local indigenous communities that are affected by the dams have become direct investors in hydro projects, by contributing their land. So also is the case in Columbia, where 20 percent of the project's revenue is allocated towards providing benefits to the displaced population.

The cases of benefit sharing, adopted in other countries, can also be practised in India, but there is lack of uniform policy for various displacing agencies. The mining, industrial, and water resource sectors have different set of policies, each to deal with displacement. The displaced people are dealt with an iron law, and their R&R is made through a policy which is not at par with the status of the law.

The compensation was to be based on historical cost along with a solatium; the concept of replacement cost was unknown. The compensation amount was not a negotiated sum but a figure fixed by the government officials under certain rules. "........enhancement of valuation in some cases (by the Court), but this was nowhere near replacement cost" (Iyer, 2007). No profit-making activity should be termed as a development activity and hence does not deserve land allocation on priority basis or at concessional rates (Reddy & Reddy, 2007).

The Ministry of Rural Development, Government of India, has framed the National Rehabilitation & Resettlement (R&R) Policy to deal with the problem of involuntary relocation in a better way. The incorporation of the provision of Ombudsman in the R&R policy is a welcome step, but the power and function of this body needs further strength. The Orissa R&R policy, 2006, is somehow an improved version and shall apply to all projects for which private land has been acquired under LAA, 1894, as well as for which land is acquired through negotiation under the policy. This policy provides a better deal in comparison to earlier policies. However, certain areas of concern still exist: Inadequate provision of agricultural land for the displaced people from mining and industrial projects, may lead to fettering away of cash compensation in a very short time period. Thus, there is a need to provide the displaced people with replacement of agricultural land. The cases of multiple displacements need special care.

Conclusion and Recommendations

The concept of economic development through industrialisation and promotion of corporate interests at the cost of agriculture, cannot bring a balanced economy in a country like India. Diversion of agricultural land for non-agricultural purposes will threaten not only the livelihood aspects of the displaced community but also the prospect of food security for the ever-growing human population. So displacement should not be looked at from an immediate short term gain point of view.

Development-induced displacements have witnessed marginalisation in the spheres of a project's benefit-sharing, jobs, backwash effects, as well as political and social marginalisation. The violation of human rights by the corporate bodies in connivance with the political parties in power and the government machinery is not an uncommon event in the annals of the development of the country. In a number of cases, the displaced people have become the target of *gundas*/mafias and police atrocities, and have lost their lives. In addition to these economic and social problems, there is large-scale depletion and degradation of natural resources and environment in the project areas, which appears to be irreparable and irreversible.

To achieve sustainable development or inclusive growth, and in order to overcome risks, arising out of the development process, without leaving them as the by-products of development, there is the need to deal with the situation properly. Displacement should either be avoided or restricted to as minimum as possible. Fertile lands and populated areas should be out of the industrial establishment. The displaced people should be provided with the replacement cost of land, rather than the market-determined price for the acquired land. Resettlement and Rehabilitation measures need to precede the construction of projects. Education and training must be imparted to the affected population, before the commencement of the projects so as to prevent hijack of jobs and other benefits by the outsiders. Reservation of seats for the children of the displaced families in professional, educational institutions will help the future generations to be better job seekers and to be part of the development process.

A proper socio-economic survey is a prerequisite to carry out a proper R&R operation. A time-bound measure is needed to achieve an all-round and higher level of development of the affected population/areas. Above all, a corruption-free administrative mechanism is highly essential to percolate the desired economic and social benefits to the bottom of the society. The private corporate units should allot share or rent for their land rather than acquiring the land and rendering the local people landless and marginalised in the face of development.

The LAA needs to be amended so as to enable the displaced people to get back their land in the event of failure/closure of the project or excess acquired land. The 'right to return' should be a part of the act, and the corporate house should come through market-determined land price, without any mediation from the state. The land losers should be paid an annual dividend instead of a one-time compensation only, so that their livelihood will not be affected adversely. Social security measures, such as, family pension, unemployment allowance, health insurance, secured education to students irrespective of their level of schooling and category of caste or creed, and food security during and after displacement, need to be introduced to all categories of displaced people, irrespective of the nature of the project. Insurance on health, life and property should be provided to the affected population. In the case of dams, land in the command area of irrigation projects must be acquired for the displaced people. The corporate houses must adhere to their commitment of discharging Corporate Social Responsibility in a vigorous manner towards the displaced people and their environment. A normative approach is necessary to prevent deprivation and marginalisation of the already displaced people. To finance displacement, measures, such as collection of special assessment from the project benefit area, particularly in case of irrigation projects, can also be taken up. The development projects should pursue the path of inclusive growth for the project-displaced people, rather than leading to their miseries.

References

Ambagudia, J. (2010): "Tribal Rights, Dispossession and the State of Orissa", *Economic and Political Weekly*, 45(33), pp. 60-67.

Baboo, B. (1992): *Technology and Social Transformation, The Case of Hirakud Multipurpose Dam Project in Orissa, New* Delhi: Concept Publishing Co.

Baxi, U. and B. Parikh (ed.) (1995): *Crisis and Changes in Contemporary India,* New Delhi: Sage Publications.

Behera, N.K. (2009): *Displacement, Resettlement and Rehabilitation*, Unpublished Thesis, submitted to Sambalpur University.

Behera, N.K. (2009): "An Introspection to the Twin Issue of Neo-Liberalisation", *Social Research Journal*, 2(2): 43-49.

Bhaduri, A. (2007): "Alternatives in Industrialisation", *Economic and Political Weekly*, 42(18), pp. 1597-1601.

Cernea M. (ed.) (1999): *The Economics of Involuntary Resettlement: Questions and Challenges, Washington* DC: World Bank.

——— (2003): "For a New Economics of Resettlement: A Sociological Critique of the Compensation Principle", *International Social Science Journal*, 55(175), pp. 37-45.

——— (2007): "Financing for Development, Benefit Sharing Mechanism in Population Resettlement", *Economic and Political Weekly,* 42(12), pp. 1033-46.

Chaudhuri, D.R. and S. Sivaraman (2007): "Nandigram Six Months Later", *Economic and Political Weekly,* 42(41): 4103-4105.

Debarajan (2008): "Is the Struggle for Livelihood a Criminal Offence", *Economic and Political Weekly*, 43(2), pp. 19-22.

Dharmadhikari *et al.* (2005): *Unravelling Bhakra,* Badwani: Manthan Adhyaayan Kendra.

Dhagamwar *et al.* (2003): *Industrial Development and Displacement, The People of Korba,* New Delhi: Sage Publications.

Fernandes, W. (2004): "Rehabilitation Policy for the Displaced", *Economic and Political Weekly,* 39(12), pp. 1191-93.

Fernandes, W. and E.G. Gunguli (ed.) (1989): *Development and Rehabilitation*, New Delhi: Indian Social Institute.

Government of Orissa (2006): *Orissa Resettlement and Rehabilitation Policy 2006*, Revenue Department Government of Orissa, Bhubaneswar.

Government of India (2007): *National Rehabilitation and Resettlement Policy, 2007*, Ministry of Rural Department, New Delhi.

Guha, A. (2007): "Peasant Resistant in West Bengal a Decade before Singur and Nandigram", *Economic and Political Weekly*, 42(37), pp. 3706-11.

Gonsalves, C. (2010): "Judicial Failure on Land Acquisition for Corporations", *Economic and Political Weekly*, 45(32), pp. 37-42.

Hussain, M. (2008): *Interrogating Development*, New Delhi: Sage Publications.

Iyer R.R. (2007): "Towards a Just Displacement and Rehabilitation Policy", *Economic and Political Weekly*, 42(30), pp. 3103-07.

Lobo, L. and S. Kumar (2009): *Land Acquisition, Displacement and Resettlement in Gujarat, 1947-2004,* New Delhi: Sage.

Mahapatra, L.K. (1999): "Testing the Risk and Reconstruction Model on India Resettlement Experience", In M. Cernea (1999), *The Economics of Involuntary Resettlement,* Washington, DC: World Bank.

Maloney (1991): *Environmental Project and Displacement of Population in India,* Field Staff (International) Report No. 14.

Meher, R. (2001): "Degenerating of the Periphery under Hegemonic Development the Case of Aboriginal in a Tribal Region", *Indian Social Science Review,* 3(4), pp. 289-325.

Mohapatra, P. (1998): *Development Induced Displacement and Rehabilitation,* Bhubaneswar: Prachi Prakashan.

——— (2006): "Displacement of Tribal People with Land Resources for Development Projects: Their Risks and Entitlement for Rehabilitation", *Adivasi*, 46(2).

Murickan *et al.* (2003): *Development Induced Displacement,* New Delhi: Rawat Publication.

Nathan, D. (2009): "Social Security, Compensation and Reconstruction of Livelihoods", *Economic and Political Weekly,* 44(30), pp. 22-26.

Pai, S. (2007): "Janadesh 2007: The Land Question", *Economic and Political Weekly,* 42(45-46), pp. 10-12.

Panda, D.K. and N.K. Behera (2008): "Development and Displacement: An Orissa Experience", *Journal of Rural Development*, 27(1):91-110.

Panwar, T.S. (2008): "Nailing the Himachal Pradesh Government's Lies", *Economic and Political Weekly*, 43(50):14-15.

Reddy & Reddy (2007): "Land Alienation and Local Community", *Economic and Political Weekly,* 42(31), 3233-40.

Sarma, E.A.S. (2010): "The Saga of Sompeta: Public Deception, Private Gains", *Economic and Political Weekly*, 45(33), pp. 38-43.

Sharma, R.N. (2003): "Involuntary Displacement: A Few Encounters", *Economic and Political Weekly*, 38(9), pp. 907-12.

Suryanarayan, M.H. (2008): "What Is Exclusive About 'Inclusive Growth' ", *Economic and Political Weekly,* 43(43), pp. 93-101.

4

Mining Industries and the Dignity of Development in Backward States: An Anthropological Search for Solution

Premananda Panda

Background

Any resource-centric development is bound to change the physical conditions of the ecosystem. Development and secured life are synonymous: Developmentrefers to the change in quality of life towards betterment; sustainable development requires that the welfare state must ensure its citizens' security, while it governs the resources efficiently. Thus, if there is any development project, be it agrarian or industrial, it must precisely address the aspirations and the problems of the mass, and more specifically, of the people at the grassroot level. Any resource-centric development with the support of higher level sophisticated technological input is bound to destabilize the hitherto harmonic life of the people having lesser technology in the area. As a result, there will not only be an altered physical geography, but also the relationship between nature and culture of the community inhabiting the area, as their integral man-area-resources corporation assumes a negative trend, which is likely to yield a variety of social evils. Often, even the high energy harvesting technology leads over other technologies, pushing the native communities towards either elimination or marginalisation.

This paper analyses the secondary data on Jharkhand mines and the development of people at the grassroots. It has been observed that the mining industries have produced many environmental refugees, caused a massive livelihood displacement. The dignity of development either simply results in a higher growth rate, or implies an elaborate bureaucratic mechanism for income transfer, to improve the distribution of income in favour of the poor. However, development rests in the efficiency of the social support system, of the people concerned. Thus, any form of development has to be viewed through an integral approach, where income growth and distribution are integral to the process of development, from the peoples' perspective, wherein the people have a say in the decision-making process, for their economy and environment. We take pride in saying, that with its immensely diverse ethnic markers, our nation has managed to consolidate its democratic system over the six decades of independence. The achievement is more striking because Indian democracy has been functioning in the context of abject poverty.

Development, in post-independent India, has resulted in development-induced displacement and impoverishment of a large number of people. The quantification of displacement is based on the size of the project: The bigger the industries, and the bigger the project, bigger is the displacement, which is based on the Land Acquisition Act, 1984 (LAA), which in turn is based on the principle of eminent domain. In Australia, this act is known as *terra nullius, and* has been declared as null and void by the judiciary. The post 1990 period has accentuated this paradigm of development, which has converted tribal and rural economy into some form of internal colonies. The development with equity in the resource-rich but poor tribal areas, logically leads to the formulation of community sector in industries.

The fundamental principle of the doctrine of globalism is economic liberty for the global players working towards industrial growth, which the state is trying to regulate in the name of public interest. Thus, any impediment coming from the people must be erased. The state power is being used to this effect, in the name of maintaining peace and order. In a sense, the free flow of trade and capital for industrial houses, treat these impediments as barriers to progress. In order to help the translational corporations to exploit labour and environment in their interest, the developing states are being pressurised by international bodies such as, the IMF, WTO and World Bank, using their power in the wake of neo-liberalism for economic development in the interest of the MNCs that are armed with the power of money, and support from state administration.

In the meantime, it is also known to us that there has been drastic reduction in government spending towards long-term investments that would enhance the quality of health, education, welfare, and environmental protection. We have witnessed the opening of the market and encouragement of the free flow of capital and labour, resulting in higher concentration of population in urban areas and destabilisation of the agrarian economy. The pride for village republic is being eroded at a rapid pace.

Impact of Land Acquisition

Involuntary displacement of the tribals from their habitat and the process in which the government undertakes acquisition of land and forest to facilitate the industrialisation processes, such as, mining have threatened the voiceless mass. The middle and rich peasants complain of labour scarcity, while the labour is forced to migrate to urban areas in search of employment asthe rich peasants adopt mechanisation in agriculture. Hence, we see that the rural and tribal peoplewho have lived for centuries in their ecology, are now in the process of transformation.In addition, it has also been observed that there has been a shift in the use of land and forest for non-agriculture and non-forest activities.During the post 1990 period, the land and forest, in states, such as, Orissa, Chhattisgarh and Jharkhand have been acquired for industrialisation. In this context, this paper intends toexamine thedisplacement issue ina few backward states and attempts to offer some arguments in favour of distributive justice in which the land and forest losers can have better alternatives in enjoying the fruits of development.

Development-Induced Displacement in Orissa

Orissa is characterised by plenty amidst plenty. This state has got the highest deposits of minerals. The major minerals in Orissa include iron ore, chromites, bauxite, coal, nickel and graphite. It has also been stated that there is low rate of utilisation of the available deposits. In order to exploit the minerals, there are 603 mines of which 343 are functional; among these, 303 mines are in tribal blocks. Regarding the type of ownership, 513 mines are privately owned and 90 mines are owned by government/public undertakings.

Till 1995, around 130 sponge iron factories were functioning in Mayurbhanj, Keonjhar, Jharsuguda and Sundargarh districts. This has increased even more in number by now. Most of these come under the Scheduled Areas. Although the consent of the Gram Panchayat has been essential, no permission from the Gram Panchayat was obtained. While on the one hand, the tribals lost their livelihood, on the other, huge concessions were given to the industries.

Most of the mineral resources are located on tribal lands and the forests. Mines have thus impacted forest-dependent tribals the most. A feature of tribal lands is that they do not have a record of their rights. Thus the tribal land losers mostly remain uncompensated. About 75%

of the displaced are tribals, as a result of industrial and mining projects; and the magnitude, of displacement in development projects, has increased to more than 4 lakhs. About 20 lakh people have lost their land, and about 15 lakh people were indirectly affected. While dam/irrigation projects displaced about 80% of the tribals, mining and industrial projects displaced about 10%.

The following table (Table 4.1) indicates the quantity of forest used for non-forest purposes:

Table 4.1 Forest Areas Diverted to Non-Forest Use in Orissa (sector-wise 2005-06)

Sl. No.	*Name of Sector*	*No. of Proposals*	*Forest Area Diverted as on 1.4.2004 (in ha)*
1	Irrigation	6	1224.664
2	Industries	2	65.039
3	Mining	13	847.05
4	Transmission line	2	8.762
5	Roads and bridges	2	5.172
6	Railway line	1	2.998
7	Total	26	2153.685

Source: http/www.orienvis.nic.in / nonforestuse.asp

The following table (Table 4.2) reveals that mining-rich industriesarealso rich in forest and tribal population. The inflow of outsiders due to large-scale mining projects has made the tribals 'a minority in their own land'

Table 4.2 Mining in Forest and Tribal Areas of Orissa

Sl. No.	*District*	*Major Minerals*	*Area under Mining (in ha)*	*Forest Cover (%)*	*Total Population (in lakhs)*
1	Jajpur	Chromite	4543.2	9.04	7.4
2	Keonjhar	Iron ore and manganese	31255.5	38.97	44.52
3	Sundargarh	Iron ore	20017.2	41.44	50.74
4	Angul	Coal	10230.5	41.66	11.68
5	Koraput	Bauxite	6297.3	17.68	50.67
6	Jharsuguda	Coal	8865.5	13.89	31.88
7	Mayurbhanj	Iron ore	5391.6	38.44	57.87

Source: Orissa Human Development Report 2004, Orissa Economic Survey 2004.

The tribal communities are vulnerable to corporate globalisation. There has been massive displacement for the upcoming industries. During 1990-1996, the Orissa Government acquired 13000 acres of land in Kalinga Nagar, of which 53.84% was private land (*The Samaj*, 21st Jan 2006), from 15 tribal villages. Between 1992 and 1997, the Orissa Government has attracted around Rs. 97,300 crores as foreign direct investment, and most of this has gone into the mining sector.

Table 4.3 The Scale of Displacement in Orissa during 1951-1995

Sl. No.	*Name of Mineral*	*Quantum of Production*
1	Coal	831.71
2	Limestone	238.26
3	Iron ore	129.73
4	Sand for stowing	26.53
5	Mica	26.19
6	Bauxite	11.79
7	Dolomite	2.57
8	China clay	1.72
9	Copper ore	0.94
10	Bentonite	0.17

Similarly, for Langigarh Project the Government of Orissa has signed up with the Vedant Company of UK for extracting aluminium from bauxite in Niyamgiri Hills. A total of 1444.666 hectares of land was acquired, of which 723.34 hectares was for the alumina refinery, and 721.323 hectares for the mines. This includes 730.961 hectares of forest land, and the project displaces a little more than 100 families. The tribals have been apprehensive of being deprived of 232.75 hectares of their land. Further, the Dangaria Kondhs of Kalahandi District are likely to lose their homes and sources of livelihood. Similarly, the Doraguda plant alone affects 2500 persons, while open cast mining in Baphlimali, is likely to affect 2500 families in 24 villages in three Panchayats namely; Chandragiri, Maikanch and Kodipari.

The Kalinga Nagar issue witnessed agitations and killings in connection with the plant's allocated land and the apprehension of the people towards being marginalised in the recent years. The Government of Orissa has acquired 10000 acres of land in 1991-92, and 15000 acres in 1995 (Orissa Report). There are pro and anti-project groups, periodically launching agitations. Similar is the casein Kashipur area of Rayagada District for Alcan Hindalco Bauxite Project, where the Government wanted to have discussions with the Gram Panchayat, but the Gram Panchayat refused to have any project in the area.

Jharkhand, India's 28th state, came into existence on 15th November, 2000, with a commitment to all-round development and prosperity of its people in general, and vulnerable communities in particular. The state is well endowed with natural resources and, therefore, has enormous potential for industrialisation with its large deposits of minerals providing a major support for mineral processing and manufacturing of heavy machinery. The state has a wide industrial base and ambitious plans, for massive investment in various industries, such as, the metal and engineering industry, energy production and non-conventional energy, telecommunications and electronics, drugs and pharmaceuticals, food processing, mineral-based industries, and the like. This has to be combined with a parallel effort to minimize pollution to prevent damaging the state's natural biodiversity. In terms of development of eco-tourism too, the state has great potential.

Jharkhand's forest-based resources and agriculture offer a panorama for agro-based industries, such as, food processing, floriculture, and medicinal and aromatic plants. The right use, of these resources and utilisation of the opportunities, both in the domestic market, as well as in the international market depends not only on the availability of trained and skilled manpower but also on the availability of quality infrastructure and suitable incentives by the government and big corporate bodies. To develop floriculture and food processing, suitably skilled manpower along with positive incentives would be required. Since each industry, provides direct employment to people, but for indirect employment, efforts should be made to set up quality education facilities for the development of skilled manpower as well as package of incentives for entrepreneurs to establish industries in the state, which will absorb the trained manpower emerging out of the institutes. This joint strategy would be far more self-sustaining than just focusing on either of the two individually.

Mining in Jharkhand forms an integral part of the economy of the state. In Jharkhand, the districts of Bokaro, Ranchi, Jamshedpur, etc., are known for their rich mineral reserves. Some of the important minerals in these areas, that form a basis for mining in Jharkhand are asbestos, mica, bauxite, manganese, china clay, fire clay, graphite, gold, kyanite, chromite, copper ore, iron ore, manganese, uranium, coal, thorium, silver, limestone, etc. Most of these deposits are found in the Scheduled Areas. Mining lease was granted to John Saminar and S.G. Huttly of the East India Company on 11th August 1774, during the British Rule, for mining coal in Ranigunj area, a portion of undivided Bengal-Bihar and Orissa unit. This unit was administrated by the Bengal Presidency under the leadership of Warren Hastings. During the 1800s many private individuals and companies obtained coal mining leases from the colonial government and started digging; and transporting outside India. There were only 91 mining companies during the 1891 Census, but by 1942, there were as many as 725 coal mines operating, in the whole country at different places. The earlier known big mine owners in Orissa were Tata Steel, Steel Authorities of India Ltd. (SAIL), and Coal India.

Through the new economic policy of 1991, the Government of India encouraged privatisation and globalisation. At the policy level there was a great shift from public to private sector, and from state monopoly to opening up of the market to global trading. The Mines and Mineral Regulation and Development Act was amended in 1993 in line with the new economic policy of the Government of India, which shifted from a thrust on regulation to development. This was again amended in 1994 and 1999, to accommodate private parties, mostly of foreign origin, with a hope of inflow of foreign funding.

The history, of the newly born state, is more accelerating today than ever before, in terms of extraction of mineral deposits, MoUs with the cooperate bodies, and also unwanted disturbing forces, such as, the naxals. Compared to the colonial forces that subjugated the native Adivasis, the country after independence has exploited the nature, more for the extraction of commercially viable mines and minerals without foreseeing the social cost incurred by the communities living in and around the natural resources. The snow clad mountains are increasing in area every day. This places mother earth at a great environmental risk, causes huge loss to the cultural ecology of the people at the grassroots, and generates a threat to the symbiotic relationship, between the resources and the people, that has existed since time immemorial. Sustainability is inherent in the practice of indigenous communities, but since it has altered through the history of political and economic subordination, the customary rights of the people on the common property resources are ignored and mutilated. Finding no other alternative, the people resort to non-traditional sources of income, resulting in the increasing participation of people in the labour market as diggers, lifters, and other labour intensive engagements, while afew unfortunate, who fail to get any scope of employments migrate across the state borders to work in brick kilns, construction units, etc.

During the early 1980s a few scholars advocated that industrialisation was the answer to the problems of economic backwardness and poverty in countries, such as, ours. However, another group of scholars were of the opinion that, since, less developed countries, depend heavily on agriculture and faced rapid growth of population and labour force compared to the industrialised nations, high priority must be given to agricultural production, in order to provide food security and generate employment for the poor. Accordingly, the Sixth Plan had both the components: the anti-poverty component and the employment plans. But the major lacunae, it had, were the weak links between the employment targets and the targets for poverty eradication. The backward linkages of industries did not work well. Many theories were articulated, mostly limited to the economic parameters; and none of them were free from criticism.

The new economic policy was announced by the Central Government in 1991. One of the development ideas was mooted in terms of core-periphery dependency theory. The explanation of the failure of the modernisation paradigm was made in the lines of in-built cultural misunderstanding and defects, and the perpetuation of inequality and disparities that continue, due to the differential accessibility to the expertise, technology, and capital investment (Mohanty, 2009). To understand the concept of development, one needs to look into the shifts in the development discourses focusing upon the natural resources exploitation and growth in the gross national product. As the government moves towards diversion of forest land for mining, there is strong opposition from the NGOs and environmentalists, who strive to save the life and livelihood of the tribals. The emerging environmental problems of resource depletion, pollution, acid rain, destruction of tropical and sub-tropical forests in a faster pace, huge loss of biodiversity and ultimately the livelihood resources, of the people, at the grassroots, have raised a lot of questions, on the cost of development as social cost is mostly undermined when such assessment is made. Let us have a cursory look at the available data in a tabulated form, in order to assess the income potential of the state. The following table (Table 4.4) reveals the details of mineral production in Jharkhand.

Table 4.4. Production of Minerals in Jharkhand in 2002-03 (in lakh tons)

Sl. No.	*Name of Mineral*	*Quantum of Production*
1	Coal	831.71
2	Limestone	238.26
3	Iron ore	129.73
4	Sand for stowing	26.53
5	Mica	26.19
6	Bauxite	11.79
7	Dolomite	2.57
8	China clay	1.72
9	Copper ore	0.94
10	Bentonite	0.17

Source: Department of Industries, Industrial Policy of Jharkhand, Govt. of Jharkhand 2001.

Jharkhand Displacement

Up to November 2007, Jharkhand has signed MoUs with 66 companies for large-scale investments. This move of the government was resisted by the people. For example, there was a massive rally in Chaibasa on 10th November 2005, by the people who proclaimed that they will not give away their land and forest for mining industries. Tata Steel was vehemently prevented from setting up their plant in Chakradharpur. The big companies are greedy to acquire more land than what is really required for their mining operations. The mineral contribution of the state to the nation, can well be imagined, when we make a comparative assessment as mentioned below (Table 4.5).

Table 4.5 Important Minerals in Jharkhand and its Share of Nation's Reserve

Sl. No.	*Mineral*	*Contribution of Jharkhand (in M. Tons)*	*Percentage Share of India's Reserve*
1	Iron ore	10052	37%
2	Coal	211593.61	32%
3	Copperore	441	25%
4	Granite	42916	21%
5	Fire clay	518	9.65%
6	Graphite	4.5	8.4%
7	Quartz and silica	2402	6.1%

Sources: Ministry of Mines and Geology, Govt. of Jharkhand, 2003.

Similarly, the pressure on forests, mostly comes from outside the forestry sector and among them one important cause is mining. Mines can occupy and despoil large tracts of land. Many mines have been opened during the last decades and still more are on the way. These affect the forest ecosystem to which the tribal communities' social support system is intimately connected. It is pertinent to mention here that according to a study made by the World Resources Institute (WRI), large scale mining and exploration of fossil fuels with their related roads and energy needs represent the second largest (after commercial logging) threat to the frontiers of forest globally, affecting 40% of all forest frontiers, classified under moderate or high threat (Bryant, Neilsen and Tangley, 1997). According to the 6th citizen report of the Centre for Science and Environment (CSE) titled "Rich Lands, Poor People:Is Sustainable Mining Possible?", almost all India's minerals are in the same region that hold its greenest forests and the most abundant river systems. These lands are also largely inhabited by India's poorest and marginalised people, who depend on the forest and watersheds for their survival (Misra and Reddy, 2009).

Jharkhand Stateis one of the top mining states that have diverted 30% of its forest land for surface mining excavation amounting to 9059.03 hectares. This is above the national average. Further, the state has a dubious distinction of clearing maximum amount of forest land for mining, leading to deforestation, loss of wildlife, damage of river systems, and above all, reducing the traditional tribal livelihood resources (collection, hunting, agriculture), and other social support systems such as kinship-based distribution of resources and mutual obligation for sharing and caring the men and materials at the village level. This altered the traditional role of women, within the subsistence communities by alienating them from the right, to cultivate traditional crops due to forest denudation.

With regard to the mining legislations in forest areas, any mining activity requires clearance from the Forest and Environment departments of the Central Government, so that the forest can be preserved; and ecological balance can be maintained. There are many land-related protective acts, such as, the Chotanagpur Tenancy Act 1908, Santal Paragana Tenancy Act 1949, the Mines and Mineral (Development and Regulation) Act, 1957 (MMDR Act) amended in 1994, in the line of new mineral policy of the Central Government in 1993, Mines Act 1952, Mineral Concession Rules 1960, Mineral Concession and Development Rules 1988, Coal Bearing Act (CBA) of 1957, Metalliferous Minerals

Regulations 1961, Forest Conservation Act 1980, National Forest Policy 1988, Environment Protection Acts and Rules 1986, and Environment Impact Assessment Notification 2006, are some of the important legislations to protect the forest and thereby protect the livelihood of the tribal people. On document, it is one of the vital measures to protect the forest. Availing the opportunities of India's liberalised approach and relaxation in the mining policy, as part of the new economic policy announced in 1991, many aspirant corporate houses expressed their interest in Jharkhand to launch their units. The Jharkhand's, State Government signed MoUs with different corporate houses, such as, Jindal, Mittal, Essar, Tatas, Birlas, and others, mostly for sponge iron and steel. Such houses that have already made entry, numbered around 70, till November 2007. There has been a mushroom growth of stone quarries and crushers all over the state.

Table 4.6 Area Covered by Major Mineral Leases in the State of Jharkhand (in hectares)

Sl.No.	*Minerals*	*No. of Leases*	*Leased Area*
1	Coal	206	129567.54
2	Copper ore	3	15857.7
3	Bauxite	41	9012,63
4	Limestone	44	9553.9
5	Kyanite	5	2500.16
6	Pyroanite	3	43.96
7	Dolomite	2	546.83
8	Iron ore	42	32438
9	Magnetite	9	357.09
10	Graphite	22	3382.16
11	China clay	33	3787.67
12	Fire clay	34	4525,38
13	Mica	15	1318.04
14	Shop stone	6	250.87
15	Sand for stowing	23	4965.83
16	Uranium	1	1312.62
17	Feldspar/Quartz	32	1782.12
18	Yellow ochre	2	40.56
19	Red ochre	1	55.43

Sources: Ministry of Mines and Geology, Govt. of Jharkhand, 2003.

Table 4.7 Displaced Persons due to Mining Projects

Sl. No.	*Project*	*District*	*STs*	*%*	*SCs*	*%*	*Others*	*%*	*Total*
1	BCCL	Dhanbad	51293	38.	22692	16.9	60290	44.9	134275
2	CCL	Haz Rachi Palamau	6630	23.4	4675	16.5	17030	60.1	28335
3	Rajmahal	Godda	3530	48.5	0	00.0	3755	51.5	7285
4	Piparwar	Hazaribagh	1358	08.8	2901	18.8	11174	72.4	15433
5	Tisco	Dhanbad	105	08.4	193	15.5	952	76.1	1250
6	Tulsidamr	Garhwal	100	25.0	240	60.0	60	15.0	400
7	UCIL	E. Singhbhum	2543	28.9	422	04.8	5835	66.3	8800
Total			65559	33.48	31123	15.89	99096	50.61	195778

Sources: Ministry of Mines and Geology, Govt. of Jharkhand, 2003.

The Indian Bureau of Mines, in its "Indian Minerals at a Glance", revealed that India earned Rs. 59509 crores from mineral production, while Jharkhand alone earned Rs. 4997 crores. According to activists, Jharkhand Region is rich in natural resources and many government and private companies have appropriated land to build a number of factories to extract natural resources. Although tribal people are supposed to receive compensation, a number of activists allege that they do not receive adequate compensation.

Displacement in Jharkhand is a continuous process. Different projects have displaced different number of indigenous people from their traditional habitat. Many private coal, bauxite iron, manganese, uranium and copper mines, leasing-in large quantums of land and forest in Jharkhand, were started prior to 1950. However, they did not maintain any record worth mentioning with regard to displacement. For a conservative estimate, coal mining displacement between 1951 and 1995 may be cited here (Table 4.7) to imagine the rate of displacement that occurred in Jharkhand.

Skilled manpower trained in entrepreneurship as well as technical skills in terms of silvi-culture, wildlife management, forest products, ecology and environment, forest management, forest science and extension, and social forestry, would be required to fully utilize the opportunities provided by these projects. Hence, the existing institutes need upgradation of intake capacity, along with massive improvements in infrastructure and skilled instructors.

All the mining industries have contributed the most to altering the physical geography that hitherto remained as the major source of livelihood for the people, at the grassroots, of Jharkhand State. It needs to be mentioned here that the reasons for deterioration of physical environment relates to the state ownership of natural resources. And though, Jharkhand is ahead of the average industrial state of the country, the shift towards tertiary sector, still needs to be made. This provides a rough road map to the policy-makers, as well as points out opportunities of growth that can be obtained by focusing on the tertiary sector. Tourism requires development of the educational institutions, as well as inviting private sector players, who can actively put Jharkhand on the map of the eco-tourists. This would create the necessary demand for the graduates while developing the tourism industry at the same time.

In the service industry too, Jharkhand can develop as a hub for higher education. Educational industrialisation is one of the long-term investments which would create an efficient human resource base, and using the existing infrastructure facilities, there can be genesis and growth of diversified economic frontiers in the state. This will work, if the state becomes pro-people and does not act as hunch inspiration for the MNCs, ignoring the basic needs of the people at the grassroots. For long-term development of the state and the people through its developing human resources, quality inputs are essential, as they would generate funds and recreate a new human resources inventory, for the sound progress of the state. The major enablers, that would push the state in this high growth sector for providing education include suitable incentives for investments in infrastructure and institutes. Further, high level education, such as medicine, engineering and management, can be provided either by inviting the private sector to invest in the state or through a public-private partnership.

Dynamism among the developed states in south India, namely Karnataka, Tamil Nadu and Andhra Pradesh, in terms of IT-based industries and IT-enabled services, must be replicated in Jharkhand. This will have a dual benefit and give impetus to the private sector to invest in the state, thus creating both direct and indirect employment, while giving incentives for educational institutions to set up bases in the state, as there would be a ready market for the newly-trained graduates.

In order to improve the quality of education, there should be major focus on strengthening the faculty in education institutes, along with heightened emphasis on vocational training and development of linkages with different industries. Further, this needs to be accompanied with a continual focus on curriculum review in order to make it relevant to the requirements of steel production, cottage industry, mineral resources, and agriculture, which are the major drivers of the Jharkhand economy.

Jharkhand directory is a vast online resource on valuable information related to the Jharkhand State, which provides website listing on various categories, highlighting business industries, trade shows and trade fairs, travel and tourism, famous hotels and resort websites, and online shopping in Jharkhand. Ready informative content, on the industries in Jharkhand through website listing, is available in this online guide. Furthermore, information related to the leading manufacturers and suppliers in Jharkhand, exporters and importers of business products, and on all important Jharkhand service providers, is also available in the Jharkhand online web guide.

Rehabilitation and resettlement can be seen from the policies, common to both Orissa and Jharkhand, that do not tally with the policy of the centre. The states have failed to provide adequate compensation for land and house, and basic amenities such as water, schools, hospitals and employment opportunities for the landless labour. The common property resources, of the people in the tribal areas, are not valued in the right perspective, and the titles of the house plots have not been made available to the displaced. Moreover, traditional rights are never given importance at the time of deciding compensation, and there has been failure to provide land for land and subsistence allowance during transition periods. There has been no public hearing or open discussion with the affected people, before they were displaced. Besides, social security, based on kinship relations, has never been taken into account while rehabilitating and resettling the displaced and affected people. There were neither selective consultancies nor consultations were ever made with the villagers and local NGOs.

Conclusion

The typical features observed inland acquisition since 1990, the year of globalism, are as follows:

- The Land acquisition Act of 1894 amended in 1984 used 'for the purpose of public domain' that was used for the public sector is now being used in favour of private profit-making industries.
- The Corporate Social Responsibility (CSR) of the industries is never followed in spirit and they feel comfortable with a few inputs given only once.
- Follow up actions are hardly taken up by the corporate houses.
- Heavy concession is given to the industries at the time of land acquisition, while land legislation and role of PESA are ignored.
- Lands are being acquired at throw-away prices. A few NGOs that initially plead for the people, later remain silent, while people's resistance is countered with *lathi* charge, imposing of Section 144, gang war, and harassment to the people who go for ventilating their grievances.

Keeping in view the above points with regards to backward states, such as, Orissa and Jharkhand, the following suggestions are made:

- On principle, and as far as possible, displacement should be avoided.
- Consultation, although limited to the fifth Scheduled Areas, should also be extended to the non-scheduled areas.
- Rehabilitation should be mandatory and should go side by side with the project.

- The loss, of common property resources and other livelihoods, should be compensated, because, the development can be justified only when no section of people suffer.
- 'Quality land for quality land' should be the basis of rehabilitation for the displaced.
- Conceptually, the tribals, living for generations should be not treated as encroachers. There is urgent need to rethink on the principle of eminent domain that land belongs to the state; the concept of public purpose needs to have a restrictive definition.
- The people's right to know in advance regarding specific proposals, that would affect their livelihood, need to be encouraged in order to avoid any further impoverishment.

The characterisation, of socio-cultural displacement as a condition of disintegration, does not imply that the displaced are unable to give meaning to their existence and suffering. They have the capacity to draw on social or religious ideals, co-operative effort, and solidarity in order to reinforce psychological and physical defence, in even the most extreme situations. This has been evidenced from many parts of the project areas. Their coping mechanisms, in response to uncertainty, anxiety and stress, may become stronger for defensive purpose as they realize the threat of the superior power (be it the central or local government authorities).

The rapid social change, experienced by the displaced, is turning into a process of alienation from cultural roots that give symbolic meaning to their existence, social control, and interaction. Undoubtedly, such an abstraction has social revolutionary potential; but without favourable socio-economic conditions, the consequences may instead become anti-revolutionary and counter-productive. Averting the destructive potential of displacement requires a strategy that entails more than evacuation.

First, rehabilitation of the project displaced must be planned and implemented. Second, the strategy for rehabilitation should consider the people's socio-economic reality. Further, the rehabilitation strategy must be sensitive to the processes, operating in the social formation and include a comprehensive plan, to release the developmental potential of the marginalised in backward states. The corporate houses must come forward to share profit with the displaced, who sacrificed for the growth of the industry.

Further, there are many factors that influence the compensation decisions made in organisations. The organisation, that acquired the land, must take initiatives to see that at the time of signing the Memorandum of Understanding (MoU), there is proportionate profit-sharing with the displaced.

Keeping in view the rapid changes in ecological conditions, sources of livelihood, and the trend to migrate, a few suggestions have been made below:

Suggestions

1. Since most of the displaced are SCs and STs, and have a history of being marginalised , displacement of the people should be avoided as far as possible. In unavoidable situations, the displaced families should be resettled in the spirit of 'community transplanted', so that they do not feel alienated from their cultural ecology.
2. The PESA Act should be extended to all non-PESA mineral belts, both rural and tribal; areas with spirit and words and non-coercive open discussion / public hearing should be encouraged and the emergent consensus should be put into action.
3. The quality, of existing human resources of the people likely to be displaced, due to forthcoming projects, should be enhanced so as to make them the beneficiaries of the projects almost at par with the project personnel on payroll.
4. Besides, the usual compensation assessments made on tangible substances of the displaced, the intangibles, such as, the loss of indigenous social support system, the cost of culture, and the cost of loss of skill and techniques should be assessed and compensatory payment should be extended accordingly.
5. After being duly rehabilitated and resettled, a fixed share of the profit incurred by the organisation should be made available to the displaced, and the acquiring body should take the responsibility in streamlining the benefits to the affected people.
6. CSR should be mandatory and should be a part of constant and continuous process to empower the affected families for at least two generations.
7. The Panchayat (Extension to the Rural Areas) Act 1996 is the most revolutionary legislation. Powers are vested in the Gram Sabhas, though the definition of Gram Sabhas is different and based on localities. Consultation, with the Gram Sabhas at the appropriate levels, before making acquisition for development projects, should be mandatory.

8. Amendment to the Land Acquisition Act in the following areas is important, the most significant amendment to the LA Act is doing away with Schedule II of the Act: Land Acquisition for private companies will not be possible in the same manner as earlier; public purpose needs to be defined with exclusive and inclusive definition. Consultation with Gram Sabhas should be made mandatory and consensus of villagers should be honoured before acquisition. Since power of restoration of the alienated land is very significant, the land, that remains unused by the organisation for five years, should be given back to the displaced and the acquiring body should be responsible to ensure that the displaced get back the unused land.
9. Training should be provided to the youth, of the likely to be displaced families, so that they can be absorbed into the organisations.
10. Societal Cost-Benefit Analysis of the Project should be undertaken before expressing the intent of any project, and the result should be widely circulated in local language to the families likely to be affected as well as the general public.
11. The formation of all evaluating committees should comprise of stakeholders, academia, civil society, and government representatives.
12. Notification should be widely circulated and publicised in the local language of the ethnic/tribal groups.
13. Compulsory Social Impact Assessment with respect to Cultivation and CPR Rights should be undertaken.
14. Compulsory Pre and Post-Environmental Impact Assessment with reference to Tribal Rights, CPR and carrying capacity should be undertaken.
15. Resettlement/Rehabilitation area should be identified in consultation with and with the participation of would-be affected parties.
16. Gender participation should be integrated fully in all the processes, consultation, design, and implementation, while achieving consensus.
17. All relocations should be in similar geographical terrains, without the loss of cultural and communitarian identity.
18. No lower limit should be laid down, for the number of households required to qualify for compensation and R&R.

19. Resettlement areas should cover or include all sources of livelihood, such as, agriculture, horticulture, livestock, fishing, forestry, artisans, CPR products, shops, SSIs, Own Account Manufacturing Enterprises (OAME), and family enterprises.
20. Resettlement sites should be fully developed before any relocation or resettlement, including houses, sanitation, schools, drainage, community halls, wells/drinking water, roads, health centres, ration shops, and common spaces, play ground, burial/crematorium ground, spaces for cultural reproduction, green cover, etc.
21. While constructing houses, the size of the family, the needs of the family, and the possibility for future expansion of the family should be taken into account. All the houses should be designed after consultation with the affected communities, and should be accompanied by homestead land. Further, the ownership rights of the house including homestead should be in the names of the husband and wife, and solely in the name of women in the case of female-headed households.
22. Compensation should include all economic and socio-cultural aspects, including monetary, land, live stocks, CPRs, priced as well as un-priced, equipment, wells, trees, houses, etc. Free vocational training and skill upgradation must be provided by the new projects from the day of the MoU with the Government, as long as the organisation exists. The amount, of compensation to the landless, should be based on man days and on the prevailing wages.
23. The resettled area should have full facilities interms of micro finance, SHGs, and extension services, with subsidies being provided for all livelihoods.
24. There should be gender parity with regard to compensation, irrespective of age and marital status.
25. Single window disbursement of beneficiary schemes should be adopted.
26. All self-governing institutions, such as, Gram Sabhas should be constituted immediately, after the rehabilitation with 50% gender representation.
27. All the rehabilitated areas should be declared as revenue villages with the power of PESA, even if it is not a Scheduled Area.
28. Compulsory employment for at least one member of the displaced community, should be made available.

References

Areeparampil, M. (1995): *Tribals of Jharkhand: Victims of Development*, New Delhi: Indian Social Institute.

Ashokvardhan, C. (1998): "Resettlement and Rehabilitation Policy of Coal India Ltd. April 1994: A Case Study of ECL Rajmahal Project", Lalmatia, Bihar, Paper presented at the workshop on *Displacement and Rehabilitation in India: Future Perspectives organised* by Centre for Rural Studies LBS National Academy of Administration, 1-3 June.

Ekka, A. (2008): "Mining and Displacement of Tribals in Jharkhand", Paper presented at the National Workshop on *Land Acquisition for the Development Projects in Scheduled Areas and Increasing Land Alienation*, organised by Lal Bahadur Shastri National Academy of Administration, Mussoorie, 3-4 March.

Iyer, K. Gopal (2008): "Land Acquisition in Orissa, Chhattisgarh and Jharkhand: A Critique and Analysis", Paper presented at the National Workshop on *Land Acquisition for the Development Projects in Scheduled Areas and Increasing Land Alienation*, organised by Lal Bahadur Shastri National Academy of Administration, Mussoorie, 3-4 March.

Malapert, L.K. (1991): "Development for Whom? Depriving the Dispossessed Tribals", *Social Action*, 41(3), pp. 271-87.

Mishra, P.P. and Reddy G.M. (2009): "Mining in Forest Areas of Orissa: A Review", Paper presented in national seminar on *Forest and Livelihood System in Orissa,* organised by the Sambalpur University, Orissa, 20-21 March.

Panda, P. (2008): "Land Alienation due to Development Projects in Scheduled Areas of Orissa: A Few Observations", Paper presented at the National Workshop on *Land Acquisition for the Development Projects in Scheduled Areas and Increasing Land Alienation*, organised by Lal Bahadur Shastri National Academy of Administration, Mussoorie, 3-4 March.

Pathy, J. (1987): "Ethnic Minorities and Processes of their Development", Report submitted to UGC, New Delhi.

Vagholidkar, N. and K.A. Moghe (2003): "Undermining India: A Report on Impact of Mining on Ecologically Sensitive Areas in India", Pune: Kalpavṛiksh.

5

Mining and Displacement Problems in Orissa

S.N. Tripathy

Introduction

Planned development, in India brought in its wake the establishment of large-scale projects in power generation, mining, industry, infrastructure development, irrigation, in addition to creating new urban settlements. However, these development projects also led to the displacement of people, mostly the tribals, from their original habitat, forcing them to migrate to new areas. This involuntary displacement of people from their productive assets (particularly land) and homes, due to industrial or infrastructure projects has been one of the social issues leading to intense debate among the academics, social activists, and planners. Though the process of land acquisition for setting up mining, irrigation, transportation, or mega-industrial projects (mostly in the public sector) is not new, the intensity of adverse effects was never comprehended in the past, as it is affecting today. The problem of Mining-Induced Displacement and Resettlement (MIDR) poses major risks to societal sustainability. Involuntary resettlement under development projects, if unmitigated, often germinates into severe economic, social and environmental risks: productive systems are dismantled; people face impoverishment, when their productive assets or income sources are lost; people are relocated to environments, where their productive skills may be less applicable and the competition for resources is greater; community institutions and social networks are weakened; kin groups are dispersed; cultural identity, traditional authority, and the potential for mutual help are either diminished or lost; and as a result, violation of human rights (Sengupta, 2001).

In the State of Orissa, which has the highest concentration of tribal population in India, after undivided Madhya Pradesh, there are 62 tribes, constituting about 23 percent of the total population in the state. The tribes in Orissa continue to remain socially, economically and educationally backward and languish at the bottom of the socio-economic ladder. Their geographical isolation and improvised economy have made them, the object of exploitation by the non-tribes. The powerful external forces of moneylenders, contractors and officials, who have links with political personnel and the police, exert dominant control over the tribes, while the poverty-stricken, illiterate, innocent tribes fail to withstand these forces and fall prey to all types of exploitation.

Though the development activities in Orissa surged as early as in the 1950's, there were about 8117 displaced families from 1446 villages, because of the development projects initiated between 1950 and 1993. The UNDP estimates that till date, more than one lakh people in Orissa have been displaced and 20 lakhs have been affected by development projects. Industrial projects, such as, the Rourkela Steel Plant (RSP), Hindustan Aeronautics Limited (HAL), and the National Aluminium Company (NALCO), have displaced people, especially the tribals (Fernades, 1994; Tripathy, 2003). A couple of anthropologists have made their investigation into the issues, related to displacement, rehabilitation and resettlement, particularly in the context of tribal society (Mahapatra, 1998, 1999; Behura, 1990, 1996; Patnaik, 1996; Ota, 1998; Panda and Panigrahi, 1989).

The Scheduled Tribes constituted about 8.1 percent of the total population in the country, according to the 2001 Census. They also constituted 55.16 percent of the total displaced population, which indicates the extent of victimisation of the tribes. Development-induced involuntary displacement of the tribes takes place in most states, mainly in the tribal concentrated regions of Bihar, Orissa, Andhra Pradesh, Madhya Pradesh, Gujarat and Maharashtra. Further, it has been observed that during the last 50 years, for various dam projects, about 6 crore people have been displaced, out of which 4 crores have practically turned into beggars in the streets (Fernades, 1994; Tripathy, 2003; Rangachari, 2006).

A significant number of tribal people, who are generally dependent on the natural and common resources, are displaced, and their ethos and life-style is dismantled and denigrated for the sake of developmental projects. Apart from the loss of land, living conditions, and life-style (of generations), displacement causes other traumatic, psychological and socio-cultural consequences, making life more miserable and impoverished (Mohanty, 2005).

In the light of the above illustrations, this study will be an effort to focus on various interdisciplinary issues as well as many lead issues, for further research in the field. Ultimately, the study will facilitate the re-orientation of the policy measures in the context of Government's initiatives, for an effective rehabilitation policy, and also suggest policy paradigms having wider implications for other development issues related to the tribes.

Mineral Resources in Orissa

Western Orissa forms a continuum, most of which is in its tribal areas, with the Northern Andhra and Jharkhand bauxite belt. Major and minor metal deposits exist in 20 of the state's 30 districts – two-thirds of them are in the tribal-inhabited Keonjhar, Sundergarh, Koraput, Jajpur and Mayurbanj districts, apart from Jharsuguda and Angul districts, where the majority of the population is non-tribal. So, mining could result in a cultural genocide, if preventive steps are not taken to ensure their development. In reality, MoUs are signed with various companies, including one of the biggest – POSCO of South Korea – for mineral exploitation and industries. In 1995, the state granted as many as 579 leases on about 281187.27 acres (113840.99 ha), including 82848.74 acres (33542 ha) for 113 leases in Keonjhar, 62708.36 acres (25388 ha) for 135 leases in Sundergarh, and 22220.12 acres (8996 ha) for 11 leases in Koraput, all three of them, tribal majority districts. The metallic ores, for which leases have been granted, include bauxite, chromite, iron, lead and manganese, and the non-metallic minerals include asbestos, dolomite, graphite, kyanite, pyrophyllite, quartz, various clays and sands, both industrial and non-industrial (Directorate of Mining and Geology, 1996: 36-43).

Mining-Induced Displacement in Orissa

It is to be noted here that not all the land of the operational mines could be identified. For example, data could be obtained for only 2334.83 acres (945.28 ha), owned by Mahanadi Coalfields (MCL) in 1995. Actually, MCL proposed to acquire 8636.91 acres, during the mid-1990s, followed by more acquisitions in the following years. Much of the land, acquired in the past as well as what was proposed to be acquired later, is either common or forest land. For example, of the 8636.91 acres mentioned above 4095.09 acres (51.7%) were private, 2499.61 acres

Table 5.1 A Conservative Estimate of Mining-Induced Displacement

State	*Year*	*Tribals*	*Dalits*	*Others*	*NA*	*Total*	*Source*
Andhra Pradesh	1980-1995	NA	NA	NA	100541	100541	Fernandes *et al.*, 2001
Assam	1980-2000	NA	NA	NA	41200	41200	Fernandes and Bharathi
Goa	1980s	NA	NA	NA	4740	4740	Fernandes and Naik, 2001
Gujarat	1980-2000	NA	NA	NA	4128	4128	Lobo and Kumar, 2007
Jharkhand	1980-1995	83543	63352	220076	00	402882	Ekka and Asif, 2000
Orissa	1960-1995	150000	45000	105000	00	300000	Fernandes and Asif,1997
Kerala	1990s	NA	NA	NA	78	78	Muricken *et al.*, 2003
W. Bengal	1960-2000	2459	99244	4373	311579	418061	Fernandes *et al.*, 2006
Total		236002	207596	329449	462266	1571630	

Table 5.2 Conservative Estimates of Displaced People during 1951- 1990 (in lakhs)

Projects	*All DPs*			*Tribals*		
	Displaced	Resettled	Backlog	Displaced	Resettled	Backlog
Dams	140.00	35. 00	105.00	53.00	13.15	39.45
Mines	21.00	05.25	15.75	12.00	03.00	09.00
Industries	13.00	03.25	09.50	02.60	0.65	01.95
Wildlife Sanctuaries	06.00	01.50	04.50	05.00	01.25	03.75
Others	05.00	01.25	03.75	01.50	01.40	01.10
Total	185.00	46.25	138.75	74.10	19.45	55.25

Source: Indian Social Institute, 1996.

Table 5.3 Displaced Families in the Development Projects

Sl.No.	*Name of the Project*	*Displaced Families*	*ST/SC Families*
1	Balimela multi-purpose dam project on Sileru River at Chitrakonda	2000	---
2	Salandi irrigation project	589	552 tribal families.
3	Rangali multi-purpose river valley project on the Brahmani River in Angul District	10,897	1710 families,1172ST families
4	Upper Kolab multi-purpose dam project on the River Kolab in Koraput District	3,179	442 SC families,1421ST families
5	Upper Indravati multi-purpose project	5,301	2223 tribal families, 796 families SC
6	Rourkela steel plant	4,251	-----
7	Talcher coal belt region in Angul District	23 villages affected by underground mines, due to open cast mining project in 38 villages	-----
8	IB valley area in Jharsuguda District	17 villages affected and 130 families displaced due to five opencast mining projects	------

Source: Pandey and Balaji (1998), Depriving the Under privileged by Development, Bhubaneswar.

(31.56%) were revenue commons, and 1326.21 acres (16.74%) were forest lands (MCL, 1995: 3-12). Similarly, almost all the land that has been handed over to Utkal Aluminium near Kashipur, Rayagada District, for bauxite mining is tribal commons (Padel and Das, 2007: 25), and so is the land used by the NALCO mines near Damanjodi in Koraput District (Fernandes and Asif, 1997: 76). Of the 410137.24 acres (166047.47 ha) used by mining till 1995, only 68328.86 acres (16.66%) were private, while the rest was predominantly tribal commons or forestland (Fernandes and Asif, 1997: 84).

Families Displaced due to Development Projects in Orissa

According to the official estimate, the total number of families displaced, due to river dam projects and other development projects in Orissa during 1950-1993, was about 81176, of which 80 percent families have been displaced, only due to irrigation projects (Pandey, 2000). The picture, pertaining to displaced families, because of various development projects in Orissa, is presented in Table 5.3.

Development-Induced Displacement in India

In other states too, limited data on displacement and deprivation could be recovered, that too only from the 1980s. The initial figure of 2.55 million, during 1951-1900 was arrived at from secondary sources (Fernandes, 1998: 231) and is without doubt an underestimate. Table 5.1 which is based on primary data-based studies, shows a little over 1.5 million mining DPs/PAPs in the 1980s and 1990s, among a total of 60 million DPs/PAPs of all the projects from 1947 to 2000 (Fernandes, 2007: 204). However, this data does not include Maharashtra, MP and Chhattisgarh, which also have high mineral deposits. Further, there have been many other projects between 1990 and 1995. When these states are studied and data on the others updated, one can expect the number of DPs/PAPs during 1947-2000 to be 5 million.

Aftermaths of Development Projects in Orissa

Landlessness takes the form of downward mobility from large to medium landholders, from medium/small to marginal farmers, and from small and marginal farmers to the landless. Further, this also has a caste-tribe as well as a gender dimension. In Orissa, for example, among the mining-displaced families, 16.7 percent of the tribals and 13 percent of the Dalit DPs became landless, against 3.6 percent of the general castes (Pandey, 1995: 180).

Data from MCL also show that the state had, by then, issued notifications for private land but took a long time to part with common land even after allotting it to MCL. For example, in 1995, only 51.43 percent of the private land, that MCL had applied for, was granted, against only 19.87 percent of the revenue commons and 17.64 percent of the forestland (MCL, 1995: 13). The state speaks of development as a public purpose, but seems to take its own precepts, seriously, only when it comes to people's sustenance, not to what it owns.

The state of Orissa has been confronting an enormous menace, from the onslaught of the projects for mining of bauxite, alumina refinery, sponge iron plants, etc. The environment, forest, and other legislations have been promulgated to protect the rights of the local communities, and their natural resource-based livelihoods. The environment seems to appear too weak to achieve this objective, in the face of the massive thrust for economic development from the state government.

The project proposal of M/s Utkal Alumina International Ltd. (UAIL) in Kashipur Tehsil, Rayagada District, Orissa (called the Utkal project here), was presented in such a manner that it ensured the proper implementation of environment, forest and pollution laws. As many as five bauxite mining and alumina projects are in the pipeline, covering five blocks of three districts – Kashipur (Rayagada District), Luxmipur and Dasamantpur (Koraput), Langigarh and Thuamulrampur (Kalahandi). Sterlite proposes to source bauxite from Sasubohu Mali of Kashipur Block; Larson and Tubro from Sijimali and Kutrumali (Kashipur Block); Birla from Kodinga Mali (Luxmipur Block); and Vedanta from Niyamgiri and Khandual Mali of Kalahandi District.

It has been estimated that the total investment, in the Orissa's bauxite projects is to the tune of Rs. 20000 crores. Taking into consideration, the present price of even just UAIL, the joint venture will reap a profit of at least Rs. 288000 crores, during the 22-23 years of the project life. While the government will get only Rs. 1300-1400 crores as royalty during that period, the tribes and dalits, of these villages will receive nothing but state repression, and a lifetime of misery and slum life.

Orissa has 90 percent of India's chrome ore and nickel reserves; 70 percent of bauxite reserves; and 24 percent of coal reserves. With no other state having such abundance of natural resources, the big business houses have no option, but to set up steel, alumina, and coal-based power projects in Orissa only. Orissa's post-reform ability to attract both private and foreign investment makes it plausible that its pre-reform failure was primarily due to ineffective or non-existent industrial policy, to exploit its mineral wealth.

However, it remains a mystery, as to why its agriculture sector grew so poorly. Despite its abundant resource wealth, Orissa is still a predominantly agricultural state, and thus its poor agricultural performance has little promise for future income growth and distribution. One possible explanation that needs further focus is the very high proportion of tribal population in Orissa. There are 62 distinct tribal groups in the state, concentrated heavily in the western hills. Around 25 percent of the state's population is tribal, the highest in the country. As elsewhere in India, these tribal populations tend to have distinctly lower social indicators of health and education, and suffer social and political exclusion.

In recent years, Orissa grew somewhat more rapidly than in its pre-reform phase – by 2.53 percent per annum, though it still remains at the bottom of the list of states in growth performance (12th during 1991-98 as opposed to 14th during 1980-90). In some ways, however, Orissa emerged as an innovator in economic reforms: it was the first state to reform its power sector, and it has a strongly set out industrial policy. Moreover, Orissa is the first state in India that has announced new agricultural and tourism policies.

In recent years, Orissa has emerged on the investment map of India, with a long list of investment proposals, largely backed by foreign investors. Apart from its new industrial policy, Orissa has also announced its agricultural and tourism policies. In the post-liberalisation scenario, Orissa was ranked 6th in foreign investments and received the largest amount of private investments in India, both foreign and domestic, followed by Gujarat, Karnataka and Maharashtra. With the state government declaring heavy industry, infrastructure, and aquaculture as thrust areas, majority of the new investments are being made in heavy industries, including steel, alumina and power projects.

The abundance of cheap labour, further, makes it an investor-friendly state. And moreover, the state government has been offering exceptionally huge subsidies to investors, in the form of guarantees, tax concessions, and investment subsidies.

Orissa needs massive financial resources and better delivery systems to uplift the living standards of its population. Because its per capita income has been far below the national average, 44 percent of its population lives below the poverty line; and 47 percent of its population has none of the three facilities – electricity, safe drinking water, and sanitation. Instead of taxing the rich, for raising adequate financial resources to support anti-poverty programmes, the state government has been offering more and more concessions to the rich, big business houses, for investments, through tax exemptions and investment subsidies.

Thus, the unreplenishable mineral wealth has been looted, leaving behind barren land and poverty-stricken people. Tribes, evicted by industrial houses, had been pushed to starvation in Koraput District and other parts of the state, while promoting the Multinational Corporations (MNCs) and big houses that destroyed the livelihood of the tribals and poor people. For example, the Vedanta Alumina Project in Langigarh, with an investment of Rs. 4500 crores, would benefit only 250 persons in the form of permanent employment, while the livelihood of around 300 villages would be affected by this project; in addition, the Bansadhara and Nagabali rivers would dry up. The tribes living in the forests should be adequately compensated in the shape of insurance coverage, educational guarantee, and future loan facilities in case of sickness, before they are displaced from their age-old habitation for industrialisation.

A study, of the infrastructure index which takes into account the power index, communications index, and transport index, shows that Orissa's aggregate of 75 falls much below the national average, which is 107. A review of the 'investment attractiveness and climate' of various states, conducted by the 12th Finance Commission in order to undertake an inter-state comparison among 20 states, ranked Orissa in the 11th position in 2001. The claims of fiscal improvement do not hold much water in the presence of about Rs. 76.18 billion, in the form of public debt as per the revised budget estimates for the year 2004-05, as given by the Ministry of Finance of the Orissa Government.

Under these circumstances, the World Bank's decision, to choose Orissa as the preferred destination for its funds, is understandable. However, the reason for this must be the dismal state of the state's economy rather than its false optimism. As far as economic benefits of new investments and privatisation programmes are concerned, the state government boasts that they will spur growth which, in turn, will help in poverty alleviation. But this argument finds little evidence in Orissa (and elsewhere) as growth in itself does not promise to 'trickle-down' to the poor. For instance, Orissa has a surplus in power and intends to be the 'Powerhouse of India'; but less than 20 percent of the people, living in rural Orissa, have access to electricity. Further, the state government argues that by attracting foreign and domestic private investments and privatisation of its public sector units, it will put more resources into the social sector, spending for poverty alleviation. However, this argument has no basis in reality. Although, the state government has withdrawn from big investments in infrastructure, this has not led to a sharp increase in the allocations to social sector programmes; and there has been no correlation between decline in infrastructure spending and increase in social sector spending.

Investigations into displacement have found nine other potential risks that deeply threaten sustainability: these are joblessness, homelessness, marginalisation, food insecurity, loss of common lands and resources, increased health risks, social disarticulation, disruption of formal educational activities, and the loss of civil and human rights. Failure, to mitigate or avoid these risks may generate 'new poverty' as opposed to the 'old poverty' that people suffered before displacement. Certain groups – especially the indigenous people, the elderly, and women – have been found to be more vulnerable to displacement-induced impoverishment risks.

The most crucial issue is that despite the development of mining industries, the inequality in the distribution of income and wealth widens and results in the concentration of poverty among the tribes in Orissa.

Conclusion

In view of the skewed distribution of income and wealth in the society and concentration of poverty, we need to provide a suitable rehabilitation strategy for the benefit of tribes, in order to ensure a strategy for their livelihood. As such, we need to rethink and reformulate our policy so as to percolate the benefits of our resources, on a sustainable basis for the greater interest of the public, particularly, in the form of employment creation and income generation, through linkage effect on industry and other service sectors.

References

Action Aid (2007): *Vedanta Cares?* Report Busting the Myths around Vedanta's Operations in Langigarh, by Action Aid.

Bandyopadhyay, D. (2004): "Rayagada Story Retold: Destitute of Development", *Economic and Political Weekly*, 39(5), pp. 408-11.

Behura, N.K. (1990): "Socio-Economic Problems and Social Change", In V. Sundersen and M.A. Kalam (ed.), *The Uprooted,* New Delhi: Gyan Publishing House.

Behura, N.K. (1996): "Environment, Displacement and Development: Case Study from Orissa", *Journal of Indian Anthropological Society*, 31 (2): 149-159.

Directorate of Mining and Geology (1996): "Mineral Statistics of Orissa 1994-95", Bhubaneswar: Department of Steel and Mines.

Downing, Theodore E. (2002): "Avoiding New Poverty: Mining-Induced Displacement and Resettlement", MMSD Report.

Fernandes, W. (1994): *Development-Induced displacement in Tribal Areas of Eastern India*, (Mimeo), New Delhi: Indian Social Institute.

Fernandes, Walter (2007): "Singur and the Displacement Scenario", *Economic and Political Weekly*, 42 (3): 203-206.

Fernandes, Walter and Mohammed Asif (1997): *Development-Induced Displacement in Orissa 1951 to 1995: A Database on Its Extent and Nature,* New Delhi: Indian Social Institute.

Goodland, Robert J.A. (2007): *India: Orissa, Kashipur: Utkal Bauxite and Alumina Project: Human Rights and Environmental Impacts*, Washington, DC: World Bank.

MCL (1995): "Status of Land Acquisition in 1995", Sambalpur: RR and LA Department, Mahanadi Coalfields Limited.

Mohanty, B. (2005): "Displacement and Rehabilitation of Tribals", *Economic and Political Weekly*, 40(13): 1318-1320.

Mohapatra, L.K. (1998): "Participatory Approach in Resettlement and Rehabilitation, Implementation", Paper presented at Gopabandhu Academy of Administration, in the seminar of 'Resettlement and Rehabilitation'.

________ (1999): *Resettlement, Impoverishment and Reconstruction in India: Development for the Deprived,* New Delhi: Vikash Publishing House.

Ota, A.B. (1998): "Countering Impoverishment Risks: The Case of Rengali Dam Project", in H.M.Mathur and David Marsden (ed.) *Development Projects and Impoverishment Risks*, New Delhi: Oxford University Press.

Panda P and N. Panigrahi (1989): "The Problem of Displaced People: A Study in the Coal Mines of Brajarajnagar", Sambalpur, Orissa, In R.N. Pati and B. Jena (ed.) *Tribal Studies in India*, New Delhi: Ashish Publication House.

Pandey, Balaji (1995): "Impoverishing Effects of Coal Mining Projects: A Case Study of Five Villages in Orissa", In Hari Mohan Mathur and David Marsden (eds.): *Development Projects and Impoverishment Risks: Resettling Project-Affected People in India,* pp. 174-92, Delhi: Oxford University Press.

Pandey, Balaji (1998): *Depriving the Underprivileged by Development*, Bhubaneswar: Institute of Socio-Economic Development.

Pathy, Jaganath (1998): "Impact of Development Projects on Tribals", In

Vidyut Joshi (ed.), *Tribal Situation in India,* Jaipur: Rawat Publications.

Patnaik, S.M. (1996): *Displacement, Rehabilitation and Social Change*, New Delhi: Inter-India Publication.

Rangachari, R. (2006): *Bhakra-Nangal Project: Socio-Economic and Environmental Impacts,* New Delhi: Oxford University Press.

Sengupta, Arjun (2001): "The Right to Development as a Human Right", *Economic and Political Weekly*, 36(27), pp. 2527-36.

Tripathy, S.N. (2000): *Glimpses on Tribal Development,* New Delhi: Discovery Publishing House.

Tripathy, S.N. (2003): "Problems of Displacement and Development", In S.N. Tripathy (ed.) the self edited, *Economic Development and Problem of Displacement,* New Delhi: Anmol Publication.

6

Social and Economic Effects of Violent Armed Conflicts on Children: Evidence from Displaced Camps in Jammu and Kashmir, India

Falendra Kumar Sudan

Introduction

Armed conflict-related displacement has significant effect on children (Alderman, Hoddinott and Kinsey, 2004; Verwimp, 2005; Bundervoet and Verwimp, 2005; de Walque, 2006; Shemyakina, 2006; Justino, 2006). Displacement often leads to simultaneous destruction of assets and serious reductions in the nutritional status of children (Alderman, Hoddinott and Kinsey, 2004; Bundervoet and Verwimp, 2005). It affects important human capital determinants, namely, education and health. This is because the disruption and destruction of infrastructure caused by violence often results in severe cutbacks in the states' capacity to provide services such as education and health care (Stewart *et al.*, 2001a, 2001b). Significant reduction in social services further reinforces the inability of households and children to fall back on state support, during THE times of crises (e.g., safetynets). Thus, displacement is associated with the destruction of lives of children (Dewhirst, 1998; Woodward, 1995). Displaced families and children are found amongst those living under the most difficult forms of socio-economic exclusion and deprivation. Children living in displaced camps, are known to face more abuse and harassment, and suffer domestic violence (Brown, 2005).

In THE situations of armed conflict and displacement, children have often been identified and acknowledged as victims (OECD, 2001).

Children's roles and contributions to their families and communities are generally unrecognised and often undermined (Lansdown, 2005; O' Kane, 2003). Recently, the importance of engaging children as social actors and the need to understand and respond to the political and social reality of children's lives haVE been highlighted (Hart and Tyrer, 2006; Boyden, 1997; Kemper, 2005; O' Kane, 2007). Children's participation is not always an easy process. It often involves challenging their traditional roles in society and transforming the relationships of power between adults and children. These changes are not always welcome at first, but through education and practical implementation, the benefits of child participation shine through (O' Kane, 2003). Children have their own valuable perspectives and priorities, which are often different from those of THE adults.

In displaced settings, it is vital to understand how young children are affected, by armed conflict and displacement, which of their rights are being violated, and what roles they take on. In order to protect their own rights and to develop the community, it is equally crucial that their views and experiences are heard. Thus, there is need to understand children's perspectives on displacement and respond to the priorities, based on their roles and responsibilities within the families, communities and in the broader society. In the present paper, an attempt has been made to document the socio-economic consequences of violent armed conflicts on non-Kashmiri young children and their experiences and views in displaced settings, so that they are heard, listened to, and acted upon to protect and promote their rights. This chapter highlights the contributions of children towards their own protection, development and well-being, as well as improving the overall environment of the community, which has serious ramifications for the child-centred policies and programmatic interventions in displaced settings.

Methodology

The study has been confined to children, below the age of 18 years belonging to non-Kashmiri displaced families living in three large displaced camps, viz. Belicharana on the fringe of River Tawi, Khanpur (Nagrota) on the Jammu-Srinagar national highway at a distance of about 10 km, and Talwara in Reasi District at a distance of about 82 km from Jammu City in Jammu Region of the State of Jammu and Kashmir. A total of 905 households are residing in three major displaced non-Kashmiri camps, viz. 284 households in Belicharana, 215 households in Khanpur, and 406 households in Talwara.The primary data and information were based on census, using pre-tested questionnaires, focused group discussions, and participatory appraisals. Both focused and unfocused observation techniques have been used. The unfocused initial observations were used in order to become increasingly familiar with the insider's world, so as to refine and focus subsequent observations and data collection. All the observations have been recorded on site and misunderstandings, if any, have been corrected thereof. Highly formal interviews have been conducted using structured interview schedules, and in-depth interviews have also been conducted to elicit opinions of stakeholders with extensive knowledge of the phenomenon under study. Content analysis technique has been used to analyze the data and information qualitatively and quantitatively (using descriptive statistics). This has been supplemented by the use of code and label field notes, sorting, shifting, constructing and reconstructing these materials.

Socio-Economic Effects of Displacement on Children

The impacts, of armed conflict and displacement on the children, have been devastating. Displaced children are inevitably viewed as victims and thus need protection. However, the displaced children are not inherently vulnerable. They have the strengths and capacities for coping with adversity.

Girls are commonly seen, as particularly vulnerable to abuse, in the situations of displacement. They are made vulnerable not by inherent qualities but through the attitude and behaviour of others. Besides, all "children" are not vulnerable. No group of children is homogenous, in terms of the risks that they face. Age, gender, class, education, language, and particular settings, place children differently with respect to the risks (and opportunities) that are created by displacement. Discrimination and marginalisation are sources of risk that obviously affect certain children more than others.

Displacement affects the lives of young children due to its impact on social structures, infrastructure and services. In displaced settings, health and health services are adversely affected. Increased poverty, higher incidence of disease and exposure to abuse are potential consequences of displacement. Displacement typically disrupts community practices and family life, all of which are implicated in the protection of children. In displaced settings, the family, the school, and the community will not be able to play their expected roles, in mitigating the threats to children's well-being. The family home may well be the scene of abuse and neglect by parents. For example, high incidence, of alcoholism in displaced communities, inevitably impacts the ability of adults to offer appropriate care. Teachers, whose lives are subject to the same stress as the rest of the community, are also known to inflict various forms of violence; for example, sexual violence directed by male teachers towards female students.

(A) Demographic Characteristics

Nearly 48% of the displaced families belong to disadvantaged groups, viz. 22.98% Scheduled Castes (SCs) and 24.20% Scheduled Tribes (STs). Some of the male heads of the households were killed in their native villages by armed militants, while some migrated to other towns and cities to eke out a livelihood, thus shifting the burden to the female member of the households. In the displaced camps, 10.24% of the females are shouldering the responsibilities of the head of households in Belicharana, followed by 6.69% in Khanpur (Nagrota), and 5.66% in Talwara. In such households, the females suffer multiple burdens, including separation from the male head of the household due to killing or migration; living in camps; managing daily household chores; feeding themselves and their family members including children; and taking care of children's education, health and wellbeing. The younger women are also at the risk of abuse by members from other households, relatives, and fellow male inmates in the camps.

On average, there are 2.77 adults per household, with significant variations across the camps (2.84 adults, 2.61 adults, and 2.86 adults per household respectively in Belicharana, Khanpur and Talwara). More number of adults implies more earning members per household. However, due to lack of economic opportunities in the camps and their surroundings, unemployment and under-employment are reportedly very high. Almost all the households are living in abject conditions of poverty and deprivation. There are 3.19 children per household, and the child-adult ratio stands at 1.15. About 31% of the children are in the adolescent age group of 13-17 years, 42.48% are in the age group 6-13 years, more than one-fifth (22.91%) are in the age group of 1-5 years, and about 0.026% of them are infants (below 12 months). Child sex ratio is estimated at 0.97 females per male child.

More than two-thirds (68.09%) of the children are born after displacement, and they have seen nothing but camp-life throughout their childhood. They are deprived of the basic civic amenities such as proper schooling, health, drinking water, hygiene, and sanitation. A greater proportion of the children, those in the adolescent age group have their own repercussions in terms of need for higher education, training, health and recreation, which are virtually absent in all camps. In the absence of these facilities, their energies and potentialities go waste; they may indulge in bad habits, or get subjected to abuse by the bad elements in and outside the camps: The adolescent males may get trapped in drug abuse and stealing, and form rouge bands, whereas their female counterparts may be lured towards sexual abuse.

Thus, there is urgent need to open avenues for their active involvement in training and skill development, so that their energies and potentialities can be channelised in the right perspective for their better growth and development. Likewise, for the children in the age group below 13 years, provision of adequate education as well as health, is a must for their proper growth. But the available education and health facilities are very meagre, and need to be supplemented through government and non-government efforts.

(B) Unemployment

Nearly 39% of the adult population is economically active and employed. Among them, 93.79% are male and the rest are female. Most of the women seek work outside the homes and camps. In Khanpur (Nagrota), the poor women from disadvantaged communities, along with their children resort to begging on particular days (Saturdays and Tuesdays) by visiting the nearby townships of Jammu, Nagrota and Katra. However, this was not reported in the other two camps. About 60% of the working age population in the three camps is unemployed; the unemployed female population is very high at 94.91%; the proportion of unemployed population in the Belicharana camp was 51.06%; it was 64.01% in Khanpur (Nagrota) camp, and 64.19% in Talwara camp. In Belicharana camp, the proportion of unemployed population is comparatively low, which is due to the fact that the camp is located on the fringe of Jammu City and the male as well as the female population has easy access to nearby industrial estates, bus stands, ware houses, shops, and establishments wherein they find manual wage employment on a temporary basis. However, more males than females are employed in Belicharana. In the other two camps, male unemployment is quite significant : 30.32% in Khanpur and 72.11% in Talwara. Thus, the incidence of unemployment is very high in these two camps, which is collaborated with the poor economic conditions. Even those who are employed earn a very small amount, given the nature of the manual wage employment they are engaged in. Overall, the extent of unemployment and under-employment is quite alarming among the displaced population living in these camps, and they should be made aware of the National Rural Employment Guarantee Act (NREGA) so that at least 100 days of employment could be provided to them.

(C) Economic Conditions

More than 96% of the households in the camps live in Below Poverty Line (BPL) conditions. However, majority of these households do not possess BPL cards and hence do not receive the subsidised ration from the Public Distribution System (PDS). In Talwara camp, more than two-thirds of the BPL households possess the BPL card and all of them avail of the subsidised ration. It appears that the displaced population in Talwara camp is comparatively more politically aware and opts for pressurising the local administration to provide them with the minimum basic necessities. They were also the first in the category of non-Kashmiri displaced population to receive food and financial assistance from the government, showing the way to others in Khanpur (Nagrota) and Belicharana.

Initially, they were not given any aid or assistance by the government, were not considered as displaced population by the government agencies, and were deprived of any assistance that was being given to Kashmiri migrants from the Valley of Kashmir. Recently, after constant and vigorous efforts, made by non-governmental agencies and social activists, they are now being provided with cash and financial assistance. To begin with, such assistance was given only to the displaced households, residing in Talwara camp; however, due to constant pressure on the government from the social activists and the groups of displaced populations living in the other two camps, the households, living in Khanpur (Nagrota) and Belicharana are also now being given food and financial assistance, which considerably eased their living.

There were recent reports of children from Talwara camp, being sold to nearby states of Punjab and Haryana. The matter was highlighted by the civil society, and after that, fresh incidents, of such trade, have not come to the limelight. However, the incidence of child labour, in the form of domestic servants, dhaba workers, rag pickers, beggars, manual workers, workshop workers, vendors' helpers, etc., is reportedly high.

(D) Age at Marriage

Marriage before the age of 18 is a reality for many young girls living in the camps. In displaced situations, parents encourage the marriage of their daughters, while they are still children, hoping that the marriage will benefit them, both financially and socially, while also relieving financial burdens on the family. In actuality, child marriage is a violation of human rights, compromising the development of girls and often resulting in early pregnancy and social isolation, with little education and poor vocational training, to reinforce the gendered nature of poverty. Due to the prevalent cultural practices and traditions, the displaced households do not adhere to the legal age of marriage. More than 18% of the households, get their daughters married before the age of 18 years,while 10% of the boys' marriages took place before the legal age of 21 years.

Early marriage for girls is due to poor economic conditions and the prevalent socio-cultural practices of marrying the daughter at puberty. Besides, displacement and living in camp situations does not provide a sense of security to the girls, due to lack of opportunities to engage in education, training, and other productive activities. The threat of sexual abuse of these young girls, within and outside the camps, also looms large on the parents. In order to avoid such threats, they marry their daughters at an early age. The young boys with poor economic conditions and improper education and training indulge in anti-social activities like theft, stealing, drugs, gangs, etc. The parents, due to lack of awareness, and in the pretext of setting them right, get them married, which, however, results ultimately in more poverty, more number of children, frustration, domestic violence, divorce, and so on.

(E) Child Survival

The system of institutional deliveries and birth registration is poor. In case of institutional birth, the health professionals themselves report the birth to concerned agency for registration. Nearly half the recent births have been registered in Panchayat records. In case of birth at home, some of the families find it difficult to register in time, due to lack of awareness, preoccupation with daily household chores, and livelihood activities. Some parents may even wait until it is necessary for their children to have formal identification; for example, prior to attending school. Proportionately, more male births (47.22%) than female births (13.33%) have been registered. Thus, there is gender bias in birth registration. Even in cases where birth has been registered, in most cases, birth certificates have not been issued. Birth registration levels are higher among children who attend early childhood education than those who do not. However, the proportion of such children is very small. Awareness-raising campaigns can help reduce the number of children without birth registration. Improving, 'mothers' knowledge and education, might benefit birth registration rates.

Immunisation of children against preventable diseases is very low. Only 51.28% of the new born children (28.57% and 77.77% of girls and boys respectively) are immunised completely. Nearly, 31% of the children (33.23% and 28.70% of boys and girls respectively) in the age group of 1-5 years have been completely immunised . Thus, there seem to exist gender disparities in the immunisation of children. The comparatively higher proportion, of immunisation in Belicharana camp, has been due to its proximity to Jammu City, better transport and communication, and visits from health professionals and members of voluntary organisations. Besides, the parents are more mobile and have regular contact with their urban counterparts. They are, thus, aware about the need for child immunisation. Displacement and poverty, lack of education, knowledge and awareness, poor accessibility, no visits from health workers, are some of the factors, responsible for non-immunisation or poor immunisation of children in Khanpur and Talwara camps. Those women who immunised themselves during pregnancy, also tend to immunize their children and vice versa. The proportion of immunised pregnant women is reportedly higher in Belicharana camp compared to the other two camps. Besides, the place of deliveries has been cited as one of the reasons for immunisation or non-immunisation. If the child has been delivered under institutional care, the new born as well as the mother is subjected to immunisation; such care is not usually taken for non-institutional deliveries. Talwara and Khanpur camps are isolated and deprived of basic health facilities; these need to be improved so that the children as well as the pregnant women can be immunised against preventable diseases.

(F) Child Development

Upon displacement, the first setback that the children experience, is lack of educational facilities. They have to travel more than 5 km to reach a school; this results in a large number of drop-outs. Enrolment of children above 6 years in the educational system is quite low and stands at 52.18%. The proportion of children enrolled, in schools in the three camps was observed to be 66.21% in Belicharana, 63.40% in Khanpur (Nagrota), and 36.07% in Talwara. Comparatively higher enrolment is seen in Belicharana, which is again due to its proximity to Jammu City and availability of private educational institutions in the camp itself. About 53% of the male children and 51% of the female children in the age group 6 plus are enrolled in educational institutions. All these paint a very ugly picture of children's enrolment in the educational system, which is far behind the national goal of education for all. Some children below the age of 6 years are also attending private schools, besides NFE centres under the CRY-funded project and *anganwadi* centres under ICDS. However, due to lack of awareness and motivation on the part of parents, and due to abject poverty conditions, they are unable to send their children to schools. The government-run educational institutions lack proper infrastructure and teachers. In the government-run schools, the teachers are quite irregular and lack interest in teaching the students, leading to a high number of drop-outs. Distance from better managed private and government-run schools also contributes to low enrolment, non-enrolment and high number of drop-outs. Thus, there is need to provide basic education along with technical and vocational skills to the children so that they could grow up as well-educated citizens and possess the skills to enter the labour market and eke out a livelihood that can support their families economically.

G. Child Protection

Even before displacement, children have contributed to family welfare in a variety of ways including taking part in agriculture and animal husbandry tasks, besides collecting fuel and fodder, fetching water, and looking after their young siblings. But a displacement breaks the traditional economic systems and as earning basic subsistence becomes more precarious, children are placed at a higher risk. Gender is another central factor. Girls are expected to be primarily or exclusively domestic workers; so household work at young ages is regarded as natural for them. Besides the domestic chores at home, they are actively engaged in remunerative work as domestic servants outside the households. In addition, displaced camps are threatening places for girls, where they are at risk of sexual harassment from close relatives, neighbours, outsiders and others. Solely by virtue of their gender, therefore, many girls are pushed into exploitative labour. Commercial sexual exploitation and trafficking of children for prostitution is also not ruled out and needs deeper probes to understand the nature and extent of the problem.

Nearly, 38% of the school children above 6 years and below 14 years are engaged in different remunerative occupations outside the home. None of the children is engaged in home-based occupations as their parents lack the money, skill and training to take up any home-based enterprise. The reasons cited, for high proportion of child labour, are displaced living conditions, acute poverty, and lack of education and availability of child-specific work near the camps. Due to inadequate earnings, aid and assistance, the children are forced into child labour, which deprives them of their basic human rights. This problem can be addressed by enforcing the minimum working age regulations; and protecting the children from economic exploitation and from performing any work that is likely to be hazardous, and interferes with their education, or from being forced to take activities that are harmful for their physical, mental, spiritual, moral or social development.

Children's Views and Perspectives on Displacement

In the following paragraphs, the children's perspectives on living in displaced camps and practical examples of children's participation in different activities, carried out under the project supported by Child Rights and You (CRY) have been presented. The project recognised the importance of listening to children's perspectives on displaced living, the practical ways in which children participate to enhance their own protection and improve the environment of their community; and respond to the roles and responsibilities of the children, provide support and help to strengthen their own protection and development initiatives, and promote their inclusion in community development processes.

Displacement is one of the most visible and disruptive effects of armed conflict in Jammu and Kashmir. Children are forced to move with their families to unknown places, that often offer harsher living conditions than those they had at home. In Jammu Region, displacement has become a problem that has spanned about two decades. All the displaced non-Kashmiri families living in camps are linked in one way or another to the ongoing armed conflict. Most of them have fled their homes during fighting or the threat of it. When there were attacks, they did not always have sufficient warning to relocate; so they quickly gathered what they could and moved to a shelter outside the affected area, be it a camp, a makeshift site, or the homes of family or friends. They are found to move because of insurgents' operations in their areas that create a general feeling of insecurity.

In some cases, the villagers are able to check on the status of the area and return when it is safe, but in others, the displacement becomes prolonged to the extent that, their homes are virtually abandoned. Fighting is frequently between two armed groups, non-state and state armed actors, but at times, villages are targeted during attacks. Some of the displaced population fled, when their homes were burned, though they could not always identify the perpetrator. Other than the direct fighting or attacks on villages, the effects of armed conflict also pushed villagers out of their homes. Displacement has had deleterious effects, on their key economic assets, land, tools, livestock and seeds, forcing them to take shelter in the camps or other safer places. In most cases, children accompanied extended families.

Most of the families have been displaced by about 80 km to 150 km. The people did not want to be too far away from their homes, so that they could check on their houses and farms whenever possible. Fathers or elderly members often returned to look after their houses that were left, or to check their crops. Many households had experienced multiple moves, before arriving at their current location. Some families had moved from site to site, before eventually ending up in the present camp. Displacement was often fora short duration, but frequent. Initially, when a militant group comes into their area or at the onset of fighting, they flee the villages to the forest or other safer places, and then move back to their homes after they feel it is safe. Some of them experienced infrequent moves. The duration of displacement varied from household to household. Most of them had been displaced, since the mid-1990s, when violence erupted in the hills of Doda, Rajouri, Poonch, Reasi and Udhampur. Children of the displaced families have suffered excessive damages on account of lack of access to education and healthcare, in addition to psycho-social problems, and loss of livelihood assets of their families.

(A) Impact on Health Status

Water scarcity is high because of irregular supply. Mosquitoes are found throughout the camps in summer and rainy seasons, because of poor drainage and sanitary conditions. Malaria fever has also been a serious problem affecting children. Access to regular sources of food is limited. The government and sometimes the local NGOs provide the camps' residents with food assistance. Majority of the families are living in a small room with no separate kitchen and bathroom. Due to lack of proper sanitation and drainage, camp dwellers are defecating and bathing in the open, in the nearby river, *nallas* or in grassy areas around their shelter. The most common symptoms of poor health reported by children are simple colds, fever, cough, and headache – all of which are communicable and preventable diseases. Diarrhoea is very common during the summer and rainy seasons. They have high incidence of skin rashes. The congestion, heat, poor vector control, chaotic conditions, and lack of ventilation, safe drinking water, and medicines, have increased the children's susceptibility to illnesses. Though access to healthcare was an issue, before the conflict and displacement, accessibility to healthcare facilities, which has now improved in physical terms, is limited in financial terms.

(B) Psycho-Social Impact

Displaced living often has a negative impact on the psycho-social wellbeing of children. It causes children great pain, grief and fear. Some children have lost interest in their daily activities; they often refuse to go to school and are quick to pick fights with their classmates. Some children have also lost their self-confidence and self-esteem. Some children feel that the fear has affected them physically. They shared that they often suffer from head-and stomach-aches, trembling, palpitations, and muscle pains. Physical symptoms of psycho-social distress are not uncommon. The insecure environment and fear have contributed to this effect. Children do not have enough space to play. The lack of space, cleanliness, and sanitation systems, have made the children very uncomfortable. Recreational and informal community gatherings are also affected. The parents do not have time to relax anymore as most of their time is spent in trying to earn a livelihood.

(C) Impact on Access to Education

Displacement has proved disruptive to children's education in several ways. The displaced children face challenges that result in part, due to their social and economic status and in part because of their isolated location. Just like the access to health facilities, although the presence of education facilities has increased, children are not always able to access them due to financial constraints. While, tuition at the government-run primary schools is free, parents in many cases have to cover the cost of several subsidiary fees, such as, school materials and uniforms. Because, the displaced families are usually unable to choose the location of their shelter, they are not always proximate to a school; they are forced into marginal areas, where communities have not yet been established and are, therefore, not conveniently linked to the mainstream education system.

(D) Impact on Livelihood Opportunities

Most, of the conflict-affected displaced households, are primarily agricultural. The displacement was accompanied, by a considerable shift from the agricultural sector into other fields. This meant a move from farming into labour, leading to higher unemployment. Majority of the camp dwellers reported themselves, as having been farmers previously; but now a large proportion of them are unemployed, due to lack of required skills and training. This does not mean, however, that people do not work. They travel a long distance to reach the nearby towns, in order to find manual work.

(E) Coping Strategies

The displaced households have not sought, to rebuild or restore what they lost. Generally, the hope, that peace will prevail and they will be able to return to their native villages keeps them from investing in long-term socio-economic activities. Some displaced families, have taken up new jobs, as manual workers, dhaba workers, domestic workers, chowkidars, factory workers, drivers, workshop helpers, etc. The displaced women and children are also reportedly seeking work and engage in all types of hazardous tasks. Women and child trafficking has also been reported. Due to proximity to the army area, national highway, tourist spots, and city, it is possible that some women and girls are trafficked into or forced to enter into commercial sex. Some of the areas, from which people have fled, are zones where poppy and marijuana are grown and where increasingly, other types of narcotics are produced. It is likely that some displaced children are involved in the transport of narcotics.

Some women along with their children have resorted to begging and depend on charity, as alternative sources of employment are hard to come by. Children are forced into begging for survival and to supplement family earnings. Some children work alone, meaning that they beg alone, but some work under close coordination with their mothers, older siblings, or other children. They use a part of the alms for themselves, mostly on smoking and for intoxicants; the rest of the money is handed over to the parents or a senior member of the household. Those who work alone are subjected to abuse by miscreants, mainly fellow children, camp dwellers, roadside vendors, workshop workers, dhaba workers, and transport workers. Those who beg in groups, mainly with their mothers and other family members, generally tend to be safer.

Some displaced people rely on aids from a variety of sources. For example, some NGOs have been helping them to identify sources of aid from the government, because not everyone knew, what was available or how to access it. Another strategy adopted by some families was to sell their valuables in the hope that they would be able to make it through hard times with this money. Some displaced families have risked return to their home areas over the period. Those who returned, often live with continued instability and threats. This coping strategy placed people at as considerable risk, since those same areas are still under continued insurgency and, many of the returnees have faced the consequences.

Experiences and Benefits of Children's Participation

The CRY project's activities in all the three non-Kashmiri displaced camps, viz. Talwara, Khanpur (Nagrota), and Belicharana, have promoted children's groups for sharing information among children on education, health, nutrition and livelihood issues. The formation of children's groups has resulted in children's participation in child protection and child right concerns. The children's groups have advocated child rights and basic life skills, among the children, adults and community members. These groups have focused on community, sports, cultural, literary and recreational activities. The groups have also raised awareness on education for girls. The members of the groups have motivated street children to go to school and have spread messages to stop child labour, and substance abuse, including drugs, sexual abuse, and harassment. They have even raised awareness, regarding HIV/AIDS and early marriages.

(A) Children's Participation in Governance

The adult facilitators have helped establish mechanisms for children's participation, by forming and promoting children's groups, using participatory activities to explore important development issues. The participatory sessions with children have helped them identify the problems, their causes, and potential solutions. Children's groups have been strengthened, to conduct weekly meetings with children in the displaced camps. Children's participation in child rights advocacy, life skills development, and community development has been encouraged.

(B) Children's Participation in Programmes

Adult facilitators have developed mechanisms, to involve young children in their own programmes. Children's groups are mechanisms, whereby the children can speak, share ideas, and develop programmes, while they also monitor and review. It enables children's participation in decision-making, programme initiatives, and developments. Children's participation in the programmes remains experimental. They participated in baseline surveys, participatory situational analysis, programme design, planning and implementation. Though, adult facilitators have had initial success, in facilitating children's participation, members of the children's groups have played a key role in all stages of planning, implementation, and review of their action programmes.

(C) Children's Participation in Identification of Problems

The participatory mapping processes have enabled children's groups, to identify positive aspects as well as problems in their camps, through participatory mapping exercises, they have identified the prevalent problems in the community, including substance abuse, sexual abuse and harassment of girls, child labour, poor sanitation, lack of toilets, bad water, bad roads, lack of health services, poor educational facilities, food insecurity and malnutrition, and absence of out of school activities. The groups have also prioritised the problems in their camps and undertook a thorough analysis of the prioritised problems, exploring how they could begin, addressing the problems, using awareness campaigns, among the communities and local leadership, and encouraging discussions among children in schools and communities.

(D) Children's Participation in Advocacy Efforts

The children's groups are involved in advocacy efforts, on issues affecting children. Through children's groups, young children learn, about their communities in active and meaningful ways. Collaboration, between children, family members, and community members has increased. Through their motivation, many children have returned to school. Children are also using creative methods, such as posters, street plays, and house-to-house visits, to increase awareness and change practices on various health and social issues with the adults in the community. The success depends on, how much the children have been involved, in developing the advocacy messages and/or how much they agree with them.

(E) Children's Participation in Action Research

Young children have been involved in participatory action research, in the displaced camps. The project organised capacity-building programmes, on child-focused participatory research for adult facilitators, followed by participatory research with children, report writing, sharing, and dissemination. The research with children highlighted many policy and programme issues, relating to education, health, child marriage, child abuse, and children's participation.

(F) Benefits of Children's Participation

The members of the children's groups have benefited, from capacity-building opportunities in child rights, communication, and negotiation skills. They are creating opportunity for girls and boys, through a platform for child participation. Adult facilitators have helped, in building the capacities of children on child rights, and giving them freedom to put their rights into practice. The members of the children's groups feel that they have gained considerably from participatory interventions, such as, information sharing about their rights; street plays, speeches and awareness campaigns on child right, and basic life skills education. With improved capacities, they raised various issues, such as, pre-and post-child birth health care, birth registration, school enrolment, child abuse, child marriage and trafficking, and health and sanitation (e.g., vaccinations, diarrhoea), with other children and community groups. They felt that their participation had brought about much change locally. The children learned that they had their own views and they were increasingly recognised within the family and community, as people with opinions and suggestions.

Girls have identified unsafe places and sought support and protection from the community's adults, to create a safer neighbourhood. This activity was undertaken, due to rise in the incidence of sexual abuse and harassment of the girls by outsiders. Initially the girls were helped to identify the places in their community that they felt were unsafe. The girls then collected evidence of harassment and their impacts. They developed recommendations to make these places safer and used them to negotiate with key persons, including the community leadership to make the places safer for girls. The girls also provided support to other girls who have suffered abuse or harassment to make sure that they are not made to feel guilty or isolated. Such peer support was crucial in rebuilding self-esteem, confidence and morale.

Over time, with experience and understanding, children's participation has considerably increased. The children have managed to overcome or minimize many of the initial challenges and have achieved some positive outcomes. Members of the children's groups have learned about child rights and basic life skills. They have learned how children can participate, in resolving family and community problems. They value collective thinking and working together, rather than acting as individuals. The adult facilitators have supported children, in identifying and analysing problems and finding solutions.

Lessons Learnt from Children's Participation

There are many practical issues and challenges involved in promoting, children's participation in displaced settings. The need for good preparation and awareness, to anticipate possible risks of children's participation beforehand and have strategies to deal with them is not over-emphasised . In the beginning, a framework to ensure ethical, meaningful and inclusive children's participation, needs to be established. This is possible by developing child-friendly information and participatory tools such as poetry, drama and songs, while making sure that children have the space to express their own views and ensuring that adults do not dominate, dictate or manipulate these views; exploring discrimination and ensuring non-discrimination; ensuring child protection issues appropriately and sensitively; ensuring children face no harm, as a result of their participation; ensuring wider accountability; and preparing adults to acknowledge the capacities of children and to respond and act upon them. Additional efforts may be required to encourage groups of children, who typically suffer discrimination, non-school-going children or children with different abilities/disabilities, to have equal opportunities of involvement. Children themselves should be encouraged to reflect on him, who is included in, or excluded from, their participatory protection and development initiatives.

(I) Children's Top Concerns in Promoting Participation

The initial phases of developing children's groups presented challenges. A general lack of support from parents was an obstacle to the children's participation, and the children had no meeting place. The children struggled to find time for the children's group activities, while attending school and extra tuition classes, and wanting some free time to play. Cultural barriers also made it difficult for them to encourage parents to allow their daughters attend the children's groups.

Children often play a vital role, in the enhancement of their own protection, and effective participatory projects can facilitate this further. The main motive of children's participation is to ensure, that their own experiences, concerns and aspirations have bearing upon the decisions that affect their lives. In displaced settings, young children have to play expanded roles and responsibilities. However, it must be ensured that an individual child is not exposed to undue risk. If such risk appears likely, then it may be necessary to consider how the views and concerns of children can be represented, without their direct involvement in person. In whichever way it is achieved, the benefits from establishing functional linkage, between child-led initiatives and the institutions and processes of governance, need to be understood and explored further.

The accountability of adult facilitators to children's concerns and priorities is required to ensure the fulfilment of children's rights to protection, participation, development and survival. Adult facilitators have the responsibility to protect the children's rights, and their accountability is reflected in increasing opportunities to listen to children, sharing information, and providing feedback to children, about how their views and recommendations, have or have not been addressed.

The development of comprehensive child protection systems, including the formation of child protection committees in communities would also enhance holistic, sustainable efforts towards child care, protection, and participation. Young children should be supported to form their own groups and the initiatives should be adhered to so that they can identify and address key protection issues affecting them, and elect their own representatives to be part of the protection committees. Capacity-building initiatives among children on child rights and basic life skills, conflict resolution, organisational development, and peace-building could also be scaled up, to support the strengthening of child-led organisations and initiatives.

Children's groups are desirous, of establishing a network of such groups in other displaced camps, to share their experiences. They are also anxious to develop better relations with local government functionaries, so that their rights could be addressed in a serious manner. Children's groups are keen to find solutions to the challenges of displacement, including livelihoods and survival with the support and intervention of authorities, at higher levels, for which they need further capacity building on communication skills, which is to be taken more seriously by adults. The young children are keen on raising some funds to increase their access to new technologies, training and information, such as, computer literacy and internet, and to start out of school programmes, like basic literacy, tuition, sports, and cultural activities. Besides, fostering children's participation beyond data gathering, participatory monitoring, and evaluation would promote self-reliance in decision-making and problem-solving, strengthening the children's capacities to take action and bring about change. As children gain experience and exposure through participating in the consultation and decision-making processes, their skills and knowledge as trainers and facilitators, on child rights and children's participation, should be recognised .

(II) Promoting Children's Participation in Local Governance

To create an enabling environment for children's participation in governance, there is a need to strengthen their involvement in the decision-making processes of schools, organisations, and local governance. The mobilisation and organisation of children's groups and promoting their networks, would increase their negotiation and bargaining powers with the local administration. Through the power base of their organisations, the children's groups and their networks, will demand effective delivery of basic amenities, such as, education, health, water and sanitation, integrated child-care services, and basic infrastructure. In order to make their groups and networks robust, they should be given representative space in local governance structures (e.g., Panchayat Raj Institutions, village development committees, and village education committees). The authorities of local governance should acknowledge the capacity of the children's groups, to contribute to local development processes and provide structural space for children's representatives, to raise issues and to influence and monitor decision-making, resource allocation, and action on issues relating to the fulfilment of their rights.

Children's participation in governance should strengthen the process of empowering children's groups and providing political space for the children to be heard. Enabling children's participation in governance requires, that local authorities should share some of the power, create space in their structures, and take children's views seriously.

(III) Promoting Children's Participation in Programming

Realising the importance of children's participation in all stages of programming, capacity-building sessions on children's participation should be organised for adult facilitators, enabling them to facilitate space and opportunities for children's participation in all areas of decision-making. Children's participation in programming should focus on the following activities: (a) education : influencing the management and running of schools; (b) life skills education : getting feedback in designing curriculum; (c) vocational training : selecting trades and managing training centres; (d) income generation programme : selecting beneficiaries; (e) alternative support : organising child fairs and competitions for children; (f) awareness generation : forming children's groups and involving community-based organisations on issues of child rights, abuse, and rehabilitation; (g) advocacy : involving children's groups in community consultations and sensitising adult duty bearers by sharing their experiences; and (h) evaluation : selecting criterion for analysing programme impact.

(IV) Promoting Children's Participation in Development Policy and Programmes

The following suggestions should be considered, while promoting children's participation in the development of child-focused policies and programmes: (a) involve children from the start and encourage their involvement throughout the process; (b) provide all the relevant information on children's issues in simple language; (c) use 'child-friendly' approach to encourage children's participation; (d) be open about resources that are available to support the process; (e) ensure that all young children, including marginalised children, are part of the processes; (f) make the process of children's participation as fair and honest as possible; (g) make sure that the adult facilitators are trained in child rights and know how to support children's participation; (h) children need to know more about how programmes work and how they can contact the right people : who, where and how?; (i) make sure that all children know about available channels of communication; (j) remember to deliver on commitments; (k) allow follow-up on consultations to let them know next actions and the progress made; (l) moral and financial support for children to stay involved; (m) training of adult facilitators to give them the confidence and skills to encourage children's involvement; (n) supporting peer (child-led) research to produce evidence that supports children's advocacy; (o) producing child-friendly versions of key documents; and (p) follow up on government promises and holding the government accountable.

Conclusion

Young children living amidst armed conflict and displacement are often at, risk of frustration, isolation and hopelessness. They have a potentially vital role, to play in enhancing their own protection and that of their peers, especially when their regular family and community life has been disrupted. Children's participation in social action that empowers them to protect themselves better, should, therefore, be considered as an emergency measure, and not as an option to be explored, when circumstances improve. In displaced settings, children's participation in social action and programming should be operationalised by taking into account the following suggestions: (a) develop a sound understanding of socio-cultural conditions, especially with respect to the involvement of the young children in social action and decision-making processes; (b) start any project through baseline survey undertaken together with children and other community members; (c) ensure that the safety and well-being of children and adult facilitators remains the primary concern at all times; (d) be prepared to suspend activities or make alterations in the light of changing circumstances; (e) adopt a gradual approach to the development of activities and allow time to gain trust and confidence, as children begin to articulate their ideas and build a solid network; (f) open up the space for children's participation by gaining the understanding and support of parents and community members; (g) develop close collaboration between community and local agencies, since they have a complimentary role to play in ensuring the success and safety of participatory projects, and facilitating the efforts of children to make contact with governmental and other bodies; (h) provide adult facilitators and children with ongoing need-based training to build their capacity; (i) encourage children to take responsibility at every possible opportunity and at each stage of the programme; (j) offer continuous support to children's activities through community-based resource persons, ready to advise and assist when requested; and (k) link existing child-led projects to the wider context of civil society and local governance.

References

Alderman, H., J. Hoddinott and B. Kinsey (2004): *Long Term Consequences of Early Childhood Malnutrition*, HiCN Working Paper No. 09, Households in Conflict Network, UK: University of Sussex.

Boyden, J. (1997): "Childhood and the Policy Makers: A Comparative Perspective on the Globalisation of Childhood", In Alison James & Alan Prout (eds.) *Constructing and Reconstructing Childhood: Contemporary Issues in the Sociological Study of Childhood*, pp. 190-229, Norfolk: The Falmer Press.

Brown, Maggie (2005): *Global Evaluation: Children Affected by Armed Conflict, Displacement or Disaster,* Norway: Save the Children.

Bundervoet, T. and P. Verwimp (2005): *Civil War and Economic Sanctions: An Analysis of Anthropometric Outcomes in Burundi*, HiCN Working Paper No. 11, *Households in Conflict* Network, UK: University of Sussex.

De Walque (2006): "The Long-Term Legacy of the Khmer Rouge Period in Cambodia", Paper presented at the First Annual Workshop, *Households in Conflict Network*, Berlin January 15-16.

Dewhirst, P. (1998): "Frozen Emotions: Women's Experience of Violence and Trauma in El Salvador, Kenya and Rwanda", *Development Update*, 2(2), pp. 1-30.

Hart, Jason and Tyrer Bex (2006): "Research with Children Living in Conflict Situations: Concept, Ethics and Method", Working Paper No. 30, University of Oxford: Refugee Studies Centre.

Justino, P. (2006): "Collective Action and Economic Development", *World Development,* 34 (7), pp. 1254-70.

Kemper, Yvonne (2005): "Youth in War-to-Peace Transitions: Approaches of International Organisations", Bergh of Report No. 10, Berlin: Bergh of Research Centre.

Lansdown, Gerison (2005): *Innocent Insight: The Evolving Capacities of the Child,* Florence: UNICEF.

O' Kane, Claire (2003): *Children and Young People as Citizens: Partners for Social Change,* Kathmandu: Save the Children South and Central Asia.

O' Kane, Claire (2007): "Supporting the Development of Children's Groups and Networks in Afghanistan: Reflections on Practice and Possibilities", *Children, Youth and Environments*, 17(1), pp. 222-37.

Organisation for Economic Co-operation and Development (2001): *The DAC Guidelines: Helping Prevent Violent Conflict,* Paris: OECD.

Shemyakina, O. (2006): "The Effect of Armed Conflict on Accumulation of Schooling: Results from Tajikistan", HiCN Working Paper No. 12, *Households in Conflict Network*, University of Sussex, UK.

Stewart, F., Fitzgerald, V. and Associates (2001b): *War and Underdevelopment,* Vol. 2, *Country Experiences*, Oxford: Oxford University Press.

Stewart, F., V. Fitzgerald and Associates (2001a): *War and Underdevelopment, Vol. 1, Economic and Social Consequences of Conflict*, Oxford: Oxford University Press.

Verwimp, P. (2005): "An Economic Profile of Peasant Perpetrators of Genocide: Micro-Level Evidence from Rwanda", *Journal of Development Economics*, (77), pp. 297-323.

Woodward, S.L. (1995): *Balkan Tragedy: Chaos and Dissolution after the Cold War,* Washington, DC: Brookings Institution.

7

Development-Induced Displacement: The Case of Moolampilly

Raju Narayana Swamy

Introduction

Mass displacement has emerged as an unfailing companion of development. With impoverishment, social disruption, and loss of access to land and resources staring the displaced people in the face, rehabilitation has been held out as a measure in mitigation. But the number of Displaced Persons (DPs) or Project Affected Persons (PAP), i.e., those deprived of livelihood without physical relocation, is growing. Many studies have pointed to the impoverishment and marginalisation of the DPs/PAPs. Development as a theory and an approach has numerous dialogues in the Indian context. As a theory, it imparts certain fundamental working principles and conceptual clarifications. On the basis of such theoretical developments and thinking, the development approach is mainly constructed and developed.

The concept of development has been defined as follows:

1. The basic purpose of development is to enlarge people's choices. In principle these choices can be infinite and can change over time. People often value achievements, that do not show up at all or not immediately, in income or growth figures: greater access to knowledge, better nutrition and health services, more secure livelihoods, security against crimes and physical violence, satisfying leisure hours, political and cultural freedom, and sense of participation in community activities. The objective of development is, to create an enabling environment for people to enjoy long, healthy and creative lives (Human Development Report, 2010).

2. For Amartya Sen, development is a process of expanding the real freedom that people enjoy. This development requires the removal of major sources of un-freedom: poverty as well as tyranny, poor economic opportunities as well as systematic social deprivation, neglect of public facilities as well as intolerance, over activity, or repressive states (Amartya Sen, 1999).

The concept of welfare-state has been progressively destabilised and discredited in the rouse of the ideological resistance between the state and market, and the shifts in the economic policy, entailed by the development of globalisation. Secularism has increasingly been under risk, as communal ideology and political forces have come to benefit, from consumerism in society and the polity. And importantly, the concept of development has come to be unfalteringly questioned, by the supporters of sustainable development strategies as well as by movements, questioning the foundation of projects, which cause large-scale displacement of marginalised people and threaten their livelihood security. The model of development adopted by the Indian state, after independence is economically inequitable, environmentally unsustainable, and politically less democratic in its denial of the rights of equal citizenship. Thus, the detractors of the projects are made to appear as anti-national, seditious, and even akin to terrorists, while the displaced are projected, as those who have to make sacrifices for the public good (Niraja Gopal Jayal, 2001).

Colonial Regime and Displacement

During the colonial regime, all biodiversity, forest and land without individual titles, belonged to the state. The state defined the public purpose[1] and deprived the individuals of their land. They opened coal mines in Jharkhand, tea gardens in Assam and Kerala (Wayanad), coffee plantations in Karnataka, etc. The Permanent Settlement 1793 and the Land Acquisition Act 1894 (LAQ)[2] were the legal changes, introduced to make land acquisition cheap and easy for the state. This deprived lakhs of people, especially the poor farmers and adivasis[3], of their livelihood.

The Post-Independence Period

The Land Acquisition Legislation in force today, is a remnant of the colonial era, when the desires of land-owners could be mistreated. The Government of India continued the practise of acquiring land against the owners' wishes for apparently public purposes. Post-independence economic development based on large projects and big industries entailed extensive displacement. The Land Acquisition Act of 1894, introduced

Table 7.1 Number of DPs/PAPs of Some States*

State/Year	*1951-1995*				*1947-2000*		*1947-04*	*65-95*	*Total*
Type	***Andhra Pradesh***	*Jharkhand*	*Kerala*	*Orissa*	*Assam*	*Bengal*	*Gujarat*	*Goa*	
Water	1865471	232968	133846	800000	448812	1723990	2378553	18680	7602320
Industry	539877	87896	222814	158069	57732	403980	140924	3110	1614402
Mines	100541	402882	78	300000	41200	418061	4128	4740	1271630
Power	87387	NA	2556	NA	7400	146300	11344	0	254987
Defence	33512	264353	1800	NA	50420	119009	2471	1255	472820
Environment	135754	509918	14888	107840	265409	784952	26201	300	1845262
Transport	46671	0	151623	NA	168805	1164200	1356076	20190	2907565
Refugees	NA	NA	0	NA	283500	500000	646	Nil	784146
Farms	NA	NA	6161	NA	113889	110000	7142	1745	238937
Hum Res.	NA	NA	14649	NA	90970	220000	16343	8500	350462
Health	NA	NA	NA	NA	23292	84000	NA	1850	109142
Admin	NA	NA	NA	NA	322906	150000	7441	3220	483567

Contd...

Contd...

State/Year	*1951-1995*				*1947-2000*		*1947-04*	*65-95*	*Total*
Welfare	37560	0	2472	NA	25253	720000	20470	NA	805755
Tourism	0	0	343	0	0	0	26464	640	27447
Urban	103310	0	1003	NA	1241	400000	85213	1750	592517
Others	265537	50000	0	100000	18045	0	15453	840	449875
Total	3215620	1548017	552233	1465909	1918874	6944492	4098869	66820	19810834

*Since the understanding of displacement has grown during the 15 years of the studies, Orissa has very few categories. They were more in the later years.

Source: Walter Fernandes, Development-Induced Displacement: The Class and Gender, Perspective Paper Presented at the International Conference on *The Emerging Woman in the Indian Economy*, Christ College, Bangalore, November 26-27, 2007.

by the British Government, still continues, with a few amendments in 1967, 1984 and 1999, and facilitates the Government to acquire the people's land, by compulsion for both the public and private purposes. In most of the cases, the Government officials have been paying the compensation to the ousters after prolonged time, while they acquire the lands with one notification and within no time. The Land Acquisition Act does not say anything regarding the type or nature of compensation payable to the oustees and the timeline for payment of compensation (Ram Babu Mallavarapu, 2006). Development-oriented projects brought about irrevocable changes in land use and in the lives of millions of its dependants. The number of DPs/PAPs has thus risen enormously.

However, no official database exists on the total and type of DPs/PAPs. In its absence, a reliable database was taken by studying development-induced displacement and deprivation in several states: In Orissa, Kerala and Jharkhand, only 60% of the projects during 1951-1995 were studied while in AP around 80% were studied. When their figures are updated to 2004, the total number of DPs/PAPs would be 3 million each in Jharkhand and Orissa, 5 million in AP, 1 million in Kerala, 100000 in Goa, 2 million in Assam, and 7.5 million in West Bengal, i.e., a total of 27 million. Once high displacement states, such as, Chhattisgarh and MP are studied, one will probably arrive at an all-India figure of 60 million DPs/PAPs during 1947-2004, from 25 million ha, including 7 million ha of forests and 6 million ha of other CPRs (Fernandes, 2007) (Table 7.1).

Rehabilitation and Resettlement Policy

Most of the Pre-1980 projects in India did not have a clear-cut resettlement plan. Resettlement was taken up on a case-to-case basis. Only a few projects offered resettlement in the form of house sites and infrastructure to the displaced. The National Rehabilitation and Resettlement Policy of 2007, notified on 31 October 2007, defines "land acquisition" or "acquisition of land" as "acquisition of land under the Land Acquisition Act, 1894 (1 of 1894), as amended from time to time, or any other law of the Union or a State for the time being in force". This upholds the sovereign power of the state, to apply the concept of "eminent domain" to forcibly acquire any private property, in any part of the country in the name of "public purpose". The 2007 Policy deletes the emergency provisions under Section 17 of the Land Acquisition Act of 1894, "used rarely", and should be applied only after considering, "full justification" of the proposed project (Clause 6.23 of the 2006 Draft Policy). Clause 7.18 of the 2007 Policy implies that land can be acquired in case of emergency, under Section 17 of the Land Acquisition Act, 1894, or a similar provision of any other Act of the Union or a State for the time being in force by keeping the affected families in "transit and temporary accommodation, pending rehabilitation and resettlement scheme or plan".

The affected persons are denied the right to make any kind of informed decision, regarding the usage of their lands, with regard to the development projects. The call for "the active participation of affected persons" (Clause 1.2), in the process of resettlement and rehabilitation, is not reflected in the process of development of the project. Only in the case of acquisition of lands in the Scheduled Areas (under Schedule V and Schedule VI of the Constitution of India) does the 2007 Policy provide that the concerned Gram Sabha/ Panchayat/ Village Council shall be "consulted" (Clause 7.21.2). However, it is important to note that the "consultation" in no sense denotes "consent". The affected persons do not have the right to say "no" at the time of determination of the project site (*ACHR Weekly Review*, 2007).

The 2007 Policy fails to define, who conducts the Social Impact Assessment (SIA) or Economic Impact Assessment (EIA). It only states that "the appropriate Government shall ensure, that a Social Impact Assessment (SIA) study is carried out in the proposed affected areas, in such manner as may be prescribed" (Clause 4.1). This lack of clarity opens the possibility for concerns, over the independence and/or capacity of those designated to carry out SIA and EIA studies. The 2007 Policy provides for the constitution of an "independent multi-disciplinary expert group", to examine the SIA report. Members are nominated by the appropriate Government. There is also no provision for consultation with the affected families, during the final preparation of the SIA and EIA reports, so that their views are reflected in the report, to be examined by the independent expert group (*ibid.*).

After the declaration of an area as an "affected area", the Administrator for Rehabilitation and Resettlement undertakes a baseline survey and census, for identification of the persons and families, likely to be affected by the proposed project. Although the Administrator is required to publish a draft of the details of the findings, to invite comments and objections from the affected persons, there is no provision for the compulsory inclusion, of any affected persons or their representatives in the survey. Wherever there is large-scale displacement, the 2007 Policy provides that the appropriate Government may appoint an Administrator for Rehabilitation and Resettlement (hereafter called

"Administrator"), who is an officer not below the rank of District Collector, to oversee the resettlement and rehabilitation plan. But the Administrator can delegate his/her powers and duties to any officer not below the rank of *Tehsildar,* or equivalent (Clause 5.6). A *Tehsildar* is the lowest ranking officer, in the state administration. That the Administrator can delegate his/her power to a *Tehsildar* shows that there is no seriousness to properly rehabilitate the affected families (*ibid.*).

On the one hand, the Administrator is vested with the power of "overall control and superintendence of the formulation, execution and monitoring of the rehabilitation and resettlement plan" (Clause 5.4), and on the other, the Administrator can only exercise his powers and functions "subject to the superintendence, directions and control of the appropriate Government and Commissioner, for Rehabilitation and Resettlement" (Clause 5.3), and "subject to any general or special order of the appropriate Government" (Clause 5.5). The Commissioner for Rehabilitation and Resettlement is appointed by the State Government and therefore, cannot be considered independent. The first and the foremost objective of the 2007 Policy is to "minimise displacement and to promote, as far as possible, non-displacing or least-displacing alternatives". But the 2007 Policy allows further displacement in the name of resettlement and rehabilitation of the project affected families. Under Clause 6.9, "The appropriate Government, shall, by notification, declare any area (or areas) as a resettlement area (or areas), for rehabilitation and resettlement of the affected families". This may cause further displacement of non-project affected persons. Although it has been mentioned that "the Administrator for Rehabilitation and Resettlement should ensure that such acquisition of land does not lead to another set of physically displaced families", displacement of non-project affected families is bound to occur, under the provisions of Clause 6.9 of the 2007 Policy (*ACHR Weekly Review*, 2007).

Clause 7.4.1 states that each affected family owning agricultural land in the affected area and whose entire land has been acquired or lost, agricultural or cultivable wasteland "may be allotted" only, "if Government land is available in the resettlement area". In other cases, the 2007 Policy only makes weak guarantees, such as, "may be allotted", "may be provided", "may be offered", etc. Clause 7.4.2 provides that: "In case a family cannot be given land in the command area of the project, or the family opts not to take land there, such a family may be given monetary compensation on replacement cost basis for their lands lost, for the purchase of suitable land elsewhere". Under Clause 7.14, the affected families could be coerced to accept money in lieu of land. It provides that : "In case of a project involving land acquisition on behalf of a requiring body, the affected families, who have not been provided agricultural land or employment, shall be entitled to a rehabilitation grant, equivalent to seven hundred fifty days, minimum agricultural wages or such other higher amount as may be prescribed by the appropriate Government". There is little guarantee for employment for the displaced persons in the projects. Clause 7.13.1 states that in case, a project involves land acquisition on behalf of a requiring body, at least one person per nuclear family, should get preference in getting employment in the project but this is subject to "the availability of vacancies and suitability of the affected person for the employment".

Moreover, rehabilitation and resettlement of the affected families, displaced by linear acquisitions in projects, relating to railway lines, highways, transmission lines, laying of pipelines, etc., is absolutely inadequate. According to Clause 7.19, the victims of linear acquisitions would be provided only ex-gratia payment, of such amount as the appropriate figure, which the Government may decide, but not less than Rs. 20,000. However, the benefits of rehabilitation and resettlement, under the 2007 Policy, will be provided to any land-owner, if he/she becomes "landless or is reduced to the status of a 'small' or 'marginal' farmer" as a result of land acquisition. The Policy provides for the establishment of the Resettlement and Rehabilitation Committee, at the project level to monitor and review the progress of implementation of resettlement and rehabilitation schemes. The Committee is not an independent body, as the state governments appoint the members and prescribe the "procedure regulating the business [.....], its meetings and other matters, connected thereto" (Clause 8.1.3). The State Government also prescribes the composition, powers, functions, and other matters relating to the functioning of the Rehabilitation and Resettlement Committee, at the district level which is headed by the District Collector/ District Commissioner of the district (Clause 8.2.1). Hence, there is no guarantee for the inclusion of the affected persons or their representatives in the District Level Committee (*ACHR Weekly Review*, 2007).

Unless, the state addresses the issues, raised by the misuse of the Land Acquisition Act of 1894, the Act will continue to be a cause of conflict. India needs development but not at the cost of mushrooming conflicts. The responsibility of the state is to provide an atmosphere, where development can thrive, but allows all stakeholders with equal opportunities to obtain rewards. The duty of the state is not to pile the odds in favour of the powerful, force land acquisition, or to dis-empower the weak and the most vulnerable. It is in this context, that we are analysing the case of Moolampilly, a small island in Kerala.

Case Study: Moolampilly

Moolampilly is an island, 6 km from Cochin, the booming city of Kerala. Around 600 families are living on this island. Most of the residents are Christians, and include peasants, agricultural labourers and fisher folk. The island is filled with Pokkali rice fields, coconut grooves, a maze of waterways, etc. The villagers use fishing rods, *kattamarams*, boats and *Cheena vala* (Chinese nets). Many of the families are poor and dependent on agriculture for their livelihood[4]. They also go to the city to work as labourers in shops. The island has a primary school, but for upper primary education, the children move to Cochin City. There is a ferry service from the island to the city, every half an hour. There is no upper primary or higher secondary school or college for the villagers in the island. The transportation facility is very poor and people have no access to car, auto-rickshaw or bus on the island.

National Highway No. 47-C links the Vallarpadam International Container Transhipment Terminal (ICTT) of Cochin Port, to two national highways. Land belonging to 22 families was acquired for the construction of ICTT from Moolampilly Island. Out of this, 12 families were compelled to part with their land for the Vallarpadam Project; they were evicted from their houses; but these evicted families alleged that they were evicted without proper rehabilitation facilities[5].

The Government promises many things before eviction. A few are listed hereunder:

1. All the evicted families will be provided with land :
   - Those, who lost less than 5 cents of land, will be allotted 5 cents of land.
   - Those, who lost more than 5 cents of land will be allotted 6 cents of land.
2. An educated member from each family will be given employment.
3. No taxes on cash compensation.

However, interviews, with the evicted families clearly show that they have been cheated by the Government. The Government later failed to provide employment to the affected families. The land allotted to them was "*kol bhoomi*[6]". This land also did not have access to basic facilities such as, road, drinking water, and electricity. Compensation given to the families was around Rs. 5000 for paddy fields, and Rs. 30,000 for one cent of land, while the real cost of the land in these areas was Rs. 2,00,000 for a cent. Out of the 22 affected families, 15 families had paddy fields. They complained that the money they got, as compensation, was insufficient for rehabilitation.

This being the reality for people, who agreed to part with their land, we now proceed to the case of those families that disagreed to move from their houses, without receiving proper compensation. The authorities (including Suseela, Special *Tehsildar* for land acquisition, the National Highway Authority of India, represented by its Project Director Sri Gajapathi Rao, supported by a force of police personnel, led by the Circle Inspector (CI) of Police, North Paravur Police Station, and the entire team including Revenue and Police officials) planned to evict 10 other families from their houses on Tuesday, 6 February 2008. The 10 houses were demolished with a bulldozer by the squads of labourers (from Bihar) and a large posse of policemen sent by the state. The whole purpose of the operation was to take over the properties of all families in the locality. Families refusing to leave locked themselves in their houses. Women and children wailed and men fumed in anger and agony. No time was given to the families, to remove their household articles and by about 3 pm, the demolition team took over the 10 houses, threatened one family (the family of Johnson) who had not given any consent or did not receive any compensation earlier. The authorities had not given the people any written agreement on rehabilitation. The eviction without proper rehabilitation was a violation of norms. All the families stood firm on their demand: "We should be evicted only after proper rehabilitation procedures."

Case-1: Jasmine, who lost her house and 2.5 cents of land, described the incident as a nightmare, which she never wanted to remember in her life. Her household utensils were destroyed by the police. They even took away her cooked food (which she had prepared for her two sons studying in 10th and 9th standards), which was thrown away by the police. Her children's books were also destroyed by the police.

Case-2: On 6.2.2008, the eviction team, accompanied by the team of police, went to the house of P.J. Celestine Master, who is the Convener of People's Struggle Committee. The parish priest and the Member of the Panchayat held several discussions with the officials and their request to postpone the eviction for a few days, was rejected. The police officers used brutal force to disburse the people and destroyed part of the house of P.J. Celestine Master, and the parish priest was seriously manhandled.

The two sons of Celestine Master were beaten up by the police. Antony Xavier, son of Celestine, was admitted in Ernakulam General Hospital for medical treatment, along with a senior citizen, who suffered a heart attack on seeing the high handedness of the two revenue officials and the police. Celestine requested the two revenue officers to show the order for demolishing the houses. But they did not show any record and they ordered the police to remove them by force.

Case 3: The house of Thettayil Subhadra, who belongs to a Scheduled Caste, was also targeted. Her son, Dileep, was later surrounded and threatened to sign the consent papers, saying that he will lose compensation, if he refuses to sign. Later, the thumb impression of Subhadra was obtained on the concerned papers, while she was unconscious, and the eviction operation proceeded at a rapid pace, giving no time to remove the household articles; their valuables were lost. The eviction team confiscated all the movable properties, including the books of children.

The children from these evicted families had to face a great tragedy. They found their houses demolished, food thrown away, their parents frightened with fear, and their books destroyed by the police. The state had not given them their rehabilitation package though rehabilitation was promised. Fr. Martin Kuttikkatt of St. Augustine's Church tried to interfere in the issue. He pleaded the authorities to stop the eviction proceedings and to give the families two or more days for making alternative arrangements. But the authorities turned a deaf ear and behaved brutally; they were in a hurry to acquire a long stretch of land cutting across Moolampilly along with five other nearby islands, and hand it over to the National Highway Authority of India (NHAI) for building the 18km NH 47-C for the ICTT project[7]. In a very brutal manner the houses of 10 families, at Moolampilly[8] of Kadamakkudy Grama Panchayat were demolished under the leadership of Ramadevi, Deputy Collector, and Suseela Jacob, Special *Tehsildar*, Land Acquisition, with the help of a large police force on 5.2.2008 at 9 a.m. without prior intimation to the residents. In view of the above facts, we conclude that there were violations of human rights by both revenue and police officials on account of which, the residents, including ladies and children suffered.

The said eviction process was carried out by violating all directions from the Court, and the Government has not given any rehabilitation facilities to the evictees. Celestine and eight others from Moolampilly Island filed a Writ Petition in WP(C). No. No. 4728/2008, before the High Court of Kerala, which directed the petitioners to file consent to

DLPC before the Land Acquisition Officer, on or before 13.2.2008, with a further direction to the Land Acquisition Officer that if they do not submit their consent for DLPC before the said date, the compensation amount, due to them, is to be deposited in the revenue deposit. The provisions of national Rehabilitation and Resettlement Scheme were not formulated and no package scheme was published, apart from the statement of the District Collector in the newspapers. The High Court of Kerala, relying upon the Judgment of the Supreme Court, in N.D. Jayal vs. Union of India (2004(9) SCC 362), held that "rebuilding livelihood by ensuring necessary amenities of life and rehabilitation of oustees under massive development projects, is a logical corollary of Article 21 and that the Government and the requiring authorities have the obligation to provide for rehabilitation of the oustees" (Kerala State Human Rights Commission, 2009).

Interference of High Court in the Issue

The High Court referred to the National Rehabilitation and Resettlement Policy 2003 and the National Rehabilitation and Resettlement Policy 2007, published in the *Gazette of India* and stated that the main object, of the National Rehabilitation Resettlement Policy 2007, is to ensure adequate rehabilitation package, providing a better standard of living to the persons, who are compulsorily displaced, on account of the exercise of powers of eminent domain, for the acquisition of their properties, for providing public facilities or infrastructure. The High Court quoted Paragraphs 1.1 and 1.2 and also referred to Paragraph 1.3. After referring to various paragraphs of the National Rehabilitation and Resettlement Policy 2007, like the definition of the expression "affected family". "Project", etc., also dealt with Paragraph 6.9 and 6.10 in Chapter VI, of the National Rehabilitation and Resettlement Policy 2007, dealing with Rehabilitation and Resettlement Plan; and referred to Paragraph 6.19, which deals with the proper implementation of the rehabilitation and resettlement scheme or plan as well as Paragraph 6.22, which deals with payment of compensation and adequate progress in the resettlement of the affected families. The Court also referred to Paragraph 7.11 in Chapter VII, which provides that each family, which is displaced, shall get one-time financial assistance for shifting the family, building materials, belongings, and cattle. Similarly, Paragraph 7.18 in the National Rehabilitation and Resettlement Policy 2007 was also referred to. The High Court also referred to Clause XVII of Exbt. R2 (a), which is as follows:

"It should be ensured that all the Project Affected People are compensated and rehabilitated as per the R & R plan, approved by the State Government of Kerala."

"That the Government Orders R2 (b) and R2 (c) have been issued in view of the Government's obligation under Clause XVII of R2 (a), to provide R&R facilities to the evictees in this acquisition."

"That it cannot accept the argument of the counsel for the petitioners, to confer rehabilitation and resettlement benefits, as per R2 or any benefit in excess of what is provided under Exbt. R1. (But held that the Government has no obligation under Clause XVII of R2 (a) to provide R & R facilities in view of the Government Order R2 (c)."

The respondents in the writ petitions were also directed to ensure, that the lands which were allotted to the petitioners in the writ petitions, irrespective of the villages from where they were dispossessed, are made fit for putting up A-class constructions, if necessary, by reclaiming the lands up to the standards of consolidation, necessary for putting up double storied buildings. The High Court further directed that in case, there was delay on the part of the respondents in obeying these directions issued by the Court, the respondents will be liable to pay rent to the evictees, for an alternate accommodation at the current rate of Rs. 5,000 per month, till such time as these directions are obeyed by the respondents. The High Court also held that the order of the High Court will not stand in the way of the State of Kerala conferring better rehabilitation and other benefits from the State (Kerala State Human Rights Commission, 2009).

Conclusion

It is necessary for the Government to nominate an officer, not below the rank of a Secretary to Government, to conduct an enquiry with regard to the above incident, for the purpose of fixing the responsibility of the officers, involved in violating the human rights. Adequate compensation, to those who were affected by such violation of human rights by the revenue and police officials, has to be implemented strictly. The compensation amount will be fixed, after taking into account the nature of damages suffered by each family. The amount, of compensation paid to the victims will be deducted from the officials, who are found guilty of having violated the human rights.

Any understanding on land acquisition should start with an inquiry, on the stakeholders in the development and their interests. The first set of stakeholders includes the land losers, the owners of the acquired land. If they find it impossible to prevent acquisition, then they try to get compensation corresponding to the replacement value of the land. The second set of stakeholders includes the requiring bodies whose interest is to get the required land in modest time and with the least possible price tag. The third stakeholder is the state, involved in preventing any law and order problem cropping up in the wake of the ensuing disturbance in status quo. The interests of the three stakeholders are mutually conflicting. But in the context of Moolampilly, we find that one stakeholder is supporting the other, who is violating the human rights, while the third remains in an embarrassing condition. As each clause has opposite effects on the different interests, it is very difficult to legislate to everyone's satisfaction on the existing model. This helps us to bring to close that any substitute to the present model should exhibit distinctiveness: it should not be unilinear, and the decision-making should be broad-based. The preferred substitute has to see that the process has not impoverished the land losers.

It is, therefore, necessary to reorganize the condition regarding peoples who are not willing to concede to compulsory acquisition and there is a need to democratize the acquisition process. There should be involvement of the people who are affected, and also of specialists, trained to lessen the communal, monetary, emotional and environmental impacts of acquisition. From the Moolampilly experience it is clear, that the colonial model with its anti-people character is not successfully complete.

Notes

1. The distinguishing feature of these laws is the establishment of state monopoly over land and other community assets and natural resources. In Australia, the principle on which this legal system is based is called *terra nullius* (nobody's land). White colonisation of indigenous land in Australia, America and Southern Africa was based on the principle, that the land without an individual title belongs to nobody as such, and can be occupied by anyone. In 1993, the Australian judiciary declared this unconstitutional. However, it continues to be the basis of land legislation in India, under its American expression of 'eminent domain'. Its first facet is that land not having an individual *patta* is state property. The second is that the state alone has the right to decide what a 'public purpose' is. But, the public purpose has not been defined till date See also Jose Murickan, *et al.*, 2003, *Development-Induced Displacement: Case of Kerala*, Jaipur: Rawat Publications, p. 30.
2. This Act gave all powers to the British government, to exercise reputed domain and did not leave any rights with the people, to oppose land acquiring.

3. The Santhal uprising, known in history as Santhal Hul, began on 28th June 1855, with 10,000 Santhals assembling at Bhagnadih in the Damin-i-koh. The attempt failed, but the enraged Santhals went on a rampage. Under the company rule, the question of common rights was never raised. The Santhal tenants were being dispossessed in mass, and were ending up as bonded labour. They targeted policemen and moneylenders for fierce attack, "...for a whole fortnight the Santhals carried fire and sword, throughout the western district." See also Vasudha Dhagamwar (2006), *Role and Image of Law in India: The Tribal Experience*, New Delhi: Sage Publications, p. 156.

4. Many cities in the Indian subcontinent, sub-Saharan Africa, and some of the poorer cities of Latin America are characterised by rapid population growth, an economy heavily dependent on the informal sector, widespread poverty and informal housing areas, basic problems of environment and public health, and difficult issues of governance. These regions are characterised by the dominance of large cities, which experience such extremes of wealth and poverty that they can be characterised as having dual or multiple economies. One economy serves the needs of the affluent and features modern technology, formal markets and outward appearance of developed countries. The other serves disadvantaged groups and is marked by traditional technologies, informal markets and moderate to severe levels of economic and political deprivation. (*See* also Geetam Tiwari, Social Dimension of Transport Planning, Transportation Research and Injury Prevention Programme, Indian Institute of Technology, New Delhi, pp. 2-8.)

5. Development-induced displacement may impact human security severely. Institutions, financing the development projects that give rise to development-induced displacement, play a considerable role in lessening the potential human security impacts of their business. Doing so, requires action at various stages of the project cycle, including in the preparatory phase (e.g., by evaluating various project alternatives for their relative human security impact), during the building and operation of the project (through appropriate mitigation and monitoring of human security impacts as they arise), and *ex-post*, through evaluation of the longer-term human security and the effectiveness of the mitigation measures. But, in general, steps have been made on paper, with many institutional policies now recognising these human security impacts and proscribing adequate responses; however, action at the project level is still lagging behind. (*See* also Georg, Caspary (2007), "The Impacts of Development-Induced Displacement on Human Security: A Study of Dam Finance", *Human Security Journal*, Vol. 4, p. 77.)

6. Land formed by reclaiming lake; unfit for building houses.

7. ICTT project of Rs. 3000 crores was built by DP World on BOT (Build, Operate and Transfer). Prime Minister Manmohan Singh had laid the

foundation for the project in February 2005.

8. The 10 affected families in Moolampilly, on account of the illegal eviction carried out by the district officials, filed H, R, M.P No. 894/2008. They complained that:

- The revenue and police officials demolished their houses and evicted them without any prior intimation. They were not given any written assurance about their rehabilitation package.
- They alleged that most of them suffered brutal torture from the police officials.
- The authorities took away their household articles, tools, and even the books of their children from their houses.
- They said that they are not against the development.
- They are ready to surrender their land and house.
- Their demand is for a clear rehabilitation package.

References

Asif, Mohammed (1999) Land Acquisition Act: Need for an Alternative Paradigm, *Economic and Political Weekly*, 34(25): 1564-1566.

Caspary, Georg (2007) The Impacts of Development-Induced Displacement on Human Security: A Study of Dam Finance, *Human Security Journal*, 4: Summer p. 77.

Common Order (HRMP 759/09,640/09,657/09,894/09/1246/09), Kerala State Human Rights Commission, Thiruvananthapuram, 4th August 2009.

Dhagamwar, Vasudha (2006) *Role and Image of Law in India: The Tribal Experience*, New Delhi: Sage Publications.

Fernandes Walter (1998) Land Acquisition (Amendment) Bill, 1998 Rights of Project-Affected People Ignored, Economic *and Political Weekly*, 33(42&43).

Fernandes, Walter (2007) Development-Induced Displacement: The Class and Gender Perspective, Paper Presented at the International Conference on *The Emerging Woman in the Indian Economy*, Christ College, Bangalore, on November 26-27.

Human Development Report 2010, UNDP, hdr.undp.org

India's Failed National Rehabilitation and Resettlement Policy (2007), *ACHR Weekly Review*, www.achrweb.org, accessed on 18th September 2010.

Jayal, Niraja Gopal (2001) The State and Democracy in India or What Happened to Welfare Secularism and Development, In Niraja Gopal Jayal (ed.) *Democracy in India*, pp. 212, New Delhi: Oxford.

Mallavarapu, Ram Babu (2006) Development, Displacement and Rehabilitation: An Action Anthropological Study on Kovvada Reservoir in West Godavari Agency of Andhra Pradesh, India, *International Journal of Human and Social Sciences*, 1(1): 35-37.

Murickan, Jose, *et al.* (2003) *Development-Induced Displacement: Case of Kerala*, Jaipur: Rawat Publications.

Sen, Amartya (1999) *Development as Freedom*, New York: Oxford University Press.

Tiwari, Geetam (2009) Social Dimension of Transport Planning, Paper Presented on *Transportation Research and Injury Prevention Programme*, Organised by Indian Institute of Technology, New Delhi, on November 29th.

8

Impact of Displacement and Rehabilitation on Chenchu Livelihoods

N. Venkata Sivaiah

Introduction

The relationship between man and his environment is as old as man's existence on earth. Man's intimate and inevitable dependency, on his environment, has taught him to respect it, and to try and achieve a balance between the resources and his needs. In the past, resources were plenty; but now, because of the increase in population and the needs, there is a disturbance in the ecological balance, and the most affected are the resource-poor persons. Hence, it is important to strike a balance between economic prosperity and ecological security. In this connection, a new direction was evolved in the field of anthropology, which is increasingly concerned with such urgent matters, that relate to human beings as a whole.

The forest and forest resources that were earlier enjoyed and controlled by forest dwellers/tribals, are now largely controlled by the state. It is not unlikely that the forest policy of the government can be influenced by the powerful industrial and commercial interests, often at the cost of poor tribals (Mahanthi, 1994). Thus, the current trends, in ecology as well as in anthropology, suggest that the macro-ecosystem level may not be appropriate for dealing with questions of human impact and resource management, except in a very broad and unspecific way. "Resource management is a site-specific task, in which social, political, legal and historical dimensions are at least as important as environmental ones" (Moran, 1984: 19-20).

It is a fact that, dependence on forest produce is of a much greater magnitude among the forest dwellers/tribals, residing adjacent to forest areas. The tribals in India, being aware of the importance of forest to their lives, developed norms and conventions, guarded by myths and folklore, which, on one hand, restrict the destruction of forests and on the other, protect and promote the forest and forest resources by maintaining the eco-system, as a divine abode and something sacred. Thus, in the past, they enjoyed forest resources without any restrictions, i.e., when they had free access to utilize the resources as their customary rights. However, this free access was severely affected, after the forest laws were introduced and implemented in the tribal areas. As a result, the 'natives' or tribals lost their rights over the forest and resources, and slowly, the indigenous practice of forest preservation also started to disappear, as they feel that the forests are not their own any more.

Besides, indirectly, encouraging non-tribals to enter and interfere with the forest resource utilisation, the government's laws and acts have also become a threat to the tribals' survival as well as the forest resources. In the same way, the modern developmental activities, that use forest resources for industrial purposes, have also become a threat to the forests as they concentrate mostly on economic profits, rather than on socio-cultural and ecological aspects.

There are some studies, which reveal the failure of modern developmental programmes, that were implemented against the tenets of tribal cultural domain, ignoring the indigenous knowledge. It was felt by Saifi Basin that, "modern industrial agriculture can be considered to reflect short-term fitted adaptations, in response to the surrounding conditions – economical, societal and ecological – part of these adaptations cannot be sustained in the long run, because of resource depletion and environmental degradation" (1997: 26). It is important to note that there is an adverse affect of this on the livelihoods of the poor tribals. It is noted by Nadakarni that : "The relationship, between poverty, environment and development, is quite complex and not amenable to easy generalisation; and we cannot take it for granted that all economic development alleviates poverty. It is possible for 'development projects' to be capable of setting up the rate of growth of Gross National Product (GNP) and yet deprive the poor of employment and even of access to their natural resource environment. Additionally, development projects may be environmentally destructive" (2000: 1184-87).

Development, at the cost of environment, may last for a short span but it may later turn out to be anti-development, causing poverty and human sufferings. Therefore, a balanced and sustainable development requires an understanding of the environmental process (Agarwal and Dube, 2002: 1).

As observed by Tracey Brieger and Ali Sauer (2000) in the case of Gujarat, the local people opposed the government's afforestation scheme by raising the slogan," jangal jangal dubadta, rupa than in kay karta" (you are submerging forests, what's the point of planting trees?). It questions the logic of deforestation by submerging the Narmada Valley in the name of development and then attempting to reforest to make up for the lost jungle. The failures, that arise out of a modern developmental programme, are not just limited to that particular programme; in the long run, they adversely affect the environment, forest and, finally, the quality of the life of the people.

The modernisation programmes fail, as they neglect the local knowledge and tradition. Local knowledge and tradition are often regarded as opposed to modernisation and as obstacles to the process of development. The failure of decades of development made the people concerned to look toward anthropologists, who have intensively dealt with environmental problems and highlighted the potentiality of indigenous environmental knowledge, and gross-root participation in environment management. It is rightly observed by Misra that : "Although there is inevitable scepticism in complete acceptance of the local environmental knowledge as alternative adaptive strategies, there is not even an iota of doubt that this knowledge has a sustainable value that has passed the test of time" (2001: 11). Thus, anthropologists have been suggesting the need to inject the indigenous knowledge in the strategic treatment of human problems, such as, ecological, economic and socio-cultural, which eventually achieves human sustainability.

In the same way, "the meaning of rehabilitation is not just confined to uprooting one thing from one place and placing it elsewhere.The planners and administrators should be clear in their minds that rehabilitation is not of a thing but of living people. When the people are uprooted from their original places and rehabilitated elsewhere, not only their economy gets affected but their social and cultural relations also get a jolt. These feelings can be observed, particularly, when the people are forced to migrate from one place to another" (Patel, 1997: 82).

Patel (1997) had studied the rehabilitated people under the Sardar Sarovar Project and felt that there are a lot of problems, difficulties in the social sphere, disturbance in community life, setback in religious life, etc., arising out of the change of locale to a place far off from their submerging homes. He argues that one should care for human and humane appraisal of social and cultural setting of the tribals, the traditions of their strength and the strengths of their traditions, and evolve suitable, people-oriented strategies for their survival in a new situation, with a sense of dignity and autonomy. That purpose can be attained, if we incorporate the urge to understand and share their notions and meanings of social and cultural life; and not to humour them into accepting something, which they hesitate to receive. Further, he suggests a real and participative understanding process of coming together to build a new society, based on the values of sharing and caring; and also mutual criticism for discovery of inner contradictions, in the logic of dislocation and rehabilitation. This alone can help us resolve the tensions, in implementing what is called social rehabilitation.

According to Patnaik, "Understanding the policy of displacement and rehabilitation cannot be complete, unless we examine the process of its implementation. In most of the cases, the beneficial provisions of the policy have remained mainly on paper and very rarely they have been operationalised." He shares that : "My field work among the Paraja, of Koraput District, who got displaced due to the construction of Upper Kolab River dam project, highlighted the negative consequences of the process of displacement and rehabilitation, mainly, due to faulty policy implications and implementations." Further, he suggests that "adequate scope and opportunity should be given to the affected persons to participate in the decision-making process" (2007 : 97).

Narayan (2002) had studied the rehabilitation process of tribal villages in Bihar by focusing on anthropological and psychological issues, which are natural outcomes of displacement, resulting in rehabilitation because of development projects. He states that "it is universally acknowledged that displacement is stressful and sometimes leads to traumatic conditions. Inspite of this, the psycho-sociological issues have been neglected in the displacement of people under various projects. Rehabilitation programmes often lack specific components of the aspects of mental health of the people. There is no evidence of discussion of the mental health problems and their implications of assessing cost and benefit of development projects" (p. 69).

He, further, says : "The displaced persons, by and large, were forced into daily wage labour. For example, the persons, displaced by the Pong Dam, who returned to Himachal Pradesh or decided to migrate to other states, in the hope of comparatively more comfortable life, were forced to become landless migrant labourers. Another example is that of 16,080 tribal families from 170 villages displaced by Ukai-Kakarpur Project on River Tapi in Gujarat and surveys reported that 42 per cent of all the families, landed or landless, were forced to migrate for work." Inspite of the intentions of the government, to provide a comfortable rehabilitation to the affected population, no attention has been paid to the psycho-sociological consequences associated with the process (p. 71 & 78).

Narendra and Sudhakar Rao (2010 : 95) while understanding resistance against Polavaram dam, a large dam under construction on the Godavari River in Andhra Pradesh, observed that some adivasis are convinced that they are hapless victims, who will be doomed. Some have resolved to leave their ancestral homes; they expect the government to at least provide what it has promised. But they have no confidence in the government. There are some who would challenge the state and ask, "Do we have to go, if they tell us to go?" This speaks of the in-built resistance and points to the possibility of a confrontation. Some feel that "it is very painful to leave after living here so long" and some say with fear that "the non-tribal people will crush us, then and there, itself". Suffice it to say that this is the predicament that is envisaged by the adivasis when they are resettled.

Thus, there is a need to understand the socio-ecological dynamics of an ethnic community and to adopt cautious steps for the protection of ethnic groups and managing the sustainability of the natural environment, as advocated by many scholars. So the strategic approach, for resettlement and development has to take into account the basic characteristic of local areas. Many of the tribal areas are remote, forested, hilly or sloppy, and the natural resource endowment is vastly different from that of the other areas.

Though the government is striving to develop the position of tribals through several measures, the benefits are not reaching them properly. The failure of these programmes can be attributed to defective planning/ conceptualisation and implementation. However, these programmes, aimed at tribal development, have both positive and negative implications on the livelihoods and resources of the indigenous population. But still, there is a need to consider the sustainable nature of the development programmes and their harmony with the local socio-cultural fabric.

In view of the above, it is formidable to look into the livelihoods, resources, traditional practices, and development, as interrelated and interdependent aspects. This sort of viewing helps us to understand sustainability of different developmental efforts among the tribal communities in general and among the rehabilitated tribals in particular. In this regard, it is proposed to study the Primitive Tribal Group (PTG) of the 'Chenchus', whom the government had displaced from the forest, on the name of rehabilitation and development, under the process of implementation of the Wild Life Act (1972) and the Forest Conservation Act (1980).

It is pertinent to note that what Haimendorf observed in the 1940s holds true even today. According to him, "It may suffice to say that, during, recent years, Chenchus' environment has begun to change and that the future alone will show how far the Chenchus will be successful in adapting to the new conditions without relinquishing altogether the traditional style of life" (1943: 16).

Significance of the Study

The Chenchus eked out their living by hunting the animals and collecting fruits, tubers, honey, etc., when the resources were abundant and when they enjoyed complete rights over the forest and its resources. However, slowly the situation changed: the forest resources became very scarce and its access was also restricted by the government. In view of the changing environmental conditions, such as degradation of forests, depletion of resources, lack of access to the existing resources, etc., the present study on rehabilitated Chenchus gains its significance. It attempts to understand the sustainability of different developmental efforts and their impact on the livelihoods of the Chenchus.

The population of the Chenchus is 49,232, and forms 0.98 per cent of the total tribal population in the State of Andhra Pradesh as per the 2001 Census (TCR & TI, 2008). They are concentrated in Prakasam, Guntur, Mahabubnagar, Kurnool, Nalgonda and Ranga Reddy districts of Andhra Pradesh. The study village 'Chenchugudem' is located in the Nallamalai Hills and in the foot hills of Amrabad upper plateau of Mahabubnagar District. It is a small tribal village consisting of 68 Chenchu households, under Laxmipalli Panchayat of Balmoor Mandal.

Methodology and Data Collection

The present study is a micro level study and lays emphasis on qualitative data, gathered through anthropological techniques, such as, observation of both participants and non-participants, case studies, interviews structured and informal, key-informant interviews and group discussions etc., along with secondary data, collected from various sources. Fieldwork was undertaken during September and October, 2003.

Displacement of Chenchus

The Chenchus have traditionally inhabited the forest tracts of the Nallamalai Hills. Historically, they were accorded special rights within the forest, including the establishment of exclusive forest enclosures and cultivation within the forest. After independence, the government took over all the lands in Andhra Pradesh and, in 1970, enacted a legislation to confer title rights to the tribals over the land they cultivated and to delineate boundaries between the villages and the Reserve Forest. With the Forest Conservation Act of 1980, however, most areas, inhabited by the Chenchus became part of the Reserve Forest. Since no immediate rehabilitation measures were taken, the Chenchus gradually lost their sources of livelihood, and some began to cultivate unproductive areas next to the forests (www.enrap.org.in/Completed.asp?linkid=97).

Thus, in 1970s, the government displaced some of the Chenchu inhabitants from their small hamlets amidst the nearby forests like Ramgiri Banda, Rampuram, Gudibanda, Bhagavantharao Bavi, Jagannadhapuram, Saipet, etc., rehabilitated them at a new place, and named it as 'Chenchugudem'. The Chenchus were given permission by the government to clear the forest to make agricultural lands for practising settled agriculture in this new settlement. The villagers said that the government officials told them not to go into the forest then onwards and placed restrictions on food gathering, hunting, fuel collection, etc., as the forest came under the Wild Life Act and was declared as Reserve Forest. After 2 years of rehabilitation, the government sanctioned them *'pattas'* (title deeds) for 3 acres of land to each family, for practicing agriculture. One elementary school was started in the year 1974 by the ITDA, to provide free education, food, clothing, soap, oil, etc., to the Chenchu children in the *Girijan Ashrama Patasala.*

Impact of Displacement of the Chenchus on Forest and other Resources

New patterns of livelihood are now emerging among the Chenchus, in place of their traditional livelihood patterns. The diversification of their livelihoods, from traditional hunting and food gathering to food production activities, made them lose their customary rights over the forest resources. While the tribals were denied access to forest resources, the non-tribals gained easy access and exploited its wood and timber. Their irrational commercial activities caused depletion of the forest and forest resources.

The villagers trace the reasons for the depletion of forests and other resources that caused changes in their livelihood patterns. According to them, the Forest Department has given permission to private contractors/ timber merchants to cut the forest trees. They say : "We have worked, day and night, as daily labour (*cooli*) for cutting the trees for the *'shavukars'* (merchants) who got the contract and permission from the government to take out the forest wood. They used to give us *'sara'* (local liquor) and 'battem' (rice) as our labour payment. Larger amounts of timber and wood from valuable trees such as 'Teku', *'Jittega'*, *'Nalla Maddi'*, *'Yegi'*, etc., were transported by them. Thus, we have lost our resource, due to government policies, and even due to our ignorance, which the *'shavukars'* have encashed. We were cheated by offering *'sara'*, our habitual weakness. We were not aware that our future was at stake. Otherwise, we would have opposed the cutting of our forest which provides us valuable resources and livelihood. As a result, we are now facing many problems in leading our lives, whereas earlier we could eat the available fruits, animal and bird species in the forest."

Nimmala Chinnamma aged about 100 years says. "In the past, the villagers used to stay in the forest in groups to safeguard the resources for our use; we felt that the forest was ours." In addition to this, the villagers used to follow the instructions and norms, put forth by the '*Peddamanchi*' (village elder) of the village, which taught them not to destroy the forest resources. But this kind of behaviour is not found these days due to the introduction of the modern (statutory) Panchayat system and due to interactions with non-tribal outsiders.

The local Chenchus express that, these days, they are not in a position to get anything from the forest to feed themselves. They say that some 10-15 years ago, they got sufficient food materials from the forest, including different animal species like, *'Udumulu'*, *'Udatalu'*, *'Kundellu'*, *'Duppulu'*, *'Adavipandulu'*, etc., and some bird species. But now-a-days, the animals and birds are vanishing, due to the depletion of the trees in the forest. Rainfall has also come down due to the forest depletion, resulting in the shortage of water resources, to the extent that it has now become a threat to the survival of the animals. They, further, say that when the forest was thick, there were plenty of tubers and roots and even their sizes were very big. One tuber could easily feed their family for a complete day. But now-a-days they are not available in that abundance, even after digging three to four feet deep; they get only very thin-sized tubers. These tubers are not that tasty, unlike the earlier ones, and also their size is small because of scanty rainfall.

One of the older respondents mentioned : "We lived by depending on the forest, completely. Earlier we got plenty of Minor Forest Produces (MFPs) like honey, gum, firewood, etc., along with hunted animals and food gatherings, to sell in the market. We spent less time and effort to get these resources, about 10-15 years ago. If we worked six hours a day, at the end of the week we were able to collect 3 kg of gum worth of Rs. 200-300; honey worth of Rs. 200; and firewood worth Rs. 100. But during the last 5-10 years, even if we worked for more than six hours a day, we are not in a position to get even half of the quantity/ amount. Since the last 5 years, we are not getting any food or MFP from the forest. So we have completely stopped going to the forest and started depending on labour works only, which we did not do 15-20 years ago. Ten years back we started going for labour, outside the village, for four to six months in a year, but since the last five years, we are completely dependent on migration labour."

After the introduction of agriculture in this village, bore-wells and tube-wells were dug for the purpose of cultivation of commercial crops which consume more water. The over-utilisation of water sources and shortage of rainfall led to low water yields from the drinking water bore-wells as well as tube-wells in the agricultural lands. This clearly indicates that the ground water resources are fast depleting. Now, out of the six bore-wells, four bore wells in this village have gone dry. Similarly, five tube-wells in the agricultural lands also have dried up.

Impact of Displacement on Chenchu Livelihoods

Displacement and relocation is not a mechanical enterprise, it is not a shift or relocation of the physical entities. Rehabilitation of people is the shifting of human beings, who already have their social and cultural roots in the milieu. They are tied to their soil and have memories and historical legacies of their own. Also they have their culture, artefacts and symbols which they love to worship and remember. That being the case, one needs to closely look into their traditional arrangements, their strengths and the viability of their social and cultural practices which have helped them to stand rooted to their soil for centuries (Patel, 1997: 89).

The drastic changes in the availability and accessibility of the resources have caused the Chenchus to look for new forms of livelihoods. As depletion is taking place from the stage of "plentiful resource" to the "lack of resource", inevitably their livelihoods have shifted to migration as labour, agriculture, agricultural wage labour, etc. Due to the depletion of resources, the food gathering activity and MFP collection has drastically come down, during the last 20 years. As a result the Chenchus have taken to new types of livelihood activities.

Table 8.1 Main Occupations of the Chenchus

Sl. No.	*Occupation*	*No. of Households*	*% of Households*
1	Migrant Labour	23	34
2	Agriculture	18	26
3	Wage Labour	15	22
4	Service	9	13
5	MFP/Food Gathering and Hunting	3	4
	Total	68	100

The above data shows clearly the changing livelihood patterns of the Chenchus. If we observe the trend of activities, such as, hunting, food gathering, and MFP collection as their main occupation, we notice a negligible number (4%) of families pursuing this sort of livelihood. Now-a-days, majority (34%) of the Chenchus have been resorting to migration in search of their livelihood. More than half (56%) of them are taking up either migrant or wage labour, as their livelihood, while about a quarter (26%) of them are practising agriculture as their main occupation. There were hardly anyone earlier, who left their home for outside works and migration works, but now it has substantially increased, and dependence on wage labour has also increased considerably.

The above discussion clearly brings out the changing livelihood patterns of the Chenchus, their vulnerable conditions of living, as a result of the loss of their earlier livelihood and customary rights over forest resources, and the uncertainty of their sustenance in the present patterns of livelihood. While they have adopted new livelihood patterns, such as, migration for labour, agriculture, and wage labour, they have also adapted some subsidiary occupations to augment their earnings. Some of the families that go on seasonal migration, practise agriculture, MFP collection, food gathering and hunting, wage labour, fishing, etc., as subsidiary occupations, when they return to the village during the monsoon.

Table 8.2 Subsidiary Occupations of the Chenchus

Sl. No.	*Occupation*	*No. of Households**	*Percentage of Households*
1	Agriculture	28	41
2	MFP collection	26	38
3	Food Gathering and Hunting	23	34
4	Wage Labour	22	32
5	Migrant Labour	21	31
6	Fishing	13	19
7	Mat Preparation	4	6

Note: *Multiple responses.

It is clear from the above that due to Forest Acts, depletion of resources, etc., the Chenchus have lost their traditional livelihoods and are forced into new livelihood patterns. Though the efforts of the government helped some Chenchu families, most of them have less sustainable livelihoods. This has turned them into hunter-gatherers in a different sense, for seeking a livelihood!

Impact of Rehabilitation/Developmental Programs on Chenchu Livelihoods

An attempt is made in this study to discuss the process of development and welfare programmes that are being implemented by the government for the Chenchus in general and for the Rehabilitated Chenchus of Chenchugudem Village in particular, and their response towards these developmental programs, in order to see how they are coping up with the changing conditions.

The Chenchus are one of the PTGs and in an effort to bring them into the developmental stream, the government has taken up many welfare programs. For effective development of the Chenchus, the Integrated Tribal Developmental Agency (ITDA), Srisailam, is working for the

Chenchus living in Kurnool, Prakasam, Guntur, Mahabubnagar, Nalgonda and Ranga Reddy districts. The ITDA takes up developmental activities, mainly in the area of housing schemes, agriculture and minor-irrigation, drinking water, animal husbandry, and vocational training. In Chenchugudem too, many developmental programmes have been taken up by the ITDA, which include agriculture, horticulture, animal husbandry, drinking water, housing, and education.

Agricultural Development

As already mentioned, the government made efforts to develop agriculture in Chenchugudem. *Pattas* for 3 acres of agricultural land were given to each household, by the government. The ITDA shouldered the responsibility for the implementation of agricultural development programmes. It dug bore-wells and provided electric motors, ploughs, and bullocks, along with agricultural implements, such as, sickle, spade, etc., and high-yielding varieties of seeds to improve production.

Initially, the villagers practised agriculture with these implements, using plough bullocks. However, within a few years, many of them discontinued the agricultural activities. The reason as stated by some was that they could not carry out cultivation as their cattle were eaten away by wild animals in the forest; others informed that the bullocks supplied by the ITDA were old and died within a couple of years. But in fact, the bullocks, carts, electric motors, and bore-wells supplied by the government were sold to outsiders and non-tribals at cheaper rates; some sold them in order to meet their personal expenses, while others sold them for drinking liquor. This was because they were not accustomed to agriculture and were reluctant to pursue the activity, as it involves hard work and does not yield immediate returns.

In the village, there are around 10 Chenchu families that have utilised these facilities well and became good cultivators. Their children were educated and became government employees. These families further developed their agricultural activities after their family members became permanent jobholders. It is observed in the village that these families are cultivating not only in their own lands but also the leased-in lands taken from the villagers, and sometimes even from outsiders from the surrounding villages. This could become possible, because these people had earlier worked as the agriculture labourers for non-tribal fields in the plain areas; when they were later shifted to the new rehabilitated colony by the government, they succeeded in agricultural activities.

Horticulture Development

Under the horticulture development programme, the government took up mango plantation in the village; 120 mango saplings were distributed to each family in the year 1990 for planting in 2 acres. Under the IFAD programme, mango plants were supplied to them to re-plant in the same fields, where the plants that were planted earlier died. Again, mango plants were distributed to 34 members in the village in 1996; to14 members in 2002; and to 20 members in 2003. As maintenance charges, each family was given Rs. 60 per month, for five years, to grow the plants.

Table 8.3. Survival of Mango Trees Planted by the Households

Mango trees that survived out of 120	*No. of Households*	*% of Households*
Below 20	12	34
20-50	9	26
50-100	8	23
100-120	6	17
Total	35	100

Though more than 50 households in the village took active part in mango plantation in their agricultural fields, only 35 households have mango trees at present. Even among them many have lost their plants and there are very few trees left now (less than 20). In fact, among all the households, only a few have almost all plants surviving, i.e., 100-120 plants (Table 8.3).

According to the villagers, there are many reasons for the loss of trees. One of the important causes was their negligence in maintaining them; others include, abuse of the money given by the government, for their personal purposes and/or for liquor. Apart from this, lack of proper water supply also affected the survival of the mango plants. Though the government provided bore-wells and motor facilities, five bore-wells were given to 18 members in five groups, while some quarrelled among themselves and sold them off, others complained that their lands were rocky and sandy and not suitable for cultivating or growing different kinds of plants. They further stated that after planting mango trees, they lost the scope to cultivate other crops in their agricultural fields, and because of this, they started going for migration works for their livelihood purpose. Due to their continuous absence from the village, they lost their mango trees, as there was no proper maintenance.

However, some of the villagers are taking very good care of their Mango trees as well as crops. They are also cultivating other crops, like castor, cotton, etc., in the same land where they are growing the mango plants, by using hybrid seeds, which only grow up to a certain level without causing harm to the existing mango plants. Thus the mango plantation programme, initiated by the government, has given inspiration to some.

GCC and Forest Department

The Girijan Co-operative Corporation (GCC) markets were started by the government for the Chenchus to sell their MFP/NTFP collections. With this provision, the Chenchus of Chenchugudem received economic benefits by selling gum, soap nut, tamarind, *nuxvomica*, *chillaginjalu*, *madangadda*, etc. But now-a-days, the non-tribals are coming freely into the forest and extracting these resources, causing further depletion. This kind of non-tribal activities are affecting the livelihoods of the Chenchus. As a result of these factors, the Chenchus of this village resorted to labour works and migration to various places in search of livelihoods. Social disorder has set in among the Chenchus of this village as a consequence of modern livelihood activities, migration works, influence of outsiders, impact of statutory Panchayat system, etc.

The Forest Department is taking some measures now-a-days for preserving the forest and other natural resources: It is taking up eco-developmental activities, such as, afforestation programmes, construction of check dams, etc. The Chenchus of this village are getting some work from the eco-development activities taken up jointly by the Forest Department and 'Eco-Development Committee' in Chenchugudem.

Culture Contrast of Developmental Programmes on Chenchu Livelihoods

No doubt some aspects of the livelihood patterns of the Chenchus of Chenchugudem are improving due to the developmental initiatives, made by the government; but they are still struggling for survival and for choosing alternative options which fit their perception.

During the last 10-15 years, migrations from this village have been increasing due to the failure of agricultural and horticultural works and also because of the depletion of forest resources, that affected their food security, including MFP collections. Thus migration has become a major part of their livelihood earnings. This has now become a trend among many Chenchu families, in order to eke out a living. About 23 families now resort to seasonal migration for their livelihoods, and for 21 households, seasonal migrations have become subsidiary economic activities. Thus 44 households, i.e., more than half (65%) of the households in the village, depend on the migrational labour works, either completely or partially, for their livelihoods. Those who depend completely on migration, for their livelihood, go to outside places such as Mumbai, Karnataka, and other towns/cities in Andhra Pradesh for nine months in a year. They are hired and transported by labour contractors, who provide meals and pay Rs. 9000 for both the wife and the husband. Though the payment is less, they opt for such work as there is no work or feeding source for them in their village. The private labour contractors take advantage of the helpless situation of the Chenchus to exploit their labour.

Fear of change of source of livelihood leads to 'occupational disruptions'. This may lead to high degree of 'occupational redundancy'. This loss, even if substituted by the new ways of managing the livelihood, often leads to a state of mental stress. Loss of agricultural land to the landowners, though providing 'economic compensation' and also new occupational opportunities under various 'rehabilitation programmes' by the government, could not fulfil the psychological loss, such as, social status enjoyed through 'feudalistic culture', the village leadership leading to psychological satisfaction. All these usually get blocked in the relocation process (Narayan, 2002: 71).

The introduction of agriculture brought about many changes in the division of labour between men and women. Women feel that their work load has increased as they now have to take up works like transplanting, weeding, harvesting, and carrying their products home or sometimes to the markets. Apart from these works, they have to look after household works, like, cooking, fetching water, washing clothes, bringing firewood, etc. Compared to earlier days, bringing firewood now-a-days takes a long time as they have to walk for long distances. The reason, for this according to the villagers, is the depletion of the forest, which is taking place, because the non-tribals are carting the forest resources. The women complained that it is becoming tough for them to prepare even two square meals that include rice and curries, because of lack of work to earn livelihood. They say that these kinds of situations happen, because of their poverty, combined with their husbands' bad habit of drinking liquor. The Chenchu men find it difficult to get food grains and other provisions, due to successive droughts and lack of availability of productive work. They feel that agricultural activities have become burdensome, as they require a lot of investment, which they can't afford. Hence, they are leaving their lands fallow.

The Chenchu men and women say that, because of all these difficulties in their farm-based livelihoods, they are forced to migrate, where they will be provided contracted wages and meals by the labour contractors. They feel that this kind of life is reflecting their earlier hunting and food gathering life style, the kind of 'hand-to-mouth' economic life or culture, as also described by Haimendorf (1943:58). Working as migrant labour, they need not procure different provisions, utensils, vegetables, etc., just as in the past, and need not strain for preparing a meal, as they do not need to cook food. Because of these reasons, they usually prefer migration works, rather than agriculture, for earning their livelihood, though they get very less amount for their work.

Thus, these kinds of "examples of people adopting or not adopting new, non-traditional livelihood strategies, illustrates that people negotiate change not only according to economic factors, but also according to the cultural and social meanings and consequences that new livelihood strategies have" (Cahn, 2006:53). In this context, it is important to note that, though the government has introduced agriculture and horticulture programmes for the development of the Chenchus, there were no full-length steps to prepare them mentally to set their lives into such economic activities, which are not part of their earlier lives or economic culture. The government has not taken adequate care to properly guide and monitor their livelihoods and well-being.

Conclusion and Suggestions

The present study concentrated on the ecological aspects, mostly on forest and other resources, in relation to the livelihoods of rehabilitated Chenchus, and their sustainability. Though there are some failures in the developmental programmes, being implemented by the government, it can be said that there is some improvement in the lives of the Chenchus compared to their past living pattern. However, there are some of the issues which should be taken up on an urgent basis, in order to bring an overall development and also maintain the ecological balance in the Chenchu areas.

The villagers urge that the government should provide different opportunities and favourable work ambience at the local level. The Chenchu people further suggest that it would be very expedient and profitable, if the government provides them with opportunities to take up apiculture as it is the occupation which resembles their own traditional kind of livelihood pattern. The government must impose and strictly implement the forest laws and make sincere efforts to prevent exploitation of forest resources by the non-tribals, in order to maintain the eco-balance, which helps the Chenchus carry on their livelihood activities, such as, collection of MFPs/NTFPs.

There is need to give more demonstrations and training programmes on cultivation of crops, etc., to the Chenchus. Efforts should be made to change their mindsets and impress upon them that they can lead a comfortable life, if they adapt to the new livelihood patterns which can be more sustainable and rewarding. The government must conduct audio-visual programmes showing live examples of people of their own tribal groups, who are developed and also about various successful programmes. There is a need to demonstrate different kinds of eco-friendly methods in agricultural activities for the conservation of land, water, etc. The villagers feel that the government must initiate rapid afforestation activities and plant useful tree species like gum trees, tamarind, *sikai, usiri,* mango, etc. This will help in MFP collections and for their economic well-being. The provision, of collecting these products, should be given to the local tribal people, and non-tribal outsiders should be strictly forbidden from exploiting these resources. There should be strict control over the private contractors who are taking the Chenchusfor migrational works and exploiting their labour.

Thus the government must take the initiative to provide different work opportunities at the local level. There cannot be a common rehabilitation package for all; it should be taken up according to the peoples' choices, experiences, traditional and cultural concerns, etc. Further, the rehabilitation activity should not be closed simply by providing land or money; there should be a follow-up mechanism, continuous monitoring, providing the support networks, and human skills, for years together, and if needed, for decades together. This can prevent the out-migration and help them in carving out a better future for themselves with more sustainable livelihoods, so that they can come out of the present distress and uncertain livelihoods. However, the recent National Rural Employment Guarantee Scheme (NREGS), works that are being provided by the government, is helping the Chenchus to get local works as well as to get immediate returns within two weeks or a month; this made them settle in their home land without migrating out in search of livelihoods. Finally, it can be hoped that sustainable development will take place among the Chenchus with the combined efforts of the government, NGOs, intellectuals, and other social activists in the very near future.

Acknowledgement

The author expresses thankfulness to Prof. R. Siva Prasad for his precious guidance, during his M.Phil course. He renders sincere thanks to Prof. K.K. Misra and all other faculty members of the Department of Anthropology, University of Hyderabad, for their encouragement in the research field all the way. Finally, the author is very thankful to the Chenchu people, who have shared their experiences with great patience.

References

Agarwal, S.K. and P.S. Dube (2002): *Environmental Controversies*, New Delhi: A.P.H. Publishing Corporation.

Bhowmic, P.K. (1992): *The Chenchus of the Forest and Plateaus – A Hunting –Gathering Tribe in Transition*, West Bengal: Samaj Sevak Sangha Press.

Brieger, Tracey & Ali Sauer (2000): "Narmada Valley: Planting Trees; Uprooting People", *Economic & Political Weekly,* 35(43-44), p. 3795.

Cahn Miranda (2006): "Sustainable Rural Livelihoods, Micro Enterprise and Culture in the Pacific Islands: Case Study from Samoa", A Ph.D thesis submitted in Massey University, New Zealand.

Haimendorf, Christoph Von-Furer (1943): *The Chenchus: Jungle Folk of the Deccan*, London: Macmillan.

Mahanthi, Neeti (1994): *Tribal Issues: A Non-Conventional Approach*, New Delhi: Inter India Publishing.

Misra K.K. and D.J. Narendra Bondla (2007): *Rehabilitation and Resettlement in India: The Tribal Emic Perspective*, Secunderabad: Centre for World Solidarity.

Misra, K.K. and M.L.K. Murthy (2001): *Peoples and Environment in India,* New Delhi: Discovery Publishing Co.

Moran E. Emilio (ed.) (1984): *The Ecosystem Concept in Anthropology*, Colorado: West View Press.

Nadakarni, M.V. (2000): "Poverty, Environment, Development", *Economic and Political Weekly*, 35(14), pp. 1184-90.

Narayan, Sachindra (2002): *The Dynamics of Tribal Development Issues and Challenges,* New Delhi: Gyan Publishing House.

Narendra D.J. Bondla and N. Sudhakar Rao (2010): "Resistance against Polavaram", *Economic and Political Weekly*, 14(32), pp. 93-95.

Patel Arjun (1997): "Socio-Culture: Missing Aspects of Rehabilitation Policy Packages, A Case of SSP", In Bhupinder Singh and Neeti Mahanti (eds.), *Tribal Policy in India*, New Delhi: Inter-India Publications.

Patnaik S.M. (1997): "Displacement and Rehabilitation Policy: The Orissa Experience", In Bhupinder Singh and Neeti Mahanti (eds.), *Tribal Policy in India*, New Delhi: Inter-India Publications.

Patnaik S.M. (2000): "Understanding Involuntary Resettlement: An Anthropological Perspective", *The Eastern Anthropologist*, 53(1-2), pp. 141-59.

Saifi Basin (1997): *Environmental Degradation and Future Global Agriculture*, Sweden: Swedish University of Agricultural Science Publication.

Siva Prasad R. and Alok Pandey (2007): "Changing Livelihoods: The Burden of Pastoralists Shifting to Agriculture", Paper presented in the *10th Sustainable Development Conference*, SDPI, Islamabad.

TCR&TI (2008): *Basic Statistics on Scheduled Tribes of Andhra Pradesh*, Hyderabad: Tribal Welfare Department.

www.enrap.org.in/Completed.asp?linkid=97.

9

Social Cost of Development: A Study on Displacement and Resettlement of the Tribals Affected under Mandira Dam Project

Madhusmita Kar and *Debendranath Jena*

Introduction

There are two contradictory debates, among the academia relating to the process of development in the recent times. They are development for human benefit, on the one hand, and the human and social cost of development on the other hand. The significant strides of development in the post-independence period have certainly brought about a revolution in the Indian subcontinent. At the same time, however, the fact cannot be denied that the model of development adopted in the name of national progress has brought benefits to the few at the cost of many; a large number of people are often forced to sacrifice for the greater good. They have never been beneficiaries of the development process; rather they can be described as the 'victims of development'. In the recent years, the issues pertaining to the marginalisation of the already marginalised sections of population have been largely called into question by researchers, social scientists, and international donor agencies. The approach towards development has been exclusionary, thus depriving a number of people of their fundamental human rights. The section of the society, which stands out prominently among such marginalised categories, is undoubtedly the tribal population. The question is not just of economic deprivation; it has also been argued that development has been a threat to the distinct identity of the tribals. The 'tribal' ethnicity is gradually being affected, due to the modern forces of change and these changes start when the development projects intrude into the tribal areas.

Moreover, while the tribal way of life is undergoing changes, it is the consciousness of the 'ethnic identity', which acts as a unifying factor for the tribal populations to stand out in agitation against the development projects. The aim of development is to bring the downtrodden sections to the mainstream social life, but hardly any project succeeds in fulfilling this objective.

A substantial number of people are displaced by the large-scale development projects intended to promote national development. The number, most commonly cited, is approximately 10 million people per year displaced throughout the world over the last 20 years (Cernea, 2000). In India alone, an estimated 25 million were displaced from 1947 to 1997 (Mahapatra 1999; cited in Koenig, 2001). Since Independence, development projects, under India's Five-Year plans, have displaced about 500,000 persons, each year, who are evicted from their lands by direct administrative actions of the government. Estimates of the total number of those displaced by development projects, since independence, reach as high as 40 million people. Further, researchers have also found that 75% of these people have not been 'rehabilitated' (Fernandes, 1991; Fernandes, Das and Rao 1989; cited in Cernea, 2000). The scale of displacement is likely to increase in the future years, thus giving rise to still higher figures. It has also been reported by researchers that the tribals, who constitute approximately 8.2% of the total population in the country, have always been the worst victims of displacement, induced by the development projects. About 40% of those displaced belong to the Scheduled Tribes (Government of India, 1990; SC, ST Commissioner's Report; Kothari, 1995; cited in Patwardhan, 1999). The tribals mostly inhabit regions rich in natural resources and do not have the power to protest against the State. As pointed out by Patwardhan (1999), the decision makers, therefore, seem to assume that they can be easily displaced without any kind of resistance regarding the deprival of their livelihood. This also explains, why fewer tribals, than other groups of people, have been resettled. Research shows that the resettlement of the tribals, displaced by the development projects, has been grossly inadequate in states, like Maharashtra, Orissa, Bihar and Madhya Pradesh. These states, having about 73% of India's tribal population, have served as laboratories for industrial experiments, and have displaced a substantial number of tribals, leaving them without adequate rehabilitation (Mehta, 2002). The most widespread consequence of development-induced displacement is the impoverishment of large numbers of people. Displacement not only takes away their land and resources, but also results in the disintegration of their social organisation and culture. Rehabilitation measures often lack a sustainable approach and the displaced people are forced to a lower economic status. The whole fabric of their lives is disrupted.

The Context of the Study: The Mandira Dam Project

The Mandira Dam Project[1], is a part of the mega steel project in Orissa which was a landmark in the state's development history in the post-independence period, i.e., the Rourkela Steel Plant, an undertaking of the Steel Authority of India Limited (SAIL). It was a milestone in the industrial development of the state, under Indo-German collaboration. For the establishment of the Rourkela Steel Plant, the Government of Orissa acquired 19,722.69 acres of land; and 2,465 families of 92 villages were displaced (Sarini, 2006). The first notifications for acquisition of the land required for the steel plant and the new township were issued in 1954. A total area of more than 30,000 acres of tribal land was acquired for the purpose of Rourkela Steel Plant, Steel Township, Railway Lines, Fertilizer Township, and Mandira Dam Project. The Mandira Dam Project is about 32 km (20 miles) from Rourkela City and is connected by road.

In 1957, notifications for the vacation of the Mandira Dam site were issued. In the year 1957-58, the work for the Mandira Dam Project was started, by the Hirakud Dam Organisation on the River 'Sankha'. The purpose of the project was to facilitate water supply to the Rourkela Steel Plant. For the Mandira Dam Project, about 11,964 acres of most fertile land was acquired by the government. The project displaced 1,193 families from 32 villages; a large majority of the people displaced, belonged to the tribal communities. For the acquisition of land for the Mandira Dam "Project, the Government of Orissa made an independent legislation, i.e., The Orissa Development of Industries, Irrigations, Capital Construction and Resettlement of Displaced Persons (Land Acquisition) Bill, 1948" and for this purpose, the Government of Orissa also established an office known as 'Rourkela Land Organisation' headed by an officer of the rank of Additional District Magistrate (ADM) who had been entrusted to look into the matter of land acquisition and resettlement of displaced families. As per the Land Acquisition Act, adequate provisions were supposed to have been made for requisition, acquisition, taking over possession, and payment of compensation (Xaxa, 2006). Out of the total number of displaced families, 639 families were resettled in six resettlement colonies. The Resettlement and Rehabilitation (R&R) scheme covered all the people displaced for the Rourkela Steel Plant, including the Mandira Dam Project. The rehabilitation scheme for the displaced people provided cash compensation for land, land for land, employment for land, and all the three categories of compensation for land. However, the benefits have been remarkably disproportionate for the affected people. The tribal families were forcibly displaced from their villages and were shifted to temporary resettlement camps having no facilities. They were allotted small pieces of rocky land that hardly gave them sustenance for three months (Xaxa, 2006). The R&R measures have not been adequate, resulting in years of suffering for the displaced tribals. Now, it has been more than five decades of the project and there are still certain issues that remain unsolved.

With this background, the study covers two important dimensions relating to the displacement and rehabilitation of the tribals affected by the Mandira Dam Project. These are: (i) Landlessness and the consequent marginalisation of the tribal families, and (ii) the effectiveness of the R&R measures in facilitating tribal main streaming.

Methodology

The study is based on the descriptive research design and the universe of the study comprises the total tribal population of the resettlement colonies. The study area covers the six resettlement colonies of the Mandira Dam Project, i.e., Laing, Ushra, Bankibahal, Jaidega, Jhandapahad and Lachchda. All these colonies, except the Lachchda resettlement colony are located within 50 km radius of the Mandira Dam Project and come under three blocks – Rajgangpur, Kuanarmunda, and Gurundia, in Sundargarh District. A majority of the people in the resettlement colonies are tribals, the number of 'Kisans' being the highest. The present study makes use of the stratified random sampling technique. The sample has been drawn from the universe using one criterion, i.e., the place of residence. As such, a proportionate number of samples have been drawn from each resettlement colony and the sample size has been fixed at 300. Then the final sample was drawn from this in various stages, using different criteria, i.e., age, occupation, and educational level. The sample covers respondents from different age groups, educational levels, and income levels. Adequate efforts were also made for the adequate representation of female respondents in the sample. The study is based on both primary and secondary sources of data. As regards the primary data, the interview method was used in combination with techniques, like, case study, focus group discussion, and participatory rural appraisal. The secondary sources include books, research reports and data from the government sources. Before developing the tools for data collection, a pilot survey was conducted which provided useful insights into the different aspects: the area and the people. For the collection of first hand information from the respondents, an interview schedule consisting of four dimensions was used, i.e., landlessness and the consequences, the inter-generational impacts, the psychological facets, and the effectiveness of R&R. Although the colonies are located in different places, there are significant similarities with regard to the characteristics of the population. As most of the people are tribals, remarkable uniformities can be seen in the patterns of their living. There are, however, certain differences between the tribal and the non-tribal families, living in the colonies in terms of their culture and life style. Table 9.1 shows the distribution of tribal population in the resettlement colonies.

Table 9.1 Distribution of Tribal Population in the Resettlement Colonies

Sl. No.	*Name of the Colony*	*Gram Panchayat*	*Block*	*Population*	*No. of STs*
1.	Laing	Laing	Rajgangpur	663	627
2.	Ushra	Dumerjore	Kuanarmunda	2449	1801
3.	Bankibahal	Dumerjore	Kuanarmunda	378	378
4.	Jaidega	Jaidega	Kuanarmunda	1110	1093
5.	Jhandapahad	Dalki	Kuanarmunda	475	466
6.	Lachchda	Kandeidiha	Gurundia	395	315
	Total			**5470**	**4680**

Source: Data from District Panchayat Office, Sundargarh.

Marginalisation: The Consequences of Landlessness

Development and marginalisation are completely contradictory terms. If one goes by the definitions, development cannot lead to marginalisation. Rather development is often understood as an opportunity for the people concerned, to improve their living standards. The World Commission on Dams simply defines development as "sustainable improvement of human welfare ... on a basis that is economically viable, socially equitable, and environmentally sustainable." There are three major tasks that development must address: (i) promoting opportunity, (ii) enhancing security, and (iii) facilitating empowerment. According to Koenig (2001), development for displaced people would need to include not only increased access to economic and social resources, but also increased local autonomy and control, as well as improving people's ability to affect their own national institutions. He defines development for those affected by displacement as follows:

(i) Increasing the availability and utility of economic resources.

(ii) Environmental sustainability implying equitable access across generations.

(iii) Respect for basic human rights.

(iv) Increasing equity between affected groups and other national groups as well as increasing equity among the different groups within affected populations.

(v) Increasing local autonomy and control.

(vi) Improving people's ability to improve their interactions with national institutions.

Marginalisation, on the other hand, is a downward process leading to social and economic deprivation. Mullaly (2007) defines marginalisation as : "The social process of becoming or being made 'marginal', i.e., to relegate or confine to a lower social standing or outer limit or edge, as of social standing. Marginalisation involves people being denied degrees of power, and suffering from deprivations that affect their life conditions. Marginalisation has the potential to result in severe material deprivation, and in its most extreme form, can exterminate groups."

Material deprivation is the most common result of marginalisation, when looking at how unfairly material resources, such as, food and shelter are dispersed in society. Along with material deprivation, marginalised individuals are also excluded from services, programs, and policies. Marginalisation can be understood within three levels: individual, community, and global-structural. However, it often takes multiple dimensions and one must recognize the intersecting nature of marginalisation and its capacity to overlap within each (Young, 2000).

Studies by different researchers have clearly shown that development projects have always been responsible for the further marginalisation of the tribals (Patwardhan, 1999; Cernea, 2000; Shankar, 2006; Chatukulam and John, 2006; Mallavarapu, 2006; Hussain, 2008). Marginalisation occurs not only in the economic sphere, but also treads into the other aspects of life, turning the life of the affected people into an isolated island, cut off from the mainstream economic and social system. It starts with the very process of displacement and the loss of land. Relocation to a different place, without adequate preparation, further aggravates the situation. People suddenly lose their access to livelihood and their standard of living starts taking a downward path. The absence of proper facilities at the resettlement sites also makes their life difficult. In the case of tribals, they are forced into a negligible status, because of the distinctive nature of their economic and social organisation.

Displacement affects the life situations and the life chances of the displaced families, in more than one ways. In this context, one of the important fields of enquiry that has attracted the attention of scholars and researchers is that of 'sustainable livelihood'. Livelihood implies the entire system of economic pursuits that characterize the life of a community. When the economic resources, on which people are dependent for their living, are taken away, the process of impoverishment begins. These include the resources that produce income, such as land or common property, as well as jobs (Cernea, 2000). For a community like that of the tribals, land is the most important resource. Thus, landlessness leads to negative consequences that continue for generations. This has been the most significant observation in the research on development-induced displacement. Because, all cases of displacement involve, in the first place, the loss of land.

A study, conducted by Nayak (2000) on the 'Kisan' tribe of Orissa, clearly showed the risks of landlessness for the tribal community and its other negative implications. From Rengali Project in Orissa, Ota (1996) reported that the percentage of landless families was more than doubled from 4.6% to 10.9%. Reddy (1997) documented that in coal mining displacements around Singrauli, the proportion of landless people increased from 20% before the displacement to 70% after. A study of Kenya's Kiambere Hydropower Project found that the farmers' average landholdings after resettlement dropped from 13 to 6 hectares. Their livestock was reduced by more than one-thirds; yields per hectare were decreased by 68% for maize and 75% for beans; and there was a significant drop in the family income (Mburugu, 1993; Cook, 1993; cited in Cernea, 2000). All these studies reveal that in those cases, where land forms the basis of productive systems, loss of land can lead to multiple risk factors for the affected communities.

For the tribals affected by the Mandira Dam Project, the problem of landlessness had significant implications. The average landholding of the tribal families remarkably went down after the displacement. Now they have only a very small amount of land that has been given as compensation and this is the main cause for their poor standard of living. Loss of land has naturally led to the destruction of the livelihood system. Table 9.2 shows the extent of land loss for the project.

Table 9.2 Extent of Land Loss for the Project

Extent of Land	*No. of Respondents*	*Percentage*
01-20 acres	147	49
20-40 acres	95	31.7
40-60 acres	35	11.7
60-80 acres	10	3.4
80-100 acres	08	2.6
100 acres and above	05	1.6
Total	**300**	**100**

Land was the only means of living for the tribal families who were displaced by the project. Loss of this resource gradually led to a state of impoverishment, which was carried over to the succeeding generations, as they lost their access to a sustainable and consistent source of living. For the poor tribals, who have no other skills, this was like throwing them out of their livelihood system. Table 9.3 shows the percentage of tribals facing joblessness after the coming of the project.

Table 9.3 Problem of Joblessness after the Displacement

Response	*No. of Respondents*	*Percentage*
Yes	220	73.4
No	80	26.6
Total	**300**	**100**

Very few people are engaged in cultivation, with the small amount of land they have. Before the tribals were displaced, they primarily depended on cultivation for their livelihood, and were also able to afford all the needs of their families. The loss of their agricultural land affected not only their standard of living, but the education and future of their children as well. Among the inter-generational impacts that have resulted in a state of marginalisation, mention may be made of the following:

(i) A significant increase in the rate of dropouts after the displacement, which shows the loss of education.

(ii) A rise in the rate of unemployment among the youngsters of the second generation.

(iii) A change in the occupational pattern of the tribal communities, wherein many of the tribals, who were earlier dependent on cultivation, are now engaged in other works, like, daily wages or small service.

(iv) A strong sense of deprivation, significantly visible, particularly among the young members, who consider the displacement to be responsible for the loss of their education and the consequent joblessness.

(v) Loss of land coupled with the lack of education and skills has resulted in a state of uncertainty, as far as, the future of the subsequent generations is concerned.

The young people, who had been the worst victims of the displacement, are struggling hard to bring their life back on the track. But it seems it will take one more generation for things to normalize. The following case explains how the life of a generation was affected, because of the displacement and the plight of the displaced tribal families in the resettlement colonies even after five decades.

Case-1

One of the respondents, aged about 70 years, was once the son of the village headman, who owned more than 60 acres of land in the submerged village of Laikera in the Laing Gram Panchayat. He now lives in the Ushra resettlement colony with his three sons. The government provided them with 20-decimil homestead land and housing subsidy for building the house. It is a small three quarter house with mud walls and bricked roofs. As the old man described the story of the displacement, tears of suffering came down his eyes, and he was completely lost in the years of the past. He has seen a sharp decline in his economic and social status; from a village headman, to a poor and helpless person, without any resources. The sense of powerlessness was clearly visible in his expressions. His family now leads a life of deprivation, and earning a livelihood is an everyday challenge. The education of the children was affected when the family was displaced. Now, the two elder sons work as daily labourers with the local contractors, but it depends on the availability of work. The youngest son is an under-matriculate and is not able to continue his studies further as the family cannot afford his education. The eldest son could not continue his studies after school; he still regrets for not being able to support the education of his younger brothers. It seems from the present conditions of the family, that their life has turned upside down, and they arenow struggling hard to ensure a secure future for the next generation.

All the tribal families expected an improvement in their economic conditions, when the project was started in the area, but no such improvement is visible. Most of them feel that they have parted with the most important asset they had : their land. As a result of displacement, they have neither the land that can sustain their life nor the jobs that they were promised in exchange for the land. They state various reasons for which most of them have not got jobs so far. In many cases, it was found that a majority of them did not fulfil the criteria for getting a job in the Rourkela Steel Plant, and in other cases, it was because of the administrative delays[2]. Having no other way out, most of them are dependent on daily wages for a living. Again, there are two sides of the picture: Those who have got employment in the Rourkela Steel Plant are leading a comparatively better life than those who have not got employment, due to the lack of required qualification or other reasons. The present conditions of the tribal families in the resettlement colonies make it evident that development has caused only deprivation. They sacrificed everything for the project, and in return they received nothing but years of suffering. There was a significant decline in their living standards after they have been resettled. While the education of the children was affected because of displacement, and most of them are dropouts from school level, the loss of education itself has been responsible for leaving them ineligible for getting the job.

They have lost their access to the traditional resources, and are not able to keep pace with the new trends of the urban industrial society. The young people in the resettlement colonies have strongly internalised the 'feeling of being displaced', even though they have never faced it directly. They have not only been economically deprived, but their community life has also been disintegrated. The traditional power structure of the tribal society was broken down bringing the community to a shattered state. The homogeneous tribal community has become quite heterogeneous both in terms of class and culture. This has created a state of disorientation in the traditional social organisation of the tribals living in the resettlement colonies.

In the absence of any opportunity for development, they have been pushed to the margin. Finding a work is a difficult task, since there is no dearth of workers in the areas. The tribal women, who were previously able to support the family economy, are now left without any work. Since the colonies are located at a considerably longer distance from the industrial centres, where work is available, it is not possible for them to go out for work everyday. Most of the young respondents in the age group of 20-35 are jobless and lack any specialised training or skills.

This kind of a situation has been responsible for developing strong feelings of victimisation among the tribals. This feeling, coupled with the sense of tribal identity, is gradually leading to the rise of a new kind of consciousness among the Mandira Dam resettlers. Most of the respondents expressed strong feelings of agitation against the project authorities and the government[3]. Table 9.4 reflects the intensity of the feelings of victimisation among the tribals in the resettlement colonies.

Table 9.4 The Project and Feelings of Victimisation

Response	*No. of Respondents*	*Percentage*
Yes	267	89
No	33	11
Total	**300**	**100**

They clearly associate these feelings with their distinctiveness as tribals and the sense of 'tribal identity'. The fact that thedisplaced persons were mostly tribals has been responsible for the rise of consciousness among the tribals as a group. 'Ethnic self-affirmation' is always related in one way or another to the defence of social or economic interests. People will assert their ethnic identity only when they gain by doing so (Behera and Pfeffer, 2008). The tribal families in the resettlement colonies have a strong sense of ethnic identity and this has also resulted in many protests in the recent past. But the protests were never well organised , and the leadership was inconsistent. It was also found that most of these protests focused on employment as the core demand. Very often, the issues have been politicised , with little benefits for the affected people. The respondents also claimed that there are many people who are making use of these issues for their own political interests. The poor tribals are not always aware of this, and in this process, they are further victimised . With the gradual growth of awareness about tribal rights, which was prominent among young respondents, a new leadership is expected to develop in the tribal belt in the future years to come.

Resettlement, Rehabilitation and the Issue of 'Mainstreaming'

It has been widely recognised by researchers, scholars, and the international donor agencies that adequate R&R of the affected people must be considered as an essential part of the project itself. But a number of research studies in this area have documented, that the rehabilitation measures have always been inadequate and ineffective, wherever displacement occurred. Resettlement and rehabilitation are considered as twin and inter-related processes. Whereas resettlement means relocation of the people to a different place, rehabilitation means to restore to the normal state. However, the usual practice is that the affected people are only resettled, while the rehabilitation measures fail to rebuild the sustainability of the livelihood system. It has now been widely recognised that displacement should not always be accepted as an inevitable consequence of the development projects, and development should not always result in the violation of human rights. Thus, it is essential to ensure that those people who are adversely affected in the process are properly compensated for the loss that is made to their lives. The projects that affect the very foundation of their lives must make adequate provisions for the restoration of their livelihoods.

Adequate R&R of the Mandira Dam oustees was the responsibility of the Government of Orissa. The Rourkela Steel Plant was involved in the rehabilitation matters only with regard to providing employment to the displaced families. The other aspects relating to rehabilitation came under the exclusive jurisdiction of the State Government authorities. The Government of Orissa developed a compensation scheme, which involved three categories of compensation; cash for land, land for land, and employment for land (Nayak, 2000).

As far as cash compensation is concerned, there were no records available with the respondents, although most of them agreed that they have received the compensation money. However, they do not remember the amount of compensation they received and how it was spent. But it was known from the accounts given by the respondents that there were many manipulations involved in the process of disbursing the compensation money. Although cash compensation was given, it was not without problems; and there are some displaced tribals who have never received any cash compensation. This fact is also substantiated by a previous research (Nayak, 2000). A second problem was that the records relating to the compensation were not made available to the respondents. Most of the respondents did not have the details of the cash compensation they have received. While these documents are essential for the purpose of claiming the job as a local displaced person, the poor tribals are being exploited by the government officials in many ways for obtaining the same. The government records indicate that plots of lands for the construction of houses were made available to every displaced family and every family was provided with housing subsidy ranging from Rs. 200 to Rs. 400 (Nayak, 2000). However, most of the tribal families living in the resettlement colonies do not have land *pattas*(records) for the homestead land although years have passed. This has posed problems for them in many ways. In the absence of such documents, it is difficult for them to obtain residential certificate from the administration, which creates an obstacle for the future education of their children.

Studies indicate that there was mention of a number of developmental activities carried out in the resettlement colonies in the government records of 1992. But the names of the resettlement colonies where these programmes were implemented, did not figure in the records of the government. The developmental work detailed in the government records were health care facilities, development of education infrastructure, drinking water facilities, well developed means of communication, recreational facilities, cultural activities and sports, and provisions for subsidies for agriculture, dairy and poultry farming, and cottage industries in the villages. However, very few of these seem to have been actually implemented (Nayak, 2000). As per the rehabilitation scheme, development of the resettlement colonies was the sole responsibility of the State Government. The field survey for the present study also did not indicate any extensive developmental work in the resettlement colonies. The people in the resettlement colonies are living in miserable conditions with a multiplicity of problems. There are no good roads to most colonies and facilities for drinking water continue to be a major problem for the people. Piped water facilities are not properly available and the dug-wells constructed under the Corporate Social Responsibility (CSR) programme of the Rourkela Steel Plant are hardly of any use to the people[4]. It seems from the underdeveloped situation of the colonies that the affected tribals have simply been relocated without adequate rehabilitation measures. It is hard to believe that they do not have access to even the basic amenities of life, after so many years of the resettlement. The colonies are like isolated locations, which are yet to see the light of development. The respondents claimed that since the colonies are located in remote areas, quite far from Rourkela City, neither the government authorities, nor the Steel Plant authorities ever visit them. During the course of the study, the researcher tried to find out the level of satisfaction of the people with the rehabilitation measures. The researcher's findings did not indicate any sign of satisfaction among the resettled tribal families. They strongly feel that the rehabilitation scheme has not been properly implemented. Table 9.5 shows the findings.

Table 9.5 People's Satisfaction over the Rehabilitation Measures

Response	No. of Respondents	Percentage
Satisfied	13	4.4%
Dissatisfied	287	95.6%
Total	300	100%

For the purpose of compensation, the Government of Orissa had classified land into four categories according to the degree of fertility and available irrigation facilities (Nayak, 2000). The 'A' class land was the 'bahal' land which was most fertile, the 'B' class land was the 'berna' land, the 'C' class land was the 'mal' land, and the 'D' class land was the 'Goda' land, which was not at all suitable for cultivation. The respondents claimed that the agricultural land acquired was A class, while the agricultural land that was given to them as compensation was D class; it is hardly of any use to them and they cannot depend on it, as a consistent source of living.

The elderly respondents claimed that their land was taken away only with verbal promises that every family will be provided with employment in exchange for the land they have given for the project. As such, Locally Displaced Person (LDP) certificates were issued to every displaced family. For the purpose of providing employment to the displaced families in the Rourkela Steel Plant, a scheme known as the T.N. Singh formula was worked out in 1958, according to which, one member from each displaced family was entitled to employment in the Rourkela Steel Plant. As per the scheme, the minimum qualification laid down for getting employment was matriculation and the under-matriculates were provided training at the Government ITI, Rourkela, with a monthly stipend of Rs. 300 (Nayak, 2000). Researchers found that with the help of such certificates, a large number of outsiders have been working in the Rourkela Steel Plant in the name of the displaced persons (Nayak, 2000; Xaxa, 2006).

Another problem that the respondents stated was that the employment for the land scheme provided for only one job per family, but it was not proportionate to the extent of land taken from each family. This has created problems in many cases, since all the sons or daughters of a displaced person had legal rights over the land, but only one of them could get employed. Similarly, in case of one son or daughter getting the job, others had to give the 'no objection certificate', which led to many family conflicts. The often-repeated argument that development facilitates the main streaming of the tribals, does not hold well in case of the tribals affected by the Mandira Dam Project. Rather, it has been responsible for the isolation of the displaced families in the social and economic spheres. Main streaming has taken place in case of those who have got employment in the Rourkela Steel Plant. But still, a number of families are struggling to get employment and this has further added to their sufferings.

Conclusion

It can be concluded that for the Mandira Dam resettlers, the process of mainstreaming is yet to begin. On the one hand, the displacement was forced upon them, and on the other hand, it has made them more powerless than before. The poor tribals were displaced from their villages, without adequate information and were made to sacrifice all their resources. As regards the R&R of the affected tribals of the Mandira Dam Project, it has been piecemeal, haphazard, and grossly ineffective. There were many loopholes, which have made the process more time taking and stressful for the poor tribals. The rehabilitation measures have been taken only as a one-time phenomenon, without any further investigation into its effectiveness. In developing the rehabilitation plan, the government has not taken into account the distinctive nature of the tribal economy and thus the sustainability of livelihoods has not been successfully restored. No significant efforts have been made to provide for the minimum facilities in the resettlement colonies. There are no roads, electricity facilities, drinking water facilities, and proper health care facilities, although years have passed; it is often taken for granted that the rehabilitation process has been completed.

It was clear from the statements of the respondents that their tale of suffering began with the construction and displacement process for the Mandira Dam Project, but there is no end to it. In fact, the Mandira Dam issue is often thought to have been settled, but the conditions of the tribals in the resettlement colonies speak volumes about the ineffective implementation of the rehabilitation measures. In recent years, the R&R of the project-affected families has been a much debated issue all over. Policies, like the Orissa Resettlement and Rehabilitation Policy, 2006, have also come into existence to provide for uniform guidelines. However, in case of development projects of the past, like the Mandira Dam Project, which do not come under the purview of such policies, the affected people have only been the losers in the process of development. Marginalisation and inter-generational impoverishment have been the obvious consequences of resettlement. Development has come their way, not as an opportunity, but as a disaster, which has completely shattered the very foundation of their lives. Development has resulted in social costs that cannot be easily compensated. The livelihood system, which was destroyed, the education that was affected, the generation that lost its future, and the culture that was disintegrated, cannot be restored again. This clearly questions the justifications of the development projects in a socialistic country like India, which guarantees social and economic justice to all its citizens.

Suggestions for Making R&R Effective

The people, who are displaced by the development projects, should be considered as the most important stakeholders. The focus should not be only on 'resettlement'; rather it should be on adequate 'rehabilitation' and creation of sustainable livelihoods. In view of the present study, the following suggestions can be given for developing better R&R strategies:

1. The Government should set up committees to look into the matters of resettlement and rehabilitation of the displaced families of the old projects (projects taken up during/after the 1950s and before 2006), where still many issues remain unsolved.
2. Land *pattas* should be issued to the families in the resettlement colonies (where it has still not been done), which are very essential for the future education of their children.
3. The National Skill Development Programme should take up skill development initiatives in the resettlement colonies on a priority basis.
4. In case of those projects, where employment is still pending, there should be a thorough investigation into the issues involved.
5. Land can provide a consistent source of living or at least economic support to the people on inter-generational basis. But once the land is taken away, there is always the risk of inter-generational impoverishment. Therefore provision should be made for providing employment to the succeeding generations of the displaced families.

6. In the projects/companies causing displacement, 30% of the jobs should be reserved for the deserving candidates from the local displaced families.
7. It has been observed in the case of many projects that the women/ unmarried girls of the displaced families have not benefited in any way. Therefore, in matters of employment, first preference should be given to women.
8. In the case of displaced families having unmarried daughters, who are not eligible for employment in the project, the rehabilitation package should also include financial assistance for their marriage. Further, provisions should also be made for providing easy loans to the affected people for clearing up their liabilities.
9. It should be made mandatory for the project authorities to sponsor the education of the deserving children from the displaced families.
10. A mandatory provision for the project authorities for taking up comprehensive Corporate Social Responsibility (CSR) activities in the resettlement colonies should be incorporated in the R&R policy.
11. The National R&R Policy 2007 should be made an Act and should be enforced with uniform guidelines in all the states of India; or the Orissa R&R Policy should be made an Act so that strict compliance can be ensured.

Notes

1. It is known as the 'Mandira Dam Project', since the dam is located near the 'Mandira' Village in the Dumerjore Gram Panchayat under the Kuanarmunda Block, in the District of Sundargarh in Orissa.
2. It is pertinent to mention here that the minimum criterion for getting jobs in the Rourkela Steel Plant was matriculation and the under-matriculates were provided with training at the Government Industrial Training Institute, Rourkela, for the purpose of getting jobs.
3. The 'project authority' in case of the Mandira Dam Project is the Rourkela Steel Plant, in Rourkela, Orissa.
4. The Rourkela Steel Plant has started a comprehensive 'CSR (Corporate Social Responsibility)'Programme, for the development of the resettlement colonies, which are among the 'adopted model villages' of RSP, but the programmes have not been quite effective in the resettlement colonies of Mandira Dam.

References

Behera, D.K. and George Pfeiffer (2008): *Contemporary Society Tribal Studies, Volume Seven; Identity, Intervention and Ideology in Tribal India and Beyond*, New Delhi: Concept Publishing Company.

Cernea, M.M. (2000): *Impoverishment Risks, Risk Management, and Reconstruction: A Model of Population Displacement and Resettlement*, Washington, DC: The World Bank.

Government of Orissa (2007): *District Statistical Handbook, Sundargarh, 2007*, Bhubaneswar: Directorate of Economics and Statistics, Orissa.

Hussain, Monirul (2008): *Interrogating Development: State, Development and Popular Resistance in North East India*, New Delhi: Sage Publications.

Josh, Chatukulam and M.S. John (2006): "Issues in Tribal Development: The Recent Experience in Kerala", In Govind Ch. Rath (ed.), *Tribal Development in India: The Contemporary Debate*, New Delhi: Sage Publications.

Koenig, Dolores (2001): *Toward Local Development and Mitigating Impoverishment in Development-Induced Displacement and Resettlement*, Final Report Prepared for ESCOR R7644 and the Research Programme on Development-Induced Displacement and Resettlement, Refugee Studies Centre: University of Oxford.

Mallavarapu, Ram Babu (2006): "Development, Displacement and Rehabilitation: An Action Anthropological Study on Kovvada Reservoir in West Godavari Agency of Andhra Pradesh", India, *International Journal of Social Sciences,* 1(1), pp. 35-41.

Mehta, Shalina (2002): "Derailed Development", *Anthropologist,* Special Issue No. 1, pp. 213-26.

Mullaly, B. (2007): "Oppression: The Focus of Structural Social Work", In B. Mullaly (ed.), *The New Structural Social Work*, pp. 252-86, Don Mills: Oxford University Press.

Nayak, Ranjit (2000): "Land Loss and Land Based Relocation", In M.M. Cernea and Christopher McDowell (eds.) *Risks and Reconstruction: Experiences of Refugees and Resettlers*, Washington, DC: The World Bank.

Ota, A.B. (1996): "Countering the Impoverishment Risks: The Case of the Rengali Dam Project", In A.B. Ota and A. Agnihotri (eds.), *Involuntary Displacement in Dam Projects*, pp. 150-78, New Delhi: Prachi Prakashan.

Patwardhan, Amrita (1999): *Dams and Tribal People in India*, Washington, DC: The World Bank.

Sariniand Adivasi-Koordination (2006): "Adivasis of Rourkela: Looking Back on 50 Years of Indo-German Economic Cooperation", Occasional Papers No. 4, Germany: Sariniand Adivasi-Koordination.

Xaxa, Celestine (2006): "Legal Issues Unsolved after 50 Years' Rourkela and after: 50 Years of Industrial Development and Social Responsibility in Indo-German Cooperation", Occasional Papers, No. 5, pp. 22-24 September, Germany: Sarini and Adivasi-Koordination.

Young, I.M. (2000): "Five Faces of Oppression", In M. Adams (ed.), *Readings for Diversity and Social Justice,* pp. 35-49, New York: Routledge.

10

Displacement and Rehabilitation of Tribals of Andaman: A Critical Review

S.K. Biswas and *Hema Banerjee*

Introduction

Displacement leads to social disorder, economic hardship, and physical uprooting of the people forever. Due to industrialisation, the tribal lands and forests, which have been the nerve centre of the tribal people's economy, become the property of the state, and people are deprived of their traditional rights, to use forests for their survival. Their displacement, not only erodes the traditional sources of livelihood and uproots people, from their traditional way of life; but also dismantles the whole system of social organisation – class of emotion, neighbourhood, community lives, etc. In the process. traditional subsistence economics and associated cultures are destroyed. Today, the tribals face displacement from their homes as well as lands, and have become economically marginalised. In the realm of modernisation and industrialisation, the role of the state has shifted from an interventionist to that of a regulatory mechanism or as a profitable institution. "Industrial revolution caused innumerable dramatic changes, in the whole range of social arrangements, from the nature of the state to the processes and purposes of the governance." (Amartya Sen, 1999).

Displacement and Rehabilitation – Conceptual Analysis

Displacement, development and rehabilitation are the buzz words, commonly placed in a single mindset. All the three are inter-related in the state of economic development and welfare society. In the paradigm of globalisation and progress of the nation, displacement of people in the name of development has become a legitimate issue from the authorities' point of view, and after liberalisation and privatisation the corporate world has also joined in this mission, with the active support and blessings of the state machineries.

Displacement has drifted away from the issue of compensation and rehabilitation to the effected people; this has drawn the attention of the social activists, researchers, electronic media, and legal experts in different aspects of the subject, and has become a sensational issue for the society at large. The twentieth century witnessed massive movements of people, dislocated by war, ethnic conflicts, natural calamities, industrial disasters, and implementation of developmental projects. "Displacement, caused by different kinds of developmental projects; is not an unforeseen occurrence; hence, the extent of displacement can be visualised and provided." (Reddy I.V.B and Chattopadhaya R.N, 1986)

Displacement requires rehabilitation, and now-a-days, the legal status of a displaced person (refugees repatriate) is crucial for determining the type of assistance, an individual is eligible to get. Rehabilitation studies provide a critical outlook of rehabilitation policies, for planners and policy-makers, especially for the tribal, vulnerable, or extinct communities. Rehabilitation is a multi-faceted and long-drawn process. It involves an incisive understanding of the problems involved and requires proper planning. It requires co-ordinated efforts of specialists, from different disciplines, voluntary associations, and social workers along with active participation of the affected population. Displacement due to social inequalities poses a different set of problems for rehabilitation. It has become a delicate issue, when rehabilitation of a small community of tribals is involved.

In the paradigm of industrialisation, majority of the private land has been acquired for mega projects. Moreover, rehabilitation of displaced families from East Pakistan to India, has once again displaced many tribal communities in Orissa, Madhya Pradesh, Maharashtra, etc. In this process, the forest dwellers / *Adivasis* are serious victims from all sides. Development-induced displacement is a traumatic experience for everyone undergoing it. Most of the development projects and rehabilitation schemes, have invariably come up in tribal-dominated areas. However, the nature and consequences, of development caused by urban development or by the development of industrial clusters, is an area that has so far received scant attention (Mahapatra, 1994, p. 237). The nature of displacement in all areas is not the same, and it is clear that displacement involves injustice to the tribal community and is a total violation of their constitutional rights. Compensation or rehabilitation is the only means to legalize the policy, but the tribal people cannot be deprived of their right to life merely by paying some money or making alternative arrangements for houses/lands at the cost of their lives. The British aggrandizement policy also indiscriminately alienated the tribals from their lands for the expansion of their economic activities.

Displacement of Aboriginals of Andamans

Prior to the arrival of the British forces in 1782 and 1858, the Andaman & Nicobar (A&N) Islands were home to aboriginal tribes. The rights over lands, forests, and sea territory were owned by these primitive tribes. With the advent of the British in these islands in 1858, the rights over lands of these aborigines were lost. The Penal Settlement of Indian Convicts was started in South Andaman, and subsequently the displacement of tribes began. The unarmed tribals were killed at gunpoint and pushed into the interior forests. Hence, the Andamanese and the Jarawas were the actual victims of the Penal Settlement Policy of the British.

During encounter with British soldiers, hundreds of Andamanese were killed, and they were victims of alien diseases transmitted from India. Both Andamanese and Jarawas were killed during the extension of the penal territory in South Andaman. "The dwindling numbers of the Andamanese, the result of several pitched encounters, was further accelerated by introduction of various diseases through the convicts and some of the naval staff cohabiting with aboriginal women and transmitting syphilis....... The consumption of opium, led to a lower birth rate, the outbreak of measles and small pox took away about half the total number of tribal of South Andaman, during 1877 "(Radcliff-Brown, 1948)." "The Andaman Home", the deadly home was made to teach them the modern way of lives and to be friendly with the British. But in truth, it was a death trap for the Andamanese. The females were sexually exploited and got infected with incurable diseases. As a result of which, there was a sharp decline in their numbers. In 1858, their estimated number was 3500, but the 1901 census recorded a total of only 625. By the time the British left the islands, the existence of the Andamanese was under threat. They were declared as endangered / extinct tribes, whose population was hardly four dozens.

The Jarawas and Andamanese were traditional territorial rivals. The British, during their time, had exploited this and utilised the services of the latter to crack down the Jarawas. They mounted punitive expeditions in the Jarawa areas, and those the Jarawas who resisted were killed and their huts were burnt. They were described as "hostile" people. The displacement of the hunting and gathering nomadic tribes of Andaman was a silent mission of the British government. The Onges, the third aboriginal primitive tribe, was not a direct victim of the British, but contact with outsiders was a big reason for their dwindling numbers. The sharp decline in the population of the Onges was alarming: from 1901 to 1931, about 63% decrease in the population was reported. During the Japanese occupation of these islands (1942-45), there was considerable destruction of their land, by poachers and timber merchants; pressure on the Jarawa territory and resources continues to this day.

In order to encroach into the Jarawa territory for rehabilitation of Bengali families in South Andaman, the local administration used the services of the male Andamanese. The Forest Department in 1949 took

Table 10.1 Demographic Growth Trends of the Andaman Tribals since 1901

Census Year	*Great Andamanese*	*Onges*	*Jarawas*	*Sentinelese*
1901	625	672	585	-
1911	455	631	114	117
1921	209	346	114	117
1931	90	250	70	250
1951	23	150	50	-
1961	19	129	(500)*	(50)*
1971	24	112	(N.F.)	(N.F.)
1981	42	97	31	(N.F.)
1991	45	101	300*	N.F.
2001	55	96	328	39

Source: Census reports.
Note: * Estimated population, N.F.: Not found.

all of them to Bluff Island and settled them there. The males were engaged by Bush Police force to defend the non-tribal settlers near Jarawa territories from hostile attacks of the latter. Further, a permanent damage was caused by the Indian Government in the lives of the Jarawas, the Onges, as well as the Andamanese. A serious lapse was seen on the part of the administration under the pressure of resettlement of Bengali refugees in Andaman Islands, while no attention was given to these unfortunate tribes. Moreover, the rehabilitation of Bengali families was affected in the heart areas of the Jarawa territories; hence, their movements have been restricted. In 1956, Andaman and Nicobar Aboriginal Tribals Protection Act was operationalised .

Population Profiles

During 1901-2001, the growth of the population of the primitive tribals is seen to have decreased very sharply. The Great Andamanese settled on Strait Island and their total population is 55, which includes two non-tribal ladies and one non-tribal gent who married the Andamanese. The Jarawa (who were once hostile) tribals, with an estimated population of 328, inhabit the Western Coasts of South and Middle Andaman Islands. The Sentinelese, the only hostile Negritos that remain isolated, inhabit the island, named North Sentinal Island. They are hunter-gathers, whose population is estimated to be 39 as per the 2001 census. The Onges have been settled in two defined areas in Little Andaman Island, and are confined to 110 hectares only. The total population of the Onges is 88 as per recent counting.

State of Primitives Tribes

For situational analysis of the tribals in India during 1960-61, the Dhebar Commission was set up. Accordingly, the Commission suggested some measures in the interest of the island's tribals. The Commission's view was that unless we look into their problems, these tribals would continue to remain prisoners of isolation in perpetual darkness. However, the Protection of Aboriginal Tribals, 1956, said that 35% of the areas of islands have to be reserved for the aboriginals. But before 1969, no concrete programmes were sorted out, for the welfare and rehabilitation of the aboriginal ethnic groups in the Andamans. No proper arrangement was made to restore the economic and hygienic conditions of these people. In the rush for the rehabilitation activities of refugees from the mainland, the administration failed to take note of the primitive Negritos, who had been living in the Islands for millennia (Krishna, 1978).

Social Condition of Primitives

Among these tribes, the Andamanese were the most affected of all. Their condition became miserable and they led a life of agony and hazards. They were forced to live in isolation. The condition of the women and girls was pathetic: The Burmese as well as Indians, from the mainland illegally used these helpless women sexually. They were forced to live with these unscrupulous people without formal marriage. Most of the male Andamanese were addicted to alcohol, opium and tobacco. The financial constraints and social disorder led them to a critical state of lives. According to Kochar, "The addiction to opium, wine and tobacco has often led the Andamanese to odd corners and subjected them to pressure of various sorts. Parents of young girls were thus forced to give their daughters to Burmese for concubinage. Many of them lived in abandoned Japanese's bunkers in unhygienic conditions" (Kochar, 1969).

Rehabilitation Programmes and Welfare Measures

In 1969, a special study team was constituted with experts consisting of anthropologists and medical specialists to look into the problems of the Negritos in Andamans. Under the special guidance of the Ministry of Social Welfare, a number of welfare and protective measures were undertaken to rehabilitate the Andamanese and the Onges. Accordingly, the Andamanese families were shifted to Strait Island, an area of 3.11 sq km, to protect them from the exploitation by the outsiders. The loss of their traditional homeland, resources and values led to a trauma. In 1967, for the first time, the Little Andaman, the exclusive homeland of the Onges was opened to the outsiders. Since 1969, hundreds of refugee families of the erstwhile East Pakistan (now Bangladesh) were resettled here. When the rehabilitation work was in progress in Little Andaman, the Onges were living in scattered places in the coastal area. They maintained a traditional nomadic life. During their interaction due to barter system with the settlers, they were often cheated and mistreated by the unscrupulous non-tribals. The Government of India was very specific about the welfare measures for the tribals in Andamans. Former Prime Minister, late Mrs. Indira Gandhi's views, in 1976, on these prevention measures were, "neither resettlement nor development should be an excuse to uproot the tribal groups...tribals are the original inhabitants" (S.M. Krishantry, 1976).

Andaman *Adim Janjati Vikas Samiti* (AAJVS) – Welfare Tasks

In order to check the disintegration of the primitive tribals' way of life, the AAJVS was formed as an autonomous body, under the

Chairmanship of The Then Chief Commissioner of A&N Islands. The main tasks of the *Samiti* were defined as:

(i) To protect the health and prevent the extinction of the primitive tribal groups.

(ii) To promote their economic and social development.

(iii) To take a comprehensive view of the problems of these tribal groups in order to develop and promote programmes in pursuance of the national policy for their development.

(iv) To develop measures for coordination among governmental, institutional and voluntary organisations for the protection of their economic and social environment, which are essential for their survival and growth.

Under this rehabilitation scheme, the Onges were allotted two small sites: one in Dungong Creak and another in South Bay. Wooden structures for individual houses with tin roofs were allotted to each family. A big coconut plantation and orchard was developed. *Pucca* wells were dug, medical facilities, *balwadi school* for children, along with other modern amenities, were provided to them. Each family was provided a quota of ration articles, free of cost, along with some pocket money. Tea, tobacco, detergents and clothes were also supplied to them.

Similarly, the Andamanese also received facilities, articles, and modern equipment, free of cost. They were asked to leave their traditional nomadic, hunting, and food gathering subsistence economy and adopt the modern way of living. Since the inception of the rehabilitation schemes, these tribals have become the "spoon fed" community. They now lead idle lives, and most of them are addicted to alcohol. A few of them are employed in the Police Department, Marine Department, schools and dispensary, but the males waste their income by consuming alcohol and drugs.

A permanent hole and irreparable damage was caused by the civil administration by constructing the Andaman Trunk Road, which affected the flow of life in the Jarawa Reserve. A committee of anthropologists made an on-the-spot study in 1981. They gave an alarming report to the administration, regarding the disturbance that resulted due to road communication into the Jarawa territory. During the construction of this road, many organised attacks were conducted by the Jarawas to discourage outsiders from continuing the work. Despite the strong resistance from the Jarawas, the administration did not stop the work. The movements of vehicles and passengers and tourists ultimately disturbed the age old nomadic lives of the Jarawas. On the basis of the **Shekhar Commission's reports, the Hon'ble Supreme Court of India passed an interim order to the civil administration to stop the road services in the territory of the Jarawas, but the local administration turned a deaf ear to this. At present the local administration is looking for an alternative route to Port Blair, the commercial town of the Middle-North Andaman.

Rehabilitation and its Aftermaths

The rehabilitation programme, that was operationalised, has shown adverse effects on the socio-economic conditions of the tribes as well as on their ecology. The new settlement has restricted their movements. The food habits, clothes, and permanent shelters turned out to be unsuitable, as far as their lives were concerned. They suffer from anaemia, diarrhoea, dysentery, and worm infections due to use of polluted water from the wells constructed for them. The free supply of rations and the pocket money has made the Andamanese and the Onges quite dependent on the government. The pocket money, doled out to them, is basically spent on alcohol and they sometimes ask strangers for more money. The Andamanese, frequently, visit Port Blair and are addicted to alcohol and other bad habits. Females are still exploited by outsiders in many ways. As their number is very less, eligible male bachelors do not find suitable mates in their communities. As a result, non-tribals of both sexes get married to the Andamanese. The coconut plantations were developed as an alternative source of income; but they are often cheated by outsiders, with whom they come into contact at the time of selling the items.

The same problems are faced by the Onges. Their settlements (Dungon Creak and South Bay) have been developed with a few hectares of land on the sea coast of Little Andaman. The local administration has developed horticulture and coconut plantations as a source of their income. But the Onges do not show any interest to take the benefits from the cash crops. Around 110 sq km of forest area was reserved for them to exploit the resources. But the populace of non-tribal settlers, who are more in number, do not allow them to move freely in these areas, or to collect any reserve articles, both from the sea and the forest areas. Most of them do not like to live in modern wooden houses constructed for them. They continue to live in unhygienic conditions, and do not wash their clothes or the other articles that they use. As a result, most of them suffer from skin and fungal infections; they are also not interested to avail the modern medical facilities. Whenever they come to Hut Bay, the headquarters of Little Andaman, they are cheated by the non-tribals in many forms. The males spend their money on alcohol and other bad habits. Their numbers are sharply declining due to alien atmosphere and other material cultures (Biswas, 2008).

The last decade of the twentieth century was a new milestone in the history of the Jarawas and the non-tribals. The Jarawas became friendly with the outsiders. They received medical aids and other food items as assistance. The Andaman Trunk Road has disturbed their tribal integrated lives. The movement of hundreds of vehicles in this area has ultimately broken the isolated and hostile lives of the Jarawas. The tourists offer gifts, food, etc., to the Jarawas; as a result, they have come out of their traditional livelihoods and surrendered to the outsiders. They have now become a show piece for the tourists. They are the centre of attraction of tour-operators to earn money from the tourists. The Jarawas openly rush to passenger buses and tourist jeeps to demand for food items. However, the sudden changes in their food habits have made them vulnerable to many diseases. Their health conditions deteriorated. The sub-committee of the AAJVS recommended for the protective role of the Bush Police to prevent unauthorised persons from entering, shooting, fishing, and killing wild life poaching by land and sea, in the tribal areas of Andaman.

In 1957, on account of the Andaman and Nicobar "Aboriginal Protection Act of 1956", the areas of the activities of the aborigines of Andaman have been reduced from 6408 sq km in 1858 to 1689 sq km in 1957. Between these times, a lot of changes have taken place in the environment of these tribes and they have lost their rights over the forests and the sea by 26%. Simultaneously, the Great Andamanese population has come down remarkably. After independence in India, under the rehabilitation scheme of the Indian refugees, the area of their activities has been reduced further and their environment has been altered. Again in 1984, about 856.72 sq km of forest area was declared as Tribal Reserve Area, which is a 50% reduction of their land in 1957. Out of the total area of 6408 sq km of Andaman Islands, the area for the movements of the Andaman Tribals has been fixed at 852 sq km, i.e., 13% of the total area, in 1984.

Though an area of 668 sq km of land has been reserved for the Onges, the area of their activities has been restricted to two small settlements, because without proper demarcation of the tribal areas, the non-tribal settlers in Little Andaman and foreign poachers often use tribal lands to exploit the forest and sea resources of the island. The Onges are not in a position to compete with the non-tribals, as they cannot establish their rights over their reserved areas. The Director of Tribal

Welfare was clear in his statement that 668 sq km in the Little Andaman Island constituted a Tribal Reserve. However, the Forest and Plantation Development Corporation records list this area as Reserve Forest, while restricting the Tribal Reserve to only 52.296 hectares. It would seem that by shifting the Onges to Dugong Creek and South Bay, the rest of the Island has been opened up for commercial exploitation.

The relationship of the tribals with forest is symbolic. Every culture, by and large, is adapted to its ecology. The islanders are supposed to belong to an Old Stone Age civilisation. Their way of life, habits, and their culture, in general, are seldom different from those of their Palaeolithic ancestors. The aborigines of these islands set the unique example of original culture of human pre-civilisation. But the Great Andamanese, the Jarawas, and the Onges have failed to sustain their Palaeolithic cultural heritage, like the hostile aborigines, i.e., the Sentinels of these islands. The new resettlement policies of the authorities have forced them to modify their primitive culture and tradition.

Further, the deforestation policies, new plantations, and the rehabilitation policies of the administration, have adversely affected the ecology of the islanders. Due to close proximity to the sea and being in the tropical rain forest zone, the habitat of the tribesmen is extremely hot. To avoid being exposed to heat, they always construct their huts in the midst of the forest, where there are large shady trees. Their huts are thatched with palm leaves. But now after contact with alien culture and atmospheres, their tastes have undergone a gradual change. New amenities were provided by the administration as demanded. These people had never used such materials before and this caused a great change in their outlook on culture and environment. The older generations could not adjust with the new styles of living in the special types of accommodations such as pucca huts with tin roofs. The settlements were made in places near the sea-shore, after cutting down all shady trees. Thus, their traditional socio-cultural behaviour lost its ground. Previously, they constructed two or three types of huts in response to their socio-cultural and economic needs. All former types of houses were made by the locally available natural materials and the labour of the islanders. The communal huts were made by their joint efforts, for living permanently and jointly. A simple art and craft walk was reflected in the making of the old thatched huts. In these permanent communal huts, they performed various cultural and ritual functions like marriages, puberty ceremonies, funeral rites, etc., by organising group dances and songs. A temporary lean type hut was erected formerly for subsistence proposed by individual efforts for seasonal use. Construction of such houses has been discarded now.

Conclusion and Findings

The on-going development activities, sudden exposure to the outsiders, import of alien economy and technology, and continuous depopulation, along with disordered socio-cultural condition, are considered to be the factors, accountable for the present pattern of social organisation of these tribal groups. Their places of settlement are remarkably isolated and congested, and so even now the tribals are restricted to their nomadic character and tradition-bound or group-like social organisation. Continuous depopulation has ruined these people for centuries, due to various diseases. The size, structure, and marital status of the respective tribal families have thus been affected (Biswas, 2008). Women feel themselves to be somewhat helpless as they are often exploited, physically as well as mentally, by the unscrupulous outsiders. Financial misery has forced the women of the Great Andamanese tribal society, to have sexual relations with outsiders, which resulted in various diseases. The youth are not ready to render help to the old by providing them with food and protection. Once socially coherent and unified, the tribal people are now suffering from distrust and disintegration in their family and social life.

Thirteen Andamanese Children are studying in Vivekananda Kendra Vidyalaya, Port Blair. Their total expenses are borne by the Government through AAJVS. Eighteen are engaged in various government departments. The Jarawa policy framed by the Government of India, notified in December 2004, is being implemented strictly to ensure protection and welfare of the Jarawas. In order to ensure a rich resource of forest-based traditional food, like wild pigs, turtles, honey, fish, etc., the Jarawa Tribal Reserve has been extended from 847 sq km to 1028 sq km (*The Daily Telegraph*). A buffer zone of 5 km radius has also been notified around the Jarawa Reserve, to ensure that they do not become unwilling targets of large-scale tourism or commercial activities. The Onges' movement to hunt and fish with their indigenous canoes, between the Little Andaman and Rutland, was quite regular, but with their resettlement and the introduction of monthly free ration by the administration made their movements become rare. Some are engaged in wage labour and some have been appointed in the administration sectors. Apparently, their friendship with the outsiders has proved to be too expensive for them.

An expert committee on tribes has raised an alarm that the tribal groups of Andaman and Nicobar (A&N) Islands are under threat from a large influx of people and burgeoning construction, which have put their traditional life-style and the fragile ecology under stress. A high level committee met at Port Blair, in the month of December 2008, to follow the court order. Ms. Madhushree Mukherjee was a member of this team, being an anthropologist who submitted a set of suggestions, entitled "An Alternative Framework for Jarawa Policy", she came out with some facts and suggestions before the administration and islanders. Experts accepted the order of the Honourable Supreme Court and agreed that the sections of the Andaman Trunk Road through the Jarawa forest should be closed. This measure was considered essential, in order to stop harmful, even deadly contact between the Jarawas and the outsiders. She opined that a vigorous and inspired organisation should replace the AAJVS, as it has failed to provide quality service to the aboriginals and personnel who are untrained and uninspired, have been dispatched to what they consider punishment postings, with no supervision. It is hardly surprising that abuses result; the personnel can be found pushing alcohol and molesting minors, not to mention lining their pockets, with impunity. In the same line, the present leader of the Great Andamanese, Mrs. Surmai observed with great concern that ferry boats coming to Strait Island from Port Blair carry liquor bottles and sell them to the Andamanese causing disruption in their family and social life. Mrs. Mukherjee reveals the fact that a social worker on Strait Island was accused, by all the Great Andamanese adults, of fathering the baby of a thirteen year old.

Note

Prof. Shekhar Singh was assigned to give a report on forestry of Andaman and Nicobar Islands. The one-man commission was set up on 23.11.2001 by the Govt. of India. The Commission submitted its report in 2003.

References

Biswas, S.K. (2010): "Political Administration of Nicobari Tribals; Post-tsunami scenario: A Study", *Oriental Anthropologist*, 10(1): 54-61.

Biswas, S.K. (2008): *The Great Andamanese and the Onges: Social Dynamism*, New Delhi: Abhijit Publisher, pp. 190-92.

Kochar, V.K. (1969): "The Great Andamanese Today", *Man in Indian,* 49 (3), p. 249.

Krishjna R. Shyamji (1978): *Survival of the Weakest, Symposium: Island Culture*, On Post Plenary Session *Xth International Congress of Anthropological and Ecological Science*, New Delhi, 10-21 Dec.

Krishantry, S.M. (ed.) (1976): *The Prime Minister and the Andaman Nicobar Archipelago*, p. 11, Port Blair: Government Press.

Mohapatra, L.K. (1996): Good Intentions or Policy are not Enough: Reducing Impoverishment Racks for The Tribal Oustees, In A.B. Ota and A. Agnihotri (eds.): *Involuntary Displacement in Dam Projects*, p. 237, New Delhi: Prachi Prakashan.

Mukherjee, Madhushree (2009): "Defending the Guardians", *Andaman Wave*, 25, pp. 2-3.

Radcliff Brown, A.R. (1948): *The Andaman Islands,* Glanccoe, Illinois: Fee Press.

Reddy, I.V.B. and Chattopadhaya R.N. (1986): "Impact of Large Projects on Displaced Persons", The *Eastern Anthropologist*, 39(2), pp. 107-14.

Sen, Amartya (1999): *Development as Freedom,* New Delhi: Oxford University Press p. 44.

The Daily Telegraph, IP&T Department, Andaman, 15th August, 2007, pp. 11-12.

11

The Impact of Kalinganagar Industrial Complex on Livelihood and Culture of the Tribal Communities in Jajpur District, Odisha

Aparajita Mishra

Introduction

Development is the founding belief of the modern world. The modern advances in science, technology, democracy, values, ethics and social organisations fuse into a single humanitarian project for producing a better world. Development means using the productive resources of the society, to improve the living conditions of the poor. According to Seers (1972): "Development means creating the condition for the realisation of human personality."[1] Development stands for economic efficiency, and the social and moral decency of achieving certain basic qualities for a society and ensuring a decent livelihood for all. Carefully planned and judiciously executed development projects are the harbingers of national progress.

In capitalistic societies, development has conventionally been measured, in terms of the size of the economy, as the Gross National Product (GNP). That is, the value of the "total final output of goods and services produced by an economy" (Peet and Hartwick, 2005:291).[2] Hence, development encompasses economic growth, establishment of industries, dams, irrigational projects, highways, national parks and sanctuaries, educational institutions, etc. Development projects are regarded as the lifeline in any developing and underdeveloped country. But, for undertaking development projects, it is necessary to acquire land from the individuals in the locality where the project is being established. In the process of land acquisition, a sizable number of people lose their homes and hearths and get physically displaced. This results in the pauperisation of people, evicted from their traditional habitats; thus depriving them of their livelihoods and access to other resources, adversely affecting their culture and kinship, built over several generations.

Since independence, India's development strategy lies in 'planned development' emphasising on public sector development projects including dams, irrigation, etc., which create large-scale displacement. In the pre-independence, era the impact of displacement was minimal because land was abundant and population was small; but displacement assumed alarming proportions in the era of planned development, after independence (Mankodi, 1989)[3]. The development projects give priority to economic efficiency, rather than to the well-being of the people affected or displaced by them. In the true sense, such projects adversely influence the life and livelihood of the oustees.

Tribal people happen to be among the most disadvantageous and underprivileged communities in India. Even after five decades of planning and development, they still remain outside the pale of any form of visible change. Thus, the effects of displacement, in case of tribals whose very survival is already at stake, are disastrous. However, socially and legally, it is agreed that the oustees should be rehabilitated to new locations with an improved economic, social, and cultural environment, which is, however, not happening in reality.

In India, the livelihood resources, of hilly communities or forest dwellers, include land and forests, which are raw materials to almost all kinds of development projects. Hence, development-induced displacement entails loss of habitats, traditional organisations and cultural ethos, with total disturbance in the socio-economic status of the affected population. Displacement forces people to start life afresh, often leading to the loss of their socio-economic conditions.

In this era of liberalisation and globalisation, the scale of involuntary displacement, due to industrial and infrastructural projects, has increased. The main causes of involuntary displacement are the building of large dams, irrigation projects, industries, sanctuaries, special economic zones, etc. During the establishment of all development projects, the Government always promises that displacement will be followed by resettlement. But in estimation, around 40 million people, of which nearly 40 per cent are STs and 25 per cent are SCs, have lost their land, due to these development projects. And still 75 per cent of them are awaiting rehabilitation.

In view of the studies, made by various scholars, this paper tries to look into the response of the development projects, which are in the process of liberalisation, mainly the private industries affecting the tribal life in many ways. Secondly, it tries to look into the risks involved in displacement (social, economic, psychological, and common property risks). Thirdly, the study focuses on the changes that take place in the livelihood pattern, socio-economic conditions and cultural life of the displaced families, in the post-displacement phase as compared to the pre-displacement phase.

The data for this paper was collected through empirical study, conducted among the Ho tribal community, in Kalinganagar Industrial Complex, who were displaced by Tata Steel, in the State of Orissa, India. The idea of Kalinganagar Industrial Complex was conceived in the early 1990s, with the advent of the liberalisation and privatisation as a part of the globalisation process. In the beginning, lands were acquired to start a steel city under public sector, but were later sold to private industries at a lower price.

As on today, there are 12 industries at different stages of construction/operation in Kalinganagar, such as, Nilachal Ispat Nigam Ltd., MESCO, Jindal Stainless, VISA, Maharashtra Seamless, Uttam Galva, Orion, Mittal Rohit, Dinabandhu and others. Tata is one of the investors that had signed a Memorandum of Understanding (MoU) in 2004, with the Government of Orissa to set up a 6.1 Million Metric Tonnage Per Annum (MMTPA) steel plant in Kalinganagar Industrial Complex, which is now considered as the steel hub of Orissa.

The Industrial Infrastructural Corporation of Orissa (IIDCO) has acquired the lands at a low price, from the local *Adivasis* (tribals) of Kalinganagar and sold 2400 acres of land to Tata Steel at the rate of Rs. 3,50,000. In the present market rate, this would amount to about Rs. 5 to 7 lakhs. After giving the authority of the land to Tata, the government left the displacement, rehabilitation and relocation activities to Tata. Thus, rehabilitating the displaced community was no more the obligation of the government; rather it was left to the private industries.

The study is mainly a qualitative one, based on the empirical evidences, which includes field surveys, observation (both participant and non-participant), case studies, and interaction with the displaced families in the resettlement camp, in the form of in-depth interviews with key informants. This constitutes the methodology part of the study.

The present study has been carried out in Gobarghati Transit Camp, established by Tata Steel, consisting of 64 displaced households. This rehabilitation transit camp is located in Mirigichara, which is five kilometers away from the main village, Gobarghati. After displacement the displaced families have been facing problems of livelihood adjustment, social disorganisation, community disarticulation, cultural changes, etc. In spite of these problems, the rehabilitation and resettlement programmes of Tata Steel have helped the displaced families to adjust with the new environment. The company has also tried to bring the community, in contact with the main stream, by providing them with various opportunities.

I

Development of Industrial Complex in Kalinganagar, Orissa

The idea of the Kalinganagar Industrial Complex was conceived in the early 90s with the advent of liberalisation and economic reforms. During the last couple of years, the Government of Orissa has signed more than 40 MoUs with various private companies, to set up steel plants in the state, where the land, acquired for public purpose, has been sold to the private industries.

The Affected People

Kalinganagar has a significant tribal and *dalit* population. Among the population in the two Blocks of Sukinda and Danagadi, 36.06 per cent and 28.19 per cent are Scheduled Tribes and 11.89 per cent and 22.31 per cent are Scheduled Castes, respectively. The data on the socio-economic condition of the people, in the three villages, who are going to be displaced by Tata Steel, and the Maharashtra Seamless, are given in Table 11.1.

Table 11.1 Socio-Economic Condition of the Villages going to be Displaced

Name of the village/ panchayat	*No. of HHs*	*Percentage of ST population*	*Percentage of SC population*	*Literacy rate*	*Percentage of cultivator labour*	*Percentage of agricultural labour*
Chandia	331	85.9	2	37.6	41	36.2
Gobarghati	558	88.8	2.1	53.5	16	37.7
Gadapur	140	97.8	0	46.7	43	13.5

Source: ADM Office, Kalinganagar.

Land Acquisition

It was observed that, the Land Acquisition Act of 1894 allows displacement for undefined public purpose, without the consent of the people affected, and Orissa is still following this act. The acquisition of land, by IIDCO for Kalinganagar Industrial Complex, began in the early 90s in different phases, and till now, about 13,000 acres of land has been acquired by the IIDCO. Of this, 6,900 acres are private lands, while the remaining area is said to be 'government' land. However, in reality, people are cultivating most of this 'government' land, for generations, for which they do not have any written evidences (*patta*). The land survey and settlement in the area have not been done here since 1928. The details of the acquired land are given in Table 11.2.

Table 11.2 List of Plants and Land Allotted in Kalinganagar

Sl. No.	*Name of the plants*	*Lands allotted (in acres)*
1	Mideast (MESCO)	530
2	Orion	150
3	Maithan Ispat	100
4	Uttam Gala	370
5	NINL	2500
6	Maharashtra Seamless	500
7	TISCO	2400
8	Rohit Ferrotech	50
9	JINDAL	678
10	VISA Industries	390
11	Dinabandhu	100
12	K.J. Ispat	50

Source: ADM office, Kalinganagar.

Compensation

In Orissa, at no stage the government has considered 'land for land' as a rehabilitation measure for the affected families. Tata Steel gave compensation in the form of homestead land of 10 hectares: house holds losing more than two-thirds of their agricultural land and entire homestead land shall receive Rs. 2 lakhs per family as compensation; families losing more than one-thirds, but less than two-thirds of their agricultural land and entire homestead land, shall receive Rs. 1 lakh per family; while all other displaced families will get cash assistance of Rs. 50,000 per family.[4]

It has, however, been observed during the field work, that the people in the transit camp mis-utilize their compensation money. When the displaced families were questioned, regarding their compensation money, different responses came from them: most of them spent their money on marriages and for construction of houses, and some used it for their daily expenditure; only a few families utilised the money for buying agricultural land. Further, some people were cheated by the financial companies, some spent it for merrymaking and festivals, while a few spent their money on alcohol.

II
Displacement and Rehabilitation

The problems associated with the displacement are the issues of rehabilitation and resettlement. The history of rehabilitation is a dismal one: most often the story of a long struggle. What, begins as a fight for compensation, turns into one for survival. Having no say in the planning or share in the benefits of the project that has completely disrupted their lives, most ousted people devolve from a state of poverty to pauperisation (Thukral, E.G., 1989: 41)[5]. Despite large-scale displacement, the resettlement and rehabilitation of the project affected people has been minimal. Among the reasons, for dismal record of rehabilitation, are the biases of project designers. Their emphasis is usually on engineering and financial aspects, and they do not take cognizance of human sufferings. Empirical evidence shows that over decades, fewer than 25 percent, of the uprooted people, have been properly rehabilitated (Hansda, 1983: 23)[6].

The Government of Orissa is yet to have a Resettlement and Rehabilitation (R&R) policy, even though there is a long and tragic history of displacement in the state, beginning in the 1950s. In the absence of a policy, rehabilitation of the displaced people is guided by mere administrative circulars, which are project specific. The relocation of households was seen as the end of the resettlement exercise. Sustainable livelihood restoration programmes or helping the resettlers, back to their feet, were not even considered necessary. With the cash given in lieu of the lands acquired, the displaced were expected to take up rehabilitation and resettlement plans on their own.

For Kalinganagar Industrial Complex, the government had issued a series of guidelines (the latest being that of 18th November 2005), to regulate the rehabilitation and resettlement of families, affected due to acquisition of land. In these guidelines, three aspectswere taken into consideration for the resettlement and rehabilitation of the displaced families: (a) financial compensation for the loss of land; (b) provision of homestead land and assistance for house building; and (c) compensation for the loss of livelihood. It needs to be noted that while the price for the acquired land, provision of homestead land and assistance for house building has been fixed by the government in the guidelines, the provision for jobs to the displaced families was not made obligatory for the companies. So, the *Adivasis* belonging to the Ho community started protesting and formed an organisation named *Sukinda Upatyaka Adivasi-Harijan Ekata O Surakshya Parishad,* or *Visthapan Virodhi Jan Manch* (VVJM), Sukinda, a group protesting against displacement at Kalinganagar. A parallel tribal organisation was also formed to counter the unity of the VVJM named *Kalinganagar Surkshya Committee* (KNSC). Due to the establishment of industries, the Ho community got fragmented into these two groups.

Process of Resettlement and its Implementation

Resettlement is understood, as the process of moving out of the existing habitat and relocating oneself to a new site, and is organised to meet the basic requirements of a clean, hygienic, and a socially or culturally acceptable environment. This creation is referred to as the rehabilitation colonies. Intermittent to this movement is a phase referred to as 'transit' and, hence, the accommodation, developed to handle this phase is referred to as a 'transit camp'. However, following are the adoptions of the Orissa Rehabilitation and Resettlement Policy 2006:

According to a release issued by Tata Steel, the displaced families would be allotted 10 hectares of land. Each family will get Rs. 1.5 lakhs for building houses along with a maintenance allowance of Rs. 2,000 per month for one year, and a temporary shed allowance of Rs. 10,000 per extended family. Tata Steel provided jobs to 29 displaced people in the Gobarghati Transit Camp, Kalinganagar, who were trained in welding technology by the company. In the camp, the displaced families are provided with drinking water, sanitation, health care, education to the children through *Balwadi/ Sishu Bachan*, adult education programme, community centres, and financial assistance as well as help to students interested in higher education.

Tata Steel also tried to rehabilitate the families economically, by providing them various livelihood options. Economic rehabilitation was planned to be achieved through employment in the industry or its ancillaries following technical training; employment following training / skill upgradation in non-farm based small and micro-enterprises; employment using traditional skills for farm-based activities; self employment following skill upgradation and exposure; and nurturing entrepreneurial potential. The company is also inspiring the women to become self dependent through Self Help Groups. Furthermore, Tata Steel is giving priority to the social life and cultural dimensions of the displaced families. In the implementation of any kind of new rehabilitation plan, Tata Steel is encouraging people's participation.

III
Rehabilitation and Livelihood Crisis

The majority (75 per cent) of the displaced people have not been rehabilitated and their incomes and livelihoods have not been restored, which implies that the vast majority of development oustees in India have been impoverished (Cernea, 1997: 1568)[7]. The studies made by Cernea (1994, 1995, 1996, 1997, 1999 and 2000) examine the Impoverishment Risks and Reconstruction (IRR) Model through a focus on livelihoods and the sustainability of the rehabilitated and the resettled population. According to Cernea, the key impoverishment risks and components, for reconstruction of involuntary resettlers' livelihoods are landlessness, joblessness, homelessness, marginalisation, food insecurity, increased morbidity, loss of access to common property resources, and community disarticulation.

Table 11.3 shows the source of livelihood of the community, before and after displacement; their primary occupation has been categorised into eight types, and a detailed analysis of changes in their occupational pattern is also given. The table shows that displacement has forced the oustees to change their traditional pattern of occupation in the post-displacement phase. However, people's engagement in primary occupation is observed to have increased after displacement. They do not posses land anymore as the land was acquired by the company; hence the oustees' engagement in agriculture is seen to have sharply declined. Now they don't have any land and, therefore, the dependency on agricultural labour work has also decreased. On the other hand, the dependency on non-agricultural labour work has increased. Employment in private service (as Tata Steel employees) is seen to have substantially increased after displacement, which was not there before displacement. There is also a substantial decrease in the selling of *Handia* after displacement; a few people also depend on the compensation money given to them, especially those people, such as the aged, who are not in a position to do any job.

Table 11.3 Occupational Changes before and after Rehabilitation

Types of Occupation		*Before*	*Percentage before*	*After*	*Percentage after*
Agriculture		39	52	02	2.25
Agricultural Labour		12	16	05	5.62
Non-Agriculture Labour		05	6.67	48	53.93
Collection of MFPs		01	1.33	02	2.25
Service	Govt. Job	09	12	09	10.11
	Company Job	00	00	10	11.24
Small Business and Other		02	2.67	1	1.12
Selling of *Handia*		07	9.33	3	3.37
Dependence on Compensation				9	10.11
Total		**75**	**100**	**89**	**100**

Source: Field survey.

Table 11.4 shows the engagement of male and female members in the households, in a primary occupation, and the man power that the community employed. Before displacement, as agriculture was the main source of livelihood for the community, there was a need of man power and during the time of harvesting all the community members, including the close kin of the family, came together to help each other. Both the male and female members worked together in their agricultural fields.

Table 11.4 Persons Engaged in Primary Occupation before and after Displacement*

Types of Occupation	*Percentage before*			*Percentage after*		
	Male	*Female*	*Total*	*Male*	*Female*	*Total*
Agriculture	39 (69.65)	32 (62.74)*	71 (66.36)	02 (3.64)	02 (7.40)	04 (4.88)
Agricultural Labour	05 (8.92)	07 (13.73)	12 (11.22)	02 (3.64)	03 (11.12)	05 (6.09)
Non-Agriculture Labour	02 (3.57)	03 (5.88)	05 (4.67)	39 (70.90)	09 (33.33)	48 (58.54)
Collection of MFPs	00 (00)	01 (1.96)	01 (0.93)		02 (7.40)	02 (2.44)
Service	08 (14.29)	01 (1.96)	09 (8.41)	11 (20)	08 (29.63)	19 (23.17)
Small Business & Other	02 (3.57)	00 (00)	02 (1.87)	01 (1.82)	00 (00)	01 (1.22)
Selling of *Handia*		07 (13.73)	07 (6.54)		03 (11.12)	03 (3.66)
Total	**56 (100)**	**51 (100)**	**107 (100)**	**55 (100)**	**27 (100)**	**82 (100)**

Source: Field survey.

* This table is about the family-wise engagement of people in primary occupation, which consists of the percentage of both men and women. The dependence, on compensation money, is not added in the post-displacement column.

But, in the post-displacement phase, we see a substantial decrease in the engagement of people in agriculture, as they do not have any land to cultivate.

We further notice that the engagement of the people as agricultural labourers has also decreased. In post-displacement phase there has been a sudden increase in the peoples' engagement as non-agricultural labourers. Most of them are mainly engaged either as labourers in the Tata rehabilitation construction site or as welders and masons in Tata fabrications. It can be observed from Table 11.4, that the engagement of female members of the community in service increased post-displacement. They get the employment opportunities, from the Tata Company, which has taken the responsibility to help the females become economically independent. Further, we notice a decline in the business of selling *Handia*[8].

Table 11.5 shows that unlike primary occupation, people's dependency on secondary occupation decreased after displacement. Mainly, there is a decline in the collection of forest produce and selling of *Handia*. This sudden reduction mainly affected the women folk, these activities were a source of extra income to their families and helped the women to become economically independent. However, there is a significant increase in the adoption of small business and other occupations, as secondary means of livelihood.

Table 11.5 Secondary Occupations before Displacement and after Rehabilitation

Types of Occupation	*Before*	*Percentage before*	*After*	*Percentage after*
Agriculture	05	8.34	02	5.56
Agricultural Labour	04	6.66	04	11.11
Non-Agriculture Labour	04	6.66	05	13.88
Collection of MFPs	14	23.34	04	11.11
Service	01	1.66	02	5.56
Small Business and Other	05	8.34	11	30.56
Selling of *Handia*	27	45	08	22.22
Total	**60**	**100**	**36**	**100**

Source: Field survey.

Table 11.6 Persons Engaged in Secondary Occupations before Displacement and after Rehabilitation

Types of Occupation	*Percentage before*			*Percentage after*		
	Male	*Female*	*Total*	*Male*	*Female*	*Total*
Agriculture	03 (21.43)	02 (4.35)	05 (8.33)	02 (16.67)	00 (00)	02 (5.55)
Agricultural Labour	02 (14.29)	02 (4.35)	04 (6.67)	02 (16.67)	02 (8.33)	04 (11.11)
Non-Agriculture Labour	02 (14.29)	02 (4.35)	04 (6.67)	02 (16.67)	03 (12.5)	05 (13.89)
Collection of MFPs	04 (28.56)	10 (21.74)	14 (23.33)	00 (00)	04 (16.67)	04 (11.11)
Service	01 (7.14)	00 (00)	01 (1.67)	01 (8.33)	01 (4.17)	02 (5.56)
Small Business and Other	02 (14.29)	03 (6.52)	05 (8.33)	05 (41.66)	06 (25)	11 (30.56)
Selling of *Handia*	00 (00)	27 (58.69)	27 (45)	00 (00)	08 (33.33)	08 (22.22)
Total	**14 (100%)**	**46 (100)**	**60 (100)**	**12 (100)**	**24 (100)**	**36 (100)**

Source: Field survey.

Table 11.6 shows that in the post-displacement period, most of the people lost their secondary occupation. More women are found to be engaged in a secondary occupation, compared to the male members in the community. Hence, the gainful engagement of the people in agriculture, agricultural labour, collection of forest produce, and selling of *Handia has* decreased in new settlement.

However, the change in the occupation was very problematic and the displaced were not swift in adapting to the new occupation. From the field survey, it was observed that, even though the company provided technical training to the people to help them get into jobs when the company will establish its plant, and most of the displaced people have taken the training, but only a few of them are working as welders and masons in Tata fabrications and rehabilitation construction site, while most seem to be uninterested. Before displacement, they were happy with their traditional occupational pattern that is agriculture, because they were not dependent on others for their needs and there was no one to boss over them. In their own words, they were "the kings of their own life". But after displacement, the jobs that they get are completely different and new. Even if the company pays them a good salary, they do not find the job interesting.

IV
Impact on Social and Cultural Life

The economic conditions of the people improved in the transit camp after displacement. This is because they get better economic and livelihood opportunities from the Tata Company, which they never got before displacement; moreover, they are also getting a chance to come into contact with the non-tribal or the main stream population. On the other hand, they lose their social co-operation; this is because after displacement, they start living an individualistic life. As it was stated in the R&R policy, major sons and the unmarried daughters are regarded as a different family. This, to some extent hampers their social and group life. Many displaced families stated that their families and relatives still live in the main village, because they do not want to leave their traditional land. Hence, after displacement families got fragmented. In hope of a better life and future, they left their close kin, and became isolated from their social as well as cultural life. After displacement they live a materialistic life, lose their social contacts and traditional life style, and try to imitate the urban ways of living. According to some of the displaced persons living in the camp, there is no enjoyment and merrymaking is left in their lives; as it was before, before displacement, mainly in the evenings all the family and friends sat together to share all sorrows, pains and happiness with each other.

According to the displaced families, the post-displacement phase, not only disturbed their social relations, but also their community cooperation. Those in favour of the construction of the plant, and accepted the rehabilitation and resettlement package, formed one community known as *Kalinganagar Surkshya Committee* (KNSC), and stood against the *Visthapan Virodhi Jana Manch* (VVJM). In this division they lost the neighbourhood relationship, and the cooperation of their kinsmen as well as their community.

Adherence to cultural customs declined invariably in all projects, during the post-displacement period. This happened when displaced community members adopted their culture with the host communities in the new place. When struggling for life and livelihood in the new locations, the observance of traditional rituals and practices has been pushed to a secondary place. Along with the change in other social institutions, the Displaced Families (DFs) in the transit camp are affected due to the impact of the non-tribals as well as the surrounding town. Even if they are recognised as Hindus, their festivals are completely different. After displacement all their traditional festivals are gradually losing importance, and along with that, their gods and deities are slowly losing importance because their places of worship are inside the forest which is far away from the transit camp. Earlier, they celebrated their festivals by consuming *Handia*, offering sacrifice, and eating meat. After displacement, all these festivals are losing their importance and even the rate of offering sacrifice has decreased. Most of their festivals, like *Mage Parab, Herra Parab, Jtara Parab* and *Baa Parab* are associated with their agricultural land, which they have lost now, cattle, *Aading* and worshiping *Marang bonga* (ancestral gods). Now Tata is inspiring them to celebrate other Oriya-Hindu festivals, which includes *raja*, *deepavali*, *dasahera*, *kumar purnima*, and so on.

Common Property Risk

Mahapatra[9] (1994) highlights that, in the process of any economic development project (i.e., dam, irrigation, power generation, or industries), the legitimate rights and interests of the people cannot be taken away, just because they are not organised , articulate or violent. Displacement invariably involves the uprooting and dismemberment of the social and economic networks of life, built over generations. In most projects, tribals constitute the majority among the displaced, followed by the Scheduled Castes. They are basically dependent on common property resources for their livelihoods, which includes forest land, grassing land, burial ground, waste land, socio-cultural places, common public services, approach roads, drinking water sources, and village deity/religious places.

The forest acts as a natural insurance which protects the tribals against crop failure due to natural hazards (Mahapatra, 1999). Loss of forest land causes the loss of grasing land, burial ground, traditional herbal medicines, and also the common land, earmarked for different community activities. The people have also lost their ancestral burial grounds (*Sasang soonom*), which gives a unique symbolic identity to each and every Ho family, as well as the community in general. So, after displacement, their concept of *Ganaen Gerang* and *Ukku Sasaan,* burying the dead has also collapsed. These days, they do not bury the dead bodies as they live in transit camps and no particular land, has yet been allotted to them, as burial ground. With help from Tata Steel Company, they are taking the bodies to Swargadwara (a holy cremation ground in Orissa) in Puri, for cremation. This system has now broken their age-old practice of burying their dead.

Before displacement, the Ho community had access to all the nearby green hills (namely, Kiajhara, Sunajhara, Badasundi, Mahagiri), from where they collected the firewood needed for their own use. These forests were also taken care of and watched by the community. In other words, the access was within the hands of the local people and the forest committee was formed jointly by the villagers and the *Athagarha* forest range. But after displacement, most of the people stopped going to these forests for firewood and other forest produce. They also lost their grazing lands and other common places they used for social and cultural gatherings.

Conclusion

This section of the paper tries to summarize the major findings of the study and makes certain suggestions to improve the efficacy of the policy implementation. This study tried to focus on the changes, shocks, stresses and trends which are involved in rehabilitation. From the field work it has been noticed, that the people who are displaced still stay in the transit camps and whatever facilities they get, are only temporary in nature. There is no assurance of these facilities in their permanent rehabilitation colony. Secondly, the rehabilitation and resettlement activity is a responsibility of Tata Steel, while the government has washed its hands off the responsibility. Thirdly, the community is now in a limbo state because they are neither a part of their original settlement nor the community has been shifted to a permanent rehabilitation colony.

The displaced should be rehabilitated with care. The rehabilitation programme and its implementation should be accomplished in a planned way, which may slow down the shocks involved with displacement. The government should involve some officials, along with the company officials which will help in successful rehabilitation. While planning and executing rehabilitation and resettlement programmes, one should also take the socio-economic, cultural, and livelihood aspects of the displaced into consideration; and before implementation, it is important to ensure the participation of the displaced people and their concerns are given priority.

A good and well-planned rehabilitation and resettlement policy, can improve the condition of the displaced and pave the way for building a just society. Only then, development has a meaning for the displaced. Finally, the government should stop selling the public purpose land/ tribal land to the private industries/ corporate houses.

Acknowledgement

I am grateful to my supervisor Prof. R. Siva Prasad for his guidance and helpful comments on this paper. I am thankful to Dr. Sujit Mishra for suggesting me ideas and helping me in writing this paper.

Notes

1. Seers, Dudely (1972): "What are We Trying to Measure? in Measuring Development", *Journal of Development Studies*, 8(3).
2. Peet, Richard and Eline Hartwick (2005): *Theories of Development,* p. 291, New Delhi: Rawat Publication.
3. Mankodi, Kashyap (1989): "Displacement and Relocation: Problems and Prospects", in Walter Fernandes and Enakshi Ganguly Thukral (eds.) *Development, Displacement and Rehabilitation: Issues for a National Debate,* pp. 135-63, New Delhi: Indian Social Institute.
4. New Progressive Rehabilitation and Resettlement Policy for the Kalinganagar Industrial Complex (Govt. of Orissa, Revenue Department, Order, No. R&REH - 2/04:_45425_/R. Bhubaneswar the 18th November, 2005).
5. Thukral, E.G. (1989): Dams for Whose Development? In Fernandes W. and E.G. Thukral (eds.), *Development, Displacement and Rehabilitation,* p. 41, New Delhi: ISI.

6. Hansda, Subota (1983): "Agricultural Development in Tribal Areas", In S.N. Mishra and Bhupinder Singh (eds.). *Tribal Area Development*, pp. 21-26, New Delhi: Society for Study of Regional Disparities,
7. Cernea, M.M. (1997): "The Risks and Reconstruction Model for Resettling Displaced Population", *World Development*, 25(10), p. 1568.
8. *Handia* is a kind of liquor prepared from rice. It is used to make offerings during ancestral worship and as a drink, which is alcoholic in nature.
9. Mahapatra, L.K. (1994): *Tribal Development in India: Myth and Reality*, New Delhi: Vikash Publishing House.

References

Cernea, M.M. (1994): "Understanding and Preventing Impoverishment from Displacement", Keynote Opening Address, International Conference on *Development-Induced Displacement and Impoverishment*, Oxford, 3-7 January, *Journal of Refugee Studies*.

Cernea, M.M. (1995): "Understanding and Preventing Displacement: Reflections on the State of knowledge", *Journal of Refugee Studies*, 8 (3), pp. 245-64.

Cernea, M.M. (1996): "Understanding and Preventing Impoverishment from Displacement", In C. McDowell (ed.) *Understanding Impoverishment: The Consequences of Development-Induced Displacement*, Oxford: Berghahn Books.

Cernea, M.M. (1997): "The Risks and Reconstruction Model for Resettling Displaced Population", *World Development*, 25(10), p. 1568.

Cernea, M.M. (ed.) (1999): *The Economics of Involuntary Resettlement: Questions and Challenges,* Washington DC: World Bank.

Cernea, M.M. (2000): "Risks, Safeguards and Reconstruction : A Model for Population Displacement and Resettlement", *Economic and Political Weekly*, 35 (41), pp. 3659-78.

Cernea, M.M. (2007): Financing for Development : Benefit-Sharing Mechanisms in Population Resettlement, *Economic and Political Weekly,* 42 (12):, pp. 1033-46.

Hansda, Subota (1983): "Agricultural Development in Tribal Areas", In S.N. Mishra and Bhupinder Singh (eds.) *Tribal Area Development*, pp. 21-26, New Delhi: Society for Study of Regional Disparities.

Mahapatra, L.K. (1994): *Tribal Development in India: Myth and Reality, New* Delhi: Vikash Publishing House.

Mahapatra, L.K. (1999): *Resettlement, Impoverishment and Reconstruction in India: Development for Deprived,* New Delhi: Vikash Publishing House.

Mankodi, K. (1989): "Displacement and Relocation: Problems and Prospects", In Walter Fernandes and E.G. Thukral (eds.), *Development, Displacement and Rehabilitation*, pp. 135-63, New Delhi: ISI.

New Progressive Rehabilitation & Resettlement Policy for the Kalinganagar Industrial Complex (Govt. of Orissa, Revenue Department, Order, No. R&REH - 2/04:_45425_/R. Bhubaneswar the 18th November, 2005).

Peet, Richard and Eline Hartwick (2005): *Theories of Development,* New Delhi: Rawat Publication.

Seers, Dudely (1972): "What are we Trying to Measure in Measuring Development", *Journal of Development Studies*, 8(3), pp. 21-36.

Thukral, E.G. (1989): "Dam: For Whose Development?", in Walter Fernandes and E.G. Thukral (eds.), Development, *Displacement and Rehabilitation,* New Delhi: ISI.

12

Industrialisation and Displacement in Kalinganagar: A Case Study of Tata Steel Parivar Colony[1]

Saswat Kishore Mishra

Introduction

The drumming out of people from their hearth and dwellings, due to the pre-planned and designed development projects, like, high dams, industries and infrastructure projects are classic examples of severe adversities doled out to the project-affected people in most parts of the world. Since, the furtherance of large developmental projects, always involves, acquiring the primary resource of land; it leads to deprivation of the ownership rights of the indigenous population. About 10 million people, annually, enter the cycle of forced displacement and relocation globally, just in sectors of dam construction and urban and transport development (Cernea, 2000). Likewise, forced displacement has become a vernacular phenomenon in India due to effectuation of many development projects (Rath, 2007). Nevertheless, there can be no denying the fact that, there is a dying need for less-developed countries to undertake multi-purpose river valley projects, irrigation projects, mining projects, power plants, large industries, transport/railways, and other infrastructure large developmental projects of the like, in order to move on in the path of prosperity, in terms of economic development.

The Government of Orissa planned, to make Kalinganagar Industrial Complex (KNIC), one of the biggest steel hubs in Asia. The idea of KNIC was conceptualised in the early 1990s, with the advent of the era of liberalisation and privatisation leading to globalisation. At present, the steel hub of Orissa has been seen to attract investors to set up industries in the complex. The Tatas are one of the investors who signed a MoU in

2004, to set up a steel plant with a capacity of 6 million tonnes per annum, in two phases, with an investment of Rs. 1,54,000 million (Sahoo, T., 2006). As per the latest report, there are 12 industries at different stages of construction/operation in Kalinganagar, such as Nilachal Ispat Nigam Ltd. (NINL), MESCO, VISA, Jindal Stainless, Maharashtra Seamless, Uttam Galva, Orion, Mittal, Rohit, Dinabandhu, and others. Though the government has allotted 2,000 acres of land to Tata, it has not yet taken possession of the entire area. Once, the entire area is acquired, hundreds of tribal families across the revenue villages will be dispossessed of their land and livelihood. In fact, as of now 815 families have already been displaced in the entire Kalinganagar complex and the number of families likely to be displaced/affected is around 5,000 (*ibid.*).

Since, resettlement refers to both the processes of physical relocation of those displaced; their socio-economic re-establishment as family/household micro-units, and as larger communities (Cernea, 2005), an income-expenditure analysis plays a vital role in ascertaining their economic well-being in the post-settlement village. Hence, it is interesting to identify the structural changes in the consumption expenditure pattern of the displaced families in the post-settlement period. Since, the conventional method of testing structural changes in regression analysis is by using dummy variables, the same has been employed in the study.

Profile of the Study Site

Tata Steel Parivar Colony (Tata Rehabilitation Colony) is located, adjacent, to the State Highway connecting Duburi and Sukinda, in Sansailo Village of Kalinganagar, Jajapur District of Orissa.

Table 12.1 Tata Steel Parivar Colony

Name of displ-acing industrial unit	*Name of village from which displaced*	*No. of DFs allotted with homestead land*	*Category*			*Remarks*	
			ST	*OBC*	*Gen.*	*Infrastructure work by IIDC Orissa*	
M/s Tata	Kalamatia	70	12	8	50	Total Area	19 acres
	Champa-koila	2	-	-	2	Total plots carved out	119
	Total	72	-	-		Plots allotted	72
						Balance	67

Source: ADM Office, Kalinganagar.

Tata Rehabilitation Colony is spread around 19 acres of land, and a total of 119 plots have been carved out. Presently, 72 families reside in the resettlement colony. Out of the 72 displaced families, 70 families belong to Kalamatia Village while only 2 families belong to Champakoila. These families were displaced from their original homes to give way to the Tata Steel project. There are 12 ST, 8 OBC and 50 general category families residing in the colony at present. The displaced families received the compensation, rehabilitation and resettlement package under the following scheme:

1. Compensation for agriculture land at the rate of Rs. 1 lakh per acre acquired.
2. Compensation for house building at the rate of Rs. 1.60 lakhs (including Rs. 10,000 for transportation) per adult male member of the family ('family' as defined in the guide lines of Kalinganagar R&R Policy).
3. Each adult member of the family to be given 10 decimals of land.
4. Financial assistance of Rs. 2,000 per month to be given, to each adult male member of the family, so long as the Tata plant does not operate.
5. Each adult male member of the family with educational qualification of 10th class or above, to be offered a training programme at a stipend of Rs. 3,300 per month.
6. Unmarried daughters above 30 years of age will be treated as separate family for the purpose of rehabilitation benefits.

Objective of the Paper

To identify structural changes in the consumption expenditure pattern of the displaced people in the post-settlement period.

Hypotheses

1. There is no significant relationship between pre-settlement household income and expenditure.
2. There is no significant relationship between post-settlement household income and expenditure.
3. There is no significant relationship between total compensation and expenditure on house building in the post-settlement place.
4. There is no structural change in the consumption function in the post-settlement period.

Methodology

The present study is contingent largely upon primary data. Secondary data has also been used along with primary data. The study focuses on the households displaced and resettled due to TISCO Project at the Tata Steel Parivar Colony, Kalinganagar, in Jajpur District of Odisha. As there was no baseline survey conducted, the data for displacement was not available and a household survey was carried out among the resettled families of the Tata Rehabilitation Colony, Sansailo, with a structured interview schedule. Primary data was collected following the sampling method and secondary data by the use of printed and internet sources.

Sample

From the total population of 72 families, residing in the rehabilitation colony under study, a sample of 36 families was selected. The procedure of 'Systematic Random Sampling' was followed, while drawing the samples. The first sampling unit was selected at random, and the subsequent units were selected at a sample interval of two, such that:

N = population size = 72; n = sample size = 36; k = sample interval = N/n = 72/36 = 2

From each sample household, the head; or an adult member of the family in the absence of the household head (who was also a member of the same family in the pre-resettlement period), was administered with the interview schedule.

Tools of Measurement

'Two variable linear regression model' was used to analyze the marginal effect of household income on consumption and expenditure during both pre and post-settlement periods. The same model was also applied to analyze to what degree the total compensation amount predicts expenditure on house building. The 'dummy variable technique' was utilised to test, whether or not there are structural changes in the consumption expenditure function, in the post-settlement period.

Data Analysis

1. Regression Analysis with Pre-Settlement Total Income as Independent Variable and Total Expenditure as Dependent Variable:

Null Hypothesis: There is no significant linear relationship between pre-settlement household income and expenditure.

H_0: $\beta = 0$

Alternative Hypothesis: There is a significant linear relationship between the said variables.

H_1: $\beta \neq 0$

Table 13.2 Anova Results

<table>
<tr><th>Source</th><th>Sum of squares</th><th>Degrees of free-dom</th><th>Mean sum of squares</th><th colspan="3">Value</th></tr>
<tr><td>Model</td><td>3288676.76</td><td>1</td><td>3288676.76</td><td>Number of observations</td><td colspan="2">36</td></tr>
<tr><td>Residual</td><td>37986878.8</td><td>34</td><td>1117261.14</td><td>F (1,34)</td><td colspan="2">2.94</td></tr>
<tr><td>Total</td><td>41275555.6</td><td>35</td><td>1179301.59</td><td>Prob>f</td><td colspan="2">0.0953</td></tr>
<tr><td colspan="4" rowspan="3"></td><td>R-Squared</td><td colspan="2">0.0797</td></tr>
<tr><td>Adj.R-Squared</td><td colspan="2">0.0526</td></tr>
<tr><td>Root MSE</td><td colspan="2">1057</td></tr>
<tr><td>tme_pre</td><td>Coef.</td><td>Std. Err.</td><td>T</td><td>P>|t|</td><td colspan="2">[95% Conf. Interval]</td></tr>
<tr><td>tmi_ pre</td><td>0.0665761</td><td>0.0388</td><td>1.72</td><td>0.095</td><td>-0.0123</td><td>0.14544</td></tr>
<tr><td>Constant</td><td>3769.582</td><td>311.873</td><td>12.09</td><td>0</td><td>3135.78</td><td>4403.38</td></tr>
</table>

Model: Yi $= \beta + \varepsilon X_i + a_i$

The estimated model is found to be

$y_i = 3796.582 + .0665761\ X_i$

$$\hat{\alpha} = 3769\ .582\ ; \hat{\beta} = 0.0665761\ \ ; R^2 = 0.0797$$

$$SE\ (\hat{\alpha}) = 311\ .8729\ ; SE\ (\hat{\beta}) = 0.0388048$$

$$t(\hat{\alpha}) = 12\ .09\ ; t(\hat{\beta}) = 1\ .72$$

$$p(\hat{\alpha}) = 0.001\ ; p(\hat{\beta}) = 0.95$$

In the model, $\hat{Y}_i$ is the estimated monthly household expenditure (pre-settlement), X_i is the actual individual household income (pre-settlement), $\hat{\alpha}$ is the intercept parameter and $\hat{\beta}$ is the slope parameter. The model shows that the marginal propensity to consume in the pre-settlement period (β) = 0.0665, indicating that if the total income goes up by Re. 1, then the average total expenditure will go up by Rs. 0.0665 only. The estimated standard errors of the slope and intercept are given as 0.0388048 and 311.879 respectively. The significance value p ($\hat{\beta}$) is 0.095, which is greater than 0.05 and the t value is 1.72. So the income-expenditure relationship is statistically insignificant at 5% level but significant at 10% level. The R^2 value tells us that only 0.0797 or 7.9% of the variation in pre-settlement expenditure of the households, is explained by the pre-settlement income. The least square estimates suggest that, the marginal effect of income on expenditure is only 6.6%. This is due to the reason that, families in the pre-settlement period relied largely upon agricultural activities. Further, income from agriculture, which is not fixed, formed a major part of the total income in that period. As they mostly consume what they produced, rice was the major crop cultivated by the people in the pre-settlement period, the income generated is largely not spent on eatables.

Hence, the null hypothesis is accepted. So our empirical model tells us that income is not an adequate measure in predicting the expenditure of the people in the pre-settlement period.

2. Regression Analysis with Post-Settlement Total Income as Independent Variable and Total Expenditure as Dependent Variable:

Null Hypothesis: There is no significant linear relationship between post-settlement household income and expenditure.

$H_0: \beta = 0$

Alternative Hypothesis: There is a significant linear relationship between the said variables.

Table 12.3 Anova Results

Source	*Sum of squares*	*Degrees of freedom*	*Mean sum of squares*	*Value*		
Model	27949313.3	1	27949313.3	Number of observations	36	
Residual	52272908.9	34	1537438.5	F (1,34)	18.18	
Total	80222222.2	35	2292063.49	Prob>f	0.0002	
				R-Squared	0.3484	
				Adj.R-Squared	0.3292	
				Root MSE	1239.9	
tme_pre	Coef.	Std. Err.	T	P>|t|	95% Conf. Interval	
tmi_pre	0.2590084	0.06075	4.26	0	0.13556	0.38246
Constant	3905.704	549.754	7.1	0	2788.47	5022.94

H_1: $\beta \neq Y_i = \alpha + \beta X_i + \varepsilon_i$

The estimated model is found to be

$$\hat{Y}_i = 3905.704 + .2590084X_i$$

$$\hat{\alpha} = 3905.704; \ \hat{\beta} = 0.2590084; \ R^2 = 0.3484$$

$$SE(\hat{\alpha}) = 549.7541; SE(\hat{\beta}) = 0.0607473$$

$$t(\hat{\alpha}) = 7.10; t(\hat{\beta}) = 4.26$$

$$p(\hat{\alpha}) = 0.000; \ p(\hat{\beta}) = 0.0002$$

The estimated standard errors of the slope and intercept are given as 0.0607473 and 549.7541 respectively. The β value indicates that if the total income increases by Re.1, then the total expenditure in the post-settlement period will increase by Rs. 0.259. The significance value *p*() is 0.0002, which is less than 0.05; and the *t* value is 4.26. So the income-expenditure relationship is statistically significant. The R^2 value tells us that 0.3484 or 34.84% of the variation in post-settlement expenditure is explained by the post-settlement income of the households. The least square estimates suggest that the marginal effect of income on expenditure is 25.9%.

The displaced families in the resettlement colony receive a fixed amount of money as financial assistance (each adult male member of a family gets Rs. 2,000 per month), and in the form of company training stipend (any adult male member who has appeared 10th board exams gets Rs. 3,300 per month) every month. Income from financial assistance and company training contributes around 42% and 23% of the total monthly income, respectively, in the post-settlement period. Here the people do make expenses on various things like transportation, education, food expenditure, house building, etc., which they never did in their pre-displacement village. So, income in the post-settlement period does influence the expenditure in the post-settlement period.

Hence, the null hypothesis is rejected and the model tells us that income can be used to predict the expenditure of the households in the post-settlement situation.

3. Regression Analysis with Total Compensation as Independent Variable and Expenditure on House Building as Dependent Variable:

Null Hypothesis: There is no significant linear relationship, between total compensation and expenditure, on house building in the post-settlement situation.

H_0: $\beta = 0$

Alternative Hypothesis: There is a significant linear relationship between the said variables.

H_1: $\beta \neq 0$

Table 12.4 Anova Results

Source	*Sum of squares*	*Degrees of freedom*	*Mean sum of squares*	*Value*		
Model	8.3057E+11	1	8.31E+11	Number of observations	36	
Residual	1.4579E+12	34	4.29E+10	F (1,34)	19.37	
Total	2.2885E+12	35	(6.54E+10	Prob>f	0.0001	
				R-Squared	0.3629	
				Adj.R-Square	0.3442	
				Root MSE	2.10E+05	
tme_pre	Coef.	Std. Err.	T	P>|t|	95% Conf. Interval	
tmi_pre	0.6863001	0.1559368	4.4	0	0.369398	1.0032
Constant	88959.25	92529.05	0.96	0.343	-99082.41	277000.9

Model: $Y_i = á + â X_i + {}^{a}_{i}$

The estimated model is found to be

$$\hat{Y}_i = 88959.25 + 0.6863001X_i$$

$$\hat{\alpha} = 88959.25; \hat{\beta} = 0.6863001; R^2 = 0.3629$$

$$SE(\hat{\alpha}) = 92529.05; SE(\hat{\beta}) = 0.155968$$

$$t(\hat{\alpha}) = 0.96; t(\hat{\beta}) = 4.40$$

$$p(\hat{\alpha}) = 0.343; p(\hat{\beta}) = 0.001$$

The estimated standard errors of the slope and intercept are given as 0.155968 and 92529.05 respectively. The β value indicates that if the total compensation increases by Re.1, then expenditure on house building will go up by Rs. 0.686. There seems to be a tendency that a family's bulk amount of total compensation amount is spent on house building. Construction of house (*pucca*) involves a lot of cost these days, owing to high costs of cement, rods, bricks, etc., in the market. From the survey, it was found that a family, on an average, spends about Rs. 4,66,805 on house building. It is obvious that, they do not rely much on the monthly salary, for meeting the expenses on house construction. So the only option left is the compensation amount, which is reasonably substantial in order to meet the construction expenses. The significance value p(β) is 0.001, which is less than 0.05; and the t value is 4.40. So the total compensation-expenditure on house building relationship is statistically significant. The R^2 value tells us that 0.3629 or 36.29%, of the variance of expenditure on house building, is explained by the total compensation received by the households. The least square estimates suggest that, the marginal effect of total compensation on house building expenditure is 68.63%.

Hence, the null hypothesis is rejected and the model tells us that, the total compensation received can be used, to predict the house building expenditure of the households in, the post-settlement situation.

4. Dummy Variable Analysis for Testing Structural Differences in the Consumption Expenditure Function of the Households in Post-Settlement Period:

Null Hypothesis: There is no structural change, in the consumption expenditure function, in the post-settlement period.

H_0: $\alpha_2 = 0; \beta_2 = 0$

Alternative Hypothesis: There is a structural change, in the consumption expenditure function, in the post-settlement period.

H_1: $\alpha_2 \neq 0; \beta_2 \neq 0$

Table 12.5 Anova Results

Source	*Sum of squares*	*Degrees of freedom*	*Mean sum of squares*	*Value*		
Model	93957990	3	31319330	Number of observations	72	
Residual	90259787.7	68	1327349.82	F (1,34)	23.6	
Total	184217778	71	2594616.59	Prob>f	0	
				R-Squared	0.51	
				Adj.R-Square	0.4884	
				Root MSE	1152.1	
com_exp	Coef.	Std. Err.	T	P>|t|	95% Conf. Interval	
d_prepo	136.1224	613.583	0.22	0.825	-1088.3	1360.51
Combi_prpo	0.0665761	0.0423	1.57	0.12	-0.0178	0.15098

Model:

$Y_i = \acute{a}_1 + \acute{a}_2 D_i + \hat{a}_1 X_i + \hat{a}_2 D_i X_i + {}^{a}_{i}$ $\qquad i = 1, 2.......72$

Here, $_1 = 3769.582$; $_2 = 136.1224$; $_1 = 0.0665761$;$_2$ $= 0.1924323$; $R^2 = 0.5100$

Where,

$D_i = 1$, if i^{th} observation belongs to post-settlement period

$D_i = 0$, otherwise

Y = consumption expenditure; X = income

If $D_i = 0$ (during pre-settlement period), then

Estimated mean expenditure in pre-settlement period is found to be:

$Y_i = 3769.582 + 0.066561\ X_i$

If $D_i = 1$ (during post-resettlement period), then

Estimated mean expenditure in post-settlement period is found to be:

$Y_i = 3905.7044 + 0.259\ X_i$

The regression result shows that the differential intercept is not significant, but the differential slope coefficient is statistically significant. It shows how much the slope coefficient, of the post-settlement period expenditure, differs from that of the pre-resettlement period. The individual coefficients are reflecting the mean differences and the *t*-test examines which of those differences are statistically significant/ insignificant. To compare the effects of income on the consumption expenditure pattern, both in pre and post-settlement periods, the dummy variable model was constructed. According to the model, as the mean income goes up, on an average of Re.1, the expenditure increases by Rs. 0.066 in the pre-settlement period and by Rs. 0.259 in the post-settlement period. This illustrates that with displacement (or in the post-settlement period); the marginal propensity to consume (mpc) has increased by 0.192.

Hence, the null hypothesis is rejected and we conclude that there is a structural change in the consumption expenditure pattern of households in the post-settlement period or the post-settlement hamlet and this is due to the change in the marginal propensity to consume.

Findings of the Study

At the end of this analysis, several main conclusions virtually impose themselves. Yet it may be proper to state that the material examined is too rich to be summarised simply. It can be looked upon as a platform of knowledge for further reflection and analysis. Firstly, it can be concluded that, income is an inadequate measure to predict the expenditure of people in the pre-settlement period. This is because, in this period the families relied largely upon agriculture activities, and income from agriculture formed a major part of their total income. However, income from agriculture is not fixed; and as they mostly consume what they produced, so the income generated is largely not spent on eatables. Secondly, the income-expenditure relation in the post-settlement period indicates that income influences the expenditure. Thirdly, the regression analysis between total compensation and house building expenditure asseverates that there is a tendency that, a family's bulk amount of total compensation amount is spent on house building. From the survey it was found that a family on an average is spending about Rs. 4,66,805 on house building. It is obvious that they do not rely much on the monthly salary, for meeting the expenses on house construction. So the only option left is the compensation amount, which is reasonably substantial in order to meet the construction expenses. With displacement, there has been a significant transition in the major source of livelihood of the affected families. Fourthly, and lastly, the dummy variable technique to test structural differences asserts that, there is a structural change in the consumption expenditure function of households in the post-settlement period and this is due to the change in the marginal propensity to consume.

Implications of the Study

The Tata Company has provided technical training, on a monthly stipend of Rs. 3,300, to all those eligible members of the families who have asked for it. Income from company training, approximately, constitutes 23 percent of the total monthly income of the households in the post-settlement period. A financial assistance of Rs. 2,000 per adult male (18 yrs or above) per month is also given to all the households in the rehabilitation colony. This financial assistance constitutes a major 42 percent of the total monthly income of the households. Despite a slump in the income from cultivation, livestock, and other specific sources in the post-settlement period, the average household income has soared up significantly in the post-settlement period. The average income in the pre-settlement period was Rs. 6,631.94, which increased to Rs. 8,386.11 in the post-settlement period. The increase in the mean household income by Rs. 1,754.11 is largely due, to the income from company training and financial assistance, which together constitutes 65 percent of the total income approximately.

The financial assistance and company training, however, are not meant for an indefinite period. The households of the colony will reap the benefits of financial assistance only, till, the steel plant comes into operation. The provision of allowance will cease to exist, once the company sets its plant. The training programme is meant for a short duration of time. So, the stipend will not accrue to the current beneficiaries in the years to come. Even though the mean income has increased substantially, and the coefficient of variation has declined in the post-settlement period, indicating more homogeneous distribution of income among the households, the possibility of sustaining this income level is very low.

The interests of the displaced families can be taken care of, only if the steel plant starts operation in Kalinganagar. Further, there is a hidden clash between the displaced families of the colony and the families who are protesting the project in the villages. If the protest does not cease and Tata backs out of the project (as in case of Tata Nano Project at Singur) subsequently, the future of the people in the rehabilitation colony of Sansailo will hang in doldrums.

New Dimensions

Land should not be considered, merely a property as several dimensions such as culture, emotions, identity and history are firmly bonded with it. One Naboghan Munda (name changed), 46, (a tribal from Kalamatia Village) a resident at the rehabilitation colony says:

> "No amount of money compensates land. We are farmers, we needed land .... We need land...... our sons need land. No compensation is good enough as it takes at least two generations to change one's life style and profession. I sold my land due to lure of cash and now feel cheated. I was a king there; happy with my three acres of land, ten cows, and two tractors. Now I shall be a *chaprasi* in a steel plant that is going to be built on my land."

What Munda posits is a question of self-esteem, dignity, self-regard and self-worth. How will the policy makers compensate him?

Notes

1. This paper is a revised version of a part of the author's M.Phil. Dissertation submitted to Utkal University in 2009. The author is grateful to Dr. Bhabesh Sen (Professor & Head, Dept. of Analytical and Applied Economics, Utkal University) who supervised the dissertation. The author is also grateful to Dr. Pulak Mishra (Assistant Professor, Dept.

of Humanities & Social Sciences, IIT Kharagpur, Kharagpur-751302) for his comments and encouragement.

References

Cernea, M.M. (2000): "Risks, Safeguards and Reconstruction: A Model for Population Displacement and Resettlement", *Economic and Political Weekly,* 35(41), pp. 3659-78.

Cernea, M.M. (2006): "Re-examining Displacement: A Redefinition of Concept in Development and Conservation Policies", *Social Change,* 36(1), pp. 8-35.

Mishra, S. (2009): "A Comparative Analysis in the Economic Condition of the Displaced People of Kalinganagar between Pre and Post Resettlement Period: A Case Study of Tata Rehabilitation Colony", Sansailo, Unpublished M.Phil. Thesis, Utkal University.

Rath, B. (2007): "National Resettlement and Rehabilitation (R&R) Policy of the Government of India for Project Affected Persons: Issues and Challenges", Paper presented on 1st International Conference on Managing the Social and Environmental Consequences of Coal Mining in India, ISM, Dhanbad in collaboration with University of New South Wales and Australian National University, Australia, New Delhi, 19-21 November.

Sahoo, T. (2006): "Industrialisation and Displacement in Orissa: Need for Resettlement and Rehabilitation with Empathy", *Journal of the Scheduled Castes and Scheduled Tribes,* Vol. 46.

13

Potential Displaced People and their Loss of Resources: An Experience from Angul, the Industrial Hub of Orissa

Nilakantha Panigrahi

Displacement is a major problem, plaguing the modern state and many a time affects the social, economic and political fabric. The State of Orissa is no exception. With the new economic approaches in the name of Special Economic Zones (SEZs), Protected Areas (PAs), Exclusive Zones (EZs), and adoption of mega-development projects in Orissa, the concept of social justice is reinterpreted, within the ambit of the Indian Constitution. The welfare commitments, of the state for the displaced have been ignored for a long time and to a greater extent, shifted to the corporate sectors during the last couple of years. In this context, Orissa has experienced fair amount of displacement across the time and space during, last couple of decades. The efforts of the Orissa Government, since 1990, to achieve development through mining and industry, have not yielded much results. These experiences indicate that the trust between the state and the people's needs is symbiotic and complementary.

With this premise, firstly, the paper briefly examines the population and natural resources of Orissa. Secondly, it reviews the development, displacement and rehabilitation history of the state, focusing mostly, on the last two decades. Thirdly, the paper gives an overview of R&R policies that are implemented by different stakeholders in the State of Orissa and provides a comparative assessment of the state and national R&R policies, of the day. Fourthly, it attempts to account the resource base of the potential displaced people and their state of agony and helplessness even under the existing R&R policy of the state, through empirical findings from a proposed open cast mining project in the district of Angul, which is the industrial hub of Orissa. Finally, the paper argues that the state must establish processes of good governance, taking into account the interests of the people. Further, the state must revamp the R&R policy to meet the requirements of the potential displaced/affected people, due to the loss of their resources. In this scenario, the state must come up with a proposal, which would align the interests of people and corporate houses and ensure that such a proposal is based on a symbiotic relationship rather than a contractual one.

I

Mega-development projects are the models of economic development across the world. Be it hydro-power projects, like, Sardar Sarovar, in Gujarat (the most controversial one in India), or the Hirakud Hydro-Power Dam Project constructed in Orissa in the 50s; industrial houses like Rourkela Steel Plant in Orissa, or Bhilai Steel Plant in Chhattisgarh (present), or BHEL in Andhra Pradesh established during the 50s; or mining projects in Orissa, which explore ores like dolomite, iron, bauxite, owned by both Private and Public Sector Companies, all development projects have immense impact on the physical, social, cultural, and psychological life of human societies, irrespective of the country in which they live and whether they are urban or rural, tribal or non-tribal. The extent of damage of both natural and man-made resources, depends on the size of the project, rate of investment, duration of the construction phase and output as planned. There was a time when many world bodies agreed that such mega-projects are the temples of economic development. Jawaharlal Nehru, the first Prime Minister of India, also called them as 'Temples of Modern India'. Perhaps the 'non-economic' threats of these temples were not visualised . Hence, more such mega projects were taken up by the state as well as the corporate sectors, perceiving them as the only panacea for economic development and growth. However, even after five decades of funding the mega projects across the world, experts from the World Bank, like Cernea (1998) found that almost 50 per cent of the World Bank funded mega projects are not sustainable largely because of non-institutionalisation of peoples' participation.

Until the 1980s, the natural resources of the world were widely seen as a blessing to the human race. Advocates of the 'Resource Curse Thesis' expressed concerns about the adverse effects of mineral dependence on growth and equity (Autu, 1993; Ross, 2008; Sach and Warner, 1995). They argued that if institutional conditions are not right, then minerals should be left in the ground (Stiglitz, 2007). However, the World Bank Group and other international financial institutions have continued to encourage countries, to commit to the growth of extractive industries as a development strategy (Campbell, 2008), and since the 1990s, over 90 countries have rewritten mining and investment codes (Bridge, 2004b). The industry has responded accordingly and many developing countries, both with and without a tradition of mining, have seen significant increase in investment. This expansion evoked responses in the form of social conflicts and political debates on mining, human rights, environmental integrity, and development. Such debates have not only influenced activists, specialist organisations, and the industry, but also have been the material for presidential campaigns (Peru, 2006), constitutional reform (Ecuador, 2008), and efforts to craft an ostensible post-neo-liberal modes of development (as observed in Bolivia).

The magnitude of displacement caused by these projects, created a lot of statistical confusions. Cernea (1996), one of the experts of World Bank on displacement, calculates that involuntary displacement due to development projects, a common phenomenon of late, is so rampant across the world, that out of 10 million affected, 6 million are only displaced, due to infrastructure development projects in the urban sector. However, this does not include the displacement due to the establishment of 'new sectors', like, Reserve Forests, mining and thermal power, and other military test ranges (Cernea, 1995). More specifically, in the Indian context, the magnitude of displacement calculated by Fernandes (2000) for the period 1951-2000 tunes to the extent of 21.3 million, while academicians like Mohapatra (1999), estimate the displacement to the tune of 25 million.

Among most displacements caused due to the establishment of development projects, during the last couple of decades, in the world, as well as in India, Orissa in particular, it is commonly observed that the projects are largely confined to tribal-dominated backward regions. Though the State imposes its right over the land, it is customarily the local tribal communities that have been enjoying the rights over the natural resources for generations. In order to substantiate the impact of such development projects on the people and the region, a couple of studies were conducted by the social geographer and economist, Sawant (1985), along with a NGO and social activists, that basically discussed the provision of infrastructure development and cost-benefit analysis. The social activists have challenged the very concept of mega-projects for the development of people, particularly for the poor. Such a challenge is basically based on the premise that the affected people largely belong to poor economic strata, and due to less or no post care services provided by the Government, these people suffer a lot in many respects. The invisible losses, incurred by these people, have forced anthropologists to examine the issues of displacement, mainly due to development projects (Scudder, 1973). However, this area was unexplored by the anthropologists in general (Beteille, 1990).

Since 1990, a couple of anthropologists have made attempts to investigate the issues related to displacement, rehabilitation and resettlement, particularly in the context of tribal societies of Orissa (Mohapatra, 1998, 1999; Behura and Panigrahi, 2001, 2002; Patnaik, 1996; Ota, 1996, 1998; Panda and Panigrahi, 1989; Panigrahi, 2008). They tried to understand the impact of developmental projects on the socio-cultural life of the oustees in general and tribal people in particular. The common risk factors that emerged out of the displacements observed by these studies, including landlessness, homelessness, joblessness, marginalisation, food insecurity, loss of access to common property resources, social disruption, and loss of various coping mechanisms adopted by the oustees, were analysed and discussed in different permutations and combinations. Thefindings have established that the constructions of big dams, mining and other developmental projects, instead of being a boon to the people, many a time proved to be the bane for most. These studies have also established that no development will be successful and sustainable, if it disrupts the social threads of the society and dismantles social institutions, social cohesion, and social security system.

Orissa: People and Area

Location

Orissa is located between 17 N to 22.3 N Latitudes and between 81.3 E to 87.5 E Longitudes. It is situated on the coast of the Bay of Bengal, and is surrounded by Andhra Pradesh on the south, Bay of Bengal on the east, Chhattisgarh on the west and West Bengal and Bihar on the north. The administrative division of the state initially comprised 13 districts, but was restructured into 30 districts in 1992, which are sub-divided into 59 sub-divisions, consisting of 314 Community Development Block, Panchayat Samitis and 56,887 villages. The state ranks 11th in terms of population, and shares 3.74 per cent of India's population, which is growing at a rate of about 2 per cent per annum. The agro-climatic conditions of the state have immense diversities; however, it can be classified into four distinct agro-climatic zones: Coastal Plains, Central Table Land, Northern Plateau, and the Eastern Ghats.

Ethnic Composition

Orissa is home to various ethnic groups, from time immemorial. There are 62 tribal communities in Orissa that have been declared as Scheduled Tribes, out of which 13 are considered as Primitive Tribal Groups (PTGs) and are entitled to special treatment. Almost 44.21 per cent of the total land area in Orissa has declared as Scheduled Area[1]. Except the coastal belt, many districts in the state have been declared either partially or completely as Scheduled Areas. The present Scheduled Area of the state covers six districts as completely scheduled and seven districts as partially scheduled. Thus, out of 314 Community Development Blocks in Orissa, 118 (37.3%) blocks are preponderantly occupied by tribal communities, which are covered under Tribal Sub-Plan (TSP). Thus, the tribal population of Orissa constitutes 22.21 per cent of the total state population. The major tribes in Orissa include Khond, Gond, Santal, Saora, Bhuiyan, Paraja, Koya, Oraon, Gadaba, Juanga and Munda. Apart from these, there are also a good number of smaller tribal communities, such as, Chencu, Juanga, Bonda, Didayi and Chuktia-Bhunjia. Tribal communities such as Santal, Gond, Munda, Ho, Birhor, Koya, Lodha, Kondha, Bhumija, Kharia and Oraons cut across the state boundaries and are also found in the neighbouring states of Bihar, Chhattisgarh, Andhra Pradesh and West Bengal, while the tribal communities like Juanga, Bonda and Didayee are found to be confined to the districts of Keonjhar and Malkangiri respectively.

Natural Resource Basket of Orissa

The major rivers of the state are Mahanadi, Brahmani, Baitarani, Budhabalang, Rushikulya and many tributaries. The state has a 480 km long coastline. Orissa has essentially an undulating topography with highland, constituting 64.2 per cent and 50.6 per cent of cultivated area in the Northern Plateau and Eastern Ghat regions respectively. Orissa is a state, rich in mineral resources. About 27 different kinds of minerals are found in Orissa. Out of the 30 districts in the state, eight districts namely Angul, Jajpur, Kalahandi, Keonjhar, Mayurbhanj, Jharsuguda, Sundergarh and Koraput are rich in mineral resources. The major mineral resources found in the state are Iron Ore, Chromites, Bauxite, Coal, Nickel and Graphite. Orissa ranks 5th and 6th respectively in terms of Iron and Coal reserves in the country. Orissa contributes to about 90 per cent of Chromites, 80 percent of Graphite, 46 per cent of Dolomite, and about one-third (40 per cent) of India's Manganese ore production.

The state tops in Bauxite production and shares 47 per cent of the total production. It stands second in the production of Pyrophylite (23 per cent), Quartz (30 per cent), Quartzite (34 per cent), and Fireclay (15 per cent) in India. The state generates about Rs. 550 crores per year from the mineral resources available within its geographical area.

Due to the large-scale deposits of mineral resources, several mineral-based industries have been set up and are operational in the state. Till the year 1950, Orissa did not have a single industry except for a few sawmills and some ice factories near Cuttack. Exploration of its natural resources began in the 1950s, with the construction of Hirakud Dam and Rourkela Steel Plant. The progress of development was slow during the first three Plan Periods. It caught pace in the 1970s and there was rapid development of industries, construction of dams and mining, which put the state on the industrial map of India.

Livelihood resources in Orissa are something more than what economists view in terms of production, distribution and consumption through transaction of goods and services. The subsistence livelihood of the tribal people has substantial linkages with man-material resources in the context of its culture, and the concept of common property resources that centres on land. The practice of corporate and joint rights over land and land-based resources did not allow the land to be a saleable commodity in tribal societies. For example, the Kutia Kondha, Bonda, Didayi, Juanga, Bhuiyans, and other tribes believe that their ancestors have given land to them and they have no right to sell it. Shifting cultivation is a form of subsistence economy, which is still in practice among many tribal communities of Orissa, like, Bhuiya, Juanga, Dangaria Kondh, Kutia, Kondh, Saora, Paraja, Didayi, Koya, Bonda and Gadaba, who derive their substantial livelihood support from shifting cultivation.

Development Disparity

The northern region of Orissa covers 11 districts, sharing 42.18 per cent of the state's total geographic area and 34.69 per cent of the state's population. The population density in this region is around 194 per sq km. The southern region includes 8 districts sharing 32.02 per cent of the state's geographic area, 17.47 per cent of the state's population, while the population density is 129 per sq km. The coastal region covers 11 districts with 47.84 per cent of state's geographical area, with a population density of 438 people per sq km. The poverty ratio for rural Orissa was reported as 48.01 per cent in the year 1999-2000. Hence, this state is recognised as the poorest state in India ahead of Bihar (43.33 per cent).

The HCR for the coastal region of rural Orissa was worked out as 31.74 per cent, but the HCR for the southern NSS region was reported as 87.05 per cent (Haan and Dubey, 2003). This has attracted the attention of researchers, policy makers, and the people's representatives.

II

Development-Induced Displacement in Orissa

The establishments of mega-projects have encroached upon land and land-based resources, displacing tribal people from their age-old habitation. These projects have immense impact on the life and livelihood of the displaced. The mega projects can be categorised as hydroelectric-cum-irrigation projects such as Hirakud (1948), Balimela (1963), Machhkund (1949), Upper Kolab (1978), Indravati (1978), Mandira, Rengali (1973), and Subarnarekha; mineral-based industries such as the Rourkela Steel Plant (1950), Hindustan Aeronautics Limited (1962); Bauxite Mining Project at Koraput (1981), National Aluminium Company at Angul (1985), and many projects related to cement, iron, dolomite and lime stone, etc.

A cursory calculation indicates that the state of Orissa, since independence, has set up 190 projects that have deforested 24,124 hectares of forestland, which is the basic source of livelihood of the tribal people (PCCF Office, Govt. of Orissa, 1999). The estimate on the magnitude of displacement of human population in Orissa, due to the establishment of various mega-projects during the period 1951-95, indicates that hydro-electric multi-purpose projects have displaced around 3,25,000 people, of which only 90,000 oustees (27.69 per cent) have been rehabilitated. Similarly, about 71,794 people were displaced in Orissa, due to industrial projects, of which only 27,300 (38.03 per cent) oustees have been rehabilitated; mining projects have displaced around 1,00,000 people, of which almost 60 percent have been rehabilitated; and around 50,000 people were displaced, due to the declaration of Sanctuary, of which only 15,540 (31.08 per cent) have been rehabilitated (Mohapatra, 1999). All these projects have immense impact on the economy, family life and village power structure of the tribal people (Panda and Panigrahi, 1986; Behura and Nayak, 1993; Mohapatra, 1998; Swain and Panigrahi, 1999; Patnaik, 2000; Behura and Panigrahi, 2001, 2002, 2008).

Globalisation and Development in Orissa

The economic reforms and liberalisation process, initiated in 1991 provided an opportunity to the state to leverage the natural resources and attract investment both domestic and international. The State Government formulated its Industrial Policy in 2001, with the objective of transforming Orissa into a vibrant industrial state by the beginning of the new millennium. Due to abundant mineral resources, long coastline inland waters, the bio-diversity of the forests and the rich cultural heritage, the State emerged as a favoured destination for industrial investment.

The new industrial policy provides single window clearance, single window information source, clearance of fast track projects, technology upgradation, interest subsidy, sales tax incentives, land bank scheme to allot land for industrial projects, waiver of electricity duty for new industrial units, reduced water rate up to 5 years, exemption of stamp duty, etc. These provisions are basically meant to attract investors for setting up industries in the state. With the formulation of new Industrial Policy and higher emphasis on industrialisation by the elected government, Orissa witnessed a huge influx of corporate giants to set up industries in the state. These mainly include Iron and Steel Industries and Thermal Power Plants. Recently, the State Government has signed MoUs with 56 Corporate Houses to set up 43 Steel Plants and 13 Power Plants in the state by leasing different mountains and resource-rich regions of Orissa for establishing mineral based industries. The state has signed these agreements with mining companies with an understanding that the state's rich mineral resources will transform Orissa from a state of poverty to affluence, and the poor will be rich. On 4-12-04, the Chief Minister declared in the State Assembly that : "No one, I repeat, No one will be allowed to stand in the way of Orissa's industrial development and the people's progress." This reflects the commitment of the government for the development of mining and industry of the state.

The major companies that have tried to explore bauxite in Orissa at different points of time, but failed, or are still trying to explore various ores, include BALCO during 1986; Utkal Alumina, INDAL, TATA, Norsk Hydro (Norway's biggest corporation), and ALCAN (Canada), and HINDALCO (Hindustan ALCO) of the Birla family. In addition, the entry of big corporate houses including TATA, POSCO, Jindal, Essar, Vedanta, Ispat and Sterilite, Bhusan, Kalinga, etc., and DFID in Orissa helped to a great extent in liberalising the processes for the companies to enter into Orissa. The role of DFID in bringing change in the fiscal management of the state health sector, reform and in overall governance in Orissa more particularly since 1990s seems to be quite significance from many perspection early to 1990, the role of DFID when it was popularly known as Oversees Development Agency (ODA). Many times, the focus of

DFID in Orissa is being questioned, whether they are for poverty eradication and development of the state or for promoting British companies like Vedanta in bauxite and metal production. The DFID co-coordinated its policy closely with the World Bank; the State of Orissa has borrowed loans more than any other state, resulting in a badly indebted scenario. The only way the state can repay the capital and interest is by borrowing further (Govt. of Orissa, 2001). Hence, the State Government in consultation with the Government of India has created couple of Special Economic Zones (SEZs) to protect the interest of the industrial houses.

In the Post-Reform period, during 1995-96, the State of Orissa, followed by Gujarat, Karnataka and Maharashtra, have received large amounts of both foreign and domestic investments. As per the 11th Quarterly Survey of Projects Investment conducted by Projects Today, Orissa is ranked 6th in terms of the total outstanding investment in the country. It is observed that by the end of June 2003 Orissa had signed 205 projects worth of Rs.1,12,261 crores which are at various stages of implementation. Orissa is among the few states in India, where investment, by the private sector for projects, is more than that of the government. The project ownership by private sector in the state is to the tune of 62 per cent, while the government owns only 38 per cent (Ibid.); participation of foreign companies in the projects constitutes about one-third of the overall investments, while the contribution of private sector investment is about 54 per cent.

It is observed that Government of Orissa approved 81 cases of Foreign Direct Investment, until 2003. In the 11th Quarterly Survey of Projects Investment, conducted by Projects Today, 2004, it was found that the new investments in the state by private sectors are more in industrial production (24.69 per cent), followed by chemical products (14.81 per cent), mining operations (12.34 per cent), power plants (12.34 per cent), etc. The data indicates that very little investment has been made in primary sectors, like, health (6.17 per cent), and food processing and marketing (6.17 per cent), which again includes fish, shrimp, water treatment, cashew nut, bakery, fruit juice, etc. No investment has been made in sectors like, irrigation, agricultural development, production of agriculture implements, communication, forestry, rural infrastructure development, etc. As regards the receipt of foreign equity, the data indicates that production of electrical equipments has received the highest share of 34.89 per cent, followed by industrial products (25.32 per cent), power plants (18.88 per cent), and food processing and marketing (10.08 per cent).

Further, an attempt was made to find out to what extent, the state has promoted Indian companies, particularly the local companies to collaborate with foreign companies. It was found that around 24.69 per cent foreign investments have been made with the companies from Orissa, while other investments have been made in collaboration with the companies from New Delhi, Calcutta, Hyderabad, Bombay, Bangalore, etc. This shows that in the process of globalisation, the potential of Orissa's natural resources have been exposed to national and international traders and corporate houses, that have established control over the state's resources. The state, instead of protecting the local interests and preserving the natural resources, helped these projects with the aim of developing Orissa. However, ecological and economic importance of these resources and the livelihood interests of the local people over these natural resources, have not been adequately taken into account, while entering into collaborations with different companies.

Angul: The Industrial Hub of Orissa

Angul District, one of the industrial hubs of Orissa, is the centre for coal-based mining projects and coal-based power production industrial units by different public and private sector companies which are at various stages of implementation. Industrial development in Angul district started with the establishment of NALCO project. NALCO in Angul Sector has acquired 4,000.98 acres of land which includes 3,409.3 acres of private land and 591.68 acres of government land. The project affected 23 villages in Banarpal Block, 2 villages in Angul Block, 12 villages from Talcher Block and one village from Oapada Block of Dhenkanal District. Of the total 4,040 displaced, 34 were locally displaced persons, while 1,381 were substantially affected persons and 2,625 were less affected persons. About 1,150 oustees have been given permanent jobs in NALCO, while 1,155 oustees have been employed on a contract basis. The NALCO-affected persons have also been allotted shops and service contracts. Furthermore, local youth from 39 villages have been trained at ITI Talcher (Samal, 1995).

Talcher coalfield, spread over an area of 1860 sq km, contains huge reserves of power grade coal (COMPDI, Geological Report, 2005). The Government of India allotted Utkal-E Block situated in this coalfield to M/s NALCO on 27.08.2004 for coal mining to meet the requirements of its captive power plants. Subsequently, a geological report was completed in April 2005, which has estimated a geological reserve of 113.393 MT. The extractable reserve has been estimated as 67.49 MT (*Ibid.*). Considering the requirement of coal for the 2nd phase of CPP expansion,

NALCO proposes to develop a coal mine in this block. Utkal-E Coal Block is situated in the south-central part of the Talcher coalfield in Chendipada *Tahasil* of Angul District. The block lies around 20°55′58″N latitude and between 84°55′49″E and 84°56′37″ longitudes; it is covered under Survey of India top sheet No. 73 D/13 on RF 1:50,000 and special top sheet L2 on RF 1:10,000.

The industrial and mining houses like TATA Sponge Iron Ltd., ESSAR Power Orissa Ltd., Jindal Steel and Power Ltd., IMFA Group Extension Plan, National Aluminium Company Ltd., and Monnet Ispat and Energy Ltd., have subsequently started their operations in the district. These companies / public sectors have acquired a total of 5,899.91 hectares of land of which 4,008.88 hectares (67.94 per cent) is private land, and 1,891.03 hectares (32.05 per cent) is government land. All these projects either, partially, or completely, have been instrumental in affecting and displacing 38 revenue villages of Chendipada *Tahasil* of Angul District (UNDP, 2008). The environmental impact of the coal-based power plants was rationalised and efforts have been made to project Orissa as the country's power home with its rich coal deposits. The state has signed MoUs within a couple of years to establish 21 coal-based power plants (till Feb, 2009) located across the districts of Dhenkanal, Puri, Jharsuguda, Sambalpur, Cuttack and Bhadrak. The total investment tunes to Rs. 1,10,000 crores to produce 25,780 MW of power in the state. The state considers power production as the enabling factor to achieve 90 percent growth in the industrial sector and plans to develop energy-intensive industrial parks with full state support.

III
R&R Policies of Orissa

The history of R&R policies of Orissa includes individual R&R packages of major development agencies like NALCO, MCL, NTPC, and the Department of Water Resources in the state. In addition, this section also briefly outlines the Orissa Resettlement and Rehabilitation Policy, 2006 and the National Policy, 2006.

R&R Policy (1994) of Department of Water Resources (DoWR)

The R&R Policy of the Department of Water Resources, 1994, has clearly laid out the difference between 'affected persons' and 'displaced persons'. The definitioncentres around the extent of loss, complete or partial, of homestead and agriculture land. Though 'family' in the policy was defined as a person with spouse, minor sons, unmarried daughters, minor brothers and sisters, and father and mother; major sons, unmarried daughters above 30 years, physically and mentally retarded persons, divorcees and widows were also treated as a separate family. The policy suggested that after a socio-economic survey of the displaced, an identity card must be issued to them. Land for land was the objective of their R&R, while emphasising on the families, who have completely lost both agriculture land and homestead, in addition to the cash grant assistance and house construction assistance. The policy of the DoWR was not committed to provide employment to the DPs and/or PAPs.

R&R Policy of Mahanadi Coalfield Limited (MCL)

The R&R Policy of MCL recognizes a displaced family, as one that has lost both agriculture land and homestead, and has been living in Orissa for at least three years, prior to the date of publication of the notification of land acquisition. The policy defines that a family consists of husband and wife and their unmarried daughters above 30 years. In addition, it also recognizes a divorcee/deserted woman or widow as a separate family that has no source of livelihood. The policy emphasised that the families are to be identified through a socio-economic benchmark survey. As a part of the package, MCL provided direct or indirect employment in the company, to nominated members of the displaced families, in order of preference, to those who have completely lost their agriculture land and homestead as well as those who lost two-thirds of their land. Further, MCL also identified displaced/affected persons to provide assistance through allotment of shops, skill development training, other related activities to the unemployed, and/or payment of one-time cash compensation, if the family refuses to avail the facilities and/or is not provided jobs. The cash compensation included Rs. 1 lakh for one-third category and Rs. 50,000 for other displaced families.

R&R Plan of National Thermal Power Corporation Ltd. (NTPC)

NTPC recognised two different categories of affected families: Firstly, those, who have lost more than one-third of their total land, were categorised as Substantially Affected Families (SAF) and the families, who have lost less than one-third of their land, were known as Marginally Affected Families (MAF). The policy considers the concept of family and separate family, but does not clarify the constituents of a family. It recognised the need for socio-economic data, which will be collected through a village survey. The compensation and rehabilitation facilities of the policy include 'land for land', depending on the adequate availability of land. Other options include training in local ITI, allotment of shops, and assistance for setting up agro-based industries like diary and poultry.

The NTPC's policy recognised all types of land losers, emphasising more on families losing one-third or more land irrespective of the present use. Taking into account, the responses of the oustees, NTPC gave importance to employment in the unskilled category, and land for land basically for SAF only.

Rehabilitation Policy of NALCO

NALCO recognizes two categories of project-affected persons: Locally Displaced Persons (LDP) and Substantially Affected Persons (SAP). The first category includes households that have lost their total landholding to NALCO, while the SAP include households left with two-thirds or less of their total landholding after acquisition.

The following are the main features of the R&R policy of NALCO:

- NALCO in principle has adopted 'job for land' as the guiding principle of its R&R policy.
- It has outlined that one person from each family of the LDP/SAP will be offered employment, subject to the vacancies and educational qualification of the nominee.
- The LDP will get preference over SAP. Employment will also be provided to the nominee under contractor.
- Allotment of shops in the company's township will be provided on preference.
- Award of petty contract jobs on preference to the affected and provision of technical training to the LDP, whenever necessary to improve the technical skill of the nominee.

The policy has clearly mentioned that the preferential assistance given to LDP/SAP will cease beyond a period of one year, from the date of commissioning of the unit and the employment-related assistance, provided to the oustees, would be confined to the unit concerned and not to another unit of the company. NALCO's R&R policy ignored the need of conducting socio-economic survey of the LDP/SAP. As a result, it generated a lot of confusion, while settling the claims of the LDP/SAP.

Orissa Resettlement and Rehabilitation Policy: 2006

Orissa Resettlement and Rehabilitation Policy 2006, published in Orissa Gazette Extraordinary No. 651, dated May 15th 2006, is a milestone in the history, of management of development-induced displacement in the state. It ensures sustained development aimed through a participatory and transparent process. The policy aims to avoid displacement, wherever possible, and minimize it; it recognizes the voice of the displaced communities, emphasising the needs of the indigenous communities and vulnerable sections; it ensures environmental sustainability through participatory and transparent process; and guides the process of developing institutional mechanisms, for implementation, monitoring, conflict resolution, and grievance redressal.

The present policy draws its strength from the experiences, gained during the last six decades of development, displacement and rehabilitation in the context of Orissa and by way of learning from the best practices from other states. A few important aspects of the Orissa R&R Policy are presented here for a brief understanding:

(a) Family-A

"Family" includesa person and his/her spouse, minor sons, unmarried daughters, minor brothers, or unmarried sisters, father, mother, and other members residing with him/her and dependent on him/her for his/her livelihood.

A separate family for the purpose of extending rehabilitation benefits under this policy includes:

(i) A major son irrespective of his marital status;

(ii) Unmarried daughters/sisters more than 30 years of age;

(iii) Physically and mentally challenged persons, irrespective of age and sex (duly certified by an authorised Medical Board). For this purpose, the blind/the deaf/the orthopedically handicapped/mentally challenged persons suffering from more than 40% permanent disability, will only be considered as separate family;

(iv) Minor orphans, who have lost their parents; and

(v) A widow or a woman divorcee.

(b) Resettlement and Rehabilitation Plan

Based on the list approved by the Government and the options given by the displaced families, the R&R Plan shall be prepared by the District Collector, after due consultation with the displaced communities in the manner determined by the Government. Such Plan should address the specific needs of the women, vulnerable groups, and indigenous communities. The same will be placed before the RPDAC for approval The R&R Plan considers the following aspects:

(1) Site for the resettlement habitat shall be selected by the RPDAC in consultation with the displaced families.

(2) No physical displacement shall be made before the completion of the resettlement work as approved by the RPDAC. The Collector will issue the certificate of completion of resettlement work.

(3) The Gram Sabha shall be consulted.

(4) Where there is multiple displacement, additional compensation amounting to 50 per cent of the normal compensation payable, shall be given to each displaced family, over and above the normal compensation in the form of *ex gratia*.

(5) Provisions, relating to rehabilitation, will be given effect from the date of actual vacation of the land.

(6) The Project Authorities shall abide by the provisions, laid down by the Policy and the decisions taken by RPDAC from time to time, provided they are within the ambits of the approved Policy of the Government.

(7) The District Administration and Project Authorities shall be jointly responsible, for ensuring that the benefits of R&R reach the target beneficiaries in a time-bound manner.

(8) The District Administration should hand over the Record of Rights of the land and house allotted to the displaced persons, while resettling them in the resettlement habitat. The District Administration shall take steps for immediate declaration of the new resettlement habitat as a Revenue Village, if it is not in an already existing Revenue Village.

(9) Steps will be taken by the Project Authorities for acclimatisation of the resettled people in the new habitat, including development of cordial social relationship between the host and the resettled communities and to ensure, as far as practicable, overall improvement of standard of living of the displaced families.

(10) Subject to the details, regarding the provision of employment as enunciated in the Policy, the project authorities shall give preference to the matter of employment, both direct and indirect, as well as through contractors employed by them, for execution, operation and maintenance of the project to local persons, as per the detailed guidelines, issued by the State Government from time to time.

(c) Provisions in Mining Projects under the R&R Act 2006

The displaced and other affected families shall be eligible, for employment by the project causing displacement. For the purpose of employment, each family will nominate one member of the family. The order of preference for employment includes displaced families losing all land, including homestead land; losing more than two-thirds of their agricultural and homestead land; losing all agricultural land but not homestead land; losing more than one-third of their agricultural land and homestead land; losing only homestead land but not agricultural land;

The Project Authorities will make special efforts to facilitate skill upgradation of the nominated member of each displaced/other family for employment in their project.

- In case the nominees of displaced families are eligible for employment otherwise, the upper age limit shall be relaxed by five years.
- The Project Authorities should notify their employment capacity in advance.
- As far as possible, the objective shall be to provide one member from each displaced/other family as mentioned above, with employment in the project.

However, where the same cannot be provided, due to some limitations, cash compensation shall be provided to the displaced/other families: The displaced/other families, who do not opt for employment/self employment, as mentioned in sub para (a), shall be provided by the Project Authorities with a one-time cash assistance in lieu of employment.

In addition, the project will also provide training for self employment, convertible preference share, making the provision for homestead land, assistance for self-relocation, house building assistance, shops and service units, benefit to landless and homeless encroachers common to all categories.

Other assistance common to all categories of projects includes: maintenance allowance, assistance for temporary shed, transportation allowance, special benefits to displaced indigenous families and primitive tribes in the form of provisions of land in natural habitation and maintenance of ethnic boundaries while making the R&R Plan.

Orissa R&R Policy, 2006 and The National Policy, 2007: A Comparison

The Orissa R&R Policy, 2006 is built upon the inputs of UNDP, and is considered as the best policy in India (Mathur, 2008; Mehra, 2007). These are the following major distinctions one finds, when comparing the State and National Policies on R&R.

- The concept of 'Family' in the Orissa Policy is more inclusive than in the National Policy. The Orissa Policy recognizes unmarried daughters and sisters above 30 years of age, a widow, or a woman divorcee as a separate family. For the benefit of rehabilitation, it also includes the physically and mentally challenged persons and minor orphans, by conferring the status of a separate family. On the other hand, the National Policy is biased against gender and social groups.

- The Orissa R&R Policy 2006 ensures environmental sustainability, through R&R processes, talks of comprehensive communication plan for awareness creation, with the involvement of civil societies at the cost of the project and dovetailing of normal development programmes, with the R&R package for the displaced/affected, whereas, the National Policy omits this aspect.
- The Orissa R&R Policy 2006 recognises that there will be no physical displacement before the completion of resettlement works, while the National Policy talks of 'adequate program' in R&R, to be ensured before physically shifting the displaced persons. The former also recognizes the need for re-establishing the cordial relationship, with the host community in the resettlement site and neutralising the socio-cultural trauma, regarding which the National Policy is silent.
- Orissa R&R Policy classifies the projects into five categories: (a) industrial, (b) mining, (c) water resources/national highway, (d) urban and linear projects, and (e) any other projects. The provision of employment is guaranteed only in case of 'a' and 'b'. It also clarifies that where employment is not possible, cash compensation with one-time assistance as per the provision shall be provided to the displaced. Therefore, the Orissa Policy seems to be valueless in providing jobs to the displaced as in the National Policy. The National Policy also provides a Rehabilitation Grant to the affected families who have not given land or employment. Both the policies opt for cash options as the most convenient mode of wriggling out of the assurance to provide land or employment (Saxena, 2008).
- With respect to the provision of homestead land and house building assistance, the Orissa Policy is more liberal than the National Policy. The Orissa R&R Policy provides for 1/10th of an acre for this purpose, along with a house building grant of Rs. 1,50,000 for projects in rural areas and 1/25th of an acre with the same house building grant in urban areas.
- The National Policy contains some provisions which are superior

to the Orissa R&R Policy, which includes the Social Impact Assessment, provision of social and physical amenities at resettlement sites, detailed enumeration of rehabilitation benefits, norms for compensation assessment, rehabilitation plan, and focus on Tribal Development Plan with restoration of alienated tribal land, settling land rights, and provision of replacing forest laws. However, both the policies have drifted from 'land for land' approach and employment even to the Scheduled Tribes. Both the policies have ignored rights of people on Community Property Resources (CPRs) for compensatory entitlements (*Ibid.*).

IV
Empirical Findings from a Proposed Open Cast Coal Mine in Angul District : The Study Universe

These findings are taken from a study carried out by the author, as part of a larger research project. The study covered two fully displaced revenue villages of Nandichhod (Gopiballavpur) and Gopinathpur of Chendipada Block in Angul District. The villages are located 38 km away from district headquarters and 9 km away from block headquarters. The displacement of the families was due to the Utkal-E-Open Cast Coal Mines of NALCO. The data was collected with the help of structured interview schedules carried out during October-December, 2008. NALCO, one of the Navaratna winners of India, is the fifth largest aluminium company in India, engaged in bauxite mining, alumina refining, alumina smelting, power generation, as well as management of port facilities. It has substantially contributed to development of roads in India. The study covered a total of 314 households consisting of eight SC, 229 ST, and 77 OBC households in two fully proposed displaced villages. The major caste groups living in the village include Dhoba, Kamar, Gouda, Chasa, Mali, Hadi, Barik and Karan, while Gond is the only tribal community living in the project villages.

Village Infrastructure

The village infrastructure includes an area of 423.435 hectares of forest, used by the villagers for collection of fuel wood and NTFP. Nandichhod Village has five cremation grounds distributed on caste/ethnic basis. The village has tube wells, ICDS centre, primary school, high school, tank irrigation (eight tanks), five temples, a public distribution service centre, three youth clubs, and six women self-help groups. A dug well as water source serves around 206 households (65.61 per cent), while the tube well serves only 59 households (18.70 per cent). The traditional water bodies play a major role in meeting the water needs of the households.

Land Resources of the Households

Of the 226.89 hectares of land in both the villages, 215.36 hectares (94.71 per cent) are agriculture land, while 11.53 hectares are of homestead type. Around 16.63 hectares of land, possessed by the households, have been encroachments for more than 20 years.

The study indicates that around 97.63 per cent have their homestead on *patta* land. The agriculture landholding status of the households shows that, 90.17 per cent (270 households) have their own agriculture land to the extent of average 1.25 hectares, while 3.97 per cent (12 households) own 1.25 to 2.50 hectares. NALCO, for its open caste coal mining, is going to acquire all the homestead and agriculture land of both the villages. Out of the 226.89 hectares of land, 127.62 hectares (56.25 per cent) are to be acquired by NALCO, 13.64 hectares are to be acquired by KCM, 77.46 hectares are to be acquired by TATA, while the remaining 7.87 hectares have been left un-acquired.

Livelihood Sources

Agriculture: Agriculture is the main occupation and the major source of livelihood for the villagers. Around 37.66 per cent of the households directly depend on cultivation, while 2.22 per cent depend on agriculture-related labour. Only 2.46 per cent of the households are engaged in business, while 6.20 and 5.26 per cent are engaged in different jobs owned by government and private agencies respectively. The average agriculture production per household is: 12.95 quintals of cereals, 0.96 quintals of pulses, 1.80 quintals of vegetables, and 0.81 quintals of oilseeds. An assessment of the disposal of agro-produce was made for the year 2006-07. The data reveals that one household disposes around 3.93 quintals of crop produce per annum, which includes 2.13 quintals of cereals, and 1.19 quintals of vegetables.

Forest Resources: Forest is another important source of livelihood for the villagers. The study found out that during 2006-07, on an average, a family has procured NTFPs to the extent of Rs. 3,431, followed by fuel wood (Rs. 2,019), food items (Rs. 1,840), and other forest produce used for household articles. The households also dispose forest produce. On an average, one household during a year disposed different forest items, like, food items (Rs. 651), and non-food items (NTFPs) to the extent of Rs. 3,076.

Livestock: Livestock resources supplement the family income basket and are substantially important for the family. Around 250 (79.61 per cent) households in the villages own different types of livestock. The average income from sheep/goat selling per household is about Rs. 1,886, followed by the sale of milk (Rs. 831). Around 18 per cent (43 households) of the households possess five or more large animals, while 28.8 per cent (72 households) rear five or more small animals.

Wage labour: Wage labour is also an important source of income which supplements the food basket of the family. During the year, on an average, one male member works for 90 person days and earns around Rs. 7,109, while one female member works for 85 person days, which supplements the family income by Rs. 5,384. The wage labour is linked to both agricultural and non-agricultural operations, and around 187 (59.55 per cent) households have job cards. Of the total households, 200 (63.69 per cent) are BPL families, which regularly receive rice from the local dealer. Of the total eligible population of 8,71,777 (89.21 per cent) have voter cards.

Thus, the income distribution of the households shows that agriculture contributes most, up to 21.68 per cent (Rs. 15,502), followed by 15.73 per cent (Rs. 11,244) from forestry, 14.84 percent (Rs. 10,608) through salary from services, 7.80 per cent (Rs. 5,575) from wage labour, and 5.25 per cent (Rs. 3,747) from livestock. The income group distribution of the households shows that 38.54 per cent are in the annual income category of Rs. 25,000 to Rs. 50,000, while 31.53 per cent households belong to the income group between Rs. 50,000 and Rs. 1,00,000. The annual income of 12.42 per cent (39 households) is above Rs. 1,00,000 per year.

Living Standard

The house type consists of brick and cement walls (47.13 per cent), mud walls (43.31 per cent), while 38.85 per cent have thatched roofs, and the rest have RCC, asbestos, and tile roofs. On an average each house consists of four rooms with separate kitchen (92.68 per cent) and cattle sheds (77.07 per cent). For 95.86 per cent of the households, wood is the major source of fuel.

Next, the economic value of assets of the households was also assessed. It was observed that one household, in the village, on an average possesses one water source costing around Rs. 8,326, livestock to the worth of Rs. 14,498 and household articles to the worth of Rs. 7,196. The average annual expenditure of the households towards food items, during the year 2006-07, reflects that in Nandichhod Village, the average annual expenditure amounts to Rs. 17,332, while the minimum and maximum of these expenses per household ranges from Rs. 2,650 to Rs. 50,350. In case of Gopinathpur Village, the annual expenditure of the household amounts to Rs. 13,933. Further, in Gopinathpur Village, the average annual expenditure towards non-food items amounts to Rs. 13,322, and rangesbetween Rs. 3,600 and Rs. 25,500. A few households have received cash compensation from TATA, which has acquired a portion of their land. The cash availability, with a few households, has influenced their expenditure pattern and raised their non-food expenditure.

V
Discussion

Earlier NALCO, a Public Sector in Angul, acquired 4,001 acres of land, including 3,409 acres of private land from 39 villages. The displacement and/or acquisition of the land was compensated with employment in NALCO to the head of each family. The local people could not see any forward and backward linkages with NALCO, due to the local development process at the household level. However, the acquired land was a source of livelihood for the people, for generations together. The shift from agriculture by all to the non-farm sector by a few, could not create any ray of hope for livelihood sustainability of the displaced, who did not get employment, and even after retirement from the job, for those who got employment. The original multiple sources of generating livelihood for the displaced, became non-existent. The villages are foreseeing unemployment in a new setup, due to the loss of agriculture, livestock, forest and other natural resources. Their poor utilisation of cash compensation, due to lack of planning as well as due to various pushed attractions for lavish expenditure, brings no rehabilitation benefits and equally concerns the potential displaced. The villagers are also apprehending that this time NALCO may not give employment to all the displaced, due to mechanisation of the work process in the mines; moreover, provision of employment under registered contractors will not be acceptable to the displaced.

The socio-cultural impact of the displacement, as foreseen by the displaced families, can be categorised as psychological impact, social impact and economic impact. Some of the social impacts pointed out by the households are the loss of community life, rise of competition among households for natural resources, loss of *jajmani* relations, rise of contractual relations, insecurity for the women and young girls, distortion of marital networks, loss of religious institution, etc. The economic impact, of displacement listed by the displaced households, can be categorised as loss of land, forest resources, water sources, loss of fuel wood supply from the forest, loss of community resources, etc.

The R&R package of the State must raise the above technical and economic contents of rehabilitation through the provision of housing and cash compensation. The package should take into account, the support for livelihood for a period of five to ten years, following the displacement. Special social and cultural rehabilitation packages may be made for the lower caste and tribal households, to reduce the degree of pauperisation among the minority communities due to displacement. The peripheral development taken up by NALCO needs to give importance to the security of migrants for their socio-economic development. People managed development institutions should cater to the social needs, economic requirements, and skill development, which may bridge the gaps and prevent further deterioration of the life and living of the potential displaced.

Such challenges are bottlenecks for the State Government. The state projects Orissa's development through exploration of minerals and establishment of mineral-based industries. In this process, the state has liberalised various policies, made them progressive, and has invited many national and international agencies/ companies/ corporate houses as the stakeholders in the development processes. The social welfare commitments of the state for the development of education, health and employment of the people, as envisaged in the Constitution of India, has been partially taken by the National Government in the name of more fund allocation. The SSA, NRHM and MGNREGA, are special schemes and are the product of these processes, in which the National Government influences the development investment in these sectors. Due to this, the State Government has partially handed over the social sector development from its own responsibility.

In the past, the state and the people have had bitter experiences of displacement and poor rehabilitation and resettlements. Prior to 2006, in many development projects, the state had little control over the rehabilitation and resettlement processes. It was taken up by the displacing agencies. The negative effects of such displacementshave been highlighted before the state, again and again, holding the state responsible for the failures. In early displacements, which were made by GoO and GoI-controlled Public Authorities, the state could not do much in streamlining the R&R situation. Therefore, in the present era when the development processes are basically leased out to the national and international corporate houses, people feel that the state may not be in a position to control and streamline the R&R situation of the state. The R&R Act, 2006 of Orissa is inadequate to safeguard the economic, cultural and social interests and identities of the displaced. This has strongly affected the mindset of the potential displaced. Hence, this calls for a revival of the relationship between the people and the state from a contractual type to a symbiotic type.

References

Autu, R. (1993): *Sustaining Development in Mineral Economies: The Resource Curse Thesis*, London: Routeledge.

Behura, N. and N. Panigrahi (2001): "Functioning of the Fifth Schedule in the Constitution of the State of Orissa", Report submitted to ICSSR, New Delhi by NCDS Bhubaneswar.

Behura, N. and N. Panigrahi (2002): "Marginalisation of the Vulnerable Tribal Communities in the State of Orissa through the Process of Sponsored Development", *Journal of Anthropological Survey of India,* 51 (1), pp. 41-72.

Bridge, G. (2004): "Contested Terrine: Mining and Environment", *Annual Review of Environment and Resources*, 29, pp. 205-59.

Campbell, B. (2006): "Reform Processes in Africa: Issues and Trends", Paper presented in the *2nd International Study groups Meeting*, Economic Commission for Africa, Addis Ababa, 19-21, May.

Cernea, M. (1995): "Understanding and Preventing Impoverishment from Displacement: Reflection on the State of Knowledge", *Journal of Refugee Studies*, 8(3), pp. 245-64.

______(1998): "Impoverishment or Social Justice? A Model for Planning Resettlement", in H.M. Mathur and David Marsden (eds.), *Development Projects and Impoverishment Risks: Resettling Project-Affected People in India*, New Delhi: Oxford University Press.

Fernandes, W. (1994): *Development Induced Displacement in Tribal Areas of Eastern India*, New Delhi: Indian Social Institute.

Govt. of India (2001): "Census of India 2001", Series-2, Final Publication Tablés, Paper-1 of 2001, Directorate of Census Operation, Orissa.

Haan and Dubey (2003): "Poverty in Orissa: Divergent Trends? With Some Thoughts on Measurement Issues", Mimeo, Paper presented at the Workshop on *Monitoring of Poverty in Orissa*, organised by Nabakrushna Choudhury Center for Development Studies, Bhubaneswar, 26-27 February.

Mallik R.M. & N. Panigrahi (1998): "Non-Timber Forest Produce: Collection, Benefits and Management in Orissa", A Study Report of NKC Centre for Development Study, Bhubaneswar, Submitted to The Ford Foundation.

Mohapatra, L.K. (1998): "Participatory Approach in Resettlement and Rehabilitation Implementation", Paper presented at Gopabandhu Academy of Administration in the *Seminar on Resettlement and Rehabilitation.*

_______(1999): *Resettlement, Improvement and Reconstruction in India: Development for the Deprived*, New Delhi: Vikas Publishing House.

Mohanty, B.N. (2009): Vedanta Aluminium Insulating Recession, *Observer*, Feb. 01-15, 9-11, Organisation for Economic Co-operation and Development (1989), Interdependence and Co-operation in Tomorrow's World, OECD: Paris.

Ota, A.B. (1998): "Countering Impoverishment Risks: The Case of Rengali Dam Project", in, H.M. Mathur and David Marsden (eds.), *Development Projects and Impoverishment Risks: Resettling Project-Affected People in India*, New Delhi: Oxford University Press.

Panigrahi, N. (2008): "Socio-Economic Survey of Project Affected Families of Utkal-E –Coal Mines Project", Nalco, Angul, Report Submitted to NALCO.

Patnaik, S.M. (1996): *Displacement, Rehabilitation and Social Change: The Case of the Paraja High Landers*, New Delhi: Inter-India Publications.

Panda, P. and N. Panigrahi (1998): "The Problem of Displaced People: A Study in the Coal Mines of Brajrajnagar, Sambalpur", in R.N. Pati and B. Jena (eds.) *Tribal Development in India*, New Delhi: Ashish Publishing House.

Ross, M. (2008): "Mineral Wealth, Conflict and Equitable Development", in A. Bebbington, A. Dani, A.deHaan and M. Watson (eds.): *Institutional Pathways to Equity: Addressing Inequality Traps,* pp. 193-210, Washington, D.C: The World Bank.

Saxena, K.B. (2008): "Development, Displacement and Resistance: The Law and the Policy and Land Acquisition", *Social Change*, 38(3), pp. 351-410.

Sachs, J. and A. Warner (1995): "Natural Resource Abundance and Economic Growth", NBER, Working Paper series No. 5398, Cambridge, M.A. *National Bureau of Economic Research.*

Stiglitz, J. (2007): "What is the Role of the State", in M. Humphreys, J. Sachs and J. Stiglitz (eds.) *Escaping the Resource Curse*, 23-52, New York: Columbia University Press.

Swain, M. and N. Panigrahi (1999): "Development Displacement and Rehabilitation in Orissa: An Overview", *Man and Life,* 25(3):163-169.

World Bank (1994): "Resettlement and Development", Washington DC: The World Bank.

Section: II
Rehabilitation Policy and Implementation Issues and Peoples' Responses

14

Land Acquisition for Industrialisation and Displacement of People in India: Role of the State

Bhaskar Majumder

Introduction

The core of industrialisation is the conscious application of advanced technologies to increasing human productivity, diminishing the limitations imposed by nature, and generally raising standards of living (Magill, 1997). The origin of industrialisation is located in pre-history, but the fundamental changes associated with industrialisation are usually derived from the industrial revolution in the United Kingdom (UK), that began in the late 18th century and subsequently spread to other countries and continents (Deane, 1984). Between 1870 and 1914, more than 50 million people had to leave Europe for US, Canada, Australia, New Zealand, South Africa, Argentina and Brazil for resettlement, after being displaced from the agricultural sector. The displacement was driven by both the push factor of land scarce Europe and the pull factor of land abundant Americas in particular (Nayyar, 2002, p. 145). In Russia, planned industrialisation after the 1917 Revolution led to the eviction of millions of peasants from their land; they were shunted into urban industries, mining, hydroelectric projects, thousands of collective farms (*kolkhozy*), and state farms (*sovkhozy*). In Japan, the path of industrialisation, based on the post-Meiji Restorations in 1868, ended Japanese feudalism (Magill, 1997). The percentage of population working on land gradually declined, not only in the UK and the US, but also in Japan and China, particularly, since the days of the first industrial revolution in the UK. By around AD 1600, about 2.76 per cent of the total land was enclosed and as many as 50,000 persons, out of a total population of around four million, were evicted in the UK. In China, since the 1950s, around 10 million people have been displaced due to hydraulic and hydroelectric projects alone (Sarkar, 2007).

The decolonised countries of the post-Second World War period accepted industrialisation, as an inescapable route for development, shown by the British industrial revolution. Industrialisation unites the workers as a working class to come out from the local economy-based inertia and start realising their own strength (Plum, 1977). In the economic history of India, modern industry was supposed to dissolve the hereditary divisions of labour based on the Indian castes and hence remove the 'decisive impediments to Indian progress and Indian power'. Industrialisation is seen, as not only inescapable but also a step forward in breaking the 'self-sufficient inertia of the villages' (Marx, 2006).

This paper deals with the dilemma in development, associated with industrialisation. Any path of development will carry with it unequal consequences for people located at different layers of the society. The paper will focus on the questions of displacement of people, following acquisition of land by the state, for industrialisation. As an immediate effect, land acquisition displaces people from the land, without their 'prior informed consent' that earlier provided them sustainable livelihood (Majumder, 2007). We have cited a few recent examples of land acquisition for industrialisation in India in this paper. The role of the State is juxtaposed in the light of that ground reality, ultimately to look into the steps for acquisition of land, and rehabilitation of the displaced people.

The rest of the paper is structured into the following sections. In Section I, we see India as a case of delayed industrialisation. In Section II we analyze acquisition of agricultural land for industrialisation and living conditions of people dependent on land in India. In Section III we present the new law on land acquisition in India and the role of the state. Finally, in Section IV, we propose safeguards, in case, land is acquired for industrialisation.

India as a Case of Delayed Industrialisation

In India, while the absolute number, of population working on land has increased, the percentage of population has remained more or less unchanged, during the post-independence sixty years. Its agriculture is characterised by a monotonically declining land-man ratio, low labour productivity, measured by money value of product and declining share of agriculture in national income over time. During the early decades of planning, the Indian economy went for the setting up of capital-intensive industries, remote from the final consumption point of the people living at the bottom of the economic ladder, and imported technology for production of goods for economic elite that left little scope for the employment of the people, who could have been released from agriculture. Thus, the capital accumulation-led industrialisation, via release of surplus labourers from agriculture and absorbed in industry, did not work. In addition to 'attached labour' on land, the limited skill of the workers, that too not much relevant for industries, prolonged the limited role of industries in providing labour employment. This led to delayed industrialisation in India, since other countries were in no mood to wait for India to catch up.

Development became production-centred, by transformation of natural resources, following collective collection-cum-consumption by human beings, who lived as natural citizens of the world, since pre-historic time. At the early stage of human civilisation nature provided enough resources to fulfil the basic needs of life. Later application of Darwinism led to discontinuation of collection, as the dominant mode of fulfilling needs. The forest-based living did not resist the emerging agriculture mode of living, and subsequent development of agro-industries. Since the scope for agriculture is limited by the size of land and its uses by type and frequency, the question arose about the setting up of industries by location and time. As opposed to limited flexibility in locating agricultural practices, the industrial set-up has higher flexibility by its location and change. Generally, industrialisation is backed by the availability of raw materials, market size-cum-access, transport and communication, availability of physical infrastructure, own industry concentration or cluster of firms for externality advantages, and inter-industry linkages (Bandyopadhyay, 2007). Annihilation of agricultural land and agriculturists' displacement are natural corollaries.

With the urban boundaries expanding to grab rural areas that circumscribe cities, agricultural land shrinks by area. This may lead to reduction in total agricultural output, because of shrinkage in total cultivable land, unless compensated by intensive farming. For countries like India that are delayed in industrialisation, there is now limited non-cultivated cultivable land. This may invite imbalance between agriculture and industry, because unless agriculture is developed enough to ensure food self-sufficiency, industry may fail to develop on a sustained basis.

Acquisition of Agricultural Land for Industrialisation and Living Conditions of People Dependent on Land in India

Late starting countries, like India in the industrialisation-led development process relative to the path traversed by the countries called industrialised today, face several economic problems, due to the falling carrying capacity of land. The initial demographic condition, in India in 1951, showed a size of population, more than that of any country in the world, except China, in time 50 years ahead of 1951. The land-man ratio in India is declining fast, because of the service sector-led urbanisation for both private and public purposes, and conversion of agricultural land for industrial purposes, in addition to the natural increase in population. Moreover, people settled in the rural regions have a history of moving out, because of various push and pull factors. Apart from the natural shift of agricultural land to non-agricultural purposes, there is the state-sponsored shift empowered by the 1894 Land Acquisition Act formulated and implemented during the colonial rule. This Act, empowers the state government to acquire any land from private hands for public purposes, decided implicitly by the state (GOI, The Land Acquisition Act, 1894). Development thus has a tendency to displace the people at the bottom, from the trajectory of development.

Acquisition of agricultural land for industrial purposes in India is not new. Since independence, the state has been executing a top down approach in development by setting up large industries and projects like mines, dams, ports, plants, and expansion of road and rail networks, each of which displaced people. Heavy industrialisation was at the core of India's planned development and hence large areas had to be acquired. The State of Orissa used 40,000 hectares of land for industry, from 1951 to 1995. The State of West Bengal used two million hectares of land from 1947 to 2000 for industry. The private sector has been targeting land mining in Orissa, Jharkhand and Chhattisgarh. Mostly, the mineral-rich as well as government land – abundant backward states are being targeted for the acquisition of land. Construction of dams to feed drought-prone areas, of which the Narmada Dam Project is notoriously known for the disputes around the Narmada River that flows into the Arabian Sea after passing through the states of MP, Gujarat and Maharashtra, led to displacement of people. The acquisition is not only for public sector units, but also for private players, such as, Reliance, ESSAR and Jaypee, for power generation as well as mining that inescapably displace people (Sharma and Singh, 2009, p. 62, 64-66). Displacement by declaration and payment of money as compensation does not make it voluntary.

The World Commission on Dams (WCD) estimated that between 40 – 80 million people had been displaced worldwide, because of large dams. The world's two most populous countries, China and India, have built around 57 per cent of the world's large dams and account for the largest number of people displaced. In India, estimates of the total number of people displaced, due to large dams, vary from 16 to 38 million people (WCD, 2000). Since independence, around sixty million persons have been victims of displacement in India (Fernandes, 2007). In India, development projects, such as, dams and canals displaced about 70.9 per cent of people, by state-led development projects up to 1989. For industrial set-up it was 6.4 per cent. Overall, about 25.5 per cent of the displaced people could be rehabilitated (Table 14.1).

Table 14.1 Displacements by Land Acquisition in India, 1947-1989

Rank (by Number of Displaced Persons)	*Number of Persons Displaced*	*Rehabilitation (%)*	*Purpose/Project*
1	1,10,00,000 (70.9%)	25.0	Dams and Canals
2	17,00,000 (11.0%)	26.5	Coal and Other Mines
3	10,00,000 (6.5%)	30.0	Industries
4	6,00,000 (3.9%)	25.0	Sanctuaries and Parks
---	12,00,000 (7.7%)	25.0	Others
---	1,55,00,000 (100.0%)	25.5	Total

Note: Figures in brackets are percentages of total.
Source: Fernandes and Rao, 1989.

Land was never considered as a factor of production in industry, either because land was abundant in supply, in relation to what was required or because the required land area was insignificant, related to the available land area of any particular economy. The relatively less area, required for setting up of industries, was also because of its high-tech nature-that moves away from dependence on land by area. Land acquisition actually implies acquisition of a physical area that covers cultivable soil area, plus plantations, water bodies, residential buildings, animal sheds, and many other assets that 'land by area and volume' carry. Land is not only a means of production but also a base of livelihood for the land-dependent people to exercise other opportunities, such as, employment and allied activities. Moreover, for the people rooted in the villages in India, land has cultural value, immeasurable by economic parameters.

The nature of displacement may also be exogenous due to war, partition, drought, flood and earthquake. What we are concerned with, is displacement for endogenous reasons, such as, land acquisition for industrialisation. State-led industrialisation displaces settled people by land acquisition. The proximity to market-cum-physical infrastructure for location of industries, means people settled by housing are displaced. While landowners give up land in the process of acquisition by the state, landless people are deprived twice, once by not getting the opportunity to work on land as agricultural labourers and the other by not being in the net of compensation. Obviously, the landless people are mainly dependent on Common Property Resources (CPRs) and are outside the purview of compensation of any type.

The immediate victims in the forward movement of technology are the people at the bottom of the socio-economic ladder. This is the section that is displaceable and is displaced by execution of any infrastructure development projects, which are usually state-sponsored and capital-based. Development thus occurs by accumulation for A and dispossession for B. B lacks the capacity to be a partner in the decision-making processes of development projects, planned by A for multiple boundaries erected, against B by obstructive education, power language (English by colonial inheritance), caste, community, height-weight-colour of the person, gender, access to institutions, and the domain of privileges. The additional factors that perpetuate the vulnerability of B are ignorance, immobility, and tradition-custom-belief. As a corollary, B fails to foresee changes. In the same process, often B symbolizes anti-change. What B fails to communicate is in equal impact of the change planned by the state; it benefits the already privileged A by the power of the purse, education and free walk on the corridors of power; it goes against B who is rooted, tradition-bound, and localised . Thus, development of A and displacement of B go together.

Unlike open agricultural space, industrial space is closed. Hence, 'abrupt' acquisition of agricultural land for industrial purposes will definitely cause twin shocks for the displaced people, one by forced exclusion from land and the other by natural exclusion from newly created industrial space. We call it 'abrupt' even after it had been notified by the state, because the stake-holders were not prepared for it, nor they could foresee it.

Displacement of population, because of acquisition of land by the state, is directly proportional to the area of land acquired, given the region-specific density of population. The land area required, in turn, is directly proportional to the type of projects undertaken. We cite here three examples of actual and attempted land acquisition in India, two for NTPC representing the public sector and one for Reliance Energy Limited in the private sector, all for generation of electricity.

Example I: Meja, District Allahabad, UP

In the power sector, the NTPC Ltd. and Uttar Pradesh Rajya Vidyut Nigam Ltd. (UPRVUNL), on the 22nd of November, 2007 signed a Memorandum of Understanding (MoU) to set up a thermal power plant of 1,320 MW at Kohrarghat of Meja Tehsil in Allahabad District of east UP. The Government of UP acquired a total land area of 2,500 acres for setting up the plant covering seven villages, namely, Kohrar, Bhagdeva, Esauta, Mai Khurd, Salaiya Kala, Salaiya Khurd, and Patai Dandi, that reportedly affected the livelihood of 469 settled households. The displacement had an immediate adverse impact on community support-cum-social integration by the loss of cultivable land, houses, wells, common grazing land, fruit trees, and timber trees. This adversely affected agricultural output, food security (self-production lost), and security of domestic animals. Further, loss of CPR led to loss of fodder and fuel. The worst hit were the landless stone quarry workers, living at the bottom of the social hierarchy, such as the Nishads, Mushahars, Kols, Chamars, Pasis, Dhaikars, Domars, Pals and Muslims, who had no entitlement for compensation post-loss of only source of livelihood.

The major reasons, for pending or delayed payment of compensations were court cases, speed money asked by the *Lekhpal*, disputes related to canal, outstanding bank loans of the displaced persons, errors in name written on the bank cheque book, objections raised by the displaced against the compensation money offered, disputes between Treasury and Senior Land Reforms Officer (SLRO), official apathy, family disputes, and expiry of validity by date shown on the bank cheque. The loss of Common Property Resources (CPRs) remains unaddressed, perhaps because, it is owned by no single individual. Most of the households were reportedly rehabilitated in areas of their choice and received compensation. The households displaced by land acquisition expect that they will be employed by the MUNPL.

Example II: Dadri, Ghaziabad District, UP

To set up a 3500 MW gas-based power plant with an estimated project cost of Rs. 25,000 cr. in Dadri Region in Ghaziabad District, Hapur Tehsil, in western UP, the Government of Uttar Pradesh (UP) acquired about 1,011 hectare of land in the year 2004, in seven villages for Reliance Energy Generation Ltd. (REGL). The villages were Dehra, Jadopur, Bajhera Khurd, Kakrana and Dhaulana. The other two affected villages, namely, Nandlalpur and Baharmandpur, were found to be uninhabited. Most of the land acquired was earlier used for agricultural purposes. Pasture or common grazing land was not acquired. The major assets covered in land acquisition were canals, ponds and wells. On July 13, 2007 the GOI gave environmental clearance to the project.

Land acquisition in Dadri was estimated to have led to displacement of over 6,000 families. The rate of compensation was fixed at Rs.150 per sq yard that was more than the market rate prevailing there, before land acquisition. The market rate immediately after land acquisition was Rs. 300 at the minimum and Rs.400 at the maximum. The loss to the cultivators for surrendering product value per year was enormous, while revenue loss on account of land rent was marginal (Majumder, 2007).

The unorganised farmers formed an association called Maharana Pratap *Sangram Sangharsh Samiti* to protest against the acquisition and claimed a compensation of Rs.500 per sq metre. They also staged a demonstration in front of the Collectorate in August 2004. On 3 January, 2006, the farmers presented their dissent against the amount of compensation. On 30 December, 2006, Reliance Energy Ltd. decided to start the construction work by digging the fields of Sripal Singh in Jadopur Village. The farmers protested against it, but the administration ignored the protest. Following the protests against the poor compensation, and based on the magnitude of loss of fertile agricultural land, the Allahabad High Court Division Bench, on the 4th of December 2009, cancelled the acquisition of land of 2,500 acres, quashing of urgency powers to acquire land, exercised by the then government. It passed an order acting on writ petitions filed by the farmers and the former Prime Minister, late Mr. V.P. Singh, claiming that the petitioners were forced to sign on documents and accept the meagre compensation offered by the Collector. The Court said that the farmers had the option to refund the compensation received.

Example III: Tanda, District Ambedkar Nagar, UP

In 1992 the thermal power plant set up in Tanda, UP was transferred from the ownership of the Government of UP to NTPC, Government of India. The geographic area of the plant remained the same since it was set up. In 2009 the NTPC Tanda thought of its expansion by acquisition of land from the adjoining nine villages, namely, Samariya, Husainpur Sudhana, Salarpur Rajpur, Keshopur Pachpokhra, Hasimpur, Sarifpur, Kakrahi, Ashopur and Ladanpur. We came to know that the people settled in the selected villages had been displaced earlier also. That means that they are facing the threat of repetitive displacement. Such displacement(s) will have unwelcome impact on social relations, impose social Darwinism by the state, empower industrial capitalists by enhancing their unhindered access to natural resources, convert marginal/small landowners into manual labour-based wage workers (supposedly unfit for industrial job), expand labour size in informal sector, and force migration to urban areas. Fixing and paying cash as compensation to the displaced is a non-substitute of life-saving land for the land-dependents. Urban-type resettlement of villagers does not help, because the domestic animals that they own need common space (CPRs) for grazing. Since village space is horizontal, while urban space is vertical, the former for low population density and the latter for high population density, urbanisation does not help the people accustomed to village mode of living. In the absence of recreation of a similar village life elsewhere by rehabilitation of the displaced, the villagers feel robbed of their earlier livelihood. Nearby rehabilitation could be the solution, but not bankable, because of unanticipated further expansion of the industrial plant. The once displaced people remain vulnerable by 'future' unanticipated displacement.

In the context of the above, we present the on-going struggle in Orissa in Example IV.

Example IV: Compensation by R&R: Posco, Orissa

Posco, the world's fourth largest South Korean steel company, had signed a MoU with the Government of Orissa in 2005 to set up a plant, near Paradip Port in Orissa's Jagatsinghpur District, that would produce

12 million tons of steel per annum. The project cost is estimated at $12 billion (Rs.55,200 cr.).

The Government of Orissa on 9 July, 2010 announced a Rs. 70 cr. rehabilitation package, for the 3,000 people who will be displaced, by land acquisition. The package has fixed a compensation of Rs. 17 lakh per acre of private land, Rs. 11.50 lakh per acre for land under betel vine cultivation and Rs. 2 lakh per acre for ponds used for prawn production. People who are alleged to have encroached on government land will also receive compensation. Further, such displaced families will be allotted a three-room *pucca* house with a cowshed and receive a Rs.5,000 relocation allowance. Larger or joint families will get bigger houses and those that do not want new houses will be paid Rs. 1.66 lakh (HT, Lucknow, July 10, 2010).

Public Response

The people, resisting land acquisition, opined that the project would destroy their livelihood that thrives on shrimp farming and cultivation of betel leaves, a highly profitable crop. The strugglers, against Posco's proposed plant, rejected the rehabilitation package for the displaceable, announced by the Orissa Government.

The Posco *Pratirodh Sangram Samity* on 11 July, 2010 decided to intensify the movement against the project and debar the entry of government officials and police into the area. The *Samity* said in a public meeting attended by about 3,000 people that the CM 'betrayed' the people by announcing a rehabilitation package without visiting the area that the project proposed to cover. The *Samity* opined that no package could replace the thriving agro-economy based on betel vine cultivation and prawn production (HT, Lucknow, July 12, 2010).

In the power structure, industry is well ahead of agriculture. The state considers agriculture as a source of surplus to feed industry by both food and intermediate inputs. Hence, the state does not hesitate to acquire land for industrial purposes that show 'forward' movement in history. Nowhere in history has, land earmarked for urban/industrial purposes, been acquired for agricultural purposes, because the accepted trajectory is conversion of rural region into urban region, agriculture into industry, hiking the economy above subsistence level, and shift from nature dependence to man dependence.

New Law on Land Acquisition in India: Role of the State

Article 31, Section A of the Constitution of India (Compulsory

Acquisition of Property) empowers the State to acquire land, based on payment of compensation, at a rate which shall not be less than the market value prevailing (The Constitution of India, p. 14). Nearly after a century, the first Land Acquisition Act 1894 was comprehensively amended in 1984. The conference, of the revenue secretaries of states that followed in July 1989, endorsed the major provisions of the 1984 Amendment. The Draft National Policy for Rehabilitation of Persons (1996) of the Ministry of Rural Development, GOI, acknowledged that cash compensation was not an acceptable proposition for most of the tribal people. The 1996 Policy observed that "majority of our mineral resources, including coal, iron ore, and manganese reserves, are located in the remote and backward regions, mostly inhabited by tribals" (Report, 1996). After a decade, the GOI approved the National Policy on Rehabilitation and Resettlement, 2007, replacing the earlier National Policy on Resettlement and Rehabilitation for Project Affected Families, 2003 (Chakrabarty and Dhar, 2010, p. 4).

The Government of India introduced The Land Acquisition (Amendment) Bill, 2007 in the Lok Sabha (Lower House of Indian Parliament) on 30 November 2007 duly signed by the Minister of Rural Development, Sri Raghuvansh Prasad Singh, that was a Bill 'further to amend the Land Acquisition Act, 1894' (Source: Bill No. 97 of 2007, Lok Sabha, website). Once passed, it will be called the Land Acquisition (Amendment) Act, 2007.

The Bill 2007 acknowledged that the acquisition of land would lead to displacement of people, deprive them of their livelihood and shelter, restrict their access to their traditional resource base, and uproot them from their socio-cultural environment. Land acquisition would have traumatic, psychological and socio-cultural consequences for the affected population, which call for protecting their rights, including those of the weaker sections of society, particularly the tribals and tenants.Rehabilitation and resettlement of the persons and families affected by involuntary acquisition of private land and immovable property, was considered in the Bill to be of paramount importance. Following the Bill 2007, 'public purpose' restricts "the scope of land acquisition under the Act to provision of land for strategic purposes relating to naval, military and air force works or any other work vital to the state, and for infrastructure projects like generation, transmission or supply of electricity, construction of roads, highways, bridges, airports, ports, rail systems or mining activities, water supply project, irrigation project, sanitation and sewerage system, any other public facility as may be notified in this regard by the Central Government in the Official Gazette" where the benefits accrue to the general public. The expression 'person interested' in the principal Act (1894) is proposed to be expanded in the new Act (2007) "to include tribals and other traditional forest dwellers, who have lost any traditional rights recognised under the Scheduled Tribes and Other Traditional Forest Dwellers (Recognition of Forest Rights) Act, 2006 and expanded to include 'persons having tenancy rights' under the relevant State laws".

The Bill 2007 pledged to make the process of land acquisition transparent, through Notification in the Official Gazette and in two daily newspapers circulating in that locality. The 2007 Bill says that the appropriate Government shall, for the purpose of providing speedy disposal of disputes relating to land acquisition, set-up by notification in the Official Gazette, the Land Acquisition Compensation Disputes Settlement Authority. The Bill 2007 mentions that the Collector of the concerned district, before acquisition should ascertain the intended land use and take into account the value of the land of the intended category in the adjoining areas, for the purpose of determination of the market value of the land being acquired.

The determination, of market value of land being acquired, is pledged to include "the market value of the buildings and other immovable property or assets attached to the land or building, which are to be acquired", "the value of trees and plants", and "the value of the standing crops damaged during the process of land acquisition proceedings". The Collector has to ensure that physical possession of the land is taken over and the amount of compensation is paid within a period of 60 days commencing from the date of the award.

Following the proposed Act 2007, the State (of India) owns the responsibility of land acquisition for which the catalyst is the District Collector and the Disputes Settlement body is the Court. The role of the Judiciary is limited by the guidelines provided by the proposed Act. By regulating the market value of the land for "the compulsory nature of the acquisition", by guiding the Judiciary in determining compensation, the state aims to execute the development model that it perceives fit for the country.

A Critique

The catalyst in land acquisition, thus, is the State in India. The 'person interested' in the context of land acquisition by the state, includes all those going to be affected by land acquisition of a particular zone.

De facto, the 'person interested' is the tribals, the original settlers on the land, who generally do not possess any land records in their hands (even many of them being not at all aware of any such needed records), the small and marginal farmers, the tenants and sharecroppers, and the agricultural wage-workers (settled in the locality and the migrants). These 'interested persons' generally do not express their 'interests'. While the migrant agricultural workers, living on the bottom-most plank, are disempowered by the new Bill by not being allowed to ask the District Collector for payment of any compensation, when his employer's plot of land is lost by acquisition for purposes other than agriculture, the employer, being a small farmer, is disempowered by being on the queue to receive compensation, the time between acquisition and compensation being 60 days. It is beyond the capacity of tribals and dalits (socio-economically downtrodden in the Indian society), unless politically mobilised , to raise voice for a compensation equal to 30 per cent mark-up of the prevailing market rate. The small and marginal farmers may feel shaky to move the Court and remain happy with whatever cash compensation they are offered. The Judiciary, due to its cobweb nature may itself be a trap for them. Fear factor works for the holders of petty property lest it is also lost in the process of bargaining and negotiating with the administrative authority. 'Public purpose' interpreted by the state becomes self-explanatory in the absence of participation from the underprivileged public. The trade-off between interests of the lightweight large public and the heavyweight few elite is weighed in favour of the latter.

For launching projects in cities, the state aims for vertical measures, such as, constructing flyovers for surface transport, underground tunnels for metro rail and tube rail so that buildings and other assets possessed by the urbane civil society, both public and private, are not affected. However, when it comes to rural areas, the state targets horizontal expansion by, acquisition of private and collective cultivable land and hence eviction of vulnerable people. It is arguable that the state followed similar measures for conversion of rural areas into urban areas in India and across countries in a time-neutral manner. But the 21st century public response and civil society is sharply different from earlier centuries, in size and density of population, as well as in democracy and voice of people. The question of 'prior informed consent' thus becomes relevant now, that might not have been relevant earlier. The state takes pre-emptive measures by 'inclusion' in the safety net of social welfare measures, those for whom, the State took initiatives to throw out of the development trajectory. Since high growth is urgent for the operationalisation of trickle down, the State first evicts people from land by its acquisition, makes them expendable and then catches them in the safety net. The objects caught in the net are never asked, if they had the right to self-determination in the development map. The map is drawn and guarded by the State.

It takes more than a generation for the households to find out a region to get settled by developing social relations. This inter-generational social identity is destroyed by one stroke of land acquisition, such lands are often under multi-cropping. By acquiring such fertile land, the development strategy of the State remains self-defeated by 'rural displacement-led urban sluminisation'. Extension of the urban boundary by such acquisition subsidizes the better off by assured supply of cheap labour from the 'newly displaced' villagers converted urban slum dwellers. Both land and necessary labour are thus curved out by one single shot of land acquisition for the industry-cum-urban economy.

It is not necessarily true that the concern of the State and the concern of the society are synonymous. The State represents only the dominant political society and camouflages it by an all encompassing behaviour. The State is strengthened internally by imposition of laws it formulates for non-or-restricted access to the original settlers in the forests and on land that is the initial insiders to the resources. The State is strengthened, in the name of protection of forests and land. On the other hand, the State has a tendency to allow private capital to convert natural resources, including land, into consumable goods for the mainstream. The sections that are declared non-mainstream now were the original insiders. These insiders were the tribals and the dalits who distanced themselves from private property understood by 'excludability'. The sections who protected these resources, since time immemorial, not backed by any state laws but as a natural practice in life, because it was not only considered to be their life-support system but also their deities, that are now evicted. By State reservation and acquisition of land, collective social ownership-cum-use is surrendered; what gets supreme is State authority.

Land carries dual meaning by its uses and by the people. Land essentially has precautionary value as opposed to immediate exchange value to its holders. For the State, land is a resource for conversion into Gross Domestic Product. In view of the affected people, it is displacement and loss of livelihood. The ultimate decision-maker is the State that calculates the costs and benefits of land acquisition. The State is also the ultimate protector of the valid citizens. Hence, forced injustice is ruled out from the action plan of the State.

Safeguards in Case of Land Acquisition for Industrialisation

We offer the following safeguards in case of land acquisition for industrialisation in India:

- The 1894 Land Acquisition Act should be repealed because it was enacted in the interest of the colonial government.
- The farmers, whose self-consumption is more than 50 per cent of self-production of food grains, should be exempted from giving up land under distress; otherwise such farmers may face the compulsion to become net buyers of food grains at a subsequent price higher than the initial sale price.
- The target for land acquisition by the State has to be the absentee landlords, the land owners with 'distress-free' double settlement, and the big landowners. The land that remains idle as estate and '*benami*' should be acquired.
- The State has to select barren land, far from human settlement, for the sake of acquisition, for industrialisation.
- The people, of the affected zone, have to be drawn as equal partners in the decision-making processes, right from the time of proposed acquisition of land by the State, with pre-notification, if it is in 'public interest'.
- Even if land-dependent people give consent to give up land, it is to be examined by an autonomous body, if the future of the nation will be endangered by deforestation, diminishing water table, emission of gas and other health hazards. It is also to be examined, if the rooted people gave consent out of fear and political pressure, or for immediate urgency to get lump-sum money as compensation.
- The real resources of a country are its land, rivers, mines, forests, the coastal belt, and above all, the people. A national 'Resource Protection Policy' has to be formulated by the State to preserve these resources.
- Paying a one-time money compensation is no solution for the people who live with land, domestic animals, water, hills and forests. The people, unsettled in the rural region by land acquisition have to be economically accommodated within a reasonable radius, through employment programmes.
- There has to be national level Land Census on a regular basis. All land records have to be computerised and put on a website.

- There has to be a Land Rights Commission, to work as a vigilant, over the activities of the government, so far as land market is concerned.
- The corporate sector as the beneficiary of land acquisition has to be guided by the State, if needed, to shoulder Corporate Social Responsibility by adoption of one or a cluster of villages.
- The compensation has to cover the land price post-acquisition, plus the cost of surrendering domestic animals and other productive assets, in addition to the cost for surrendered opportunity, to have access to common space (CPRs) along with the cost for security loss.
- At least 50 per cent of India's total non-water non-forest surface area, has to remain reserved for agriculture for the production of food and cash crops. A national policy needs to be formulated in this regard.

For the persons who are displaced by land acquisition, the government should in a time-bound manner:

- ensure food security by provision of BPL cards to the displaced families, as a component of India's general food security;
- develop indigenous technology at the resettlement site, through formal and informal institutions for the displaced;
- develop physical infrastructure at the rehabilitation zone;
- ensure micro-credit for the displaced potential entrepreneurs, with no property mortgage;
- promote vocational education and training to the youth, before the acquisition of private land for industrial purposes;
- provide low-cost rural housing to the displaced, at the resettlement site and link it with development schemes; and
- promote resources for repetitive, durable and multiple uses for the development of agro-industries in the resettlement zone.

The suggested measures need to be components of a National Policy on R&R (Annexure-I).

Acknowledgement

I thank M.G. Gupta, Tinku Paul, G.N. Jha, S. Jaiswal, and A. Singh for the field-work. The usual disclaimer applies.

References

Bandyopadhyay, D. (2007): "A Political Choice", *Mainstream,* 45 (13): 4-6.

Chakrabarti, Anjan and Anup Dhar (2010): *Dislocation and Resettlement in Development, From Third World to the World of the Third,* London and New York: Routledge.

Constitution of India (1982): "As Amended up to the Constitution (45th Amendment Act)", Allahabad: Central Law Agency.

Deane, Phyllis (1984): *The First Industrial Revolution, Cambridge*: Cambridge University Press.

Fernandes, Walter (2007): "Singur and the Displacement Scenario", *Economic and Political Weekly*, 42(3), pp. 203-206.

Fernandes, Walter, J.C. Das, and Sam Rao (1989): *Displacement and Rehabilitation : An Estimate of Extent and Prospects,* New Delhi: Indian Social Institute.

GOI, Forest (Conservation): Act 1980 (with amendments made in 1988).

GOI, The Land Acquisition Act, 1894 (as amended up to 1985).

Hindustan Times, 2010, July 10, 12, Lucknow, India.

Lok Sabha, The Land Acquisition (Amendment) Bill, 2007 (Bill No. 97 of 2007).

Magill, Frank N. (ed.) (1997): *International Encyclopedia of Economics*, Vol. I and II, London: Pergamon.

Majumder, Bhaskar (2007): "Development Hydra, Two Cases of Forced Industrialisation in India", Report submitted to G.B. Pant Social Science Institute, Allahabad, India (Mimeo).

Marx, Karl (2006): "The Future Results of the British Rule in India", in P. James and D. Phillip (ed.), *Globalisation and Violence*, Vol. 2, London: Sage Publication.

Nayyar, Deepak (2002): "Cross-Border Movements of People", in Deepak Nayyar (ed.), *Governing Globalisation, Issues and Institutions,* New Delhi: Oxford University Press.

Plum, Warner (1977): *Industrialisation and Mass Poverty: Points from Two Centuries of Debate* (Translated from the German by Lux Furtmuller), Bonn: Friedrich-Ebert-Stiftung,

Sarkar, Abhirup (2007): "Development and Displacement, Land Acquisition in West Bengal", *Economic and Political Weekly*, 42(16), pp. 1435-42.

Sharma, R.N. and Shashi Singh (2009): "Displacement in Singrauli Region: Entitlements and Rehabilitation", *Economic and Political Weekly*, 44(51), pp. 70-78.

World Commission on Dams (2000): *Dams and Development : A New Framework for Decision-Making,* London: Earthscan Pub. Ltd.

Annexure-I: R& R Policy – Some Selected Issues

Issues	*NTPC Policy*	*GOI Policy*
Administration, and supervision of R& R policy	• Land Acquisition Group under Project Human Resources (HR) department will interact with the State Govt., for land acquisition, including mutation and vacation of the acquired land. Estate Officer will ensure prevention of any encroachment.	• In case of *en masse* displacement of 500 families in plains and 250 families in hills, the State shall appoint an officer, not below the rank of District Collector, to be the Administrator for R&R.
Socio-economic Issues for R&R	• Socio-Economic Survey • Institutional arrangements to be provided, for timely implementation of compensation, R&R measures.	• Survey of PAPs and preparation of R&R. • The Administrative Officer shall minimize displacement of persons and ensure the interests of the PAPs.
Focus on ST in a new social set-up	• Additional benefits to ST PAPs for loss of customary rights of forest produce: • financial assistance equivalent to 500 days of MAW; and • efforts to resettle PAPs close to their natural habitat.	• Each ST PAF shall get preference in allotment of land, shall get additional FA equivalent to 500 days MAW, will be re-settled near their natural habitat, and shall be compensated for loss of customary rights over forest produce.
R&R package	• Preparing certification list of PAPs • Resettlement Package • Self Resettlement: • 5 times of basic compensation, payable for the house-solatium and interest (under LA Act) Rs. 50,000 to Rs. 1,00,000.	• A PAF owing a house to be allotted house site, free of cost, not more than 150 sq m in rural and 75 sq m in urban areas. • PAFs may be resettled with the host community and preserve its own identity.

Issues	*NTPC Policy*	*GOI Policy*

R&R package	• *En masse* resettlement (for HSOs over 100, who have not opted for self resettlement):
	• Allotment of government land for Resettlement Colonies (RCs)
	• Allotment of plot in RC to HSOs on free hold basis.
	• Each HSO – 200 sq m plot in RC, free of cost.
	• Additional Resettlement Benefits:
	  • Shifting Grant
	  • Resettlement grant
	  • -Assistance for transit accommodation ? emergency acquisition.
	• Rehabilitation Package:
	(i) land for land; or
	(ii) rehabilitation grant	

Assetless PAPs	• Landless but dependant PAPs on acquired land for livelihood ? grants + incentives on stamp duty and registration charges up to 1 acre for purchasing land. • For rural artisan/small trader/self emp. having shop ? one time financial assistance of Rs. 15,000 + Resettlement Grant	• Each PAF of only BPL category shall get a one-time FA of Rs. 25,000 for construction of house. • Each wage-labour PAF shall be provided a one-time FA, equivalent to 625 days of the MAW.

Issues	*NTPC Policy*	*GOI Policy*
		• Each displaced PAF shall get a monthly subsistence allowance equivalent to 20 days of MAW per month for a period of one year up to 250 days of MAW.
Basic Amenities to be provided at resettlement zone	• In case of cluster resettlement, infrastructural facilities to be provided along with CD Works.	• PAFs shall be provided the basic amenities and infrastructural facilities at the resettlement site as per norms, specified by the appropriate government.
Employment	• NTPC has no obligation to provide employment.	• GOI has no provision for employment.
Transparency in planning and implementation	• Share information and carry out consultations – Public Information Centre (PIC), VDAC during RAP.	• Transparency in policy, through media and Publication of Official Gazette. • Declaration of resettlement zone.
Capacity Building	• Capacity Building, based on need-assessment will be made for PAPs.	• The PAFs shall be provided training for self-employment as part of R&R benefits.
Extension programme	• Welfare activities to be ensured by promotion of: (i) education with emphasis on girl children, Scholarships; (ii) health through dispensaries in villages; (iii) special efforts for vulnerable persons, women-headed households; and (iv) adoption of village.	• The PAFs shall be provided necessary training facilities for development of entrepreneurship for self-employment at the resettlement zone as part of R&R benefits.

Issues	*NTPC Policy*	*GOI Policy*
Grievance Redressal System (GRS)	• A Village Development Advisory Committee (VDAC) comprising representatives of PAPs, State Government and NTPC shall be formed.	• Constitution of GRS under the chairmanship of Commissioner R&R.

Note: FA = Financial Assistance, MAW = Minimum Agricultural Wages, PAFs = Project Affected Families, CD = Community Development, RC = Resettlement Colony.

Source: Government of India, Ministry of Rural Development, 2003, National Policy on Resettlement and Rehabilitation for Project Affected Families – 2003 (Published in the *Gazette of India*, Extraordinary Part – I, Section 1, No. 46, dated 17th Feb., 2004). National Thermal Power Corporation Ltd. 2005, Handbook on Resettlement and Rehabilitation, June.

15

Ultra Mega Power Plant in Orissa: Some Unanswered Questions

Sujit Kumar Mishra and *Nata Kishore Mishra*

Introduction

It is an undeniable fact, that violent displacement of large numbers of people, in the name of development is not unknown in Orissa. Increased attention has recently been given, to the successful rehabilitation component of development intervention. However, in spite of all development, the only process, which is not changing, is the agitations due to development-induced displacement. The local people at the project site do not always welcome the project; the obvious anger being against the manner in which the problems of displacement are being tackled. For example, the Rengali Dam's resettlement blue print was acclaimed to be one of the best in India. However, in reality, it was a failure at the implementation level.

A number of factors affect the success of a resettlement process. These factors include proper implementation of a policy, proper monitoring of the process, equitable distribution of rehabilitation benefits; and above all, sharing of information at the grass-root level and decision-making power at the bottom level. Effective sharing of information leads to effective *ex ante* or preventive decision-making mechanism, which will have an adaptive solution in a sustainable manner.

Ultra Mega Power Plant: An Overview

India is a country of chronic power deficit. To tackle this, the Government of India has planned to provide 'power for all' by the end of the eleventh plan. The Ultra Mega Power projects, each with a capacity of 4,000 MW or more, are being developed with the aim of bridging this gap. Nine such plants are going to be established in Chhattisgarh, Gujarat, Karnataka, Madhya Pradesh, Maharashtra, Andhra Pradesh, Orissa, Tamil Nadu, and Jharkhand. Out of these, three plants will be set up in Tamil Nadu, Chhattisgarh, and Orissa in the first phase. After a discussion between the Central Power Minister Sri Sushil Kumar Shinde and the Orissa Chief Minister Nabin Pattnaik, it was finalised that a plant will be set up in the Lankahuda, Bhedabahal and Kirei Gram Panchayat of Sundargarh District in the State of Orissa. The National Power Finance Commission will set up the project in association with Orissa Integrated Power Corporation. Coal produced in IB Valley will be used in this project and the project is estimated to cost Rs. 16,000 crores (*The Samaj*, September 10, 2009). After the project is set-up, most of the power requirement will be fulfilled.

The Issue of Rehabilitation: Some Questions and Agitations

Three consecutive Gram Sabhas were held to acquire a total of 2,140.470 acres of land in Sadar Block of Sundargarh District, and also to get consent from the Gram Sabha for the proposed coal-based thermal power plant of 4,000 MW capacity at Lankahuda Village of Sundargarh District to be jointly set up by the Central Electricity Authority and Power and Finance Corporation. The meetings were attended by the Additional District Magistrate (ADM), the Block Development Officer (BDO), Sadar Tahasildar, and the Land Acquisition Officer (LAO). The officers of Industrial Infrastructure Development Corporation (IDCO), responsible for acquiring land for the project, in addition to the project-in-charge and the Associate Vice-President of the Ultra Mega Power Plant were also present in the meeting. There is a requirement of 2,447.98 acres of land for this project, out of which 2,107.47 acres is non-government land and 321.423 is government land. The land to be acquired village-wise is shown in Table 15.1.

Table 15.1 Villages to be Affected and Amount of Land to be taken

Sl. No.	*Village*	*Total Land Proposed to be Acquired (in acres)*
1	Bhedabahal	219.917
2	Kandabahal	257.680
3	Semna	155.385
4	Kirei	138.623
5	Kopsiga	481.829
6	Lankahuda	263.090
7	Japanga	540.755
8	Rupidihi	372.210

Source: Sambad, Monday, September 14, 2009.

The types of land proposed to be acquired are: (a) Forest – 59.38 acres, (b) Gochar land "123.25 acres, and (c) Road" 24.96 acres. For the acquisition of the land, Gram Sabha meetings were held during mid-September at Lankahuda, Bhedabahal and Kirei villages respectively.

At the outset, the project in-charge gave some information about the project in all the Gram Sabhas. He further said that the proposed projects would be undertaken with the cooperation of the people. However, the first Gram Sabha called at Lankahuda Gram Panchayat (GP) ended in pandemonium. The meeting was opposed at the very outset, by the *Krushak Sangha Samiti* that declared that they would rather die than leave the village. The people present in the meeting supported the *Krushak Sangha Samiti* in one voice. When questioned, the concerned MLA said that the people were not in favour of the project and as people are opposing the project, he also opposes it, irrespective of the fact that the project belongs to the Central Government. Some of the people likely to be displaced said they would be ready to part with their land, provided they were paid Rs. 6 lakh per acre as compensation.

Even in the second Gram Sabha, it was quite clear that the people whose land was to be acquired by the project, were ready to offer their land, if proper compensation was provided to them. However, this meeting also came to an end with protests from the people. Discussion about the compensation was the main aim of the meeting, but nothing was discussed. Later, a resolution was written, rejecting the setting up of the project and it was signed by everyone present.

In the third Gram Sabha, the project authorities tried to convince those who will be displaced by the project, by providing information about the Rehabilitation Policy of the State Government, and suggesting that they should protest only after fully weighing the losses and gains of the project. Aware of the fact that if the project is opposed without any reason, it will go out of hand, the Sub-Collector explained the displacement and rehabilitation policy in detail. He also replied to the questions of the villagers. Sri Nabin Naik, a villager from Japanga said that 90 percent of his land will be acquired, but the homestead land will not be acquired; as such he will not come under 'A' category and therefore, no one from his family will get employment in the project. Sri Dinabandhu Naik from Kandabahal said that he inherited the land from his ancestors and therefore, the compensation is not sufficient. He suggested that just as government land is taken on lease basis, private land should also be taken by the project on lease, and the owners of the land should be shareholders in the project. Sri Ramchandra Naik of

Kandabahal explained that irrespective of the category, they should be assured of employment in the project. A letter to this effect may be assured by the district administration, so that the people could seek redressal in Court, if this condition is violated. He insisted that if this is not fulfilled, the people will not be ready to give their land. Krushna Chandra Patel living in Kirei said that 24.35 acres of his land in Kandabahal will be acquired by the project; but his homestead land and house will not be acquired, he wonders what his situation would be. He feels that this has been done on purpose by the company. In the same way, Baikuntha Patel and Judhistir Naik from Rupidihi Village asked many questions, related to the plant authorities.

Finally, a resolution opposing the project was passed, laying certain conditions. To sum up, the important questions put forward in the Gram Sabha were:

1. Can the company give share to the affected families in the Plant?
2. Will the value of land, registered in the recent past be considered as the compensation amount?
3. Can the district administration give a written assurance of providing employment to all the affected families, so that, people can go for legal action, if the assurance is not fulfilled?

These are some of the unanswered questions, raised in the three Gram Sabhas, for the acquisition of land, for Ultra Mega Power Plant, in Sundargarh District of Orissa.

Agitation against Ultra Mega Power Plant: Causes and Consequences

The main reason for the agitation is the manner, in which the problem of rehabilitation was tackled in the past and also the promises which were not fulfilled: A steel plant was set up in 1959 at Rourkela by the Hindustan Steel Limited (HSL), and to supply water to the steel plant, a dam was built at Mandira. It is alleged that the persons displaced, due to the construction of the dam, have not yet been properly rehabilitated. In the same way, the people displaced by 45 sponge iron and steel plants, and more than 50 mines are still fighting for their peripheral development and pollution control.

In this context, the people in Sundargarh are apprehensive, that setting up of a 4,000 MW Mega Power Project will upset the environmental balance of the area. The rise in temperature in Talcher area, because of the Thermal Power Plant and coal mines, causes panic in the minds of the people; they are afraid that the same situation may arise here (*The Samaj*, September 10, 2009). Already, because of the dust and smoke from the sponge iron plant, the sky in Sundargarh remains smoky and as such, the people are afraid that the situation will further deteriorate, after the Mega Power Project is set up.

Secondly, in all the past projects of Orissa in general, and Sundargarh District in particular, the resettlement agency was under enormous time and resource constraint, as a result of which the quality aspect of resettlement was compromised to achieve quantitative targets (Garikipati, 2000; Mishra, 2005). There was no consensual discussion with the affected people, prior to their displacement, a factor that undoubtedly contributed to the poor overall outcome.

All these are examples of the failure of the classic 'Bargaining Theorem', propounded by Pigou, which talks about the bargaining procedure of two parties or agents. In this approach, the authorities have to commit themselves, not to carry out the resettlement, unless a mutually agreeable resettlement plan has been devised. However, in almost all the projects implemented in Orissa, the role of one agent was nil, whereas the other agent (project authorities) has showed his discretionary power.

Thirdly, the most important point is, lack of proper dissemination of information. Because of this, some clever people reap the benefits, leaving others behind. The awareness of the community at the grass-root level is very minimal. So, they should be sensitised about the real cost and benefit, about the projects by the project authorities. At times, some people create problems and instead of bridging the gap between the planners and the resettlers, they widen the gap. This leads to anger, disbelief and frustration about the project among the people. For example, in the present context, an incident took place, for which a press conference was called by the villagers of Japanga of Lankahuda GP, who protested against an application submitted to the Collector, Sundargarh, by three Panchayats, in support of the proposed Ultra Mega Power Plant. In the meeting, the villagers complained that the application submitted to the Collector was a conspiracy and the signatures were forged. There are '*dalals*' who try to confuse the common man. All this happens, because of lack of transparency, between the planners and the villagers. These activities will linger the process leading to unforeseen situations, such as, strikes and agitations, which ultimately lead to unnecessary expenditure.

From the above discussion, on agitation in the present context, few issues came to the picture: (i) lack of information about the rehabilitation policy, which is the first and foremost impediment in the proper understanding of any type of development intervention; (ii) proper compensation; (iii) jobs in the company; (iv) share in the company; (v) proper dissemination of information; and (vi) community participation at the grass-root level in the decision-making process. Each of the issues mentioned above are interlinked with each other. The first four are absolutely on proper implementation of policy, where proper and just compensation is the main component, which should also address the equity aspect of the socio-economic lives of the displaced people. The last two are, proper monitoring of the process. For years together, these have been the basic problems, arising in all types of land-based developmental interventions.

The two major questions that arise here are: (i) who will decide the compensation? and (ii) what are the components of adequate compensation? These are the major undecided factors, in all kinds of resettlement studies. However, there is still enough time left to include the grass-root communities in the decision-making process. As this was absent completely, the people lost their confidence on project officials of the ongoing and future projects. As a matter of fact, they are expressing their unhappiness, through strikes and agitations, against forthcoming projects, like, the Mega Power Plant.

Minimizing the Impact: Proposed Solutions

At present, only one law pertains to the regulation of land, acquired by development projects. The basic act, which has guided the regulation of land in India, has been the Land Acquisition Act (LAA) 1894, which was passed by the colonial government, to make it possible for the state to acquire private land for 'public purpose'. Albeit this, the term 'public purpose', that figured in this act, is not defined properly. In fact, the absence of an explicit and proper guideline, which defines the term 'public purpose', makes the application of the whole act, an arbitrary one.

However, as far as rehabilitation experience in Orissa is concerned, the past experiences show, that in some of the industrial projects, only a handful of the people, who got the jobs, received training to upgrade their skills. Furthermore, in some cases, a few of the displaced people have received neither land, nor job, nor cash. It is clear that mere passing of laws does not help the people directly in distress situations. Hence, in this context, a system has to be created, where both the parties, i.e., the project authorities and the affected get to decide the different components of adequate compensation. This will be achieved through the process of

the urban middle class, have always taken a pro-industry stand for rapid industrialisation. In the general elections, both national and regional, political parties of the state have been making false promises to provide jobs to the growing number of unemployed educated youths. It may be recalled, in the 1980s, when the first child sale due to hunger and starvation was reported from Kalahandi, the then Chief Minister of Orissa announced 1,000 industries to be set up in 1,000 days. But public sector, mega aluminium plants were set up in Anugul and Koraput districts, only in the early 1990s, and these two industries displaced more people than the jobs they provided (Meher, 2008).

The development activities in Orissa began in the late 1940s and gained momentum in the early 50s, with the introduction of the Paradeep Port Plan. The major development projects, which induced large-scale displacement in the state, are the industrial projects including the Rourkela Steel Plant, the Hindustan Aeronautics Limited (HAL) and the National Aluminium Company (NALCO); multipurpose dam projects such as the Hirakud, Rengali, Upper Kolab, Upper Indervati, and Balimela; thermal projects such as, the Talcher Thermal Power Station, Ib Thermal Power Project and Talcher Super Power Project; and the coal mining projects in the Talcher and Ib valley coal mining areas. The state's endeavors aimed at encouraging private investment at any cost, have been vigorous. During the last five years, the State Government has signed 43 Memorandums of Understanding (MoUs) with private companies. Notable among them are international and Indian corporate giants, namely POSCO (Korea), Vedanta Aluminium (UK), Rio Tinto (UK), BHP Billition (UK-Australia), Alcan (Canada), Hindalco, Jindal, Tata and Sterlite. Mining projects worth Rs. 3,000 billion have already been launched and projects worth a further Rs.11,000 billion are in the pipeline. Thus, Orissa is fast emerging as a major site for foreign direct investment and multinational development projects, violating the rights of the indigenous population in the hill districts and mineral reserves areas of Orissa (Sahoo, 2005).

Development has been both, mantra and myth, as thousands of crores of rupees have been ploughed into millions of projects, while the promise of employment and prosperity has remained elusive. Agriculture being the source of income and employment, for 85 percent of the people in the state, never was a priority. It has always been suffering from extreme poverty and central neglect, in terms of the economic sphere, due to the unequal allocation of resources. According to an estimation, the poverty ratio, in the state in 2004, was 46 percent, the highest in India.

The cultivable land in Orissa has declined. During 1980-2000, about

26,500 hectares of forest land was destroyed for mines and industries. In addition, the juggernaut of development reduced them to ecological refugees and victims of strategy growth, forcing them to pay the price of development, while others else reaped the benefits (Fernandes, 2005).

The Continued Suffering

The relationship between development and displacement is an ironical one. The State of Orissa, in the process of development, has been experiencing the grim truth of displacement due to development projects. A glaring revelation of displacement in the state is that a significant number among the displaced people is that of tribals, and other economically marginalised rural people, who depend upon the natural resources for their livelihood (Fernandes, 2009). The sacrifice, of millions of displaced tribals, who gave their land, houses and source of livelihood, and suffered in the national interest, will only be recorded as footnotes in the history of the country's development. Their pain and suffering will all be forgotten, in the government's project files and will never find a mention anywhere, as is evident from the stories of the displaced persons at Hirakud and Rengali.

One need not go into a detailed analysis, of the various 'developmental' projects, initiated after independence, and the development mania which continues even today. The fact remains that nobody cares for the DPs. It is only their sheer resolve to build lives in spite of all the adversity and their spirit of struggle to keep pushing for better rehabilitation measures that things have improved. The struggles of the DPs either in Rengali, Upper Indravati, Kashipur and Kalinganagar, or all over the state, has gone a long way in broadening the envelope of the development discourse, as well as contributed to deepening of the democratic norms and ethos in the country. One might not talk here of the Hirakud development project, which affected 285 villages, 18,432 houses, and 1,12,038.59 acres of cultivated land, as they were submerged in the Hirakud Reservoir, affecting 22,144 families. However, all such sacrifices made by the displaced people, will only be counted as a footnote, in the history of the country's 'development' (Baboo, 2006).

Even though the State Water Commission brings out a detailed directory of the various power and irrigation projects, there is no information available about the numbers of DPs and PAFs. Whatever data is available exists only, because of the efforts of the people's movements, NGOs, academics, and researchers. It has been estimated, that in Orissa a total of 14 lakh people, most of them *Adivasis*, have been displaced by the development projects so far (Pandey, 2008). The total number of displaced people in Orissa, during 1951 to 1995, on account of various projects, is approximately 5,46,794 out, of whom 3,25,000 were displaced by dam projects only. Further, Fernandes, Das and Rao put forth, that by 1985-86, around 8,07,500 people were displaced, due to major projects like Hirakud, Balimela and Upper Kolab. The details of displacements and rehabilitation from 1951 to 1991 in Orissa are shown in Table 16.1.

Table 16.1 Displacements and Rehabilitation in Orissa, 1951-1991

Category	*Displaced*	*Resettled*	*Per-centage*	*Backlog of Settled*	*Backlog in Percentage*
Dams	3,25,000	90,000	27.69	2,35,000	72.31
Industries	71,794	27,300	38.03	44,494	61.97
Mines	1,00,000	60,000	60.00	40,000	40.00
Misc.	50,000	15,540	31.08	34,461	68.92
Total	**5,46,794**	**1,92,840**	**35.27**	**3,53,955**	**64.73**

Source: Fernandes and Asif (1997).

The data presented in the table is, only until 1990, but the situation has not changed, much in terms of continuance of displacement, due to developmental projects; in fact, it has increased in this hyped up economic boom, as never before. The situation with regard to rehabilitation is in no way different. The percentage of those rehabilitated is still as low as 25-30 percent of the total number of displaced population. The magnitude of displacement put above, by various groups/individuals, shows the seriousness of displacement in India and Orissa as well, and thus calls for special attention. In the age of liberalisation, privatisation and globalisation, the future will certainly witness more cases of displacement in Orissa.

Displacement and Rights

Development-induced displacement, inevitably leads to violation of human rights. Displacement predominantly affects those, who are politically, economically and geographically marginalised (Mathur, 2006).

The push of globalisation and the state's development policies in the recent decades have, however, endangered the continuation of traditional life-styles. The displaced people are victims of serious human rights violations, as a consequence of the dispossession of their lands and natural resources, widespread violence and repression, and assimilation.

In accordance with international law, Indigenous Peoples and Minorities enjoy all the fundamental human rights and freedom like the people, besides certain international laws which made specific legal provisions to secure and protect their rights. The Declaration on Right to Development in 1986 states that right to development is an inalienable human right. The right to participation is based on various articles of the International Bill of Human Rights, which includes the Universal Declaration of Human Rights (UDHR), the International Covenant on Civil and Political Rights (ICCPR), and the International Covenant on Economic, Social and Cultural Rights (ICESCR). More specifically, the 1991 International Labour Organisation Convention Concerning, Indigenous and Tribal Peoples in Independent Countries (ILO Convention 169) stipulates (Article 7) that indigenous and tribal peoples shall participate in the formulation, implementation and evaluation of national and regional development plans, that affect them (Velath, 2009).

The process, of development-induced displacement in Orissa, takes away many rights from the displaced, that, in fact, are granted to them by the Indian Constitution. Ironically, Article 19 (e) of the Indian Constitution guarantees to its citizens, the freedom "to reside and settle in any part of the territory of India" and Article 21 says that "no person shall be deprived of his life or personal liberty except according to procedure established by law". Thus when the state takes away land, it deprives CPR dependent communities of their livelihood on the assumption that the natural resources are state's properties: "the right the state has appropriated to itself goes counter to the citizen's fundamental rights" (Fernandes and Paranjpye, 1997).

Under Article 19 of the Indian Constitution, all people have the right to freedom of assembly, and freedom of expression and speech. But the Orissa Government and private companies, have consistently disrupted peaceful democratic meetings, by using police and paramilitary forces, which is a violation of the right to peaceful assembly (Meher, 2006). In the last two decades, Orissa has witnessed many struggles, to protect the life and livelihood of people (for example, in the towns of Balipal, Gandhamardan, Chilika, Indravati, Gopalpur, Kashipur and Kalinganagar). The police firing at Gopalpur, Maikanch and Kalinganagar that led to the loss of poor and tribal lives % of those, who opposed mega development projects, can be seen as denying them their basic rights of livelihood, and as an ongoing conflict between the two sides, those favouring 'industrialisation', led by the government, and those opposed to it. If the democratically elected continue to violate the rights of the tribals, which from the perspective of the subaltern is very democratic. The gap between the rich and poor will be further widened the weaker sections of the society will be more dehumanised and excluded, resulting in resistance movements, including violent protests (Samal and Das, 2006).

Land Alienation and Rights of Local People

Land is a particularly contentious issue, with regard to development projects, especially in the areas with tribal populations, and it is important to understand the constitutional provisions here. The tribal land, water and forest alienation took place through a process of gradual, systematic and dubious appropriation of these rights, under the British colonial state's penetration into the domain of customary communal property resources. Due to large-scale industrial and infrastructural projects, the tribal and poor people were displaced, from their productive assets and homes. The Land Acquisition Act of 1894 (amended in 1984) empowers the government to acquire the people's land, by compulsion, for both public and private purposes, also termed as 'national interest'. This Act serves the State, as a weapon for immediate land acquisition. It is in pursuance of this principle of 'eminent domain' by the Indian State that, the property or ownership rights of the State, came to infringe on the rights of the displaced peoples (Ramanathan, 1996).

The eastern Indian state of Orissa appears to have been the latest example, of the immaturity and ineptness that define many of India's democratic institutions. Some of the large-scale acquisitions, in the years succeeding independence, include those for the Hirakud, Machkund and Sileru dams and Rourkela Steel Plant in Orissa. For the Hirakud Dam in Orissa, 1,12,038.59 acres of cultivated land was acquired in the 1950s and today 50 years later, according to the Orissa Government, approximately Rs. 6 crores (out of the assessed compensation of about the Rs. 9 crores) has not reached the 3,098 affected families. The Orissa Land Reforms Act 1960, Section 22 prescribes restrictions on alienation of land, by members of the Scheduled Tribes to non-Scheduled Tribe members. This becomes more important, in the context of the rights of tribals in upland areas, who have enjoyed these lands as their ancestral domain from time immemorial, but the sovereign domain of the government alienates the people from their traditional sources of sustenance livelihood and social networks causing untold hardship and miseries (Sharma, 2003).

The recent protest movements, against land acquisition for Special Economic Zones (SEZs) in Kalingnagar since 2006 have stirred a national debate on the rights of those displaced and brought recognition to the fact that development-induced displacees are stakeholders in development and should be entitled to rights as equal partners (Pandey, 2008). In May 2006, the Orissa Government announced a new draft policy on Resettlement and Rehabilitation (ORRP), which provides for *inter alia*, 'land for land' compensation for the acquisition of land for development purposes and SEZs and employment to at least one person from each affected family. But in Orissa, the resettlement programme neither acknowledged this loss, nor compensated properly, and thus deprived them of their right to livelihood. Besides, the R&R policy endorses a patrilineal view of property rights by giving land entitlements only to major sons above 18 years of age and unmarried daughters or sister solder than 30 years. This raises major issues of social justice and equity.

The Constitution of India does not explicitly recognise any right to be protected from losing one's habitat and livelihood. Article 21, which confers the right to life, is undoubtedly one of the most read into provisions of the Constitution. It is up to the states to determine the extent to which the communities, that are dislocated and suffer loss of habitat and livelihood, can have a say in the matter of being compensated for livelihood losses.

Constitutional Provisions and People's Rights

Local institutions are socially embedded and thereby function in the context of social and economic inequalities. In the process, the local institutions can be advantageous, functioning as an important actor in the implementation of the R&R Policy. Under the Orissa's adaptation of Central Panchayat Extension to Scheduled Areas Act, 1996, (PESA), for the first time in Orissa, it was legally provided that the Grama Sabha or *Srama Sasan* will exercise ownership rights over the minor forest produce. The Act provides an extensive power to the Gram Sabha and Panchayats in the Fifth Scheduled Areas. It mandates consultation with the Grama Sabha and/or Panchayats in the case of land acquisition for development projects, as well as before preparing a resettlement and rehabilitation package for the project affected tribals (Bandopadhya, 2004). The PESA seeks to provide significant protection to the tribals in the Scheduled Areas against arbitrary, discretionary, and motivated action by the State relating to land acquisition. However, the State has never consulted on the type of development people desire, thus violating the right to decide their own priorities as part of right to development, as an inalienable human right (Bharati, 1999).

The Government of Orissa is signing MoUs with a number of companies to set up mega projects. The mining lease given to UAIL, Vedanta Aluminium Limited in Lanjigarh Block of Kalahandi District is illegal, and in fact, unconstitutional. The area where the lease has been given is a Scheduled Area, that is to say, territory governed by the Fifth Schedule of the Constitution of India. In these areas, the Governor is empowered to make the regulation, repeal or amend any law of parliament to prohibit or restrict the transfer of land by/amongthe members of the Scheduled Tribes, or regulate the allotment of land to members of the Scheduled Tribes in such areas (Sahu, 2008).

The Supreme Court in Samatha vs. State of Andhra Pradesh (AP), 1997, categorically held, that transfer of land, by any means including lease by the Government to a non-tribal, is impermissible under the Fifth Schedule. It was held that the executive, while exercising the constitutional power to dispose of its property, should equally be cognisant of the constitutional duty, to protect and empower tribals. Therefore, the Court is required to give effect to the constitutional mandate and legislative policy of total prohibition, on the transfer of the land in Scheduled Areas to non-tribals.

Rule of Law

The rule of law remains eminently measurable, in terms of governance transparency and public accountability of the class of developmentalists, though not fully the theory of development, which may, and does indeed, counter the idea of the rule of law (Baxi, 2009). Thus, a blatant double set of values is apparent in the application of law. Under Article 19 of the Indian Constitution, all people have the right to freedom of assembly, and freedom of expression and speech. The not-so-hidden cost, of development in the State of Orissa's design of developmental governance, escalates state investment and dedication of disproportionate resources in police, paramilitary, and related security forces. The police and paramilitary forces, along with *goondas* hired by companies, have consistently disrupted peaceful democratic meetings, which is a violation of the right to peaceful assembly. The Orissa Government's security forces have been responsible for a reign of terror against the *Adivasis* by arbitrary arrest, torture, custodial death, maiming, rape, and extrajudicial killing. The armed police march past villages and conduct the regular patrols as a way of instilling fear in villagers and extorting their consent. The Government of Orissa has chosen to rely on police power, rather than democratic dialogue: they have launched a concerted campaign, to silence and suppress opposition to the project, through the excessive use of force (Padel and Das, 2009).

The police forces are arresting community leaders, activists, and others, identified as opposing the project, including women and minor % protestors against the UAIL, POSCO, and Tata projects were arrested, under countless false cases. The majority of the arrests appear to be based on trumped up charges, involving dacoity or arson and stringent interpretations of the law. The arrest of Bulka Miniaka, a respected member of the community of Kashipur, on charges of a dacoity on 2 December 2004; the murder of anti-POSCO activist Dula Mandal by pro-POSCO goons on 21 June 2008; the gunning down of social activist Amin Banara near the Tata factory site on 1 May 2008; attacks on several leading activists % some were even murdered % by company hired goons; or State's suppression by force, has been the hallmark of bauxite-mining projects in Orissa, and this underscores coordinated efforts to ensure that bauxite-mining projects proceed as planned, with or without the consent of the local people. The collusion of the Government of Orissa with private companies, in repressing the voices and desires of the people explains the culture of impunity surrounding the incidences of violence. The Government of Orissa should uphold the rule of law, specifically to enforce the Samatha Judgment, cancel any unconstitutional mining leases, and refrain from granting any further constitutional leases on *Adivasi* land in the future (Goodland, 2007).

Forest Rights in Orissa

The National Forest Policy 1988 [2] made provisions to safeguard the rights and interests on forest land of the tribals. The Scheduled Tribes (Recognition of Forest Rights) Bill, 2005 was drafted, to fulfil the need for a comprehensive legislation to give due to recognition to forest rights, % to hold and live in the forest land, under the individual or common occupation for habitation or for self-cultivation for livelihood, by a member or members of a forest-dwelling Scheduled Tribes or other traditional forest dwellers. The Act has thepower to undo what the colonial forest regime had done and provides for the right to conserve, protect and regenerate. It also attempts to re-distribute power, between communities and bureaucracy, and seeks to create a new democratic system of forest governance (Saxena, 2006).

Orissa has had a very long history, of customary rights over forest. Ignoring the symbiotic relationship between tribal people and forests, and establishing industrial projects, laying railway tracks, building towns, and collecting raw material for industries, gave birth to a process of deforestation, rendering insecure, the livelihood of the tribal and indigenous communities in the hilly areas and tribal belts of Orissa. The Orissa Government's agreement with Vedanta Aluminium to allow mining of bauxite deposits in the Niyamgiri Hills, the home of the Dongaria Kondha Tribe, is an example, of how corporate interests, backed by State, support are trampling on tribal livelihoods and threatening an ecologically rich and important region (Sahu, 2008). However, if the recent stand of the Orissa Government towards the UAIL and SIIL is any indication, then the agreement has violated the forest rights act, as the State Government has not taken the local communities, especially the tribals into consideration. It meant the loss of rights earlier by the tribal community over the forest and land resources around them (Mohanty, 1998). In the process, the rights of the working class and the marginalised were violated in the mad rush for exploitative growth. So it becomes the responsibility of all the concerned people to join efforts for building collective and long-standing resistance, against ideas and actions that deprive the people of their rights to life and livelihoods.

Intellectual Property Rights

The predominant tribal people of Orissa are the Khond, the Saora, the Bhuiya, besides the Gond, the Munda, the Dongaria and the Santal, who have good indigenous knowledge. The new development paradigm has separated the large traditional ethno-biotic knowledge and skill base, possessed by the tribal communities of Orissa from the mainstream (Mahapatra, 1994). The assertion of intellectual property rights of the tribals is an apt way of surviving in the market economy. Intellectual Property Rights (IPR) encompass the preservation of indigenous knowledge bases in fields, such as, medicinal plants, agricultural bio-diversity and environmental management, and compensation to indigenous people for the use of their expertise. Apart from plants, the indigenous people have drawn attention to new varieties of crops, organic pesticides, sweeteners, new fruits, preservatives, and perfumes.

In the age of liberalisation, researchers and professional gene hunters sub-contracted by international companies, visit and talk to the tribals and take away their samples. When the samples are processed and a product is made, the so-called discovery is patented and the rights are under the control of the company backing the project. The National

Environment Policy 2004 in Section 5.2.2, envisages the legal recognition of the tribal IPR, but still the traditional knowledge base of the tribals is either ignored or not legally recognised by the foreign sources.

Environment Cost and Sustenance of Livelihood

Environmental protection is clearly provided in the Constitution of India and judicial interpretation has strengthened this mandate. Despite India's commitment at the Climate Convention, green house gas emissions in Orissa have skyrocketed. Orissa's environment and social fabric, are severely threatened by large-scale mining and industrial activities; and they are expected to further intensify in the coming years (Goodland, 2007). Presently, the state emits a significant per cent of the world's greenhouse gases. By 2020, this figure is expected to rise by 1 per cent, at the current rate of development. Environmental clearances were granted to UAIL, POSCO and Sterlite industry, without the use of rapid environmental impact assessment, creating a conflict of interest and violating the judicial principles of the National Environment Policy 2006. It has been seen in the past, that because of the improper environment impact assessment study, the NALCO smelter in Angul has come to be established in a place where the fluoride level in the ground water was already high, and 11 villages were identified that were affected by the increase in fluoride levels, which can have serious health risks.

Besides causing drastic climatic changes and a decline in wildlife habitats, mining in Orissa has undermined the livelihood of thousands of *Adivasis*. It deprives future generations of the benefits of the state's mineral resources. Marginalised people are forced to live with a scarcity of water, as rivers are diverted for industrial use. Furthermore, the ash ponds, red mud stacking, and chemical effluents, disposed into the rivers not only contaminate the water, making them unfit for human and animal consumption, but also causes harm to their agriculture lands and destroys their produce (Samal and Das, 2006). Loss of habitat and livelihood, environmental hazards, inadequacy of the compensation packages, irregularities in the planned rehabilitation scheme, and the socio-cultural impacts on the people are the direct impacts of development activities. When people directly affected by pollution or development projects, are made to participate in the decision, along with the representatives of industry as well as government officials, the industry and the developers cannot exploit the local landscape or disregard the community. Development, in such a context, is more likely to be ecologically-sensitive and justice-oriented.

Conclusion

The human rights dimension, of the development process, has often been sidelined, because it does not fit well within the prevailing conceptions of development. In the recent years, the plight, of indigenous people in Orissa, has become a specific issue of concern, in the international human rights agenda, as well as in domestic legislation and policies.

However, displacement is not on the wane; ironically, the development policy presumes that displacement is inevitable. There is an attempt to justify it, as 'national interest, though it actually diminishes poor people's ability to control and gainfully use natural resources. The technocratic model of development, adopted by the Orissa Government, was thoughtlessly derivative and has proven to be economically iniquitous, environmentally unsustainable, and politically less than democratic, in its denial of the right to livelihood and sustenance.

Development is necessary and indeed, crucial to improving the living conditions of Orissa's marginalised communities. However, it cannot take place without the participation of those who may stand to lose a significant portion of all that is valuable to them. What is thus needed, is an alternative model of development, a model that believes the 'small are beautiful' and effectively counters the 'large' that symbolises unsustainable and elitist development. It has to be man-centred and nature-centric. The fruits of development should not go to the privileged beneficiaries only; all the affected people should be given every opportunity to be a part of the benefits. Resettlement and rehabilitation measures should be participatory, so that all stakeholders are involved in the process of resettlement. Compensatory policies should not be half-hearted and should provide a suitable environment, employment opportunities, education facilities, food security, and health care facilities for the displaced.

The entire issue of displacement, must be seen, as an issue of complex human rights, including political, social, economic, and cultural aspects, and not merely as an administrative issue. Displacement policy, practice, and research need to focus, not merely on the risks and impact of displacement, but also on developing institutional mechanisms that will protect and strengthen the rights of the displaced women and men, including their right to information, shelter and development. The challenges, faced in the process, require strong determination, sustained political commitment from the government, resources, and capacity.

Therefore, it is the responsibility of the State to ensure that the processes of change and goals of development are so guided, as to achieve the constitutional goal of creating a vibrant socialist welfare society.

References

Baboo, Balgavind (2001): "Dams, Displacement and Violation of Human Rights: Case of Hirakud Dam in Orissa", in P.M. Katare, and B.C. Barik (eds.), *Development, Deprivation and Human Rights Violation*, pp. 195-208, New Delhi: Rawat Publication.

Bandopadhya, D. (2004): "Rayagada Story Retold: Destitute of Development", *Economic and Political Weekly*, 39(5), pp. 408-11.

Baxi, Upendra (2008): "Development, Displacement, and Resettlement: A Human Rights Perspective", *Indian Social Development Report 2008*, Council for Social Development, New Delhi: Oxford University Press.

Bhakthavatsala Bharati, S. (1999): "Human Rights and Development Projects in India", *The PRP Journal of Human Rights*, 3(4), p. 20.

Fernandes, Walter (2005): "Rehabilitation as a Right: Where is the Policy?" *Social Action*, 55(2), pp. 123-37.

_______(2009): "India's Half-century Search for a Resettlement Policy and the Right to Livelihood", in Renu Modi (ed.), *Beyond Relocation: The Imperative of Sustainable Resettlement*, New Delhi: Sage Publication.

Fernandes, Walter and Asif, Mohammed (1997): *Development-Induced Displacement in Orissa 1951 to 1995: A Database on its Extent and Nature*, New Delhi: Indian Social Institute.

Fernandes, Water and V. Paranjpye (1997): *Rehabilitation Policy and Law in India: A Right to Livelihood*, New Delhi: Indian Social Institute.

Goodland, Robert J.A. (2007): "India: Orissa, Kashipur: Utkal Bauxite and Alumina Project: Human Rights and Environmental Impacts", Library of Congress: Washington, D.C.

Mahapatra, L.K. (1994): *Tribal Development in India, Myth and Reality*, Delhi: Vikas Publication House.

Mathur, Hari Mohan (2006): *Managing Resettlement in India: Approaches, Issues, Experience*, New Delhi: Oxford University Press.

Meher, Rajkishore (2006): "Globalisation, Industrialisation and the State: A Sociological Study of Tribals Reaction to Industrial Development in Orissa", Paper presented at the Seminar on *Towards a Sociology of South Asia*, New Delhi, 27-28 January.

Mohanty, Monoranjan (1998): "Orissa's Tribal People: Politics of Disentitlement", in Raj Sebasti L. (ed.), *Contemporary Social Movements in India: Achievements and Hurdles,* New Delhi: Indian Social Institute.

Padel, Felix and Samarendra Das (2008): "Cultural Genocide: The Real Impact of Development-Induced Displacement", *Indian Social Development Report 2008*, Council for Social Development, New Delhi: Oxford University Press.

Pandey, Balaji (2008): "The Kalinganagar Tragedy: Development Goal or Development Malaise", *Social Change*, 38(4), pp. 609-26.

Ramanathan, Usha (1996): "Displacement and the Law", *Economic and Political Weekly*, 31(24), pp. 1486-91.

Sahoo, Sarbeswar (2005): "Tribal Displacement and Human Rights Violation in Orissa", *Social Action*, 55 (2), pp. 153-66.

Sahu, Geetanjoy (2008): "Mining in the Niyamgiri Hills and Tribal Rights", *Economic and Political Weekly*, 43(15), pp. 19-21.

Samal, Kishore and Karthik C. Das (2006): "New Mega Projects in Orissa: Protests by Potential Displaced Persons", *Social Change*, 38(4), pp. 627-44.

Saxena, N.C. (2006): "The Resettlement and Rehabilitation Policy of India", in H.M. Mathur (ed.), *Managing Resettlement in India*, New Delhi: Oxford University Press.

Sharma, R.N. (2003): "Involuntary Displacement: A Few Encounters", *Economic and Political Weekly*, 38(9), pp. 907-12.

Somayaji, Sakarama (2008): "Man-Made Disasters: Displacement, Resettlement and Rehabilitation in Orissa : Reflection from the Field", *Social Change*, 38(4), pp. 689-704.

Velath, Priyanca Matur (2009): "Development and Displacement: Rights-based Theoretical Analysis", in Renu Modi (ed.), *Beyond Relocation: The Imperative of Sustainable Resettlement*, New Delhi: Sage Publication.

Xaxa, Virginius (2001): "Empowerment of Tribes", in Singha Roy and Debal K. (ed.), *Social Development and the Empowerment of the Marginalised Groups: Perspectives and Strategies*, New Delhi: Sage Publication.

17

Development and Displacement: A Note on Special Economic Zones

Vinita Pandey

Introduction

India was one of the first countries in Asia to recognise the effectiveness, of the Export Processing Zone (EPZ) Model in promoting exports – Asia's first EPZ was set up in Kandla in 1965. With a view to overcome the shortcomings, experienced on account of the multiple controls and clearances; absence of world-class infrastructure, and an unstable fiscal regime; and with a view to attract larger foreign investments in India, the Special Economic Zones (SEZs) Policy was announced in April 2000. This policy intended to make SEZs an engine and accelerated force for economic growth, supported by quality infrastructure, complemented by an attractive fiscal package, both at the central and state level, with minimum possible regulations. In order to instil confidence in investors and signal the Government's commitment to a stable SEZ policy regime, and with a view to impart stability to the SEZ regime, thereby generating greater economic activity and employment, a comprehensive draft SEZ Bill was prepared after extensive discussions with the stakeholders. A number of meetings were held in various parts of the country, both by the Minister for Commerce and Industry as well as senior officials. The Special Economic Zones Act, 2005, was passed by the Parliament in May, 2005, which received Presidential assent on the 23rd of June, 2005. The draft SEZ Rules were widely discussed and put on the website of the Department of Commerce, inviting suggestions/comments. Around 800 suggestions were received on the draft rules. After extensive consultations, the SEZ Act, 2005, supported by the SEZ Rules, came into effect on, 10th of February,

2006, providing for drastic simplification of procedures and for single window clearance on matters, relating to central as well as state governments.

The main objectives of the SEZ Act are:

(*a*) generation of additional economic activity;
(b) promotion of exports of goods and services;
(c) promotion of investment from domestic and foreign sources;
(d) creation of employment opportunities;
(e) development of infrastructure facilities;

It is expected that this will trigger a large flow of foreign and domestic investment in SEZs, in infrastructure and productive capacity, leading to generation of additional economic activity and creation of employment opportunities. The SEZ Act, 2005 envisages a key role for the state governments in export promotion and creation of related infrastructure. A single window SEZ approval mechanism has been provided through a 19-member inter-ministerial SEZ Board of Approval (BoA). The applications duly recommended by the respective State Governments/UT Administrations are considered by this BoA periodically. All decisions of the BoAs are made with consensus.

SEZ Rules

The SEZ Rules provide for different minimum land requirements for different classes of SEZs. Every SEZ is divided into a processing area, where the SEZ units would come up and the non-processing area, where the supporting infrastructure is to be created.

The SEZ Rules provide for:

- Simplified procedures for development, operation and maintenance of the SEZs and for setting up units and conducting business in the SEZs
- Single window clearance for setting up a SEZ
- Single window clearance for setting up a unit in a SEZ
- Single window clearance on matters, relating to central as well as state governments
- Simplified compliance procedures and documentation with an emphasis on self certification

The major contributions of SEZs for the development of the economy are briefly accounted as follows (Majumdar, 2007):

1. Attracting Foreign and Domestic Investment in Enclaves: Because of the provision of facilities and amenities on the one hand and incentives on the other, the capital flows in.
2. Stimulating Exports: This is the major purpose of the SEZs.
3. Creation of Employment: The SEZs cannot be counted as a solution to the unemployment problem; they are, nonetheless, a viable source of employment creation.
4. Leading to Balanced Development: Though it is good to develop all the regions simultaneously, such balanced development requires a lot of resources at a time. So regional development can be undertaken in stages. Thus, developing certain areas as leading areas like SEZs is a solution.
5. Fostering Linkages with the Economy: Deepening backward and forward linkages with the rest of the economy may bring in technological development and quality production of goods when SEZs interact with Domestic Tariff Area (DTA). New production sectors and catalytic effect to export are induced into non-SEZ areas due to demonstration effect.

Table 17.1 Exports from the Functioning SEZs since 2005

Year	*Value (Rs. in crores)*	*Growth Rate (over previous year)*
2005-2006	22,840	25%
2006-2007	34,615	52%
2007-2008	66,638	93%
2008-2009	99,689	50%
2009-2010	2,20,711.39	121.40%

Source: Department of Commerce, Ministry of Commerce and Industry, Govt. of India.

A Planning Commission study has shown that 73 per cent of the cultivable land in the country is owned by 23.6 per cent of the population. With more and more farmers being displaced through land acquisitions, either for SEZs, food processing and technology parks, or for real estate purposes, land is further getting accumulated in the hands of the elite and the resourceful.

The government has very conveniently taken refuge behind an NSSO study that says that, some 40 per cent of the farmers have expressed the desire to quit farming. After all, what the government is facilitating, is to make it easier for the farmers to abandon their land. It believes that a rehabilitation policy for the farmers, therefore, is the need of the hour. What is, however, not being seen through, is that an agrarian economy like India cannot afford large-scale displacement of farmers. It will lead to social unrest of a kind which has not been witnessed. What India needs desperately is a policy paradigm that restores pride in agriculture, stops take-over of agricultural lands, and ensures sustainable livelihoods for 600 million farmers.

Development, Displacement, SEZs, and other Concerns

Every development project essentially requires the large chunks of land, which leads to displacement of local inhabitants, having immense social, economic, psychological, environmental, and cultural implications. There has been little analysis of how to integrate people into development, since the development is for people. There are four essential components in the human development paradigm, as put forth by Mahbub ul Haq. They are: equity, sustainability, productivity and empowerment (Haq, 2000). Unfortunately, none of these paradigms are considered seriously, when people are being displaced for development projects. Displacement deprives the oustees of the community life and thus development becomes relatively irrelevant for the displaced. "...Displacement can be conceived as the total deprivation of the community life, amenities, facilities, assets, access to natural resources, and the hardships involved before, during and after the process (Verma, 2004)".

Michael Cernea identifies the various risks of impoverishment due to displacements % landlessness, joblessness, homelessness, marginalisation, increased morbidity and mortality, food insecurity, loss of access to common property, and social disintegration (Cernea, 1996). By giving the examples of a few projects (dams) Enakshi Ganguly Thukral narrates the trauma of displacement and the inhuman and cruel approach adopted by the project authorities. The psychological preparedness for displacement is never given consideration. The process of rehabilitation is itself leading to more displacement. She also highlights the problems of women in displacement. She writes, "Land Acquisition Act 1984, the main law of acquisition reveals a gender bias, which seems to reinforce the existing situation of women's lack of ownership of land and property. Similarly, lack of gender sensitivity is present in almost all the policies that govern rehabilitation and resettlement (Thukral, 1992)." Highlighting the plight of tribal communities, Hari Mohan Mathur says, "Nowhere are the effects of displacement more disastrous than in the case of the tribal people, whose very survival is already at stake with their land, their sacred shrines, the historic monuments, their homes and villages affected; their whole life falls apart (Mathur, 1995)." Thus many displaced tribals drift towards the nearest city to join the burgeoning number of slum dwellers.

The imminent displacement of thousands of people and livelihoods in the countryside, where these SEZs are slated to come up, shall lead to massive protests. It is worth noting that, while a fact sheet on SEZs on the Government of India website, gives details of the number of approved and proposed SEZs, their land requirements as well as export and employment potential, there is no mention of the number of people to be displaced by these zones, leave alone how the government intends to attend to the issues of displacement. Indeed, the entire website, dedicated to SEZs by the ministry of commerce and industry, makes no mention of this necessary 'first step' for the establishment of a SEZ. In fact, in a special issue of seminar magazine dedicated to SEZs, in February this year, the minister for commerce, Kamal Nath, has gone so far as to say in an interview that SEZs have nothing to do with displacement (Gopalakrishnan, 2007). The silence, as well shall see below, is in keeping with the discourse of independent India's development 'for the greater common good'. It is a silence, however, that in fact has been bitterly contested in the country, especially, since the 1980s, with the emergence of people's struggles for justice against large-scale development-induced displacement. (*Ibid*., 2007)

The increasing role of the state as the promoter of corporate-led economic growth is underlined by the acquisition of land for SEZs and the transfer of ownership of this land to 'developers'. Displacement thus gets pushed to a private arena with compensation, potentially negotiated by the market and without the state's responsibility for rehabilitation. Considering that these SEZs will acquire thousands of hectares of land with little regard to land ceiling provisions, with upto a minimum of 1,000 hectares for multi-product and 100 for service sector SEZs, the displacement and disruption of livelihoods to be caused by SEZs and their grave implications are emerging, even as the country witnesses steadfast resistance by peasants; and state violence and repression in West Bengal,

Orissa, Andhra Pradesh or Maharashtra.

Let us discuss some of the case studies, wherein SEZs have led to displacement of people, livelihoods and environment.

The Steel Plant and Port – Erasama Block, Kujang Tehsil, Jagatsinghpur District, Orissa

The South Korean Pohang Steel Companies (POSCO's) investments in Orissa state have been marred with controversy, violence and stiff opposition. News about tension in Jagatsinghpur has been flashed over days in different newspapers and television channels. While local resistance against the project is a critical aspect of the issue, a new dimension to POSCO's plans has emerged which deserves more scrutiny. There are serious social and environmental issues embedded in and around this project. The Government of Orissa actually accepted a project which was rejected by Brazil on the grounds that the company was not ready to pick up ore at market prices, according to report in *The Hindu*. But the Orissa Government laid down the red carpet and offered SEZ status to the project, along with several privileges, including export of iron ore, sale of raw material at cheap rates, and so on. The setting up of the South Korean Pohang Steel Company, POSCO and port at the cost of Rs. 55,000 crores required a diversion of 1,253.255 hectares of forest land for non-forest use. There is a mandatory procedure to be followed for the clearance of the forest land as per the Forest Conservation Act, 1980. The grant of clearance would mean felling of about 2,80,000 trees.

Located about 10 kilometres from the famous Paradip Port, the proposed plant and port area would affect 3 Gram Panchayats of the Erasama Block. These include 7 revenue villages with 11 hamlets. While the official figure of the number of families being affected and displaced is quoted as 'up to 400', according to the local leaders of the movement against the POSCO project, the entire population of 22,000 will be affected by the project, due to displacement of livelihoods based on a thriving agricultural economy. Apart from paddy cultivation, the most critical livelihood support is provided by the cultivation of *paan* or betel leaf. The local cultivators say that betel leaves are a substantive source of income for the people, generating income in lakhs of rupees. This is corroborated by a detailed field investigation on the matter. In addition, cashew nut cultivation and pisciculture (fish breeding) are other important livelihood sources for the people of the area. The proposed port at Jatadhari (Estuarine region of Erasama) would also directly displace the livelihoods of several fishing communities, as the Jatadhari estuary serves as a spawning and breeding ground for several species of fish. It will also cause irreversible damage to the coastline. The port activities will include construction of jetties and extensive dredging in areas, which are currently fishing grounds for the people of the area, and will, therefore impact the entire coastal ecosystem of the region. Furthermore, one of the most prime issues has been the threat to the nesting habitat of the endangered Olive Ridley turtle, as a result of this project. Several conservationists have pointed out that if the port is allowed to come up, it will adversely affect the turtle nesting beaches in the Gahirmatha Marine Sanctuary, where nearly 4,00,000 Olive Ridley species come every year for nesting. For the last two years, environmentalists have been highlighting the massive impact that the POSCO steel project and captive port will have on the coastal ecosystem and the Gahirmatha Sanctuary along the east coast a breeding ground for the endangered Olive Ridley turtle.

POSCO's plans include setting up a steel plant, mining operations, a captive port and allied activities in Orissa. With the delay in the grant of Special Economic Zone (SEZ) status, POSCO began pursuing environment and forest clearances for its two components – steel plant and port – separately in May and June 2007. Both these components have, since, been granted environment clearance by the Ministry of Environment and Forests (MoEF), despite opposition at the mandatory public hearing in April 2007. And neither of the clearance processes tried to look at all the three components of the project as part of the same 'plan'; nor were the environment and social impacts assessed cumulatively.

Displacement and Destruction of Livelihoods in Nellore District, Andhra Pradesh (India) due to SEZ and Expansion of Port

An International Fact-Finding Mission (FFM), comprising eminent civil society representatives from Thailand, Malaysia, Philippines and India, visited Nellore District of Andhra Pradesh and expressed great concern over the displacement and loss of livelihoods of the poor and landless tribal communities in those districts, due to construction of Special Economic Zones (SEZ) and expansion of a port in Krishnapatnam. The mission observed and verified violations of the right to food and livelihood in Midderevu, Ramalingapuram and N.M. Kandiga ST Colony in Nellore (in Tada) and concluded with a set of observations and recommendations to the Andhra Pradesh Government. The mission observed that due to expansion of the port, four villages are facing threats of imminent eviction and altogether 14 villages were exposed to the threats of livelihood loss.

These villages were mainly inhabited by poor landless tribal and traditional fisher folks, who had poor assets and no land titles. They were largely dependent on Common Property Resources (CPRs) and fishing in back water and sea for survival. The eviction would result in complete destruction of their livelihoods and would expose them to extreme vulnerable conditions. The state government had proposed a relocation site for the four villages, far away from the back water and sea, which would endanger their livelihoods as fisher folks. Moreover, the landless fisher families, who would be victims of marine and back water pollution, would not receive any compensation and/or rehabilitation. The FFM team observed that these poor villagers were largely uninformed about the expansion of the port during the planning and initial phase of allotment of land, and no consultation took place at the grass-root level, to enable them to voice their opinions. It was further observed by the FFM team, that the state authorities did not pay any attention to the villagers' pleas of restricting further expansion of the port. The villagers also demanded for land and financial assistance from the state to pursue their livelihoods in a better way; but these demands too failed to generate any response.

The FFM team concluded that the new port would create very little employment opportunities for the local people, as this would be highly mechanised and the activities in the port would result in large-scale pollution of the surrounding environments. The dredging done by the authorities for expansion of the port, had already destroyed the breeding ground of the fishes in the backwater and the fisher folks were suffering from poor catches. In brief, the FFM team concluded that expansion of port in Krishnapatnam violated the Right to Food (RTF) of hundreds of households in 14 villages, by restricting their access to food and food producing resources and by polluting these resources.

Coastal Environmental Concerns (Displacement of Coastal Communities)

The three states that cornered the maximum number of approvals were the coastal states of Maharashtra, Andhra Pradesh and Karnataka (followed closely by Tamil Nadu). The scale of activity along the coast is bound to displace coastal communities. The fishing community has come out strongly against SEZs, because forced land acquisitions and destruction of the shoreline have affected their livelihoods.

Coastal Andhra Pradesh

The Coastal Corridor of Andhra Pradesh, as the new attempt at industrialisation of the coastline is called, will be a combination of SEZs, a Petroleum Chemical, Petrochemical Investment Region (PCPIR), private ports, airports, and a sea port corridor, known as the Vadarevu-Nizampatnam Industrial Corridor (VANPIC). The land to be acquired for the corridor is a staggering 50 lakh acres. Destruction of the coastline has already started insidiously. Several SEZs have come up in the stretch from Ichapuram to Tada and the locals are already fighting, mostly losing battles with big businessmen, supported by the government in a desperate attempt, to protect their villages, dwellings and livelihoods, and to stop the displacement of the communities. At stake is the future of lakhs of people along the coastline, including fishermen, farmers, labourers and others. The destruction is taking place bit by bit. The SEZs and ports have displaced large numbers of farmers all along the coast. Now, a stretch between Bheemunipatnam and Kakinada (132 km) is being converted into the PCPIR. This will be followed by VANPIC in the second phase. For the PCPIR, a whopping 600 sq km of land is to be acquired to locate industries. The Polavaram Project in East Godavari, conceived ostensibly to provide drinking water, will see its left main canal actually meeting the needs of water-guzzling industries. Fishermen in villages along the coast are going to be hit hard, very hard, and as many as 49 villages in Visakhapatnam District and 10 villages in East Godavari District will be affected.

The other aspect of the corridor project is the death of an ecosystem. After the petrochemical industries come up, the effluents will be flushed out into the sea. There are claims that the industries will treat the water by reverse osmosis, but this is rarely done. Since pharmaceutical companies have already come up on the coast, the fish population has come down. Fishermen mention sightings of thousands of dead fish. In Achyutapuram, Visakhapatnam District, people are fighting attempts by the Brandix SEZ to release effluents into the sea. According to the Visakha District Traditional Fishermen's Federation, about 700 Olive Ridley turtles and 11 dolphins were found dead in February, 2010 at the place in Parvada Mandal, where the NTPC releases its effluents. The federation estimates that so far about 36 tons of fish have died of pollution-related causes this year. Environmentalists believe that the project will sound the death knell for the ecosystem. The coastal ecosystem is going to be hit and the estuaries where fish breed will become uncongenial to various species. There are seasonal streams in Bheemunipatnam that carry micronutrients into the sea. When the streams flow, the fish swim closer to the coast and fishermen catch them. If such streams are tinkered with, there will be no fish according to environmental activists.

Even the environment impact assessment studies are based on parameters that will not hold good, when industries are set up along the coastline. The reports only look for toxicity levels that might endanger humans. If they are below such parameters, the studies clear such emission levels, without realising the threat to other species and the ecology by extension. This will definitely influence the livelihoods of the coastal communities and in many cases, displace them involuntarily for livelihoods." The wildlife experts are concerned about the deathblow to the bird preservation sites in Andhra Pradesh due to SEZ units. Sites such as Naupada swamp, Telineelapuram in Srikakulam, and Veerapuram in Anantapur, which are home to pelicans; and Kondakarla Ava in Visakhapatnam, and Uppalapadu in Guntur, which are habitat for migratory birds, are likely to get affected. The proposed SEZ in Mangalgiri Mandal in Guntur District where Uppalapadu Bird Sanctuary is situated, will be affected since a SEZ leads to increase in pollution. The AP Biodiversity Board also took up the issue in Anantapur District, owing to the violation of Bio-Diversity Act." (Report by U. Sudhakar Reddy in *Deccan Chronicle*, 22nd September, 2008)

The Case of Gujarat

Another SEZ project that received notification despite the company having a history of environmental violations, is Adani's Mundra SEZ in Gujarat. The company, which had a presence in the area for almost a decade, has destroyed mangrove forests, along the Mundra Coast, in Kutch District in order to construct a port. The Adani Group has already been allotted around 19,768 acres of land for the project, making it the biggest landlord in Gujarat. Most of the acquired are a comprises grazing land and creek land, belonging to 15 villages along the coast. The project is also within the coastal regulation zone and has displaced the fishing community and a fishing economy worth over Rs.9 crores. The Jaths, the local fishing community, had been struggling to protect the traditional paths to their fishing creeks that were going to be acquired for an airstrip for the Adanis. They had even filed a case, but were forced to settle for a compromise under intense pressure from the company.

The Case of Karnataka

In Karnataka, SEZs are planned at Tadri in Uttara Kannada, Padubidri in Udupi, and Baikampady in Dakshina Kannada. Padubidri was where Cogentrix was to set up its power plant. The Barge Mounted Power Plant (BMPP) and the expansion of Tadri Port have been, and continue to be, severely criticised by the local people for the negative social, economic and environmental impacts they can have. Tadri is situated on the banks of the fertile and productive Aghanashini Estuary and the villagers fear the fallout of such 'development' on their rice-fields, salt-pans, fisheries, clam collection, and mangrove diversity. Tadri, in fact, had a ship-breaking unit in the early 1990s. This was shut down under public pressure, on grounds of ecological damage, and is reflective of what the people of this area consider more important.

Food Security Threat

The SEZ Act, by allowing acquisition of (so-called single cropped) agricultural land for such zones, is threatening the food security of the country, with the stagnation of food production and reduction in yields for a decade, even with the SEZs.

National Policy on Resettlement and Rehabilitation, 2007

Following the killings in Nandigram in West Bengal, displacement because of the SEZs, became the focus in India. The Prime Minister, Dr. Manmohan Singh, referred to the formulation of a policy for rehabilitation of the displaced persons, but failed to give any assurance on the repeal of the draconian Land Acquisition Act of 1894 (LAA) and its amended form of 1984. On 11 October, the Union Cabinet approved the National Policy on Rehabilitation and Resettlement (NPRR) 2007, to replace the existing National Policy on Resettlement and Rehabilitation for Project Affected Families, 2003.

Displacement for the "greater common good" was the phrase enshrined in the developmental state's history by independent India's first Prime Minister, Jawaharlal Nehru, as he charted his vision of progress and modernity for India. Exercising the powers of eminent domain, as articulated by the colonial government, the state dispossessed at least 50 million people of their land and livelihoods under the colonial Land Acquisition Act, 1894. Most of these people are now untraceable and they or their descendants form the millions living in urban shanty towns across the country. Years of popular and mature agitation on the issue however, have not translated into a law on the issue of displacement, Resettlement and Rehabilitation (R&R) in the country. The first central policy on R&R was put in place in 2004 and the newest one, National Rehabilitation and Resettlement Policy (NRRP), more recently towards the end of 2007.

The Spirit of NPRR

It states: "...There should be a clear perception, through a careful quantification of the costs and benefits that will accrue to society at large, of the desirability and justifiability of each [development] project. The adverse impact on affected families – economic, environmental, social and cultural – needs to be assessed in a participatory and transparent manner. ...The aim should be to minimise large scale displacement, as far as possible. Only the minimum area of land commensurate with the purpose of the project may be acquired. Also, as far as possible, projects, may be set up on water land, degraded land or un-irrigated land. Acquisition of agricultural land for non-agricultural use in the project may be kept to the minimum; multi cropped land may be avoided to the extent possible for such purposes, and acquisition of irrigated land, if unavoidable, may be kept to the minimum." (http://www.prsindia.org)

Despite these caveats of concern for the displaced and the democratic process, however, nowhere is the right to inform consent legalised in the policy or in any other related law, such as, the LAA, 1894. Iyer (2008), outlining some basic principles for a policy and law regarding displacement emerging from the struggles of the people displaced by large dam projects (the logic may be extended to displacement due to SEZs) has argued, "Where the LAA 1894 is used for acquiring land, the acquisition needs to be made (a) contestable (not merely in regard to compensation, but also in relation to the public purpose, which is the justification for displacement); (b) procedurally, more humane and equitable; and (c) justice in terms of compensation, with due regard to the amount, needed for buying land or property (house, shop) in the resettlement area." He adds, "There is a cruel irony, in describing the involuntary and helpless victims of a project as stakeholders, and this is compounded, when they are put on the same footing, as those who stand to benefit from the project. Let us not forget that, while in the case of the former, existing rights (i.e., natural and often centuries old rights of access and livelihoods) are taken away, in the case of the latter, the project, by diverting river waters through canals, confers new rights not earlier enjoyed. The former are stake-losers, whereas the latter are stake-gainers."

Highlighting the lacunae of policy planning in India, Cernea says: "Worst consequence of displacement-impoverishment and violation of basic human rights happen most, when national resettlement policy guidelines are not effective. The key to sound resettlement is to adopt a people-centered development policy, not a property compensation policy" (Cernea, 1996). By emphasising on compensation package, there seems to be proposal of cash compensation only, instead of resettlement facilities. The entire compensation is used for immediate consumption purpose, leaving the displaced with nothing, to replace their lost income-generating assets and opportunities. In a report published by the Asian Centre for Human rights, on the review of Draft National Rehabilitation Policy(NPR), 2006, a detailed analysis of the draft has been carried out:

Preamble of the Policy: India's **Draft National Rehabilitation Policy 2006 (NPR)** in its preamble recognises "traumatic, psychological and socio-cultural consequences on the displaced populations, which calls for affirmative State action for protecting their rights", the need for "the active participation of affected persons", "Social Impact Assessment", Environmental Impact Assessment", "the desirability and justifiability of each project", "Tribal Development Plan", etc. The preamble promises all happiness the displaced communities could desire for. But the promises in the "Preamble" are not reflected in the operative part of the Draft Policy and hence do not provide safeguards.

Exclusion of the Displaced: The call for "the active participation of affected persons" (clause 1.2 of the Draft Policy), in the process of resettlement and rehabilitation, is not reflected in the processes of development of the project. First, the affected persons do not have the right to be consulted, prior to finalisation of their lands as the project site. Under Clause 6.1, in cases where displacement involves 400 or more families *en masse* in plain areas, or 200 or more families *en masse* in tribal or hilly areas, Desert Development Program (DDP) blocks or areas mentioned in Schedule V and Schedule VI of the Constitution of India, the Appropriate Government shall declare, by notification in the Official Gazette, the area of villages or localities as "an affected zone of the project". The affected persons have no say in the process of determination of a project site, even if it is on their lands or even if there might be other alternative sites.

The Draft Policy also calls for preparation of Social Impact Assessment (SIA) report and Environmental Impact Assessment (EIA) report by the Requiring Body, for all projects (except linear projects) involving physical displacement of 400 or more families *en masse* in plain areas, or 200 or more families *en masse* in tribal or hilly areas, DDP blocks and areas mentioned in Schedule V and Schedule VI of the Constitution of India. But there is no provision for inclusion of the affected persons or their representatives, while conducting the EIA and SIA. The Draft Policy provides for the constitution of a "multi-disciplinary expert group" to examine the SIA and EIA reports. Members are nominated by Central and State governments. There is no accountability, independence or transparency in the process of examination of the SIA and EIA reports. There is also no provision for consultation with the affected families during the final preparation of the SIA and EIA reports, prior to their submission, to the expert group for examination.

Exclusive Powers: Clause 4.6 of the Draft Policy gives sweeping powers to the Ministry of Defence, to acquire land in connection with national security and the Ministry of Defence is exempted from conducting any SIA or EIA. Therefore, if a nuclear plant is set up for national interest or defence purposes, no one can oppose it. The Draft Policy also lays stress on the State's power to "compulsorily acquire any land under the Land Acquisition Act, 1894" by application of the emergency clause of the Act. Clause 6.23 of the Policy provides that "Emergency provisions under Section 17 of the Land Acquisition Act, 1894 should be used rarely". However, experiences of the application of the Land Acquisition Act, since 1894, show that invocation of Section 17 of the Act is the rule and its non-application is a rarity.

Administrator for Resettlement and Rehabilitation: Wherever there is large-scale displacement, the Draft Policy provides that the State Government shall appoint the Administrator for Resettlement and Rehabilitation, who is an officer not below the rank of District Collector, to oversee the resettlement and rehabilitation plan. But the Administrator for Resettlement and Rehabilitation may delegate his/her powers and duties to any officer, not below the rank of *Tahsildar* or equivalent. This will seriously impact the rights of the affected persons as an officer of the rank of *Tahsildar*or equivalent, usually does not have the knowledge to understand the magnitude of the problems, to oversee the resettlement and rehabilitation plan.

Enhancing Displacement: One of the principal objectives of the Draft Policy is to "minimise displacement". Contrary to the objectives, the Draft Policy allows further displacement of non-project affected persons from their land, in the process of resettling the project affected families in a particular resettlement zone. Sub-clause (b) of Clause 6.11 states, "If sufficient Government land is not available there, then land may be purchased or acquired under the Land Acquisition Act, 1894 for the purposes of resettlement and rehabilitation scheme/plan." This implies that the State has the power to evict anybody from his/her land, in order to resettle the project affected persons. The Draft Policy also lays down that the State can use its emergency powers, under the Land Acquisition Act, to evict such people. On the other hand, the Draft Policy is silent on the rehabilitation of these displaced persons from the resettlement zones. This will create an endless cycle of displacement, rather than solving the problem.

One of the functions of the Administrator for Resettlement and Rehabilitation is, to "acquire adequate land for the project" (sub-clause (vi) of Clause 5.5). This is in conflict with one of the main objectives of the Policy which states, "To minimise displacement and to promote, as far as possible, non-displacing or least-displacing alternatives" (sub-clause (a) of Claus 2.1). It is clear that more the land is acquired for the project; more will be the number of displaced persons.

Lack of Safeguards: The Draft Policy fails to provide adequate safeguards to the displaced persons. Under sub-clause (iv) of Clause 6.4, only those project affected families, who are/were having possession of forest lands prior to the 25th October, 1980, will be included in the survey of the Administrator for Resettlement and Rehabilitation. In effect, only the affected families, who are/were having possession of forest lands prior to the 25th October, 1980 will be entitled to the benefits of the NRP-2006. This is not in consonance with the Scheduled Tribes and Other Forest Dwellers (Recognition of Forest Rights) Act of 2006, whose cut, off date for ownership of land rights is 13 December 2005. The Draft Policy does not guarantee land for land or adequate lands to the Affected Families (AFs). Clause 7.4 states that each AF owning agricultural land in the affected zone and whose entire land has been acquired "may be allotted" agricultural land or cultivable wasteland to the extent of actual land lost, subject to a maximum of one hectare of irrigated land or two hectares of un-irrigated land/cultivable wasteland, "if government land is available". The phrases like "may be allotted" and "if government land is available" give enormous discretionary powers to the governments.

The compensation package is ridiculous: Clause 7.7 of the Draft Policy provides that in case of allotment of wasteland/degraded land in lieu of acquired land, each AF shall get a one-time financial assistance of only Rs.10,000 per hectare for land development. In effect, an AF can get a maximum of Rs.20,000 compensation. Also, in case of allotment of agricultural land, one-time financial assistance of only Rs.5,000 per AF is provided. The state governments have been acquiring the lands under the Land Acquisition Act of 1894 and selling these appropriated lands to make profits. There is little guarantee for employment for the oustees. According to Clause 7.11, employment will be provided by the Requiring Body, only to those affected families who have lost their employment due to the project. Also, such employment will be "subject to availability of vacancies and suitability of the affected person for the employment". Clause 7.12.1 states that Affected Families who have not been granted employment or agricultural land, shall be entitled to a Rehabilitation Grant, equivalent to 750 days' minimum agricultural wages.

Impact on Weaker Sections: According to the definition of "affected family" as provided in sub-clause(s) of Clause 3.1 of Chapter III, the affected family, among others, must have been "residing continuously for a period of not less than three years preceding the date of declaration of the affected zone". Tribals who practice traditional mode of agriculture, such as shifting cultivation, which requires temporary shifting from one place to another place every year for the cultivation of crops, and other nomadic forms of life, may not be "residing continuously for a period of three years" at a particular place and hence may not come under the strict definition of "affected family" to get the benefits under this Policy.

The Draft NRP-2006 has dealt with displacement of Scheduled Caste and Scheduled Tribe families separately. But the Policy does not provide for collection of disaggregated data, about the number of SC and ST families, amongst those affected population in the survey to be conducted by the Administrator of R&R. The Draft Policy provides for setting up a Tribal Development Plan, for the development of the SC/ST families in their resettlement zone, in cases where the displacement is 400 or more families *en masse* in plain areas, or 200 or more families *en masse* in tribal or hilly areas, or DDP blocks or areas mentioned in Schedule V and Schedule VI of the Constitution of India. But no benefits have been provided to the displaced SC/ST families in projects involving linear acquisitions.

Although the Draft Policy provides that, concerned Gram Sabha(s) should be consulted in all cases of acquisition in the Fifth Schedule Areas, including acquisition under the emergency clause of Land Acquisition Act, the Policy does not provide such safeguards in cases of land acquisition in the Sixth Schedule Areas. The Draft Policy also does not provide guarantees, for land for land compensation even to the STs and SCs. Clause 7.18.3 states that land would be allotted to SCs and STs only "if available".

Redressal of Grievances: The Resettlement and Rehabilitation Committee, to monitor and review the progress of implementation of resettlement and rehabilitation schemes, is constituted by the State Government under the chairpersonship of the Administrator of R&R. But the Committee is not independent of the State Government, as the latter prescribes the rules and procedures of the Committee. The Grievance

Redressal Cell under the chairpersonship of the Commissioner for Resettlement and Rehabilitation is also not independent. It is constituted by the State Government, and all its rules and procedures including composition, powers, functions, and other matters relating to its functioning are prescribed by the State Government. Furthermore, the Grievance Redressal Cell is financially dependent on the Requiring Body. Hence, the Cell may not be able to ensure proper implementation of the R&R plan. Also, there is no nomination of civil society organisations or of representatives from the affected persons into the National Monitoring Committee which is constituted by the Ministry of Rural Development of the Central Government.

Conclusion

The process of development is important for the progress of any society. However, in the over enthusiasm of attaining development, we usually tend to forget the cost we are paying for development. SEZs definitely have a positive role to play in enhancing exports, investments, and creating employment and economic growth. Unfortunately, the entire process of SEZs in India has become synonymous, with displacement of people, loss of livelihoods, and severe socio-economic, environmental, psychological, and cultural impacts. The need of the hour is to strike a balance between development and containing displacement. For this to happen, we need to find first an answer to: "Development for whom and for what?" If we have convincing answers, development shall never create negative displacement – effective resettlement and rehabilitation of the communities will not hurt the displaced communities. There is a necessity to put much thought into the planning process, so that displacement is kept to the absolute minimum and if possible, avoided. In fact, most of the development plans would be more easily acceptable and implemented, if they were more focused on people rather than on production and power. Development plans must contain a human framework for analysing their performance, for which human development indicators should be given importance.

References

Aggarwal, Aradhana (2006): "Special Economic Zones: Revisiting the Policy Debate", *Economic and Political Weekly*, 41(44), pp. 4533-36.

All India Fact Finding Committee (2007): *Repression and Massacre Instead of Dialogue and Democracy,* Vijayawada: AIFFFC.

Baneerji, Rahul (2008): "Reconciling Displacement and Rehabilitation", *Social Action*, 58(3), pp. 246-53.

Bhaduri, Amit (2007): "Development or Developmental Terrorism?" *Economic and Political Weekly,* 42(07), pp. 552-53.

Bidwai, Praful (2007): "Blood on their Hands", *Mainstream,* November 23-29.

Cernea, Michael M. (1996): *Eight Main Risks: Impoverishment and Social Justice in Resettlement,* 10-19, Washington, DC: The World Bank.

Chowdhury, Neerrja (2007): "Nandigram: CPM Exposed", *Mainstream,* 45 (50), pp. 11-12.

EPW (2007): "Piemeal Tinkering", *Economic and Political Weekly*, editorial 42(16), pp. 1399-1400.

Gopalakrishnan, Shankar (2007): "Special Economic Zones and Neoliberalism in India", *Man and Development,* 29(4), pp. 25-40.

Haq, Mahbub ul (2000): *Reflections on Human Development,* New Delhi: Oxford.

Iyer, S.H. (2008): "Analysis of the Structure and the Practice of the Legal Machinery : Special Economic Zones and their Impact on Labour", *Labour File Journal*, 6(4-5), pp. 14-18.

Majumdar, Manab (2007): "Approaching Special Economic Zones: The Debate, Dimensions and Determinants", *Man and Development,* 29(4), pp. 1-24.

Mathur, Hari Mohan (ed.) (1995): *Development, Displacement and Resettlement: Focus on Asian Experiences,* pp. 19-20, New Delhi: Vikas Publishing House.

Nayak, A. Kumar (2008): "SEZs and Displacement", *Social Action*, 58(3), pp. 254-63.

Rajagopalan, T.N.C. (2008): "SEZ Policy Should be allowed a Reasonable Run", *Business Standard*, September 29.

Rajkishore, Mahana (2008): *Pain, Politics and Distress of the Displaced*, Working Paper 209, pp. 5-40, Chennai: MIDS.

Ramachandran, H. and Debatosh Biswas (2007): "Locating Land for Special Economic Zones", *Man and Development,* 29(4), pp. 51-64.

Rustogi, Anupam (2008): "The Infrastructure Sector in India 2000", in Anupam Rastogi, Prem Kalra and Ajay Pandey (eds.), *India Infrastructure Report 2008*, pp. 30, New Delhi: Oxford University Press.

Sampat, Preeti (2008): "Special Economic Zones in India", *Economic and Political Weekly,* 43(28), pp. 25-29.

Sarma, E.A.S. (2007): "Help the Rich, Hurt the Poor: Case of Special Economic Zones", *Economic and Political Weekly,* 42(21), pp. `1900-1902.

Sawant, P. B. (2007): "Special Economic Zones Act and What It Means", Speech at a Seminar at Arthagyan Prabodhini, Pune, January 28.

Sen, S. and B. Dasgupta (2007): "SEZs: Modern Enclaves to Reward Capital by Exploiting Labour and Displacing Livelihood in the Agrarian Economy", *Mainstream*, 45(19):5-9.

Sharma, Vineeta (2007): "Implications of a Special Economic Zone on Project Affected People", *Man and Development,* 29(4): December.

Singh, Mahi Pal (2007): "Nandigram: A Dangerous Chapter in the History of Human Rights", *Mainstream,* 45 (50), pp. 9-11.

Singhvi, Sanjay (2006): "Special Exploitation Zones", *RED Star,* March.

Thukral, Enakshi Ganguly (ed.): (1992): *Big Dams Displaced People: Rivers of Sorrow, Rivers of Change,* pp. 24-25, New Delhi: Sage Publication.

Verma, Manish (2004): *Development, Displacement and Resettlement*, Jaipur: Rawat Publications.

18

Development Induced Displacement: Evidence from Sardar Sarovar Project

D.C. Sah

Introduction

The debate on relocation and rehabilitation of tribals in Narmada valley, is informed by numerous sources, including print and electronic media, the state, the Greens, Morse and Berger Independent Committee, and the pro and anti-dam activists. Each of these agencies has its own perspective and source of information. More often, the aim of these agencies is either to discredit R&R, making it an impossibility, or proclaim that everything with respect to R&R is as planned. The facts are, however, in between the two extremes. The Sardar Sarovar Project[1] (SSP), because of these, has been controversial, since its inception[2]. Of late, right to livelihood of the Project Affected Persons[3] (PAPs) has become a moot question, wherein insensitivity of the major agents towards grass-root needs, have allowed judiciary to play an active role. Human rights of the poor, for one or the other reason, have always been disregarded by the Indian State, under the ruse that these rights have different meanings for different societies and the western concept cannot be imposed on us. This argument is unique to states that have little sensitivity for human misery. Unfortunate though it may seem, the state as well as the civil society has failed in protecting the livelihood rights of a section of PAPs. Consequently, the Supreme Court interpreted some of the rights buried under Directive Principles and made them enforceable. This paper, using findings of rehabilitation experience of Sardar Sarovar affected people of Gujarat (Sah, 1997; 1998; 1999), aims to understand interaction among state, civil society, and the PAP community in meeting the repercussion of access failure to food in the relocation sites.

The Civil Society and State

The SSP is the product of varied and mixed experiences; good at the level of policy, fairly acceptable in the implementation of relocating 4570 PAPs from 19 submerging villages, and poor in case of their rehabilitation (Sah, 1997). Although the compensation package offered by the SSP has been better than other irrigation projects in the country[4], its success at various levels is a product of coming together of many minds. The R&R policy of SSP has evolved over a period of time and after a long struggle by activists in Gujarat for a better deal for the displaced population. Lack of uniformity in dealing with R&R of displaced oustees has been the hallmark of the development process. Till recently, the Land Acquisition Act initiated by the British government in 1894 guided the rehabilitation of oustees. For monetary compensation to oustees, the Act recognised only the individual owners whose names figured in land revenue records. As a result, those whose livelihood was based on Common Property Resources (CPRs), sharecropping, cultivation on encroached land and farm labour, were not considered as project affected people. The compensation to legal owners of land was based on Government Resolutions (GRs) which varied from state to state and within a state, from project to project. Once the compensation is paid, the oustees are left to resettle without proper support for social and economic adjustments with the host communities. The oustees, a large proportion of whom is tribal, unaware of the intricacies of law and markets in the new environment were left to fend for themselves.

The deteriorating situation of the PAPs of various development projects resulted in militant tribal unrest, mobilisation of tribal groups, and its wide coverage in the media. These concerns were reflected in the Narmada Water Dispute Tribunal (NWDT) Award of 1978. Taking into account the directives of NWDT Award, the Government of Gujarat issued orders under resolution dated 11 June, 1979 for granting facilities at new sites of resettlement to PAPs of major and medium projects.

The GR of 1979, though accepted 'land for land' as a concept and defined a PAP as one who had been residing or cultivating or carrying on any trade or occupation in the submerging area, in its definition of family considered only the major married sons as separate families. Moreover, the GR of 1979 had provisions for a compensation package to the oustees of Maharashtra and Madhya Pradesh, but had no specific provisions for the oustees of Gujarat. Thus, with reference to SSP, the GR of 1979 had four major problems. First, the award was available to PAPs other than those originating from Gujarat submergence area. Second, the definition of family was such that only married sons were considered as separate families, hence, entitled for compensation package. Adult unmarried sons of a family had to share the compensation package with their parents. Third, joint landholders and sharecroppers were not considered as separate families. Only the legal owners of the land were considered as PAPs. And lastly, the relocation sites were not necessarily to be in the command area of the SSP, and, consequently, the GR was not committed to provide irrigable agricultural land to PAPs.

The role played by NGOs – Arch Vahini, Rangpur Ashram, and Rajpipla Social Service Society – in forcing a just R&R policy is well documented (Arch, 1988; Sheth, 1995; Patel, 1995). A prolonged struggle forced the state to accept a just R&R. The involvement of NGOs in R&R in Gujarat can be seen in two phases. The first phase ends by 1987, when these NGOs were able to organise tribal population to force the policy, makers to come out with a just R&R policy. The second phase is that of post December 1987 when the R&R package was accepted by the Government of Gujarat and these NGOs decided to become active partners in the relocation process.

Notwithstanding the fact that left to the state, the implementation of R&R package would have been as indifferent as has been in other projects in the country, a fair amount of success in the execution of the relocation of PAPs certainly would not have been possible but for the support provided by the Non-Government Organisations[5] (NGOs), who had earlier fought for a just R&R policy for the SSP.

It is quite possible that the success of the SSP relocation process may emphasise the inevitability of NGOs' involvement to ensure a fair deal to the PAPs elsewhere. This may be a premature conclusion, as it is possible that, what led to the success of a process, may end up in its demise, when the process is replicated. The working of NGOs reveals a heterogeneous pattern. The NGOs, working in rural reconstruction are a mixed lot; some like Arch Vahini, had delivered the services keeping their ideology of social reform, but many more are simply participants in what may be termed as 'market of development programmes' (Shah and Das, 1986). The difference in the actions and ideology of the NGOs are built within the character of the people running these organisations. Such variations result in indifference in delivering what the organisation is supposed to deliver with sensitivity. Importantly, the concept of sensitivity is not static; it varies not only across organisations but also for an organisation over time. Thus, it will be a futile exercise to presume consistency in approach. A policy decision to involve NGOs arrived in good faith that the grassroot level understanding would be helpful in the successful implementation of programmes that may be self defeating and may not ensure sensitivity as shown by some NGOs, in the case of SSP.

There is another dimension to NGO involvement in SSP; R&R in the case of SSP provides an opportunity in understanding the relationships among the state, NGOs, and the community actions in coping with the shocks of relocation. A participatory approach in R&R would create alternatives to either top-down development approach of the state or PAPs' own approach. This interactive approach to development will bring the desired flexibility in policy environment where changes in policy are systemic.

Institutional Innovations

It may be argued that the emergence of NGOs, sensitive to the actual needs of the PAPs, has changed the political process of empowering the poor. In fact, shedding of the built-in inertia to act with humane values in the case of SSP is an outcome of a combination of forces: a strong grassroots movement and initiative of NGOs; an in-depth understanding by academicians of socio-cultural needs of the affected people, to generate alternatives in policy formulation; and pressure by the foreign funding agency – the World Bank – to allow for various options, have played important role in developing an acceptable R&R policy. It is least likely that such interplay of forces can be accommodated in many development projects so that a just R&R becomes part of the project. For, not only the existence, but also a change in the nature of initiative from various participants could result in a different R&R policy frame.

In a normative sense, after accepting the R&R package, the first institutional intervention was to introduce accountability in land acquisition and relocation. Barring a few exceptions in the front of providing land, the state and the NGOs did a creditable job; the PAPs did get what was due to them in terms of land and infrastructure. But a policy frame cannot solve all the problems of the society; it, nonetheless, reflects the concerns we have and the type of society we believe in.

Viewing the R&R with the backdrop of SSP experiences, there are many positive features also: The land for land policy of compensation is one of the most important of all. By accepting land for land, subjectivity in price fixing, can safely be avoided. Tribal groups residing often in remote undulating areas, sustain themselves under low yield equilibrium. Cultivating larger areas compensates for the low yields. Through the R&R policy, the procedure of compensating on quality-based pricing of land would bring not only subjectivity, but also meagre compensation to the PAPs.

Planning development projects with sensitivity needs establishment of strong linkages, with those processes and institutions that identify and address the disequilibria created by the projects. First, lack of provisions in the project design to monitor second generation environmental problems and their remedial measures may render the project non-functional, as, such problems become a threat to the environment and the people. This happens over time especially, when no specific organisation is formally responsible for providing remedial measures. It is desirable to make provisions to avoid such occurrences as an essential part of the project document itself. Such a measure will not only compel the planners to identify second generation environmental problems to the maximum extent at the planning stage, but would also call for fund allocation in order to respond to such problems, as and when they arise. Secondly, in the prevalent paradigm of development, market plays an important role. PAPs who are mainly tribal people, are unfamiliar with market forces and remain alienated from these processes. Consequently, they are required to bear a variety of associated costs without being benefited. This increases economic inequality, not only between hosts and new settlers but also among the resettlers. Provisions necessary for economic integration are also missing from the present R&R policy of SSP. Development has been so isolated from displacement in the present R&R policy that, these issues are not even recognised. What is, therefore, needed, is a development policy wherein displacement and rehabilitation become part of a policy frame.

The R&R policy of the SSP has subdivided the implementation plan into a relocation plan and a resettlement plan. In doing so, it has disassociated the relocation process from the project construction. The R&R policy states that this plan would be ready at least a year before the start of land acquisition. In the process, as experiences show, relocation takes place, simultaneously with submergence. This is referred to as *paripassu*. The problem with *paripassu* is that the project authorities turn indifferent to the needs of the PAPs as time passes. But the *paripassu* clause cannot be avoided. Thus, a project should commence only after ensuring equal treatment and package to early as well as late resettlers.

The early years of relocation were of extreme hardship to the oustees owing to the breaking up of usual informal exchange structures of submerging villages. To mitigate this hardship, the relocated households are given cultivation rights, till submergence commences without resorting to an official sanction. This economic support may ease the hardship associated with early shocks of relocation. Also, the process of acquiring land in the command area for relocated PAPs should be complete before the commencement of the project. Though, to some extent, this will restrict the choice of site for resettlement by the oustees, it will smoothen the planning of the relocation process.

Missing Rights

When the R&R policy of SSP proclaims that the tribal community would, strictly, be settled in the area of their choice, it empowered the state to break the social fabric, associated with the village, peer group, and family[6]. The relocation process could be seen from two different angles: first, the traditional social linkages and economic institutions, in the submerging villages, had an important place in the life of the oustees. These arrangements had helped in the sustenance of the society in the submerging villages. The randomness of relocation and the absence of the traditional arrangements at the new sites could make the oustees vulnerable to exploitation. Second, the existing policy is inappropriate. The people, associated with resettling the oustees, may defend the policy and the process by reiterating that the decision of shifting is an individual decision. The strength of the argument is drawn from the fact that the tribal village is not a homogeneous unit; even in a *falia* people do not always want to shift together. And since the oustees may be shown land in different locations, their moving to the new sites is voluntary, as the oustees have preferred the land they want to cultivate in the new sites. The argument could have been accepted, if there were methods in avoiding the randomness of the relocation.

It may be argued that the R&R policy of SSP provides avenues and instruments of choosing the new site. The fact is that oustees certainly may have a choice: to choose the best amongst the worst. Thus, the migration, in absence of proper social and economic arrangements, may not only be involuntary, but also an outcome of the policy frame, incapable of safeguarding the risks of social disruption. This is what can be termed as lack of interaction within a rigid policy frame.

Lack of interaction among the agents was not only present during site selection but also in gender issues. While interpreting 'member dependent on land', unmarried women, widows and divorcees need to be identified as adult members. This is just not a question of justice and equality, but also reflects the attitude of policy, makers towards the needs and participation of women. This attitude further manifests in the form of ignoring the gender perspective in choosing relocation sites, selection of sites for house plot, locating drinking water sources (pumps and wells) at the new sites, etc. In tribal communities, female participation in day to day decision, making, as also in economic activity, is equal to that of males. But the patriarchal norms of non-tribal societies restrict mutual decision, making. Hence, revisions recognising women's need and concerns, and ensuring their participation in decision, making have to be incorporated in the R&R policy.

In fact, the relocation and rehabilitation must be recognised as participatory processes and this must be realised by policy, makers through appropriate and effective interventions. The term participation has been used here as the right of the displaced to participate in a process, which is affecting their livelihood. This also presupposes that there exists mutual trust between institutions involved in R&R and the affected community. This may result in better living conditions, with respect to choices of migration, identification of new sites, agricultural land, house plots, and location of social amenities. The proposition was well founded, but the reality shows that, though the interaction between state and the civil society existed, it was missing at the community level. Hence, exclusion and marginalisation were the obvious outcomes.

The experience of SSP has shown that, the well-intended policy statements remain unimplemented, owing to failure of identifying instruments for their execution. The R&R policy of SSP also lacks necessary linkages that make such policies implementable. For example, with respect to land rights of the PAPs, and their cultural losses, the policy does not ensure how the right for entitlement of land free from encumbrance would be enforced. Neither does the policy spell out as to how cultural losses, owing to relocation and social and economic integration with the mainstream, would be taken care of. Almost always, these statements show well-intended concerns, but these have emerged as rhetoric that clearly lack the necessary institutional arrangements for their implementation. And thus, when land rights are being discussed in the R&R policy, issues such as checking: (a) the size of allotted agricultural land; (b) whether canal, road, or any other project is not on the land allotted to a PAP; (c) whether the same land which was shown to a PAP has been allotted to him; (d) for encumbrance on it; (e) if the right of a minor in the father's property clashes with the right of a major son, have remained outside the purview of the present policy. This creates ambiguity in the minds of the PAPs, about their status as landholders. Therefore, identification of institutions which shall carry out such verifications cannot be over emphasised.

The PAPs, despite being tribal, are not a monolithic entity 7; they vary significantly in terms of their languages, customs, beliefs, perceptions, needs and capabilities. The SSP failed to address the needs of the groups, which had remained unexposed to the market economy and modern agriculture – the Bhil, Nayaka and Vasava of Zones II and III. The extension wing neither differentiates between hosts and PAPs, nor among the different groups in tribal population.

Relocation allows only movable heritage to shift along with the displaced. Relocation of PAPs as a community demands reconstructing immobile cultural icons in the new site. This is possible when: (a) it is recognised that the community has to be relocated rather than the PAPs; and (b) freedom of cultural necessities becomes part of the development process. Both the above prerequisites are difficult to achieve, for one, we keep on forgetting the concept of heterogeneity amongst the PAPs, and for other, there may not be many social scientists, who would like to be associated with the process of identification of relevant necessities – social, cultural and economic – to be included in the development process. Empowering the PAPs is a process which may not fascinate many social scientists, for the research agenda in this case is guided by tangential pressures from funding agencies, and the 'publish or perish' syndrome from peer groups. Having cautioned about the dangers, help from trained social scientists – anthropologists, sociologists and economists – in the process of planning itself is not considered an undesirable option. In fact, such inclusion may improve chances of identifying meaningful alternatives.

For providing amenities in the relocation sites, the R&R policy of SSP states that water supply for drinking and cattle, fodder and grazing land, schools, approach roads, electricity connection, health centres, religious places, cemetery and grave-yards, Panchayat house, etc., should be made available. More often these facilities are linked to a minimum number of relocated families. The relocation process, as experiences have proved, does not always contain the minimum number of specified families, required for the provision of a particular facility at a new site. This easily leads to non-compliance in providing these amenities. Another major problem in the new sites has been lack of maintenance of created services. This not only marginalised the inhabitants but also resulted in the exit of an NGO from R&R scene[8].

India is a signatory to ILO Convention 107, adopted in 1957 as a convention, concerning the protection and integration of tribal population. The ILO convention affirms the right of the tribal people to their land and proclaims that if they are displaced due to national interests, the displaced will be provided with land suitable for their present need and future development. We, in India, also believe that all people are free and equal in dignity and that all people contribute to the diversity and richness of Indian culture. Any doctrine of cultural superiority, therefore, is legally invalid and socially unjust.

Despite the fact that the relocation package of SSP reflects the idea that relocation will not adversely affect the standard of living, and also reflects the development of human rights, the displacement due to SSP has reportedly resulted in human rights violations. The first serious protest against the violation of human rights originated from Manibeli (PUCL, 1993).The PUCL report viewed the process of relocation infringement on right to life, right to information, right to struggle, as well as violation of NWDT recommendations. This was followed by a Gujarat PUCL (1993) report, which found the observations of the PUCL report to be factually incorrect and concluded that the allegations of coercion were baseless. The Gujarat PUCL cited the findings of the Fact Finding Team's report on Manibeli incident (A charya *et al.*, 1992). "The Fact Finding Team observed that there is a rupture of dialogue between the two groups, who are socially and culturally the same, and this was aggravated by the intervention of outside agencies. Police intervention became inevitable to help the group that wanted to shift to a new site. Bulldozers were used more for operational purposes than intimidation. The committee found no visible signs of violence nor was violence reported by any party, during the operation. Police was not used for any dismantling or shifting operations.

There are also other references to human rights violations ranging from the rights of non-PAPs (Soni and Appa, 1993); right to struggle; violation of Court Orders (HRCN, 1993); right not to be forcibly evicted; right not to be forcibly staying; right to information; and right not to be physically harassed (Bhatia, 1997). These reports, from pro and anti dam groups, are equally persuasive. But when Bhatia (1997) reported of forced eviction from Antras submerging village of Gujarat, where 30 families were refusing to shift; the violence against Budiben – a PAP of Antras and Narmada Bachao Andolan activist – and her subsequent rape to psychologically threaten her to shift; and forcible stay of Malu PAPs, who wanted to shift to their submerging villages Gadher and Vadgam – the drama was being staged for evidences to stop the dam, the texts were neither mediocre in nature nor were the sentiments behind it trivial. But the way, the whole set of evidences served the ideology, a sense of patronage towards PAPs was more dominating than the possibility of rehabilitation.

But more disturbingly, evidences confirm that abnormal weather in the region results in severe yield fluctuations. The food security implications are serious, if the PAPs have also experienced yield stagnation in two consecutive years. Even during normal years, the risks, involved in technology adoption, are so high that the PAPs, by and large, prefer to avoid adopting the new agricultural technology in dry areas. As a result, the cushion available, from good years, is not enough to neutralise the risk of food insecurity during abnormal years – erratic weather induces wide yield fluctuations. During abnormal years, nearly half the PAPs face total crop failure. The yield of major crops registers a sizeable; households' access to food grains reduces by about 20 per cent, and the level of consumption and calorie intake fall by about 17 per cent (Sah, 1997). During scarcity years, the PAPs' coping mechanism focuses on: (a) reducing farm expenditure; (b) decision of household members to work as casual and agricultural labour; (c) seasonal migration of some family members; and (d) borrowings and distress sale of cattle. But these adjustments are not enough to maintain the households' calorie intake. The role of the state in the PAPs' coping mechanism has been marginal. Moreover, agricultural growth in this dry zone is riddled with moderate increase in production and recurring crop failure. The pressure on land is immense and agriculture alone is unable to sustain the households' consumption in a weather cycle[9].

Pressure on land forced the PAPs to augment their land resources by multiple cropping. A fifth of the cultivable area is double cropped (Sah, 1998). Though irrigation is important, in the diversified farms, the extent of multiple cropping on dry land is three times more than that in the irrigated area. While irrigation is consequential for diversification, it is the quality of irrigation which governs diversification. Two other obstacles in crop diversification are lack of exposure to modern technology, hence access to extension support; and constraints in labour availability. The process of crop diversification has been left to PAPs, wherein the role of state as an agent of change and NGOs as its catalyst is negligible.

Crop diversification, instead of adversely affecting food security, has brought about positive changes in terms of increased farm yield, additional surplus for non-food expenditure, less market dependence and increased calorie intake for all farms, other than cotton dominated farms. But in the absence of a viable technology, crop diversification could not reduce yield risks. Since the understanding on the new technology varied amongst different tribes, Tadvi and Rathwa used it well to adapt to their needs, while the Vasava, Bhil and Nayaka were unable to adopt the technology. This increased inequality between the tribes. Moreover, the economy as a whole, though could absorb the seasonally unemployed in the farm sector, the pace and intensity of growth of the non-agricultural sector in the vicinity was not robust enough to bear the employment imperatives of crop failure. Consequently, some of the family members had to migrate to distant places for some time[10]. Seasonal migration supports the consumption levels of the non-migrating members of the households at a respectable level. In order to get the best out of their unproductive land[11], some PAPs have developed institutions unknown to them in their respective submerging villages. Short-term land transactions, such as, sharecropping, fixed rent, or land mortgage[12] are such institutions developed in the new sites owing to market failure.

The PAPs' consumption response to income changes is similar to the one observed in case of the mainstream society: a decline in the share of food in the total family budget. Although cereals and pulses still account for over three-fourths of the total calorie intake, superior cereals are replacing coarse cereals among all the income groups, more so during abnormal years. This substitution is more an upshot of the availability of superior cereals through PDS, rather than a matter of choice. What is most disturbing is the fact, that even during normal years, about a fifth of the PAPs have reported per capita intake of less than 2000 calories per day, while during abnormal years, the calorie intake of half of the PAPs remains below this norm. Not only the incidence of poverty is high during these abnormal years, but also the intake gap within the vulnerable group of the poor, further deteriorates and inequality indices show a sharp increase. In order to bridge the poverty gap, a mixed policy focusing on rapid agricultural growth and the expansion of non-farm employment is desirable.

These second generation problems of involuntary migration were known to the policy-makers, and yet inaction on their part for strengthening the coping mechanism of PAPs only indicates their insensitivity. The State, it seems, instead of participating at the time of the short-term shocks, believed that their interaction with community at the time of these crises is outside the R&R purview.

Decision Making

In order to utilise the findings of information support, for policy reorientation, it would be mandatory on the part of the project authorities, to participate in the discussion and dissemination of field realities. Such dissemination would lead to: (a) identifying the deviations, from expected norms; (b) understanding implications of the observed deviations; (c) causes of such deviations; and (d) measures to be adopted for minimising the associated risks. Devoid of such participatory process, the PAPs, as has been the case in the SSP, would find themselves in a perpetual state of poverty[13].

In order to plan for integration of the oustees into the mainstream economy, it is desirable to distinguish between institutions at the new sites and their access to PAPs. For, the second generation, problems of resettlement, such as, access to market and technology, yield risk, access failure to food, pressures on land, leasing out land, seasonal migration, etc., need a different treatment than the usual top-down development approach. The basic failure of the existing rehabilitation policy of SSP is the policy- makers' overconfidence about their organisational capabilities to respond to the problems related to rehabilitation. The organisational setup responsible for economic integration, in the absence of participation of PAPs, NGOs, agricultural scientists, and the community, is unable to comprehend the complexity of the process and is unfit to deal with the resultant negative consequences.

For those associated with development planning, the R&R in any guise is soothing; for it lends to the philosophy that: (a) development is sacrosanct enough to be overtly insensitive to various problems created by it; and (b) the distortions so created can be ironed out by policy interventions. The R&R policy of SSP is also riddled with policy instruments waiting for execution, owing to lack of institutionalisation. The forgoing analysis calls for fresh debate, not only on the R&R policy of a development project, but also on how the mid-course corrections can be accepted by policy makers. It has also been argued that in the absence of public support, the risk, of access failure to food, has serious implications. Yield fluctuations in the dry zone are high and it is not uncommon that, though the total food availability is normal, a sizeable section of PAPs may have poor yields. For some, owing to the poor quality of agricultural land[14], this could be a perpetual phenomenon. This renders them unfit to cope up with their lack of access to food. If the policy-makers are serious in minimising the adverse effects of such access failure, it could be a perplexing task. Otherwise, they could choose to ignore the indications provided by the capability of the allotted agricultural land and availability of alternative employment in the area and remain complacent.

Does it mean that the total food production and availability, other things remaining the same, have no poverty implication? The situation can be puzzling, when despite a substantial improvement in the total food production, some households may be facing access failure to food. Sen (1981) has put forward the entitlement approach as an alternative theory to the cause of famines. He defines entitlement as a set of different commodities that a person acquires through the use of various legitimate means in his position. In an open economy, his endowment and ownership of productive assets shall, in normal situation, provide access to a number of commodities, through economic exchange and production, for his consumption. Abnormal situations like crop failure, severe fluctuations in macro-economic indicators like total availability of food stock, and changes in pattern of normal stock market and hoarding, may result in affecting his endowment – through land alienation, ill health and the ability to work; or his exchange entitlement mapping, which is affected adversely – through wage reduction, increase in food prices, loss of employment, and crop failure. Production in relation to ownership pattern, agricultural land with severe problems, access to alternative employment and wages, and more importantly, the short-term measures initiated by the state, provides insights on households' capabilities.

The above argument aims at initiating policy changes. The observation in certain quarters that the relocation package is generous enough to tackle problems, relating to resettlement, is a misplaced proposition. The relationship between agricultural growth and poverty, notwithstanding, depletion of assets, seasonal migration, reduction in current consumption and input use are not unimportant indicators of the process of increasing deprivation. Their inclusion, in the analysis, would make our understanding richer, and their influence in policy formulation would have far-reaching implications. The inability to command food, even if it is available through PDS, is an indicator of the want of public action in the form of creating short-term employment. This will not only provide the much-needed purchasing power, but also improve productivity of land. But in the long run, land alone should support livelihood. To make this happen, factors, constraining technology transfer in agriculture, cannot be ignored. The important question is how to institutionalise these processes.

The foregoing analysis indicates that interactions among the state, NGOs as the main component of the civil society, and the community on the issue of livelihood adaptation has been insubstantial. Consequently, the state's responses to PAPs' own coping mechanism has been insensitive. Public actions are reserved for occasion when the whole region is facing access failure to food. The civil society, as an extended arm of public action, has remained superficial in the community's coping mechanism. In the process, the community is forced to take decisions on the consequences of impoverishment risks. This apathy, owing to lack of participation, resulted in exclusion and marginalisation of the affected PAPs in the short run. In the long run, the state and the civil society's actions confirm increasing anxiety, to insulate the economy from year to year fluctuations of rainfall. This indicates some optimism for a process which would lead to a closer interaction among, state, civil society, and the community in the long run.

The absolute failure of the Indian State became visible, when the Supreme Court forced the state to accept the Grievance Redressal Authority (GRA). The aim of the GRA is to look into every aspect of R&R of Gujarat's oustees, including poor quality of allotted land and livelihood adaptations. Over 9000 cases have been addressed by the GRA till date. This reflects on the inventory of complaints[15] that the state has left for the GRA to attempt.

Conclusions

The R&R experiences, of the Sardar Sarovar Project, have also provided us a rich data on how displacement forces livelihood adaptations. In the normal process, people adapt to new ways, in order to improve their material wealth. But in abnormal situations, like involuntary migration, people adapt their livelihood, because they can no longer cope with the impoverishment risks. Involuntary migration due to large dams creates incompatible forces which disregard civil society's equity and justice norms; the benefits to the command area are at the cost of misery to the displaced population. In the process, though it improves the economic condition, owing to irrigated agriculture, the displaced have to undergo a number of negative consequences, both material and cultural. These negative consequences not only outline the inequitable access to benefits, but also reflect distortions in the relationship among the state, NGOs, and the community.

The civil society was omnipresent in SSP either as alternative paradigm of development – as the case was pre-1987 – or as an extended arm of bureaucracy, as the case was post-1987. The super-interaction between the state and the civil society post-1987, undermined the existence of the PAPs. This has led to the exclusion of community in the rehabilitation process. In the absence of help from the state, as well as the NGOs, the excluded community is forced to initiate their own coping mechanisms. The Sardar Sarovar Project has shown us that when the interaction of the state and the civil society with the community is insignificant, a diffident outcome in the form of the ever-changing institutional rules emerges. The increasing attention being paid to the rights of the displaced people, of late, is largely because of the pressures on the State from the Supreme Court. The Grievance Redressal Authority appointed in Gujarat under the Chairmanship of Justice Desai, proves that when interactions among the three important agents – the state, the civil society, and the community – are insignificant, judicial activism tries to fill the vacuum. The legality of the emerging process, notwithstanding its consequences to role and responsibility of state, is debatable.

The SSP experience has reconfirmed that a comprehensive policy framework is inevitable, if impoverishment risks have to be avoided. The solution to the problem is difficult and complex. Three processes have to be started simultaneously: First, creating avenues for irrigation and efforts for adapting agricultural technology for the agro-climatic conditions of the new sites; Second, organising PAPs so that they respect the rules of open markets; and Third, strengthening the farmers' adjustment mechanisms for coping with scarcity, by creating more avenues for non-farm employment so that the interactions among the state, civil society, and the community result in safeguarding the livelihood rights of the marginalised. Even after doing so, it is likely that emerging impoverishment risks warrant revisions. The sensitive society dealing with involuntary migration will have to make room for this. Recognition by policy-makers that these are potential risks is the first step towards avoiding the risk. A policy frame with provisions to identify the impoverishment risks, associated with resettlement, and to counteract them is needed for acceptable rehabilitation. These concluding observations deserve attention of the policy-makers who ultimately will develop the National Rehabilitation Policy for the people affected by development.

Notes

1. Sardar Sarovar Project is one of the largest irrigation projects, costing the state a sum of Rs. 84080 million in 1986-87 prices. It is estimated that it would: (a) irrigate 1.8 million hectares of land; (b) provide drinking water to 4720 villages and 131 urban centres; and (c) generate 1450 MW power. All these benefits in monetary terms would be Rs.14000 million of additional production per year.

2. The controversy started in late 1960s on sharing the benefits and cost of the project between Gujarat, Madhya Pradesh and Maharashtra. This was followed by an agitation fora R&R policy for the project between 1982 and 1987. During late 1980s and early 1990s, the project again remained controversial owing to estimation of social cost and economic benefits. The opponents of the Sardar Sarovar Project argue that this project hides its social and environmental costs and over estimates its benefits; they believe that even under heroic assumptions, this project is nothing but an environmental disaster. These activists have been critical of the techno-economic feasibility of the project. Their criticism has also been directed to: (i) large area of submergence; (ii) destruction of forest and wildlife; (iii) interruptive approach to the natural flow of river and the resultant sedimentation; (iv) problems of water-logging and salinity; (v) seismic problems due to large reservoir; and (vi) risk of water-borne diseases to downstream population. Anyone, who is following the SSP debate would substantiate the fact that second generation R&R problems created because of SSP are equally important. The fate of over 30,000 people, who have been displaced from Gujarat and reallocated in the command area, need concentrated efforts. Currently, violation of rights to livelihood of some of these PAPs, who have poor quality land, is under debate.

3. It is estimated that about 40.7 thousand families from Gujarat, Maharashtra and Madhya Pradesh will be displaced from their habitat, owing to construction of SSP and out of this, a majority belong to tribal population. Experiences relating to R&R of SSP displaced people are far from encouraging. A review of the R&R of displaced population of development projects reveals that in absence of a National R&R policy, inadequate legal provisions for land and property acquisition, and lack of institutional provisions to relocate and rehabilitate, the displaced population faces bureaucratic insensitivity and loss of livelihood. The livelihood adaptation by communities, either in improving management of commons (Jodha, 1981), or in creating an alternative to top-down approach of state (Susan and Hossain, 1997), or in scarcity management (Desai, Singh and Sah, 1979) have earlier been attempted.

4. A few *Sarvodaya* activists, who took the cause of the oustees of Ukai Dam in south Gujarat, were concerned about the future of the PAPs of SSP. They along with other non-party activists began to work in the

area and mobilised tribal population for a 'better deal'. The discriminatory provisions of the 1979 GR were highlighted. Public demonstrations of the tribal people were organised. A writ petition was filed in the Supreme Court. The Court appointed a commission to inquire into the availability of alternative land for rehabilitation. Media and researchers repeatedly raised issues for proper rehabilitation. As a result of growing pressures from NGOs world over and their concern for environment and tribal people, the World Bank evolved guidelines for rehabilitation for the projects, supported by the Bank. Moreover, by the early eighties, the Government of India began to pay attention to the problems of tribal oustees. In 1984, it formed a committee for evolving a policy of rehabilitation for tribal oustees, displaced by development projects. The R&R package of SSP is a 'land for land' compensation package, which recognised every adult in the submerging village as a PAP and provided five acres of land in the resettlement site, along with a house plot and temporary shed plus transportation, plinth construction, village civic amenities, one-time up-keep allowance of Rs. 4500, and implement grant. But this package was accepted after a prolonged struggle. This flexibility demonstrated by the Government of Gujarat, in liberally defining the PAPs, was forced. To begin with, the Narmada Water Dispute Tribunal Award recognised only legal land owners in submerging villages as PAPs and hence, only these were entitled for a compensation package. Pressures from NGOs, social activists and the tribal protest forced the state to recognise encroachers, grown, up sons of the PAPs, and share-croppers, as a separate family affected by SSP.

5. ARCH-Vahini was the first NGO in Gujarat to mobilise the tribal community, in order to protect their right, to livelihood. Recognising that the then existing norms do not recognise the landless labourers, share-croppers and forest encroache as PAP, ARCH worked relentlessly for forcing a just R&R policy for four years starting from 1983. In December 1987 the Government of Gujarat was forced by this grassroots movement to announce a new R&R policy. ARCH was joined by two other NGOs, Sarmik Vikas Sansthan and Rangpur Ashram, to help the state in relocating and rehabilitating PAPs after 1987.

6. A total disregard for social implications of relocating PAPs from 19 submerging villages to 120 plus new sites, is paradoxical. The relocation process could be seen from two different dimensions: first, the traditional social links and economic institutions, in the submerging villages, had an important place in the life of PAPs. These arrangements had helped sustaining themselves in the submerging villages. The randomness of relocation in the absence of these arrangements at the new sites, has made the PAPs vulnerable to exploitation. The second dimension to the process is the appropriateness of the existing policy. The people associated with resettling the PAPs defend the policy and the process

by reiterating that the decision of shifting is an individual decision. The strength to the argument is drawn from the fact that the village is not a homogeneous unit; even in a *falia the* people do not always want to shift together. And since the PAPs were shown land in different locations, their moving to the new sites is voluntary, as the PAPs have preferred the land they are cultivating in the new sites. This argument could have been accepted, had there been some method in the randomness of the relocation. It is often argued that the policy provides avenues and instruments of choosing the new site. The fact is that PAPs certainly had a choice: to choose best amongst the worst. Thus, the migration in the absence of social and economic arrangements is not only involuntary but also an outcome of a policy, incapable of safeguarding the risk of social disruption. The misery could have been avoided with adequate policy frame and planning.

7. Displacement in Gujarat is from 19 villages located in three zones: Zone I villages were most developed among all the submerging villages. The main tribe living in this zone, Tadvi, being close to the non-tribal area, had experience of modern markets and modern agricultural production technology. The villages in Zone II, where Tadvi and Dungaree Bhil were the main tribes, were under-developed. On the other hand, Zone III comprising eight interior villages (with Rathwa, Dungaree Bhil and Nayaka as the main tribes) was most backward among all the three zones.

8. A large number of problems were cropping at the field: there were widespread complaints of shortages in drinking water, frequent break downs in hand pumps, poor quality of roads and drainage in resettlement sites, water-logging and out-break of disease during monsoon, etc. These were communicated by the concerned NGO to the state, for necessary actions. But in action from state resulted in deteriorating well-being of PAPs (Patel, 2001).

9. Apart from poor quality land in the case of about 15 per cent of the PAPs, 43 new sites are outside the command area of the project. In both these regions the livelihood adaptations are only community induced. The state and the civil society have no role in this adaptation.

10. Pastoral nomads of north Gujarat, Narvies from Saurashtra, road workers from Panchmahals, query workers from tribal Bharuch, and tribal workers from south Gujarat are seen in major industrial towns of Gujarat, the seasonal migrants seldom cross district boundaries and work as farm labour in irrigated areas and casual, semi-skilled casual labour in industrial towns. It has been argued that migration may be motivated by desire to seek skill and leads to development through a process of urban migration leading to socio-economic development which ultimately results in the overall development of the area. The other proportion argues that inclination to migrate is determined by difference in the income between source and destination of migration, and may result in equating expected

income. In Ambavadi and Piparvati, two villages where seasonal migration is relatively higher, about 53 per cent of relocated households have reported out, migration compared to 14 per cent in the sample as a whole. The out, migration in these two locations, is owing to low productivity of land and inability of land to support all the family members. During the summer of 1996, about 1 out of 5 members of the households, in these two locations, had migrated for 1 to 4 months in search of jobs, as masonry helpers, nursery hand and sugarcane cutter in Surat, Ankleshwar, Dam site and Vadodara.

11. This is one of the major problems faced by the PAPs in the new sites. The origin of this problem is lack of participation of the PAPs, in the process of land selection.

12. When compared to non-tribal Gujarat, leasing out land, in relocated villages, is three to four times more prevalent. Preliminary findings of a study on short, term land transition reveals that 75 per cent of such land is leased out on share-cropping basis, bearing all the cost including labour; and the produce is shared between the landlord and the tenant, depending upon their agreement at partnerships ranging from 50:50 per cent to 67:33 per cent. Over 70 per cent of such contracts are due constraints like capita, labour and bullocks, while 30 per cent of such contracts are owing to land-related problems, such as, low productivity. Three new sites Malu, Ambavadi and Piparvati have a large proportion of households who have leased out their land on fixed rent or sharecropping and moved out to submerging villages to cultivate land, which has not yet come under submergence. A bulk of these households perceive that by not opting to move to their submerging villages, they are taking an unwarranted risk of yield fluctuations year, after year, either due to water logging or crop failure. All of them would want to come back but would like to relocate to new sites with irrigation facilities (Sah: 1998).

13. In a developing economy like ours, one of the two sectors (agricultural sector) is traditional. It produces wage goods (foodgrains) and has excess supply of labour. The non-agricultural sector is modern and draws capital and labour from the traditional sector. The productive accumulation in the economy can be faster, if agricultural sector performs. This is so because only then: (a) strong input-output linkages, between the two sector would be established; (b) terms of trade between sectors would support surplus transfer; and (c) demand for non-agricultural goods in the traditional sector would increase. The overall growth of the economy, in the long run, would be constrained if: (i) technology in the traditional sector remains stagnant; (ii) market links between sectors remains weak or the terms of trade remain unfavourable, for resource transfer to non-agricultural sector; and (iii) contribution of various parts within the agricultural sector is unequal. The above constraints, in the

short run, would also increase social and economic inequality. Although it was observed that high agricultural growth reduces rural poverty and higher consumer price aggravates it, the process may be affected if: (a) early growth takes place under extreme inequality and its benefits may not 'trickle down' to large rural masses; and (b) oligopsonistic influence of landowners distorts the rural labour market, dampening the on-farm employment opportunities and wage rates. Indian concept of poverty has moved from identifying a minimum normative absolute living standard, in terms of per capita consumer expenditure – it may be the normative food basket or the minimum calorie intake – towards explaining poverty. It should, however, be noted that cross-sectional analysis of calorie intake by individuals of PAP households contain noises despite the large sample. Moreover, this approach of poverty measurement does not give adequate emphasis to quality of life: PAPs' access to services, their environment relating to law and order, access to justice, the environment where they live, the air they breathe and the water they drink. In the absence of these concerns, the measurement of poverty is partial, reflecting only the food insecurity of PAPs.

14. As for the poor quality land, the Sardar Sarovar Punarvasavat Agency (SSPA) reports that to mitigate the problem, necessary measures are under consideration. A technical committee under the chairmanship of the Director (Canal) of Sardar Sarovar Narmada Nigam Ltd. (SSNNL), was appointed by the Executive Committee of SSPA. Subsequently, a task force with the Director (R&R) and CEO (SSPA) has already been constituted by GoG to take corrective measures. To begin with, 21 sites were jointly inspected by the field officers of SSNNL and SSPA, and remedial measures were outlined for each new site. The remedial measures have been taken in 43 sites, and work except for major structure in one or two cases, has been completed. The impact of these measures is yet not clear. Although, the present analysis reveals widespread dissatisfaction amongst the PAPs, with respect to land quality, official documents do not show that PAPs have registered their complaints with SSPA. The SSPA received complaints only from seven new sites. As a result, tractorisation or partial or entire relocation, in these new sites has been in progress. Still this is an issue that needs to be resolved as early as possible. As the progress, in identification of poor quality land and corrective measures, was too slow, the Supreme Court came into action.

15. Even the National Policy on R&R has not raised these issues. For a detailed discussion on the first and second-generation problems, see Sah (1997; 1998; 1999).

References

Acharya, S., S.P. Punalekar, N.K. Gourah, and N.V.V. Char (1992): "Report of Fact-finding Team appointed by Ministry of Water Resources on Manibeli", New Delhi: GOI.

Bhatia Bela (1997): "Forced Eviction in Narmada Valley", in J. Dreze, M. Samson and S. Singh (eds.), *The Dam and the Nation, New* Delhi: Oxford University Press.

Davies, Susanna and Naomi Hossain (1997): "Livelihood Adaptation, Public Action and Civil Society", IDS Working Paper 57, Sussex: Institute of Development Studies.

Desai, G.M., Gurdev Singh and D.C. Sah (1979): "Impact of Scarcity on Farm Economy and Significance of Relief Operations, (Mimeo)", Ahmedabad: Indian Institute of Management.

Govt. of Gujarat (1992): "Human Rights Issues at Manibeli: Fictions and Facts", (Mimeo) Report by Gujarat PUCL on behalf of Human Rights Group of Narmada Abhiyan.

Jodha, N.S. (1981): "Role of Credit in Farmers' Adjustment against Risk in Arid and Semi-arid Tropical Areas of India", *Economic and Political Weekly*, 16(42-43), pp. 1696-1709.

Patel, Anil (2001): "Resettlement in Sardar Sarovar Project", *Water Resource Development*, Vol. 17(3), pp. 315-28.

Mohanty, M. and C.C. Kalara (1993): "Drowning of Manibeli", *PUCL Bulletin*, 12(7).

Sah, D.C. (1995): "Displacement: National Rehabilitation Policy", *Economic and Political Weekly*, 30(48), 3055-58.

Sah, D.C. (1997): "Second Generation Problems of Involuntary Migration", *Indian Journal of Agricultural Economics*, 52(4).

Sah, D.C. (1998): "Avoiding Impoverishment Risks: Towards a Policy Frame of Dam Affected People", *Review of Development and Change*, 3(1).

Sah, D.C. (1999): "Pressures on Land, Employment and Migrations", *Review of Development and Change*, 4(2).

Sen, A.K. (1981): *Poverty and Famines*, Oxford: Oxford University Press.

Shah, G. and Biswaroop Das (1986): "Voluntary Organisation Development", (Mimeo), Surat: Centre for Social Studies.

Shah, G. and Biswaroop Das (1988): "Voluntary Organisation in Gujarat", (Mimeo), Surat: Centre for Social Studies.

Sheth, Pravin (1995): "Politics of Narmada Project", (Mimeo), Ujjain: Madhya Pradesh Institute of Social Science Research.

Soni, Trupti and Appa Gautam (1993): "Sardar Sarovar Project Downstream Impact", Paper presented in workshop at *Narmada Forum*, organised by Delhi School of Economics and Institute of Economic Growth.

19

Involuntary Urban Displacement and Vulnerability Risks – Voices of the Displaced

Nanda Kishore M.S.

Introduction

In the context of economic liberalisation and a rapid increase in international productive integration, India is widely being criticised for her lack of inclusive development. For example, the impressive development of the service sector has concentrated strongly in a selected number of urban centres, causing not only a strong rural to urban divide, but also a growing schism between the modern and the traditional sectors. Consequently, underlying social and economic inequalities are exacerbating as the rural, uneducated, and the socially marginalised population is excluded from new development opportunities. Over the next 20 to 30 years, dramatic population increases are forecasted to take place in the world's urban areas in general, and in the mega-cities of the Third World, in particular. Economic growth will be accompanied by a declining share of agriculture, in the total output and employment, and by acceleration in the rate of urbanisation. A considerable increase will occur in the number of metropolitan conglomerates, with over four million people each. Mega-city formation will be more massive and rapid in the developing countries than in the developed ones, thus continuing to increase the population glut in many Third World cities. Although ongoing rural development policies and programmes attempt to stem the flow of rural migrants to cities, this flow continues. A manifestation of this phenomenon is the direct social effect of mega-projects. While mega-projects are vital enablers for India's economic growth strategies, for its function in attracting corporate investments and enhancing productivity, they engender widespread human displacement. In India, displacement for development projects is notoriously prevalent; an estimated 60 million people have lost their land and/or hearth in the name of development, since Independence, in 1947. This is regarded as severe social injustice and a human rights violation and, above all else, highly contrary to the principles of development.

Forced displacements have remained to date as relatively silent companions of urban growth. Yet the frequency and magnitude of compulsory displacement are likely to increase in the developing world, as the trend towards urbanisation grows stronger. This work examines the social issues raised by involuntary displacements and relocations, their causal mechanisms, the typology of displacement processes, and the policy issues involved in guiding forced resettlement. The dramatic disruptions caused by displacement – loss of home, often loss of jobs, destruction of income-generating assets, or separation from site-related informal network services. Development projects that are oblivious to the perils of impoverishment through displacements, are shown to be in conflict with the poverty reduction goals of, urban growth strategies. Urban poverty is likely to increase, when displacement occurs unless such displacement is guided by correct policies for population resettlement. Is displacement justified? How is it against the philosophy of justice? Despite displacements, how do we have sustainable development along with displacement? For whose development such displacements are made? Why are only those living in the slums inside a city displaced, most of the time? These are some questions for which the research has found a few answers, and the whole process of displacement has been put through the prism of justice and impoverishment risks theory.

Urban growth involves reordering of city spaces, improved transportation networks, new industrial estates, new water and sewage systems, and much better environmental services. The need for investments in basic urban infrastructure and equipments will increase dramatically, and they will require changes in land use. This, in turn, will entail intra-urban compulsory relocation processes. Relocation of urban populations has happened until now as well, but it can be predicted that involuntary population displacement will become more significant than it has ever been on the Third World urban agenda; and requires more attention to policy, institutional, and research concerns. Urban compulsory relocation raises critical issues: land availability, job losses and job creation, reconstruction of housing stocks and of viable new neighbourhoods, adequate equipments for environmental management, as well as major financial and political issues.

Rooted in this topicality, this research explores the displacement effects of one such recently completed mega-project, an international airport that is located on the periphery of Hyderabad, the booming capital and IT centre of the State of Andhra Pradesh. In so doing, this research not only elucidates the aforementioned issues, but also explores in detail how rural populations make the transition from livelihoods shaped around rural livelihood activities to urban livelihood activities. As much land is acquired in peripheral urban areas in India in order to develop the infrastructure for Special Economic Zones and IT Parks, such regions experience a rapid degree of transformation, which, in turn, has a profound impact on the livelihoods of the directly and indirectly affected population.

Theoretical Underpinnings

The theoretical foundation of this research centres on two interrelated research domains. The first discusses the economic and social role of development-induced displacement projects, such as, the airport and IT companies. The second inquires into whether and in what situation human displacement, which is often a direct consequence of development-induced displacement, is justified; and how the ill effects thereof can be remediate. Mega-projects in transport infrastructure are the most prevalent as they are considered pivotal to contemporary society and international production networks. They facilitate the integration of production processes across national boundaries, allowing developing countries to take on specialist role within the production value system. These production functions tend to converge in urban conglomerates, where a higher concentration of specialist infrastructure facilities are available and where corporation can benefit from agglomeration economies. The state in particular plays a central role in developing world-class (transportation) infrastructure facilities in order to develop location-specific competitive advantages. In this respect, airports, for instance, are expressly being developed into commercial hubs, where investment incentives and complementary infrastructures are provided. This, in turn, attracts international capital, creating jobs and numerous spin-off developments; thus, providing a strong impulse to the regional economic development.

Despite their undeniably important economic function, one of the criticisms on mega-projects is that due to their sheer scale, they often require the displacement of people, residing on the designated land. This, in turn, is considered by many, a gross social injustice and human rights violation. It is argued that displaced populations often face the risk of impoverishment, when they are unable to reconstruct their livelihoods. For instance, when income levels are not restored, as jobs, land, or other productive assets are lost; when communities are forced to disperse, breaking down social networks and cultural practices; when access to health care or educational facilities deteriorates; or when people do not have access to new housing. Successful livelihood reconstruction typically depends on the resettlement and rehabilitation schemes, individual capacities, and the opportunities created by the development project. When these impoverishment risks are not sufficiently reversed, it becomes clear that the gains and losses of mega-projects are not equitably distributed, raising the question whether it is justified to sacrifice some for the so-called 'greater good'.

Legal Framework for Land Acquisitions

In India, private land can be acquired through the Land Acquisition Act of 1894, a law formulated during the British colonial period. Essentially, any state department can acquire land, either for itself or on behalf of a private party, if the land is required for a project that meets the public purpose provision. Therefore, if the project is a 'scheme of development' that serves the greater public good, land acquisition is permissible. However, no social impact analysis or any form of public participation is required in determining the extent of a project's contribution to the public good. The public purpose provision is so arbitrary that, in practice, the state can acquire land for any purpose it sees fit.

The procedure for acquiring land is divided into three distinct phases: notifying the public and hearing protests, making the final declaration of the land and assets to be acquired, and formulating and passing compensation. Persons losing private land are eligible to be compensated for the market value of the land they lost, for the structures on their land, and are eligible for a small transition allowance. By and large, it is argued that monetary compensation is an ineffective tool for the full rehabilitation of the affected persons, as it cannot account for and monetise intangibilities, such as the adverse social effects. This requires benefit-sharing programmes or development interventions. This Act, however, does not require the government to pass any other form of support other than cash compensation. Additionally, due to severe land market distortions in India, the level of compensation for land lost does not allow displaced persons to obtain equal replacement lands, which is particularly devastating for the livelihoods of rural communities. Furthermore, the Act only recognizes persons with legal title to their land, thereby excluding any persons occupying government land from compensation. These persons are typically already the most vulnerable and marginalised in India.

In order to address some of these shortcomings, the Government of Andhra Pradesh has enacted an amendment to the Land Acquisition Act and a Resettlement and Rehabilitation Policy. The former permits private land owners to negotiate with the government in determining the height of the compensation payable, while the latter attempts to address the resettlement and rehabilitation problems of some of the more vulnerable households. However, this policy was enacted in 2005, after the acquisition procedures for the airport were finalised. Despite the positive contributions to the Act, the land acquisition framework, as it applies to Andhra Pradesh, is severely subordinate to best practice resettlement and rehabilitation principles, as formulated by, amongst others, including the World Bank and Asian Development Bank. Most importantly, it fails to adequately define and assign entitlements and excludes many genuinely affected and vulnerable households from any form of remediation.

The Case of International Airport Project in Hyderabad

This is one of the most devastating and biggest displacements in a mega city like Hyderabad. The Government of Andhra Pradesh under the leadership of the Chief Minister Chandra Babu Naidu of the previous government, run by the Telugu Desam Party (TDP), had proposed the plan for an International Airport in the year 2000, but it did not get any type of assurance as the leadership was changing in the state. The TDP lost the elections and the Congress Party came to power in the year 2004 under the leadership of the present Chief Minister Dr. Y.S. Rajashekara Reddy, who instantly got the approval for the project from the Central Government as it was also led by the Congress Party; the work was started soon after. Ironically, the second and the third cases of displacements occurred under the same legislator, Smt. Sabita Indra Reddy. Just 15 days before the displacement, people of all the four villages were informed through a notice. The short notice came as a shock although the people were anticipating the project. The people were not in a position to take any precautionary measures. Smt. Sabita Indra Reddy assured the people of proper compensation and resettlement as all these people owned land. She also explained the inevitability of having such a project and made it clear that the project was certain to happen. As all these processes were going on, the people were unable to decide, if they were to move or stay back and protest.

Most people from all the affected villages were dependent on agricultural crops. They were flower-growers and sold their produce in the city of Hyderabad, and most of the people, even those with the landholdings of two or three acres, made enough profit. They used to employ 10 to 12 people a day for the work. The whole process of displacement and resettlement was supposed to take place under the special officer of IAS cadre, Mr. Prabhakar Reddy. The Collector of Ranga Reddy District was also involved in this. After the given time of 15 days, the authorities arrived with police forces and asked the people to vacate. But people had several ceremonies fixed before the notification. On their request to the concerned legislator, they got a grace period of 15 more days to vacate. On 13th May 2004, with the help of more than 500 Special Police Forces, the people were asked to evacuate; and all of them were shifted in lorries like animals; and the land was forcefully acquired.

The Politics of Displacement and Compensation

The uniqueness of this specific case study and other cases has been the fact that people from 11 villages, most of them with landholdings, some of them with assigned lands, and a very small number of people with no land were displaced. The Government of Andhra Pradesh acquired 5,480 acres of land for the project and more than 11 villages were affected either fully or partially. Out of the 5,480 acres of land, 3,400 acres belonged to the private owners, who have *pattas* (registration document or official land titles), while the other 1,600 acres are said to be government land, occupied 50 or 60 years ago by the local people, specifically people belonging to Schedule Castes and other Backward Classes for the sake of agriculture. The government made it very clear through the special officer Mr. Prabhakar that there will be no land for land compensation.

The people of the locality decided to organise a struggle against the government. However, the caste stratification in the place is also according to the different political parties – the Reddy group people largely supported the Congress Party as it is led by a person belonging to Reddy caste, while the BC and SC (Backward Class and Schedule Caste) groups largely supported the TDP (Telugu Desam Party). Due to this division amongst themselves, the plan to organize a struggle did not happen in a very strong manner. But as the compensation policy was quite clumsy and there was fear among the people of losing their assets, they decided to start an association of their own. This led to the inception of SIALLWEL (Shamshabad International Airport Land Losers Welfare Association).

The talks on compensation measures started on a very low note, as the officials had made it clear, that there will be no 'land for land' compensation – the compensation for land would be in terms of money. The government fixed prices for the land under categories A, B, C and D. The initial compensation rate of Rs. 2 lakhs per acre was protested against, and the people did not agree. A district committee was formed, led by the Collector, but it was a failure as the compensation money didn't move beyond Rs. 2 lakhs. This led to the formation of a state committee. The committee raised the compensation from Rs. 2 lakhs to Rs.4 lakhs, in the months of February and March 2002. The four categories and their compensations were distinguished on the basis of the quality of the land – A: Irrigated Land – Rs. 4 lakhs; B: Semi-Irrigated Land – Rs. 3.5 lakhs; C: Unirrigated Land – Rs. 3 lakhs; and D: Assigned Land – Rs. 65,000. This compensation is, however, not at all justifiable. The land actual value is far higher than the price offered by the Government. At that time, land value was up to Rs. 60 lakhs per acre.

Due to illiteracy and the fear of losing everything, most people agreed but wanted some of their demands to be fulfilled. The demands were as follows:

- Giving employment opportunity to two members from every family: The Collector of the Ranga Reddy District agreed to the same and promised that it will be fulfilled.
- Land for construction of house within the city limits: This was also agreed and the land was allotted closer to the Shamshabad main road.
- Demand for compensation to be given at one time: Even this demand was agreed.

The assigned land was also divided into three categories: (a) Rs. 80,000 + 30% = Rs. 1,04,000 (wet land); (b) Rs. 25,000 + 30% = Rs. 78,000 (rainy crops); (c) Rs. 50,000+30% = Rs. 50,000 (waste land). In the mean time, there were some tensions in a place called Kothaguda or Rashidguda. After the survey and the compensation policy was spelt out, an elderly person from the Muslim community filed a case showing some old references and saying that all the land in the village belonged to him. Some other person also filed a case saying that the land belonged to him. This virtually stalled the compensation process and a large amount of tension prevailed in the village. The people were confused and eventually feared that they may not get any compensation, if all the lands belonged to a Muslim man. This led to another type of consequence, where a villager committed suicide. This was a quite disturbing factor for the Congress Government as the foundation stone was going to be laid by the Prime Minister, Dr. Manmohan Singh and the Congress President, Ms. Sonia Gandhi. The government fearing the backlash and the repercussions would delay or stop the project, immediately asked the officials to take action and restore the compensation process. Because of this, a special G.O. was issued and although the case was still going on, the compensation process was also initiated simultaneously. So the people with *lavani patta*[1] also got a compensation of Rs. 65,000 per acre.

Table 19.1 Components of the Regular Compensation Package for Private Land Owners

Component	*Description*	*Specifics*
Category A Land (Wet)	Lands which have assured source of irrigation for two crops which are under cultivation	Rs. 4,00,000 per acre
Category B Land (Semi-wet)	Lands which have assured source of irrigation for one crop under cultivation	Rs. 3,50,000 per acre
Category B Land (Dry)	Lands under rain-fed cultivation or in waste lands	Rs. 3,00,000 per acre
Solarium	To cover immediate (transition) expenses and possible damages	30 per cent of total land value
Interest	To compensate for an increase in market value of land	12 per cent per annum of total land value
Structure Value	Houses, sheds, farm houses (wells and pipes excluded)	At fixed rate of Rs. 100 per sq yd
Tree Value		As per market value
Floriculture Value	Flowers under cultivation	As per market value

Source: Brief on International Airport Project, Ranga Reddy Collectorate, 21-11-2006.

Table 19.2 Extent and Type of Land Acquired for HIAL

Sl.No.	*Name of Village*	*Land Handed Over to HIAL (in Acres)*				
		Private Land	*Assigned Land*	*Encroached*	*Vacant*	*Total*
1	Shamshabad	31.12	25.24		2.81	**59.71**
2	Manneguda	25.22				**25.22**
3	Anantha Reddyguda	358.30		174.17	82.79	**615.26**
4	Gollapally Khurd	539.37	154.16	126.23	96.28	**916.04**
5	Gollapally Kalan	966.53		23.25	117.6	**1,107.38**
6	Muqthabahadur Ali	136.17			7.89	**144.06**
7	Rasheedguda	134.04				**134.04**
8	Khajaguda	31.38			3.99	**35.37**
9	Mamidipally	902.11	5.02	910.54	136.38	**1,954.05**
10	Mankhul	392.15				**392.15**
11	Village sites of Gollapally Khurd, Anantha Reddyguda, Gawlaguda		43.09			**43.09**
12	Lands under internal roads				64.03	**64.03**
Total		**3,516.39**	**184.42**	**1234.19**	**447.74**	**5,489.86**

Source: International Airport Project, Ranga Reddy Collectorate, Vigilance Report No.108, 22-09-2007.

The incident narrated was a case of rare happening, there were also constant debates regarding the site of the resettlement colony. After several rounds of discussion and strong protests against moving the people away from the city limits, the government identified a place which comes under the GHMC (the then HUDA) and fixed 250 square yards of land per family. The locality is 6 km away from one of the displaced villages called Chinna Gollapally, 8 km away from Galvaguda, 7 km from Anantha Reddyguda, and 9 km from Seethamma *Thanda*. The sites were allotted according to their survey numbers. However, certain groups remained away from the present resettled colony.

Further, there were some tensions during the time of displacement. The displaced people from all the villages together requested for a separate Panchayat. The authorities did not agree for such an arrangement. This again had its own political tinge. The groups were already divided, and this worsened after the separate Panchayat demand was denied. The people had a point to make: The lands of the people that were closer to the airport had different market value compared to other lands. For example, the land at Shamshabad cost around Rs. 50 lakhs at that time, whereas in Mankhul, the land value was below Rs. 5 lakhs. However, the government did not make any such distinctions, and paid the same amount to all lands. This was also one of the factors, why the displaced people were not very happy with the attitude of the officials.

The Resettlement Colony of International Airport Project

Immediately after the displacement, people could not find a place to stay. They were promised sites in a place which will be named as Airport Colony. Due to this, most of the people accepted and decided to vacate (the people were also threatened with the use of police forces). More than 550 families from four villages have been given a place to stay. Presently, 400 families have built houses in the Airport Colony. As this took place during the summer holidays, the transition period did not have much impact on education. Most of the people, who belonged to the Reddy group, did not build houses; instead, they invested their money in real estate business and started living in rented houses. Just before the news of the displacement, the rent in the area was just Rs.1400 to 1500. But once the displacement occurred and people realised that all the people from 11 villages would come to Shamshabad for shelter, the rents were increased.

On the day of resettlement itself, the displaced people were paid the compensation money at one go. This was one positive thing that happened to these people. The problems faced by the residents of the new colony are discussed below:

Problems in Airport Colony

Most of the displaced people belong to the agriculture group at large, especially floriculture – most of them were trained in these areas only. This was a major problem for the people as they do not know any other work. They are all semi-skilled labourers. The other problems faced by the oustees are listed below:

- School facility is available only till Class 4.
- All the children have to go to Shamshabad which is 4 km away from their locality for education and there is no transport facility.
- The transport facility is so bad that there is no single bus being operated by the State Government and the people have to rely upon private vehicles and autos.
- There is no primary health centre in the colony. People have to go to Shamshabad, even for small illnesses like headache and fever.

Problems of Caste and Political Parties

The biggest tragedy of this specific displacement and resettlement has been that of the people getting separated in the name of caste and political parties. As mentioned earlier, the displaced people comprise Reddys, who are upper caste people; yadavas of Backward Class; and Scheduled Castes. The Reddys are in favour of the Congress Party, while the other group of Backward Classes is in favour of the Telugu Desam Party. The Scheduled Caste group is divided between both the parties. Due to this division in political alignment, the resettlement process also saw some major differences. According to the survey numbers, the plots were distributed, but the Reddys, did not build houses in the resettlement colony as they have to live with the SC and BC people; instead they have been living in a place called Madhura Nagar near Shamshabad. This is just one dimension to the whole problem.

The other problem is, that the political rivalry among the groups has gone up to the level, that they do not even interact with each other. The Chairman of the Shamshabad Panchayat is from the TDP background; hence he is supported by the BC group and opposed by the Reddy group. Although the Reddy group denies the charges, the issue is true and it has been revealed by the BC group.

Displacement Leading to Vulnerability

Displacement, by nature, leads to vulnerability, and if it is in the urban area, the agony cannot be explained; it needs to be experienced. Vulnerability can be explained as "The degree to which an exposure unit is susceptible to harm, due to exposure to a perturbation or stress, and the ability (or lack thereof) of the exposure unit to cope, recover, or fundamentally adapt (become a new system or become extinct)" Kasperson (2001). This is the same situation faced by the displacees of all the three crucial cases taken in this study. It is a fact that all the people lost their job and their very existence came under threat. Many a time, men and women used to work simultaneously to earn bread for the family, but the new conditions were not conducive enough for the women to work. First of all, the people, in the first and the second case studies, are economic migrants and they had come in search of work to survive. Along with this, after 20 or 30 years of stay in the localities, this displacement came more as a shock and it has made them weak mentally and physically. With regard to the people who got displaced due to the airport project, their conditions have become worse as they do not have work to do. Moreover, after having had several employees working in their own fields, it has become extremely difficult for them to accept that they themselves have become daily wage labourers now.

The vulnerability level, at the resettlement colony, is the worst part of the whole process. The people are living in huts without even a proper roof. The huts are so small that a person cannot stand, and these have been built with small wooden sticks and leaves. The worst part was during the summer that year, when it rained incessantly in Andhra Pradesh. The belongings of the displaced people got washed away along with the huts and they had to take shelter in a building which was under construction. As the people had tapped the power from the electric poles directly, many children got electrocuted – in one such incident, a boy called Ravi passed away, and he was the only son of the family. The resettlement colony made people extremely vulnerable during the nights. Moreover, the resettlement colony is far away from the city and is surrounded by small forests; several snakes sneaked into the houses, or were sighted on the small roads of the colony. There have been several incidents of elderly people and children getting bitten by the snakes.

Vulnerable within the Vulnerable

The resettlement colonies have made the people vulnerable, due to the environmental conditions in which they are living. The places are not clean and the residents are prone to all types of disease. The 'Urban Basic Services' have not been provided to the people. The displacement has led to several vulnerabilities and that include cultural alienation, dispossession of land resources, human rights abuse, and lowering of living standards.

Due to the crosscutting nature of the displacement, no social/equity and distribution analysis can proceed without a discussion of gender. Thus, a growing constituency of policy-makers, social advisers, and gender scholars talk of gender main streaming and 'engendering' activities. They use gender conceptually and practically, to approach a whole array of issues, ranging from forced migration to development co-operation and health.

In the following section, we look briefly at the long process which led to the main streaming of gender – at least at the *de Jure* level – in national development. The tragedy of displacement due to development projects is compounded, because the affected bear the cost, but have no share in the benefits. Women, of course have even lesser access; they are mere passive recipients in the fallouts.

Vandana Shiva[2] (1993) puts the other facts in a very strong way, by saying that women's underdevelopment was not due to insufficient and inadequate participation; rather it was due to their enforced but asymmetric participation, whereby they bore the cost but were excluded from the benefits. The concern is that women are not consulted, and have been neglected in the policy process of displacement and resettlement. The authorities in charge of the relocation do not understand the women's problems of adjusting to the new locality. Since even, under normal circumstances, the society has yet to treat women equally, the displaced women will need some extra attention to cope with the changed circumstances, till such time that they can begin as equals. The traumas of displacements have direct connection with the rights of the women and their civil liberties. There is a necessity for upholding the social rights of all those who are vulnerable, but the required attention is not paid.

Ursula Oswald Spring[3] (2006) addresses this problem and says, "human rights and its phases of development do not guarantee minimal life conditions, but reinforce the individualisation process, increasing social vulnerability. On the contrary, social rights reinforce networks and create within the diverse cultural contexts and cosmo visions options for resilience building, reduction of social vulnerability, self reliance and peaceful conflict resolutions." The women have become vulnerable within the vulnerable. The concept may sound slightly different, as the argument

Table 19.3 Core Human Rights Challenges of Development-Induced Displacement

Human Rights Provision	*Elaboration*
Right To Development-DRD	"All persons are entitled to participate in, contribute to, and enjoy economic, social, cultural and political development, in which all human rights and fundamental freedoms can be fully realized" (DRD). Broadly speaking, often development in reverse is experienced by affected persons; they are also often excluded from ensuing developmental opportunities."
Right To Participation -ICCPR, Article 25	This allows affected persons to participate in decision-making processes that affect them, relating to, for instance, all resettlement and rehabilitation procedures. In most situations, very little equal and transparent participation in this regard is extended to affected persons.
Right to Life -UDHR, Article 3, 17, 23	In certain situations, physical coercion (both public and private) against civil disobedience can violate the right to life. Additionally, when people are deprived of their livelihood through loss of home and means to make a living, their right to life is also violated.
Right of Vulnerable Groups-UDHR, Article 2; ICCPR, Art. 2	Displacement often affects the most vulnerable groups disproportionately. Pre-existing gender inequalities can exacerbate when their ownership rights are not recognized; indigenous and minority groups who often lack formal land titles, lose access to Community Property Resources (CPR) and are excluded from employment opportunities.
Right to Remedy -UDHR, Art. 8; ICCPR, Art. 2	As most decisions that affect the livelihoods of affected persons are taken without their knowledge or consent, it is essential that institutional and legal frameworks are in place that permit the affected population to halt and/or prevent future right violations.

Source: Adapted from Rajagopal (2000) and Robinson (2003).

is that all the people displaced are vulnerable, but the truth is that the women are the first hit due to the fact that they need time to adjust with the new community and all the communities are not that safe for the women. For example, the men in the resettlement colonies, that do not have toilet facilities, will go out to the fields to finish their ablutions, but this is not that easy for the women. If this is one example of vulnerability there are several more examples, to prove that women are the worst hit in any developmental project.

The financial insufficiency of compensation, as a means for restoring and improving livelihoods, is by now well, known by the understanding we had through the chapter on three case studies. It is fully predictable that the outcomes will continue to be de-capitalisation and impoverishment, with countless people becoming worse off. To continue a financing pattern, based on compensation alone, means largely to continue financing the certainty of repeated failure and further impoverishment. Financing is in itself a factor of such paramount importance, for achieving economically sustainable resettlement that, when flawed, it causes failure, even if other necessary factors of success are present. Certainly, money alone would n't solve all resettlement problems either. But the absence of adequate financing foreordains failure by definition. Avoiding altogether or reducing displacement, whenever possible, remains always the desirable and paramount goal. But when compulsory displacement becomes unavoidable, these mechanisms are crucial for placing the people, who are physically or economically displaced on a new and economically robust productive foundation. Endowing development projects that cause displacement with the budgeted financial resources, needed to correct the harm through sustainable resettlement, is nothing more than a normal, elementary prerequisite for creating the capacity to do the job. Yet although this is a fundamental premise, project economists underestimate it.

Analysis of the compensation principle and practices, followed in the case studies of Hyderabad, cannot but conclude that compensation is structurally insufficient to achieve full restoration and is even less capable of generating improvements in livelihoods. Empirical findings show beyond any doubt, that the delivery of compensation is subject to structural dysfunctions, diverting practices, delays, etc., leaving the goal of oustees' reintegration and reconstruction unachieved. Given that the historical record of forced displacements is a reliable predictor, the absence of legislation mandating benefit sharing in public sector projects causing displacement means, in unambiguous terms, accepting in advance that resettlement will most likely fail to achieve restoration of livelihoods. Equally starkly, it means not repaying in full, the society's debt to those expropriated and condoning cost-externalisation and impoverishment.

Notes

1. Certificate that allows the farmers to use Government land but not to sell.
2. Shiva, Vandana (1993) Impoverishment of the Environment: Women and Children in Last, In Maria Mies and Vandana Shiva, Eco feminism-Kali for Women, pp. 70-91, London: Zed Books.
3. Spring, Ursula Oswald (2007) Climate Change: A Gender Perspective on Human and State Security Approaches to Global Security – Concept Paper for International Women Leaders, Global Security Summit. See http://www.afes-press.de/pdf/Oswald_Climate_Change_gender_perspective_abs.pdf

References

Bhatia, Bela (1997): "Displacement and Resettlement in the Narmada Valley, Forced Eviction in the Narmada Valley", in Jean Dreze, Meera Samson and Satyajit Singh (eds.), *The Dam and The Nation*, pp. 267-321, Oxford: Oxford University Press.

Cernea, M.M. 1986. "Involuntary Resettlement in Bank-Assisted Projects: A Review of the Application of Bank Policies and Procedures in FY 1979-1985", Projects, Agriculture and Rural Development Department, Washington, DC: World Bank.

Cernea, M.M. (1988): "Involuntary Resettlement in Development Projects: Policy Guidelines in World Bank-Financed Projects", World Bank Technical Paper No. 80, Washington DC: World Bank.

Cernea, M.M. (1990): "Poverty Risks from Population Displacement in Water Resources Development", HIID Development Discussion Paper No. 355, Cambridge, MA: Harvard University.

De Wet, Chris (1996): "Economic Development and Population Displacement, Can Everybody Win?" *Economic and Political Weekly,* 36(50), pp. 4637-46.

Downing, Theodore E. (1996): "Mitigating Social Impoverishment when People are Involuntarily Displaced", in C. McDowell (ed.), *Understanding Impoverishment Providence,* Oxford: Berghahn Books.

Fernandes, Walter, J.C. Das, and S. Rao (1989): "Displacement and Rehabilitation: An Estimate of Extent and Prospects", in W. Fernandes and E.G. Thukral (eds.), *Development, Displacement and Rehabilitation*, New Delhi: Indian Social Institute.

Fernandes, Walter (1991): "Power and Powerlessness: Development Projects and Displacement of Tribals", *Social Action*, 41(3), pp. 243-70.

Fernandes, Walter (1995): "An Activist Process Around the Draft National Rehabilitation Policy", *Social Action,* 45(3), pp. 277-98.

Fernandes, Walter (2000): "From Marginalisation to Sharing the Project Benefits", in M. Cernea and C. McDowell (eds.), *Risk and Reconstructing Livelihoods, Washington* DC: The World Bank.

Mathur, Hari Mohan (1999): "The Impoverishing Potential of Development Projects", Resettlement Requires Risk Analysis, Development and Cooperation No. 6, Frankfurt: Deutsche Stiftung für Internationale Entwicklung.

Mathur, Hari Mohan and David Marsden (eds.) (1998): *Development Projects and Impoverishment Risks* Delhi: Oxford University Press.

Reddy, I.U.B. (2000): "Restoring Housing under Urban Infrastructure Projects in India", in M. Cernea and C. McDowell (eds.), *Risks and Reconstruction*, Washington DC: The World Bank.

Thukral, E. (1996): "Development, Displacement and Rehabilitation: Locating Gender", *Economic and Political Weekly,* 31(24): 1500-1503.

20

Coal Economy, Displacement and Rehabilitation: A Hard Look in Talcher Coal Mines Area of Orissa

Kabita Kumari Sahu

Introduction

Mining is one of the most common activities in the modern world, which helps in industrialisation and tertiarisation of the economy along with rapid growth of national income. The activity has been expanded by leaps and bounds, due to rapid rise in human population and the various development activities around the world. Coal is one of the essential mining products, used popularly for domestic cooking and industrial heating. Out of the various mineral deposits in Orissa, coal occupies the second place, so far as coal fields in Orissa such as Ib Valley and Mahanadi Coalfields are concerned. The coalfield of Talcher located in Angul District plays an important role in boosting industrial development in this area. The huge reserve of power grade coal in Talcher has led to the establishment of a large-scale thermal power station in this area. These coalfields are of great significance not only to Orissa but also to Andhra Pradesh and Tamil Nadu. Talcher coalfields are located in the central part of Orissa, extended over an area of 1813 sq km; the total reserve of coal in the area as estimated by GSI is 25485.18 million tons.

The coalfield extends over an area of about 1800 sq km and is endowed with huge reserves of inferior grade non-coking coal in thick seams, lying at comparatively shallow depths. The total reserves are estimated at 22800 million tons and the coalfield has been divided into 30 blocks for detailed exploration. The present mining operations cover an area of 100 sq km with four underground and six open-cast mines. The coalfield is well connected by rail and road to important centres of India. Apart from coal mining, the major industries in the area are thermal power generation and the production of fertilizers and aluminium. The area is rapidly growing into a large mining and power complex, together with downstream industries. About 97% of the total coal production is from the large open-cast mines. The coal-to-overburden ratios (stripping ratios) are very favourable and the production capacity can be achieved in a comparatively shorter period with open-cast operation.

However, open-cast mining causes substantial impact on the land, forests, and water resources, in terms of quantity as well as quality, and on air in terms of quality. Besides, the acquisition of land, on a large scale for mining, will inevitably lead to the displacement of people. Several other industrial activities in the area, including power generation, are likely to give rise to environmental degradation. A survey carried out in the coal mines area indicated, that reserve forests constitute about 14% of the mining area in this coalfield. Future expansion of mining activities requires an estimated land area of 2580 hectares, of which 300 hectares would be forest area. This large-scale acquisition of forest land for mining, would have to be linked to a forest restoration programme through appropriate land reclamation, top-soil build up, and plantation. Compensatory afforestation is being carried out on degraded forest land within the mining area.

Coal mining, in the Talcher-Angul belt, has encouraged rapid urbanisation of the rural landscape and has led to extensive degradation of forest land. Open-cast mining, which is carried out in densely populated, areas, has a direct effect on human settlements and the demographic endowments in the area. The forest cover in the MCL mining area in Talcher was 160 sq km in 1975, but is now only 54 sq km, which indicates that there was a loss of 106 sq km of natural forest due to mining (Action Plan for District Action Group by Indian Environmental Society).

The area affected by mining is classified into: (i) Active Mining Area (ii) Abandoned Quarry (iii) Coal Dump (iv) Overburden Dump. The mining is carried out by open-cast and underground mining methods, causing large-scale displacement of people; their rehabilitation is a continuous process in this area. So this research paper is a humble attempt, to investigate the rehabilitation and resettlement policy of Coal India, for the people displaced due to the coal mine projects.

Coal Mines in Talcher Area

There are six operating open-cast mines and four underground mines in the area. The open-cast mines cause more displacement and health hazards comparatively. The list of open-cast mines with area and production is shown in Table 20.1.

Table 20.1: Open Cast Mines, Acquired Area and Mineral Reserve

Sl. No.	*Name of the mine*	*Year of operation*	*Total lease hold area (in ha)*	*Area already acquired (in ha)*	*Decoaled area (in ha)*	*Active mining area (in ha)*	*Total mine able reserve (in mt)*	*Present produ- ction (in mt)*
1	Bharatpur OCP	1985	1237.18	1119.795	162.197	65.0	167.8	5.0
2	Balanda OCP	1960	1045.75	1045.75	245.0	40.0	31.0	1.2
3	Kalinga OCP	1991	1117.36	739.5	105.5	160.0	166.0	6.5
4	Lingaraj OCP	1994	1248.5	249.18	20.02	70.14	319.0	5.0
5	Ananta OCP	1988	810.0	296.17	97.38	65.0	148.0	6.0
6	Jagannath OCP	1971	423.08	423.08	186.06	53.79	107.0	5.5
	TOTAL		5881.87	3873.475	816.157	453.93	1139.3	29.2

Source: Annual Report of MCL, 2009.

Balanda OCP is the oldest and started operation in 1960, followed by Jagannath OCP in 1971, and Bharatpur OCP in 1985. The total active mining area is 453.93 hectares and the present production is 29.2 million tons. These open-cast mines have already acquired 3873.475 hectares of land in 76 villages under both Land Acquisition Act and coal-bearing areas (acquisition and development) Act, 1975. But compensation, rehabilitation and resettlement have been taken up only in 35 villages. The people displaced from the coal mines area are rehabilitated as per the R&R policy of Mahanadi Coal Fields Ltd. A study made by Walter Fernandes and Atif from 1951 to 1995 reveals that in the mining projects, 60% of the displaced people have been compensated, while only 27.69% in irrigation projects, and 38.03% in factories have been compensated. Hence 72.31% of the displaced in irrigation projects and 61.97% of those displaced by industries in Orissa are not compensated, which reflects the wrong R&R policy of the Orissa Government. The rehabilitation is relatively better in the coal mines area in Orissa.

Land Acquisition, Displacement and Compensation

If mining is the most crucial activity that has to be undertaken in a specific area, the state has to consciously provide for a proper plan of relief and rehabilitation, which is acceptable to the communities affected; and the land acquisition procedures have to ensure a complete Environment Impact Assessment (EIA) and Environment Management Project (EMP), inclusive of compensating for women's livelihoods and development losses in a manner, which enhances the existing social and economic situation, rather than degrading it further. Land is acquired from the villagers and private persons, under the provisions of the Land Acquisition Act, for important public/private projects in the fields of irrigation, power-hydel, industries and mining, etc., resulting in the involuntary displacement of indigenous people from their land to an unknown place. Since land acquisition is essential for development, displacement of the local inhabitants to a place unknown to them cannot be avoided. The state has to also ensure, that the industries and mines first implement complete relief and rehabilitation, in the existing and abandoned projects, before fresh leases are granted for mining more lands and displacing more people in the green field areas. This is the first step towards building the commitment of the industry and the state that is responsible for mining-induced impacts. With the expansion of mining, displacement is still continuing in Talcher Block. The compensation includes financial compensation for the loss of land, provision of homestead land and assistance for house building, and compensation for the loss of livelihood for at least one member of the affected family. Rehabilitation colonies have been developed by MCL and others, where infrastructure such as roads, schools, tube wells, etc., have been provided. However, those, who have chosen to settle elsewhere, have been deprived of such infrastructure. There are many people employed as drivers, stone crushers, etc., and are daily wage earners. Earlier at least one member, from every household amongst the Project Affected People (PAPs), was eligible for a job; however, employment is no longer being offered as an option by MCL these days.

Displacement of human settlement not only creates hardship but also disturbs their former life-style and socio-economic condition. A World Bank report states, "All involuntary displacement destroys previous way of life, production systems are dismantled, community structure and social network are weakened; traditional authority and the individual social contract and economic inter-dependencies among families and kinship groups are ruptured." In a welfare state like India, it is the responsibility of the government to ensure that the displaced persons are rehabilitated and resettled properly so that their standard of living improves and they are placed better than before. The basic philosophy of rehabilitation and resettlement is to compensate the land losers and other PAPs in such a way that they get enough scope to reconstruct their socio-economic system. The Government of Orissa has already laid down well set guidelines for the rehabilitation of the displaced persons arising out of different types of projects, such as, industries, mining and irrigation, etc. Through its rehabilitation and resettlement policies for the project displaced/affected persons, the government intends to safe-guard the PAPs, so that they do not suffer from adverse effects and at least regain their former standard of living and earning capacity, after a reasonable transition period – the transition period is to be kept to a minimum. After the Kalinga Nagar incident in Jajpur, the Government of Orissa has made drastic changes in its R&R Policy for better welfare of, displaced people.

Regarding rehabilitation and resettlement, it is admitted that everywhere the affected population is under-estimated and not paid proper attention, by the project which takes away their land and thereby their livelihood. Experience has proved that rehabilitation and resettlement is always second in priority to the construction and execution of the project. In Mahanadi Coalfields Ltd., although land acquisition is a continuous process which would lead to large-scale displacement of human settlements, it is seen that the rehabilitation and resettlement agency is not properly equipped and gets the least priority. In the MCL project area,

995 families have been resettled and 2513 persons have been provided employment in different jobs. The details of project-wise employment and resettlement of families are shown in Table 20.2.

Table 20.2: Employment and Resettlement of Families

Sl. No.	*Name of mine*	*Total employment*	*Resettlement of families*
1	Kalinga OCP	791	
2	Bharatpur OCP	459	464
3	Jagannath OCP	382	510
4	Ananta OCP	247	21
5	Hingula OCP	102	---
6	Lingaraj OCP	497	---
7	Talcher UGP	35	---
	Total	2531	995

Source: Annual Reports, MCL, various years.

In Kalinga OCP, 791 affected people were given employment in coal mines, followed by 497 in Lingaraj OCP, and 459 in Bharatpur OCP. In comparison to the number of displaced people, the number of employed is seen to be very less in the mines area. A total of 510 families displaced from Jagannath OCP have been resettled, followed by 464 from Bharatpur OCP.

Rehabilitation and Resettlement Policy of the State Government in Coal Mines Area

Mining in Talcher area has resulted in large-scale displacement of people, who lost their land. There is an urgent need to assimilate these land oustees, by means of rehabilitation and resettlement and to undertake specific measures for mitigating their problems and removing the psychological feeling of alienation. The Revenue and Excise Department of the Government has formulated uniform guidelines, for rehabilitation and resettlement of the displaced persons/families, due to acquisition of land by MCL Projects in the state. A brief outline of the policy is given below:

A family/person shall be eligible for rehabilitation benefits if:

(a) All the lands of the family have been acquired;

(b) More than one-third agricultural lands along with homestead land have been acquired;

(c) Only homestead land has been acquired; or

(d) The family/person is homestead less but residing in the village.

This is to be ascertained through joint enquiry by a committee consisting of representatives from the MCL and the Government (Collector of the District). A family in the aforesaid context shall include the husband/wife as the case may be and their unmarried children, but does not include major sons who have been separated from the family, on or before the date of notification under Section 4(1) of the Land Acquisition Act, 1894, in respect of area/village. Such people shall be treated as a separate family.

Job and Self Employment Policy for Displaced People

Employment to the displaced people is an important method of rehabilitation, because it provides a continuous flow of income to the suffered family. MCL Project has given top priority to job and self employment to substantially affected people in the coal mines area.

The employment policy of coal mines projects is as follows:

(i) One member from each family, sustaining loss of dwelling house, homestead land and agricultural land, no less than, one-thirds of the total holding, shall be provided with employment on a priority basis.

(ii) One member from each family having sustained loss of three acres of non-irrigated land and two acres of irrigated land shall be provided with employment on second priority.

(iii) In case of families having lost only homestead land or the total agricultural holding, one member from each family shall be provided with employment according to availability.

(iv) In case of families who have lost one-thirds of their total agricultural holdings, one member from each family shall be provided with employment according to availability.

(v) Rehabilitation of other displaced families shall be made through self employment schemes.

Each displaced family shall be allotted government land of up to 10 decimal for homestead purpose, free of cost. Street lights, school buildings, health centres, provision of drinking water, recreation centres, ponds, tanks, play ground, veterinary centres, tree plantation, and shopping centres shall be provided according to necessity. Each displaced family shall be given assistance at the rate of Rs. 2000, for the construction of a temporary house. Expenditure in respect of rehabilitation shall be borne by the MCL.

R&R Policy of MCL

Coal India Limited (CIL) has also enunciated a rehabilitation and resettlement policy defining the project, affected persons and their entitlements. In the said policy, although the CIL has made provisions for, extension of, rehabilitation and resettlement benefits to a wide range of persons, it still remains confined only to the sphere, of employment and provision of resettlement plot or one-time cash grant of Rs.50,000 in lieu of resettlement plot to the category of 'A', 'B', and 'C' land losers and homestead oustees respectively. Coal India in its policy recognizes an adult individual as the unit of entitlement.

The project affected persons are classified into the following categories:

A. Land owners including those with whom government land is settled:
   (i) Persons from whom land is acquired including tribals cultivating land under traditional rights.
   (ii) Persons whose homestead is acquired.

B. Landless who derive their livelihood from the land to be acquired for a minimum of three years prior to the date of notification (of intention to acquire land):
   (i) Sharecroppers, the landless, tenants, and daily labourers.
   (ii) Tribes that depend on forest produce.
   (iii) Persons whose homestead is acquired.

To be eligible as a project affected person, one has to produce a written legal document or reference to a legal record, such as, Revenue Officer's Certificate, Electoral Roll, Ration Card, or School Record. The compensation and rehabilitation entitlement options are stated below, along with the category of persons affected by the project:

I. Persons (including tribals cultivating land under traditional rights) from whom land is acquired category, all land owners with titles will receive monetary compensation for the land acquired from them. The value of the land is determined on the basis of the prevailing legal norms.

In addition:

(a) If possible the company will offer employment as per their own policies (Package-A).

(b) PAPs identify and purchase, with the assistance of the company, equivalent replacement land using their land compensation (Package-B).

(c) The company will assist a PAP to establish non-farm self employment through the provision of infrastructure, petty contracts or formation of co-operatives (Package-C).

(d) If none of the above other packages are available, a PAP with less than two acres would receive rehabilitation assistance in the form of subsistence allowance or grant to be used for productive investments provided that his income from other sources does not exceed Rs.12,000 per annum (Package-D).

II. A person whose homestead is acquired:

The PAP will receive the replacement cost of homestead and the structure on it. In addition, the company acquiring the homestead will provide:

(a) An alternate house site measuring 100 sq m per family or a one-time cash grant of Rs. 50,000 in lieu of the acquired land (recent addition).

(b) Assistance in designing the new house if so desired by the PAP.

(c) A shifting allowance to cover the full cost of transporting his belongings to the relocation site (Package-E)

III. Sharecroppers, landless, tenants, day labourers and Landless tribals.

Package-C or job with contractors – contractors will be persuaded to give job to eligible PAPs, on a preferential basis where feasible.

In addition, the company will shift the tribal community as a unit and provide facilities to meet the specific needs of the tribal community to allow them to maintain their cultural identity.

Welfare Measures of Coal Mine Projects

Coal India limited has implemented its policy for the affected people and has made the following efforts for the welfare of the affected people:

1. Land for Land (Package-B)

Wherever possible and if so desired by the PAP who are land owners, the PAPs will identify and purchase land with assistance from the company. The land and its area should be such that it provides better or at least the same income to the PAP as was derived from his original land.

The modalities in this package are:

(i) A PAP who opts for this package is not entitled to any other rehabilitation options. However, shifting allowance at market rate, to cover the full cost of transportation, will be provided to the PAPs for moving to the new area.

(ii) The PAP may purchase land, on a willing buyer willing seller basis, within a limited geographic area and specific time period.

2. Non-Farm Self-Employment (Package-C)

For PAPs who opt for the non-farm self-employment package, the company will assist in developing such options as diary and poultry production, shops and petty contractors.

3. Subsistence Allowance

For PAPs having less than two acres of land, the subsidiary would provide rehabilitation assistance to ensure that the PAPs are able to regain their former standard of living or earning capacity. The assistance would be in the form of subsistence allowance or a lump sum grant to be used against productive investments.

4. Community Facilities

The company will provide at the resettlement site, the following infrastructural facilities:

(i) School building

(ii) Road with street lights

(iii) Pucca drain

(iv) Pond

(v) Dug well and/or tube well for drinking water supply

(vi) Community Centre

(vii) Place of worship

(viii) Dispensary

(ix) Grazing land

(x) Play ground.

5. Socio-Economic Survey

A base line socio-economic survey is required to be carried out to identify the PAPs and ensure restoration of income. This survey is to be conducted prior to the notification, under the relevant land acquisition acts by the company, with the help of reputed independent institutional agencies, that are well versed with the social matrix of the area. The objective of this survey is to formulate a viable and practical RAP for the affected persons to ensure the restoration of their income and the quality of life.

Gender Issues in Rehabilitation

The rehabilitation programmes taken up so far have been entirely insensitive to gender concerns, whether in providing land, housing, jobs or cash. The rehabilitated colonies provide no space for women, who need privacy, toilets, washing, domestic, health, recreation, and educational facilities. Neither have these provided for taking up economic activities on their own, not only because the forests are too far away from the colonies, but also because the people have no space for livestock rearing or for storage of forest produce in their resettlements. The rehabilitation programmes have been implemented with complete disrespect for social relationships and cultural beliefs. The approach of both industries and governments towards communities, with regard to rehabilitation, has always been one of performing magnanimous favours than with a sense of duty or responsibility. Hence, gender needs have never been a priority in the rehabilitation programmes.

The greatest impact of displacement, due to mining, has been the transformation of Adivasis from a close association and symbiosis with nature, to culturally and ecologically degraded communities. This degeneration of association from nature has led to the degeneration in cultural values, ceremonies and social celebrations, and common property management practices. Festivals have lost their significance as the people's association is now with mine-pits and not forests. A critical issue with regard to the legal rights of Adivasi women over lands is the problem of '*benami*' form of marriages – the Adivasi women are lured into marriage by non-tribal men even in non-mining situations, in order to enjoy rights to lands and properties. Land alienation, in many of the Scheduled Areas in the Adivasi regions, took place in this manner, where the non-tribal families reap the rewards of the lands owned by tribal women who, on the other hand, remain as mere concubines. It is feared that if legal rights are provided to Adivasi women over their lands, this could result in more land, passing into the hands of non-tribals. This becomes an issue of serious conflict when fighting for women's rights to rehabilitation and compensation. Especially in a mining area like Talcher, the infiltration of migrant labourers and non-tribal populations into Adivasi regions, places women in more vulnerable situations.

Conclusion

Talcher is a peculiar place, so far as land acquisition and consequential rehabilitation and resettlement are concerned. The rehabilitation and resettlement polices of Coal India Ltd. in Talcher coal mines area are good but they are not properly implemented. There are frequent strikes by the affected people, in different coal mine areas for compensation. Although employment is a major thrust in the coal mines area, no other activities are provided for over-aged persons, spinsters, physically handicapped, mentally retarded, orphans, widows, divorcees, encroachers, etc. There is no also separate policy for the SC and ST communities on a priority basis.

Hence, the following suggestions are forwarded for better rehabilitation in the coal mines area:

1. Special attempts are required to ensure, that the project affected women get adequate access to income-generating opportunities.
2. The settlement locations should be adequately outside the coal bearing area. These locations should be pollution free with good wind speed and directions.
3. The resettlement colonies should have adequate facilities for future growth of housing, infrastructure, commerce, recreation, etc. They should be nearer to the place of work and administrative centres.
4. Special rehabilitation and compensation should be provided to SC and ST communities, old people and children, widows and divorcees, mentally retarded and physically handicapped persons.
5. More hospitals and dispensaries should be established in the mining area to provide health care facilities, especially for respiratory, skin and eye diseases.

6. Sufficient plantation and water spray in the summer season should be provided for the welfare of the people.

Displacement is basically a human problem, which affects the people economically, psychologically, culturally and socially. So the rehabilitation and resettlement policy in the coal mines area, should be handled carefully to provide a better standard of living to the affected people.

References

ADB (1998): *Handbook on Resettlement: A Guide to Good Practice*, Manila: Asian Development Bank.

Agnihotri, A. (1996): "The Orissa Resettlement and Rehabilitation of Projects Affected Persons Policy, 1994 – An Analysis of its Robustness with Reference to the Impoverishment Risk Model", in A.B. Ota and A. Agnihotri, (eds.), *Involuntary Displacement in Dam Projects*, pp. 19-42. New Delhi: Prachi Prakashan.

Asif, M., L. Mehta, and H. Mander (2002): "Engendering Resettlement and Rehabilitation Policies and Programmes in India", A Report of the Workshop held at the India International Centre, New Delhi on September 12 and 13, 2002 by the Institute of Development Studies and Action Aid, India with support from DFID.

Baruah, B. (1999): "The Narmada Valley Project: Displacement of Local Population and Impact on Women", *Natural Resources Forum* 23(1), pp. 81-84.

Cernea, M.M. (1997): "The Risks and Reconstruction Model for Resettling Displaced Populations", *World Development*, 25(10), Great Britain: Pergamon Publication.

Ekka, Alexius and Mohammed Asif (2000): "Development-Induced Displacement and Rehabilitation in Jharkhand, 1951 to 1995: A Database on its Extent and Nature, A Study Supported by Oxfam (India) Trust", New Delhi: Indian Social Institute.

Fernandes, Walter (1996): "Development-Induced Displacements and Marginalisation in Orissa", in A.B. Ota and Anita Agnihotri (eds.) *Involuntary Displacement in Dam Projects*, New Delhi: Prachi Prakashan.

Fernandes, Walter (1991): "Power and Powerlessness: Development Projects and Displaced Tribals", *Social Action* 41(3), pp. 243-70.

Government of India (1996): "Draft National Policy for Rehabilitation of Persons: Displaced as a Consequence of Acquisition of Land, A Document of Ministry of Rural Development", Published in *Economic and Political Weekly*, 31(24)pp. 1541-45.

Government of Orissa (1994): "The Orissa Resettlement and Rehabilitation of Projects Affected Persons Policy", Department of Water Resources, Bhubaneswar.

Goyal, Sangeeta (1996): "Economic Perspectives on Resettlement and Rehabilitation", *Economic and Political Weekly*, 31(24), pp. 1461-67.

21

Between Two Nations: Chakmas and Their Settlement in Arunachal Pradesh

Chunnu Prasad

India is the largest nation experiencing refugeehood. During her liberation in 1947, an estimated 10 million people took refuge from neighbouring countries. Ever since, India has been hosting refugees; however, it is not a state party to the UN Convention, relating to the status of refugees 1951 or its Protocol of 1967. There is also no domestic legal framework to deal with the issue of asylum and refugees. Although there are a few provisions in the Indian Constitution, which could be translated for the protection of refugees, there is a lack of common understanding on those (Chimni, 2000). In this backdrop, there is a point for India for accession to the UN Convention, relating to the status of refugees in 1951 and adoption of a normative legal framework. The Convention is the basic instrument of Refugee Laws, that defines a refugee, and sets out their rights, and the responsibilities of states that grant asylum (Year book, 2005).

The Ministry of Home Affairs formulates the policies and programmes for relief and rehabilitation of people of Indian origin displaced from other countries. It has also been entrusted the work of providing relief to the Tibetan and Srilankan refugees; and various relief and rehabilitation schemes are being implemented by the Ministry of Home Affairs, through the State Governments and Union Territory Administrations. A wide range of measures was taken for the resettlement of '*old migrants*' during the period from 1948 to 1961. These included agricultural schemes, vocational and technical training schemes, and rehabilitation loans for small traders, businessmen and professionals, and provision of housing, medical and educational facilities. Another measure was taken to resettle the '*new migrants*' who arrived between January 1, 1964 and March 25, 1971 (Constituent Assembly of India debate, 1948). All these migrants largely resettled in the eastern and north-eastern states of India. The settlement wing functions as a Subordinate Office of the Rehabilitation Division of the Ministry of Home Affairs and deals with residuary matters of resettlement of displaced persons, from, former West Pakistan under the Displaced Persons Compensation and Rehabilitation Act, 1954, and the rules framed thereunder (Compensation and Rehabilitation Act, 1954).

As far as India's refugee regime is concerned, she should frame its refugee law and place her refugees in different categories, on the basis of their historical divide and injustice. The Chakmas are such a category. The Chakmas, who settled in 1964, almost more than five decades from now, are reclaiming their basic human dignity, which they were denied on various occasions, by the State Government as well as civil society groups (Chimni, 2005).

The Chakmas are the tribals of the north-eastern states of India. They are settled mainly in the states of Mizoram, Tripura, Assam, Arunachal Pradesh, Meghalaya and West Bengal. The Chakmas are believed to have migrated from the Chittagong Hill Track (CHT) of West Bengal to the Mizo Hills. It is also believed that the Chakmas migrated from the Champa Kingdom in Cambodia, where the Lushais called them Tui-Chek, which means the people who lived near water. The Chakmas have close resemblance to the Mongolians of the Tibeto-Burman groups. Khyangtha and Thangtha are the two groups within the Chakmas. They are classified on the basis of the places where they live. Khyangthas live on the bank of the river, while Thangthas, also called Jhumias live on hill tops. The Chakmas believe in Buddhism and have a language of Burmese and Sanskrit scripts. Agar Tara, a version of Buddhist scripture, is their oldest scripture. It is read on the special occasions, like marriages, funerals, etc. (Incredible India from www.india.com).

The Chakmas are the Mongoloid tribes, probably of Arakanese origin. The name Chakma sometimes is spelt as *'Tsakma' Tsak* or *Thek* in Burmese. They might have migrated from a place, somewhere in South-East Asia. The Chakmas, though the original inhabitants of the CHT, are perhaps the least known people of Asia, being the residents of a remote and backward area, which is of little political or economic consequence. This place has been the homeland of the Chakmas, for centuries. Though the origin of the Chakmas is not very clear, their history connects them with the mountainous kingdom of Kapilnagar in the Himalayan ranges. It is learnt that during AD 1052 the Chakmas started moving from Arakan into the bordering area of Bengal, right down the plain areas of Chittagong (Bangladesh) and made it their home (Talukdar, 1994).

There is very little documentation available on the early history of the Chakmas. However, there is evidence of the mention of a place known as *'Chacomas'* in central CHT, probably referring to the land inhabited by the Chakmas, in the 1550s, where a Burmese king claims himself to be the "*highest and most powerful king of Arakan, Tippera (Tripura), of Chacomas and of Bengala*" (Talukdar, 1994).

In 1947, Radcliff ceded the CHT District to Pakistan on the basis of religion, when the Indian subcontinent was partitioned into Islamic Pakistan and secular India, though the district was 98.5 percent Buddhist (Think India, 2006). On the 15th of August 1947, the Chakma youth under the leadership of Sneha Kumar Chakma hoisted the Indian tricolour at Rangamati, while in the south, six days later the Pakistanis lowered the Indian tricolour at gunpoint (Bhattacharya, 2001).

On the another side, Jawaharlal Nehru promised Sneha Kumar Chakma, the representative of the Parbattya Chattogram Jana Samity, that the Bengal Boundary Commission had no jurisdiction over the CHT. Before India's independence, Sneha Kumar Chakma had met Sardar Patel and Jawaharlal Nehru in July 1947 and was promised by both, that CHT would remain with India. However, on 18 July 1947, when the Indian Independence Act was published, Radcliff had not listened to the submissions of the two Hindu members of the Bengal Boundary Commission, Justice Bijon Mukherjee and Charu Biswas, that CHT should be with India. Sneha Kumar went to Delhi after hoisting the Indian Tricolor at Rangamati on the 15 August 1947, to meet the Indian leaders to try and revise the decision of Radcliff (Talukdar, 1988). He met Sardar Patel, who told him that he was with him but he should meet Jawaharlal Nehru. It took 50 days for Sneha Kumar Chakma to meet Nehru. When he finally got an audience and told Nehru the CHT should be with India; that the Chakmas were ready to fight for this and asked for India's help with arms, Nehru got up in anger and shouted, "*Do you propose to bring India under foreign rule again?*" That decision sounded the death knell for the hapless Chakmas. Thus, the Chakmas had to unwillingly cede with Pakistan (Prasad, 2010).

Chakmas Settlement in India

As far as history is concerned, the Chakmas' problems in India dates back to post 1971 and post Bangladesh issue. Chakma influx into India can be traced to the partition of the subcontinent from the beginning, as '*inconsistency and political expediency*' governed India's CHT policy. The first influx of the refugees took place shortly after partition, when 40,000 Chakma families fled to India (Singh, 2001a). Having housed and absorbed a large number of non-Muslim Chakmas from East-Pakistan, India did not treat the Chakma differently and resettled them, first in North India and later in North-East India. The manageable number of the Chakmas, their widespread dispersal in the sparsely populated North-East and their ethnic proximity largely mitigated any potential opposition from the indigenous population. Furthermore, absorption was feasible partly because ethnic consciousness in the North-East was still in its infancy (Singh, 2001b).

The present demand for the grant of citizenship and Scheduled Tribe status by the Chakmas, clearly shows that they are not only unwilling to move out of the state, but are also politically conscious and quite determined to stay permanently in the state. However, their desires have not been fulfilled even after five decades; they have been denied citizenship at several occasions, even after the Indira-Mujib agreement of 1972, which makes mandatory for the Indian Government to treat their applications lawfully for the grant of citizenship (Prasad, 2006). Under the Indira-Mujib agreement of 1972, it was decided that the Chakmas who came to India from the erstwhile East Pakistan before 25 March 1971, will be considered for the grant of citizenship. Moreover, the Supreme Court in its ruling of 9 January 1996 has directed the State Government to forward all applications of the Chakmas, for citizenship to the Government of India and not to evict any of them, while their application is under consideration. M.M. Jacob, while expressing the view of the Central Government stated that, "The presence, of these Chakmas in the area, has also not resulted so far, in any major law and order problems, though some isolated instances of friction between, locals and these Chakmas have come to our notice.... That the Central Team, which visited Arunachal Pradesh to study the problems of these refugees, expressed the view that the grant of citizenship would introduce an element of responsible social behaviour in these refugees (Singh, 1996)." He further added, "Refugees from Bangladesh who came to India between 1964 and 25 March 1971, are eligible to the grant of citizenship, according to the policy of the Government, as most of the migrants have already been granted citizenship." Further more, he asserted, "Keeping the above in view there is no question of deporting these refugees from the State of Arunachal Pradesh. The general public in the state will have to be convinced, that the burden of rehabilitation of the refugees will have to be shared by the country as a whole, including Arunachal Pradesh" (Singh, 2001b.).

Districts/Villages where Chakmas are Concentrated in Arunachal Pradesh

Changlang District has the highest in number of Chakmas – with a population of 40,000 – followed by Lohit district with 15,000, and lastly Papumpare District, which has only 5,000 people. According to the Government of India's record, their population is approximately 60,000 (Census of India, 2010). Presently the Chakmas are resettled in the three districts/villages, as shown in Table 21.2.

Table 21.1 Chakmas in other Parts of the World

Country	*Total Population*	*Total Percentage*
All Chakma Population	**5,50,000**	**100**
Bangladesh	3,00,000	55
India	2,00,000	36
Burma	20,000	5
Other parts	30,000	4

Sources: UNHCR Report on Migration, Global Resettlement, 2009.

Table 21.2 Status of Chakmas in the North-East and Eastern States of India

State	*Status*	*Scheduled Status*	*Total Population*	*Ethnic (Rank)*
Arunachal Pradesh	Refugees	Refugees	60,000	II
Assam	Citizens	ST	5,000	IX
Meghalaya	Citizens	ST	610	IIV
Mizoram	Citizens	ST	71,283 (8.5%)	II
Tripura	Citizens	ST	64,293 (6.5%)	III
West Bengal	Citizens	ST	3,000	XI

Source: Office of the Registrar General, Government of India, 2001 on Population. Also see Migration Report, 2009.

Papumpare

It is the most developed district in Arunachal Pradesh, because the capital city Itanagar falls in this district. Largely, the Nyishis are the majority community in this district. It has a border called Balijan and Kokila, which divide Arunachal Pradesh and Assam. It is one of the most conflicting areas as far as state boundary and land is concerned. Earlier Chakmas were largely settled in Balijan, but over a period of time, they were shifted forcefully and resettled to the new place called Kokila, which is a flooded area. For a period of minimum four to five months, this area remains under floods and heavy rainfall. Being a low-lying area, the Chakma-inhabited region is always under a deluge.

Changlang

Changlang, the biggest district of Arunachal Pradesh, has the maximum population, largely of Buddhist origin. Most Chakmas are concentrated in Diyun and Mieo. The condition of Chakmas here is better off, as compared to the other two districts, due to active involvement of civil society groups particularly the SNEHA. The following are the villages in this district where Chakmas are found: Gautampur, Santipur, Joytipur, Abhaypur, Dumpani, Rajnagar, Joshnapur, Dumpattar, Udaypur, Modoideep-I, Modoideep-II, Kamakhyapur, Vijoypur-1, Vijoypur-II, Vijoypur-III, Dharmapur-I, Dharmapur-II, Ratnapur, Golakpur and Milanpur.

Lohit

Lohit District also has a good number of Chakma people. They live in three *bastis* (villages), which are always under the threat of flood every year; loss of life and property is very common. My field work found that the oldest people who migrated from CHT and Rangamati are living in these three *bastis* (street) of Lohit District:

(a) Chakma *Basti*-I

(b) Chakma *Basti*-II

(c) Chakma *Basti*-III

Socio-Economic and Political Conditions of Chakmas in the Settled Areas

The social condition of the Chakmas of Arunachal Pradesh, in particular, and India, in general is very rich. They do not have caste system or any type of division, we see in other religions. Socially, they live together, eat and participate in all the occasions, without any differences. They marry freely without any restriction based on caste, sex, tradition, rich, poor, etc. The Chakmas are largely Buddhists. During my field work, I did not find a single Chakma, who was not Buddhist, and there was no report of conversion to any other religion. It is also appreciable that, though they are facing huge discrimination from the state, as well as the Central Government, and everyday violence by the AAPSU activists and Arunachalees, they have a strong and deep feeling that they are in good religion and one day definitely things will change.

Politically, very few Chakmas are enrolled in the electoral list. Many Chakmas, who are born in India are still waiting for their enrolment in the electoral rolls, but their application has been rejected many times, starting from 2004, and in 2007 and 2008. In 2004, the Election Commission warned that it would not hold assembly polls in Arunachal Pradesh, unless the State Government includes the Chakmas in the electoral rolls. As a result of this, from 2 January 2004 onwards, the commission has stopped its ongoing revision of the electoral rolls in four assembly segments that also form parts of the Lok Sabha constituencies, in both East and West Arunachal Pradesh.

The commission ruled that the conduct of any and all elections, in the four assembly constituencies of Doimukh, Chowkham, Bordumsa Diyum, and Miao, along with all election-related work, including the preparation or revision of the electoral rolls there, shall stand suspended until further orders, in an order dated 2 January 2004 (Rana, 2004). The commission was compelled to take this drastic measure, as the State Government officials, engaged in the electoral roll revision, in an unprecedented step, refused to entertain the commission's repeated instructions to include the Chakmas. Their refusal was based on a State Cabinet's decision, taken on 14 May 2003, not to include non-Arunachalese people in the electoral roll, unless they possessed the Inner Line Permit, issued under the Bengal East Area and Frontier Regulation, 1873 (Prasad, 2007a). Terming the decision as '*wrong*' the commission has pointed out that, even the Supreme Court of India and the Delhi High Court, in their respective orders on two different petitions, dealing with the question of the settlement of the Chakmas in the state and granting of Indian citizenship to them, have held that the Chakmas, born in India on or after 26 January 1950, but before 1 July 1985, and living in the state, are to be treated as residents of the state and are entitled to be registered in the electoral roll of the state. The commission had also met the Arunachal Pradesh Chief Minister on 28 August 2003, and on the basis of the Supreme Court Order dated 9 January 1996 and the Delhi

High Court order dated 28 September 2000, had conveyed to him that as long as the Chakmas were ordinary residents in the state, they could not be denied their Constitutional right of enrolment in the electoral rolls of the state. Subsequently, in September 2003, the commission had also conveyed through an official communication, that the preparation and revision of the electoral rolls was a constitutional duty, conferred on the commission by Article 324 (1), and the State Cabinet's resolution, refusing voting rights to the Chakmas was a hindrance to the commission's constitutional obligation, to prepare and revise the electoral rolls. This, in turn, will adversely affect the free and fair conduct of the elections, said the commission in its September 2003 communication to the State Government, requesting it to suitably amend or altogether scrap its Cabinet resolution. The State Government's refusal to comply, resulted in an impasse (Supreme Court Judgment, 1996).

The economic condition of the Chakmas is so poor and unfortunate that even after 50 years, some sections of the society are living under poverty and just surviving with a one-time meal in a day. They are living Below Poverty, Line (BPL) and the government does not have any plan for these marginalised sections of the society. Neither the Government of India, nor the Government of Arunachal Pradesh, nor any civil society has attempted to bring some necessary economic changes, to improve the conditions of the poor Chakmas, in all the three districts of Arunachal Pradesh. It is unfortunate that the entire settlement of the Chakmas is largely on the bank of the river, which is flooded during the rainy season – in Kokila (Papumpare) the Chakmas are settled on the bank of the River Hollongi; in Diyun, Changlang, it is called Neo Deheng River and in Lohit it is called Darang River (Prasad, 2010).

Incidence of Discrimination

Discrimination is largely connected to the term '*adequate*', which means that these services are available, accessible, acceptable and adaptable.

Availability means that the goods and services are made available to the affected population in sufficient quantity and quality.

Accessibility requires that the goods and services are: (a) granted without discrimination to all in need; (b) within safe reach and can be physically accessed by everyone, including, vulnerable and marginalised groups; and (c) known to the beneficiaries.

Acceptability refers to the need to provide goods and services that are culturally appropriate and sensitive to gender and age.

Adaptability requires that the goods and services are provided in ways, flexible enough to adapt to the change, of needs in the different phases of emergency relief and reconstruction (Babu, 2008).

During the immediate emergency phase, food, water and sanitation, shelter, clothing, and health services are considered adequate, if they ensure survival to all in need of them. The concerned authorities, after reasonable verification, shall issue to the affected and, displaced persons all documents, necessary for the enjoyment and exercise of their legal rights, such as passports, personal identification documents, birth certificates, death certificates, and marriage certificates. Any lack of access to such legal documents or not having such legal documents, shall not disentitle them for recompense. But it was found during my field work that none of the concepts applies here, when it comes to the Chakmas. I found a huge list of intentional discrimination by the AAPSU as well as State Regime.

I present a few points and analysis which I experienced in my field work, when I interacted with these excluded people:

1. There is not a single case registered in the Kokila, Papumpare Police Station of the violence done by the AAPSU, on many occasions. When I asked about the views on AAPSU, one of the senior Chakmas told, "*I do not understand what criminalisation is! And how Chakmas are criminal*". He asked the definition of crime. He said that one small boy of his village, below the age of 18, had just stolen four bananas and for that he was kept in prison for at least four years without trial and order of the court.
2. At first, the Chakmas were allowed to settle in Ledu (Changlang), the hilliest and densest forest areas. Over a period of time, with their hard work, they made it a place suitable for habitation. Later, many Singpho came from other parts of Arunachal Pradesh and started claiming that the Chakma-settled areas were theirs and started torturing the Chakmas to leave the land. Finally, in October 2007, when the conflict turned violent, the Deputy Commissioner of the District, Mr. Lokhande mediated between the Chakmas and the All Arunachal Mismi Student Union (AMSU) and created boundaries for the Chakmas and the Mismis. Both groups had accepted the solution, but a few months later, the AMSU stated that it does not accept the solution given by Mr. Lokhande and claimed all rights on the land; the Mismis, forcefully, took away even the agricultural produce of the Chakmas.

3. As per Arunachal Panchayati Raj Institution, the head of the village is called the '*Gam Bura*', but in Chakma village, he is the '*Head Man*'.
4. Chakma students are unable to continue their education beyond the 8th grade, because there are only 15 primary, two secondary schools, and one higher secondary school in Changlang, which is 10 km from Diyun (Chakma settlement area). And over all, it is 25 to 30 km from all the primary and secondary schools, if we take an average of all the Chakma settled areas. Many primary schools, where Chakma children study, have shortage of regular teachers; andthe Chakmas themselves manage the teachers by paying money.
5. There are no roads in all the three districts where Chakmas are settled.
6. The Chakmas are facing flood situation in their areas and the government has not initiated any programme to control floods even after four decades.
7. There is no electricity.
8. Not a single Chakma works as a government employee in the state.
9. No security for their life and property is provided, either by government, or by non-government organisations.
10. All the central, as well as international organisation programmes have been suspended in all the three Chakma settled districts, including Anganwadi Programmes, *Sarva Siksha Abhiyan*, National Rural Guarantee Scheme, National Health Mission Scheme, and many more.

Categorisation of Chakmas

The Chakmas of Arunachal Pradesh are concentrated in three districts particularly in Papumpare (Urban), Changlang and Tirap. The Government of Arunachal Pradesh has been violating all the basic rules and laws defining in their own way, by categorising these Chakmas into three categories:

(a) Chakmas who settled originally in the year 1964.

(b) Chakmas who after inter-district migration, have settled in Papumpare, Changlang and Lohit.

(c) Chakmas, who after inter-state migration have settled in Tripura, Mizoram, Assam, West Bengal.

Firstly, the Chakmas who directly migrated in the year 1964 and settled in various parts of India and were later brought to NEFA (present Arunachal Pradesh). Secondly, the Chakmas, who, because of situations like floods, life threat, livelihood etc., migrated within the state and mixed with the other Chakmas, settled in the districts, namely, the Changlang, Lohit and Papumpare. And lastly, intra-district migration: for example the first Chakma exodus happened in the year 1947, just after independence; they were granted citizenship as well as Scheduled Tribe status, and mainly settled in the states of Assam, Tripura, West Bengal and Mizoram; but later migrated for job, education, or other purposes; and married and settled in Arunachal Pradesh over a period of time.

The Arunachalees have the misconception that the Chakmas look like Bengalis, since they are from Bangladesh; so they do not consider them as tribals like themselves; however, this is not true. The Chakmas were given land in Arunachal Pradesh by the Indian Government with the intention of permanently settling them – the government hoped that the Chakmas can again build their shattered life in the state. Thus, the Chakmas were settled in the state on humanitarian basis. The government also expected them to be comfortable in the state, as they were also tribals and Buddhist by religion. That was one of the reasons they were settled near the Khamtis and Singphos, who were also Buddhist and tribals.

From the time, the Chakmas were settled in the state, they were given employment opportunities mostly in paramilitary forces, whilesome were given government jobs. There was no problem and no question of citizenship as they were given equal opportunities, like any other Indian citizen. There was also no discrimination towards them, since Arunachal Pradesh was a Union Territory (NEFA) at that time. The problem began only after it was made a full fledged state (Prasad, 2007b).

Under the Chief Minister-ship of Gegong Apang, slowly all the facilities given to the Chakmas by the Union Government, such as, ration cards, free books for the students, drinking water, electricity, etc., were withdrawn – the Circle Officer of Diyun gave a circular ordering the Chakmas to surrender their ration cards, which added more misery to the life of the community. Almost all the Chakmas were dependent on agriculture, but even after toiling for days together, they could not produce enough rice to sustain themselves throughout the year. So they depended on the PDS for rice and kerosene oil – for lighting their homes at night. Thus, snatching away these facilities resulted in hunger among the community. This was not only a crime against the helpless Chakmas, but also a crime against humanity. In order to add more misery to the already piled mountain of miseries, the Arunachal Pradesh Government ordered the closure of most of the schools in the Chakma areas. The Chakma children were also prevented from taking admission into other nearby schools, such as, in Chowkham. This inhumane step taken by the State Government resulted in a generation of illiterate children among the Chakmas and till date the middle school is lying vacant to be re-opened (NHRC, 2002).

Not only the Chakmas of Lohit District, but also their fellows in Changlang and Papumpare districts, suffered such injustice. In Changlang District, the Chakma students were prevented from taking admission into any of the government schools. Some of the students studying in Miao Senior Secondary School, Innao Senior Secondary School, Namsai Senior Secondary School, etc., had to leave the school in the middle of the academic session. Till date, the Chakma students are denied admission in any of the government-run schools for secondary education. The only school, that was open to the Chakmas in Changlang District, is the Diyun Secondary School, where more than 150 students study in a single class room (NHRC, 2002). In grade six, more than 250 students sit in a single class room. Also, all the schools in Chakma areas have neither teachers nor a proper school building. Only one teacher is allotted for a primary school to maintain discipline in five classes at the same time. Such is the pathetic condition of the Chakma students. It is because they are born in the Chakma community of Arunachal Pradesh, that they have to go through this ordeal (Chakma, 1996).

Former Arunachal Pradesh Chief Minister Dorjee Khandu requested the Prime Minister Manmohan Singh to constitute a high-level committee to solve the Chakma problems in the state. It is really difficult to understand, whether the committee will be made from the Centre or from the State Assembly – already a high power committee had been constituted in the state, a few months ago, with Setong Sena as the Chairman. As the problem is political in nature, it can be solved only if there is political will. Merely, constituting a high level committee, will not help (newsoneindia.in).

The question, that persists in the minds of all those, who believe in humanity is that being born and brought up in India, according to the Citizenship Act, 1955, and also the Citizenship (Amendment) Act, 2003 of Section 3-1(a), by which every person born in India on or after the 26th day of January, 1950, but before the 1st day of July, 1987, shall be citizen of India by birth (Rodrigues, 2005). Why are the Chakmas of Arunachal Pradesh not considered to be Indian citizens? Why do they have to go through the trauma of being labelled as refugees? Also according to International Convention, a person should not be denied citizenship, on the basis of caste, community and religion. Then why are the Arunachalee Chakmas are denied nationality? It has been almost five decades, but still the Chakmas in Arunachal Pradesh are living in doubt: whether they are Indians or refugees. Ironically, all other Chakmas settled in other parts of India are leading normal life like any other Indian citizens. Then, why is such injustice, being done to the Arunachalee Chakmas? Because of this injustice the future of thousands of Chakma children is hanging in balance. The Chakmas don't have any source of employment, as the Arunachal Pradesh Government has stopped providing employment to them. It is also difficult to find jobs outside the state. Chakmas are frustrated, when they see their friends from other communities getting jobs, just after passing Class 10 or 12, while they are unemployed even after completing graduation. Is not this pure *'discrimination'*? Despite being more educated and qualified, they are being ignored in job opportunities, even in their place of birth (Prasad, 2007b).

Now-a-days, there is a lot of debate regarding the issues of development in Arunachal Pradesh. The Chief Minister Dorjee Khandu has taken the oath to root out corruption, streamline the PDS, and ensure time-bound accelerated implementation of power projects and other critical on-going schemes, related to developmental activities, which have direct bearing on the lives of the rural poor in the state. The people have very high expectations from Dorjee's regime and changes are expected to be seen very soon. But whatever developmental activities and projects are going on, are mainly centered in the western and central parts of the state. There are no development projects slated for Changlang and Lohit districts, as the development of the three districts is not considered to be equally important, as any other districts – this is because the Chakmas are largely concentrated in these districts (newsoneindia.in).

India's refugee regime represents a particularly salient case for exploring the role of interconnections between issue-areas, as an independent variable in cooperation. This is because of the absence of a binding normative framework on burden-sharing, and the fact that states have few interests in contributing to burden-sharing for its own sake, which means that the prospects for international cooperation have been determined, largely, by the ability of UNHCR to use linkages to connect refugee protection to states' interests in issue areas, outside the immediate scope of the regime (Bose, 2000).

Two conceptual conclusions of particular relevance for the role of complexity, emerge from this case study: Firstly, structural interconnections between issue-areas play a role in cooperation, because they enable and constrain the ability of actors to appeal to linked interests within bargaining; and secondly, institutional interconnections (such as nesting, parallel and overlapping institutions) are but one special case of structural interconnections.

It is surprising that India's refugee regime has not been given greater prominence in international relations. There was a fundamental contradiction between the principles of sovereignty and human rights, but argued that, this conspiracy is mitigated by the practice of granting rights of asylum to foreign political refugees. Refugees actually buttressed a territoriality-based conception of sovereignty, because states could allow unwanted populations to flee without taking more extreme actions, and the international community could assist refugees, without direct intervention. Refugees were, in essence, a necessary relief valve for the system of sovereign states (Chimni, 1999).

The plight of the refugees, irrespective of whether they are looked after, either by the UNHCR or the Government of India, is abominable, to say the least. The condition of the refugees, who are not recognised, either by UNHCR or the Government of India, is the worst. The lack of legal mechanisms and policies on refugees, is one of the fundamental flaws of refugee protection in India. But the courts in India have awarded judgments to abide by international principles on refugee protection including non-refoulement (Chimni, 2005).

However, the cardinal problem arises, when both the UNHCR and the Government of India violate their own standards and principles. While it is possible to bring the Government of India under the scrutiny of the quasi-judicial bodies like the NHRC and the judiciary, there is no such mechanism to scrutinize the UNHCR in New Delhi. Official rules and procedures have become an excuse to raise the '*veil of secrecy*' and to resort to arbitrariness at the expense of the refugees. It is a well-known fact that none of the regions of South Asia including India, Bhutan, Maldives, Nepal, Myanmar, Sri Lanka and Bangladesh is a party to the 1951 convention or to its 1967 protocol, as stated before (Oberoi, 2006). It is also true, that there are no national refugee legislations and administrative provisions, related to the protection of refugees, despite the positive example, set by India's generous naturalisation of Afghan refugees of Sikh or Hindu ethnic background in 2007 and 2008. For countries hosting refugees, local integration continues to remain a very limited option (*The Hindu*, 2009).

The ratification, of the 1951 convention relating to the status of refugees, is a statement of intent, unless it is enforceable in domestic courts. Since, the Government of India is not even considering the ratification of the 1951 Refugee Convention, its enforcement in domestic legislation or development of a refugee legal regime is a far cry. A consistent legal framework is vital to the prevention of political adhocism, which often translates into forcible repatriation for the refugees. The issue is not only development of domestic legislation, but how to ensure that both the UNHCR and the Government of India strictly abide by their own standards and principles. For the refugees, the latter remains the immediate concern and the UNHCR has manifestly failed to address the issue of protection (Oberoi, 2006).

As voluntary repatriation still remains elusive in these situations, UNHCR continues, as in 2007 and 2008, to promote resettlement as a durable solution, for most of the refugee camp population in Bangladesh, Thailand and Nepal. Within the context of strategic resettlement, special attention is also given to the protracted refugee situation in Malaysia and India. UNHCR also hopes that in 2009, resettlement countries will provide support to address the protracted situation of Afghan refugees in Iran and Pakistan – the two countries hosting the largest number of refugees, worldwide. It is also hoped that considerable progress in strategic resettlement of these case loads will open new opportunities for increased asylum space (Chaudhury, 2003).

The basic findings of the research suggest that there should be right to life with dignity and access to uniform treatment to all the refugees so far settled in India over a period of time. Civil societies need to work independently without any pressure. India requires immediate implementation of national migration and refugee laws and policies with the support of NHRC and international organisations. Whatever the case may be, as far as my understanding is concerned, I have a firm belief that in the coming days, India's refugee regime would be more loyal towards the refugees who settled in India in general and the Chakmas in particular. This also plays a more important role in the entire South Asia and brings some of the very effective policies and laws to minimize the gap of denial of the refugee rights. So far as my hypothesis is concerned, it has been proved through my field work that India's refugee regime is yet to evolve a transparent framework linking rights, laws and policies, in order to encumber the great prevarication between policies and practices. The treatment of refugees by the refugee regime, widely differs in India from state to state and is subject to much pressure from civil society groups.

Regarding migration, which is a consequence of human nature, whoever comes first and settles down, claims to be the original settler. The Chakma problem is nothing but a political and policy problem in Arunachal Pradesh, in particular and the North-East, in general. This can only be solved once both the state and centre sit together and think over deeply in a sense to solve the problem without involving any political interest. My extensive field work has proved that the Chakmas are legal migrants, particularly the second and third generations. The Chakmas fall within the ambit of the citizenship rights acts of the Constitution of India. They should be given citizenship rights as well as Scheduled Tribes status, so that they can live with dignity. The refugee regime in India should also keep in mind that the solution is democratic and not only satisfies the Chakmas but also the tribals of Arunachal Pradesh, so that conflict situations do not arise in the future.

References

Babu, Justice S. Rajendra (2008): Address as Chairperson, "National Human Rights Commission", India, at National Conference on Relief and Rehabilitation of Displaced Persons, Organised by National Human Rights Commission, at India Habitat Centre, New Delhi India, 24 March.

Bhattacharya, Swapna (2001): "The Refugee-Generating Chittagong Hill Tracts: Past, Present, and Future", in S.K. Roy (ed.), *Refugees and Human Rights*, pp. 317-44, New Delhi: Rawat Publication.

Bose, Tapan K. (2000): "India: Policies and Laws towards Refugees", 10(10), Article appeared on the website of Human Rights Solidarity, www.hrsolidarity.net.

Chakma, Suhas (1996): "Information Displayed by the Asian Centre for Human Rights", Application written by Suhas Chakma to Justice A.S. Anand, Chairman NHRC, Complaint for full implementation of the Supreme Court Judgment in the Case of NHRC *vs.* State of Arunachal Pradesh (CPW 720 of 1995) of 9 January 1996, New Delhi, p. 3.

Chaudhury, Sabyasachi Basu Ray (2003): *Uprooted Twice: Refugees from the Chittagong Hill Tracts*, in Ranabir Samaddar (ed.), Refugees and the State; Practices of Asylum and Care in India, 1947-2000, pp. 249-80, New Delhi: Sage Publication.

Chimni, B.S. (1999): "From Resettlement to Repatriation: Towards a Critical History of Durable Solutions to Refugee Problems", UNHCR.

——(2000): *International Refugee Law: A Reader*, pp. 146-52, New Delhi: Sage Publication.

——(2005): *Outside the Bounds of Citizenship: The Status of Aliens, Illegal Migrants and Refugees in India*, in Rajiv Bhargava and Helmut Reifeld (eds.), Civil Society, Public Sphere and Citizenship, Dialogues and Perceptions, pp. 277-313, New Delhi: Sage Publication.

Constituent Assembly of India (Legislative) Debates, Vol. 1, February, 1948, p. 187.

Incredible India, www.india.com.

Judgment of Supreme Court of India (1996), Original Civil Jurisdiction, Writ Petition (Civil) No. 720 of 1995, Between NHRC vs, State of Arunachal Pradesh, 9th January, New Delhi.

NHRC (2002): NHRC vs. State of Arunachal Pradesh & Annr. (720/1995) and the Present Plight of the Chakmas of Arunachal Pradesh, Committee for Citizenship Rights of the Chakmas of Arunachal Pradesh.

Oberoi, P. (2006): *Exile and Belonging: Refugees and State Policy in South Asia*, pp. 77-103, New Delhi: Oxford University Press.

Prasad, Chunnu (2006a): Victims of Partition: A Case of Chakma and Hajong Refugees of Arunachal Pradesh, *Think India*, 9(4): 59-71.

——— (2006b): Migration and the Question of Citizenship: People of Chittagong Hill Tract in Arunachal Pradesh, *Indian Journal of Political Science*, 67(3): 471-490.

——— (2007a): Arunachal Pradesh and the Inner-Outer Line Regulation of 1873-1874 of North East Frontier Agency, *Third World Impact*, 18(173): 15-19.

——— (2007b): Student Movement in Arunachal Pradesh: A Case of Chakma-Hajong Refugee Problem, *Economic and Political Weekly*, 42(15): 1373-1379.

——— (2010): *India's Refugee Regime and Resettlement Policy: A Case of Chakmas in Arunachal Pradesh*, Thesis submitted to the Centre for Political Studies, Jawaharlal Nehru University, New Delhi.

Rana, Ajit (2004): Election Commission throws Chakma Spanner, *The Pioneer*, 23 January.

Rodrigues, Valerian (2005): Citizenship and Indian Constitution, In Rajeev Bhargava and Helmut Reifeld (eds.), *Civil Society, Public Sphere and Citizenship: Dialogues and Perspectives*, pp. 209-235, New Delhi: Sage Publications.

The Hindu, 20 June, 2009.

Singh, Deepak K. (1996): The Arunachal Tangle: Migration and Ethnicity, *Journal of Peace Studies*, 3(18-19): 54.

—— (2001a): Stateless Chakmas in Arunachal Pradesh: From Rejected Peoples to Unwanted Migrants, *Social Science Research Journal*, 9(1): 47-82.

—— (2001b): Refugee question in Arunachal Pradesh: Some Conflicting Currents, *Journal of Anthropological Survey of India*, 50(4): 95-102.

Talukdar, S.P. (1988): *The Chakmas: Life and Struggle*, p. 47, New Delhi: Gyan Publishing House.

———— (1994): *Chakmas: An Embattled Tribe*, New Delhi: Uppal Publishing House.

Year Book of United Nations (2005): *Towards Development, Security and Human Rights for All*, Vol. 59, pp. 711-908, New York: United Nation Publication.

http://news.oneindia.in, urges-centre-to-resolve-contentious-refugee-issue, February 1, 2008.

22

Development Projects and Tribals: A Critical Look from Uttar Pradesh

Rudra Prasad Sahoo

Introduction

The Kaimur Range (Hills) which passes through Madhya Pradesh (MP) and Uttar Pradesh (UP) is surrounded by Chhatarpur in the west, Robertsgunj in the east, Mirzapur in the north and Rewa in the south. UP's naxal and Maoist-infested Kaimur mountain range, spreads across Sonebhadra, Mirzapur and Chandauli districts, is witnessing a silent revolution. Recently, tribal women of 500 odd villages have taken over 20,000 hectares land for cooperative farming, claiming ownership, as they are the original inhabitants of the forest. This region is now in news, because this region is said to be in the grip of coal, mineral and forest mafia. The mafia allegedly under the protection of forest and police officers indulge in illegal cutting of trees and mining of sand. Some naxal groups are also part of the nexus. The tribals have been declared encroachers in their own land. This has happened due to lack of information and communication gap among the tribals. It has created a sense of insecurity and pessimism for the future, says Fernandes. In his words: "Many of them lose hope in their future and develop a fatalistic attitude (Fernandes, 1989). The ignorance about the mainstream society and the fear of the unknown, add to their self-perception of inadequacy." In this scenario, the tribals of Kaimur region, like in any other region of India, are facing the dual problems: first, is that of a low self-image in their original habitat, where they are unable to deal with the outsiders; and second, these tribals begin a new life with a sense of powerlessness.

In the name of developmental projects, the original inhabitants are being forcefully resettled and relocated to another area. This is no ordinary crisis: this hampers the community network and can be considered a crisis of civilisations. This is a fundamental clash between our knowledge systems: of beings, of nature, wisdom, technology, and the demonic tendencies. Those who believe that development is simply materialistic, for them, the world rests on ideas of power, territories, boundaries, profit, exploitation and oppression. This popular paradigm of development has created a madness which is coterminous, with the discourse of development of rationality, with the advancement of science and technology, irrespective of the cultural, social and political ideologies of the nations.

However, India as a nation, six decades after its independence, has achieved nothing substantial. The delusion and disappointment around the much hyped notions of development, in the long run, only echoed; and the miscellany of the idea still dominates the social, economic and political discourses at the official level. Through this paper, an attempt is made to analyse the very structure of the development policy.

The established perception of development has been nothing more than a myth – a misconceived enterprise; so what is required, is to come out of these imaginary credos and take on the real challenges. Because adherence to a false-consciousness approach, based on the concept that whatever is big, capital-intensive, modern and industrial is the best, can lead to incalculable and irreparable loss to humanity. The notion of increased production and creation of wealth, against a background of national (government) interest and security, with an intention to develop the society as a whole, focuses primarily on those having land and the resources to invest. However, all this is at the cost of the disadvantaged and the poor in the society. The resources are extracted by the elites of the society; and those who are 'poor' have no involvement in this process and the so-called 'development' has not brought much meaningful change in their lives and livelihood. In fact, they are reduced to mere 'objects' of development, and are lamented as what one might call 'people out of progress'.

In such context, this paper is an endeavour to highlight some of the pertinent issues, which the tribals in the Kaimur Range of Uttar Pradesh are facing, and to explore and provide some strategy for its solution. The paper is divided into four main parts: The first part deals with the idea of the so-called 'development' found in the western literature and in the mind of the Indian policy planner; the second part deals with what development means to tribal people; the third part deals with the issues, pertaining to the Kaimur Range tribe, their problems and their recent demands; and the fourth part suggests some alternative solutions to their present problems.

The Idea of Development

Stressing to its genesis, the idea of 'development' has been mostly materialistic; and the industrial revolution, which exploited nature, and treated nature and men alike are the common points to understand the development. But in the true sense of the term, development refers to economic, social, political and cultural processes of change in human societies. Their happening is both inevitable and necessary, but the questions that they bring in their wake too need to be answered. Questions such as, what exactly is development, form a monolithic and stereotype viewpoint in conceptualising or defining development, but do not solve the very purpose of the downtrodden, who struggle every day to fulfil their basic necessities. But a relative consensus, with regards to developmental objectives, revolutionises the idea of development, which seeks to satisfy the spiritual and material needs of man. So development implies that it is for the benefit of the human beings in all aspects, tangible as well as intangible.

The dominant paradigm of 'development' is based on a belief in the superiority of the West (of their knowledge system, and their progress and achievement made in science and technology, and their culture and civilisation as a whole).

Development rhetoric, based on the triumph of western science and technologies, bewildered the whole world, during the post-war period – the 50s and 60s constitute the period of the economic and political recovery. Large amounts of capital were injected into third world countries, to strengthen their infrastructural sectors, so as to facilitate the development process (by establishing big industries). This period was marked by an emphasis in the linear, evolutionary model of modernisation, in theory as well as in praxis. The dominant model was inherently myopic; its emphasis was on industrialisation, science and technology, ruthless exploitation of natural resources, and letting loose of market forces, completely ignoring the cultural and social sensibilities of its subjects. Vandana Shiva once said, "The natural world is absent from the economic model, used by the development planner." By the late 60s and early 70s, the optimism of the western 'modernisation theory' of development began to fade, because the Indian leaders felt that the experience of the west never replicates here, as there is a large gap between the rich and the poor. The development policy, which the state adopted from the west, does not trickle down to the poor and the disadvantaged sections of the society.

From this above explanation, it is clear that the development theories, based on the western model of economic growth, were profoundly inadequate. The experience in the developing countries, particularly India, showed a polarisation between the poor and the rich classes. And, therefore, the focus shifted to the 'poor people'. The feasibility of the western paradigm of development, that has inexorably affected the common masses in India, has been questioned in the last couple of decades. In order to give consolation to the voice of the poor, an emerging paradigm of development came into the picture, in the discourse of development. Now the focus has been shifted, in favour of, well meaning individuals and communities' relationships, helping them to live in harmony with nature and to live without impoverishing or endangering future generations, leading to what has come to be known as 'sustainable development'. This was the beginning of the larger debate on: Should the dominant model of development be kept in the back seat? Has the new idea percolated to popular perception? Will people's participation bring any real change in the dominant model of development?

This emerging paradigm of development, which focuses the social aspect before establishing any new project, was debated in the early 80s and their importance was underscored at the World Summit on Social Development, held in March 1995 at Copenhagen. In this summit, the whole idea of social development acquired a new meaning. It was apparently more comprehensive than mere economic development; it aimed at the attainment of much wider social objectives: Social development in the UN quarters broadly refers to improvement in human well-being, brought about by a modification in societal conditions. Development thinking during this period had come to accept, that it should be human centred. Social change which would create a conducive atmosphere for the eradication of poverty, promotion of productive employment and acceleration of social integration, was the key to social development. Policies were to be aimed at reducing and eliminating polarisation of societies, social exclusion, unemployment and poverty, and to provide opportunities for the disadvantaged groups, to improve their living conditions (UNESCO, 1994:10).

So the construction of a new project is not a problem; but the problem that the development has created is enormous and its effects are visible on human beings over the time. Today the problem is not confined to construction of dams or industries, but they are of different types: to name a few, some are the increase in the heights of dams, careless mining induced by industrialisation, unplanned urban settlements vis-a-vis natural disasters, mega infrastructural projects, like the national road quadrangle and the river interlinking, are the list of activities that require careful planning before its implementation in a particular area. In addition, globalisation, privatisation and creation of Special Economic Zones (SEZs), are the result of contemporary manifestations of mainstream development, which is creating hindrance to achieve sustainable development.

The paradigm shift has actually exposed the inability of the established notions of development, to answer the larger economic, social, political and ethical questions. The whole discourse of the dominant model of development has created a gulf between policy and practice, besides alienating the poor from the developmental process. Moreover, the role of democracy, as a political system, has been neglected and has missed the attention of the social scientists, anthropologists and the activists alike in this whole debate. To what extent do democratic processes, decentralisation of power and local self governance reach the vulnerable and marginalised sections of the society, becomes imperative to dwell upon, irrespective of the political ideologies. The answer to this could help in countering the blind run to 'materialistic development', and to understand the phenomenon in its totality.

Development (What it Means to Disadvantaged People) and Development Debate

What development means to the disadvantaged people? Most of the developmental projects operate totally in opposite directions, making a vast majority of the Project Affected Families (PAFs) feel insecure about their lives. This is only due to poorly planned and haphazard execution of rehabilitation plans. Their resettlement and rehabilitation becomes almost difficult in the absence of a state level policy. The legislative mechanism must create some avenue for these vulnerable groups, before undertaking any grand project. Even as development creates wealth for a few, it leaves these poor masses with an irreparable sense of loss and impoverishment. And when these people make an attempt to resist, they inevitably come into conflict with the law. Already marginalised, they are further faced with the daunting task of facing the state power, and lastly by a politically articulate community, comprising mostly of an educated, urbanite middle class, impregnated with the rhetoric; whereof 'development' is synonymous with 'progress' and 'modernisation' is the panacea for all the ills.

In India, the law, relating to compulsory land acquisition for public purpose, is a more problematic one. Particularly for a developmental project, whether it is infrastructural or industrial, taking land from the poor without providing alternative means of generating livelihood, which substantially benefits the poor, has created a sense of insecurity among the marginal mass (PAFs). The government makes a decision which suits it, and never listens to the voice of these people, who are the real victims, the decision.

So, the development debate from the angle of 'real people' is that, they are the ones who actually bear its 'real costs', till long after the matter has settled for the rest, "and also touch upon its legal, social and environmental ramifications. For most part, the problem is studied through the eyeglass of a few big projects and the violence wrought in their wake".

About a decade ago, the world community came up with alternatives to the prevalent model, suggesting designs that shifted the emphasis away from the 'economic' dimension of development. The alternative visions: 'sustainable' and 'social development' effectively challenged (still to do that in praxis) the supremacy of the economic growth model. To quote Elie Wiesel, "I swore never to be silent whenever human beings endure suffering and humiliation. We must always take sides. Neutrality helps the oppressor, never the victim. Silence encourages the tormentor, never the tormented".

Development, from the foregoing conclusion would then amount to a realisation of human potential. And furthermore, the juxtaposition of human rights with development implies that, it is something that can be identified, measured and implemented. How then do we measure development? Antony N. Allot invented the 'General Felicity Index' (GFI), according to which, the measure of development is directly proportional to the measure of felicity of the individual. One measures "not just the increase in the number of factories or expansion of services, but whether life is happier and more fruitful and enjoyable for the individual. In doing so, one has to balance one factor against another".

The most pertinent questions, in such a situation, that arise here are: Does development always mean the same thing to all parties? And what are the consequences of the processes, set off by the dominant paradigm that could be acceptable as 'progression' to realise our dream of development, which was once cherished by our ancestors who brought freedom to the nation? An answer is not too forthcoming; but one aspect is more or less resolved: the need for a change in the dominant paradigm.

When the whole issue of development is debated in different forums, its impact on culture has never been given any importance. The search, for a homogenous process of development, has been accompanied by a deepening erosion of cultural identities. The western paradigms have, adversely, affected the cultural distinctiveness of the developing countries, and the 'modernised' version of development has succeeded in establishing the hegemony of essentially occidental cultural constructs, as if the destiny of the West is to civilize and convert the backward peoples of the earth, to the truths, vouchsafed to the West alone. The issue of obdurate traditions and cultural constructs, that resist change, are sometimes cited as reasons for the failure of development strategies premised on economic growth. It must, however, be remembered that not everything in tradition is negative and therefore it would be imprudent to reject tradition as a whole, in order to facilitate an alien culture that promotes gross materialism and personal consumption, at the cost of social justice, which by no means is an assertion of the "everything's great about our culture", syndrome but an acceptance of the fact that culture *per se* has critical functions that development does not offer adequate replacement for, and, therefore, it cannot be dispensed with to promote growth. In fact, any worthwhile growth would, by necessary implication, have to take into account relevant cultural factors, and coexist with them.

In connection with social development, two allied concepts have found mention in the current debate: that of 'human development' and 'sustainable development'. The concept of human development implies people-centered development, where people are empowered to make their own choices. It emphasizes the relevance of local knowledge and values as guidelines and tools for making these choices, thereby equipping people with the requisite knowledge and resources to take charge of their own destinies. Sustainable development, on the other hand, is its extrapolation into a broader idea as is very aptly and ideally elucidated by the UNDP Report (1994; 4): "Sustainable development is development that not only regenerates economic growth but distributes its benefits equitably; that regenerates the environment rather than destroys it; that empowers people rather providing their participation in decisions affecting them. It is development that is pro-poor, pro-nature, pro-jobs and pro-women and pro-children."

A major step, in the direction of human development, was the articulation and adoption of the Millennium Development Goals (MDGs), by the UN General Assembly in 2000, at a special meeting attended by 147 heads of state or government. The aim of MDGs are as follows: (1) eradication of extreme poverty and hunger; (2) achieving universal primary education; (3) promotion of gender equality and empowerment of women; (4) reducing child mortality; (5) improving maternal health; (6) combating HIV/AIDs and other diseases, such as, malaria; (7) ensuring environmental sustainability; and (8) developing a global partnership for development. These goals have sought to reorder priorities across the development spectrum.

The policy planner must keep all these issues in mind, before planning for any rehabilitation of this vulnerable section. Emphasing on the importance of policy planning, David Marsden says: "Baseline surveys are important for a number of reasons. They should provide an accurate record, of who the project affected persons are, how they gain their livelihoods and also create the boundaries of entitlement by delineating all those, who are eligible for benefits and by definition, excluding all others" (Verma, 2004). In the Indian context, where illegal and unauthorised encroachment is a major issue, such boundaries of entitlement allow the cost of resettlement and rehabilitation action plan to be more accurately gauged. The major problem in India is that very few socio-economic baseline surveys have been undertaken in the past in the project, affected site. As a result, the people, who are not really affected out of the development project are the real beneficiaries, while the victims lead a more pathetic life than ever before. As the tribes are more innocent than other people and almost all are illiterate, their language is a barrier to have their grievances redressed before the governance system. In such a situation, the tribes are the worst victims, who not only lose their dwelling place but also the very hope of living on the earth. Particularly, the women folk (within the tribal community) are the worst victims of this process. In the tribal areas, women are responsible for collecting food, fuel, fodder, etc. They are more mobile in collecting household management goods from the forest. But once they are deserted, the government policy does not give any legitimate claim to lead a secure life. The biggest problem is that the policy in Uttar Pradesh is even more gender biased (Singh, 1992). If a couple holds property separately, they will be considered as one unit and will receive only one package. In this situation, the women forego their right to the package, as the government gives land only to the head of the family: the man.

The recent wave of globalisation has touched each and every national boundary across the globe. In India and particularly in backward states like Uttar Pradesh, globalisation's effect is visible. The increasing demand to turn land to Special Economic Zones (SEZs) and other industrial-related projects is a threat to the vulnerable sections, because they will lose their assets and means of livelihood to such projects, which pushes them to further vulnerability.

Tribals of Kaimur Range of Uttar Pradesh: Their Problems and Demands

The natural resources and the forest, spread over Robertsgunj, Mirzapur, Sonebhadra, Chandauli, and other forests bordering Uttar Pradesh, fall under the Kaimur Range. This area is the original homeland of the Kol tribes. Their population is very less, and they live in small and scattered settlements. The forest and small fence characterizes the hilly and undulating landscape, and the tribal people of the region were mainly engaged in subsistence agriculture and collecting minor products from the forest.

Tribal Problems

Pre-independence

During the colonial rule, Lord Cornwallis, the then viceroy, introduced "Permanent Settlement" in India. This rule was also applied to this region, which curtailed the freedom of the Kol tribes. But their real alienation from their inhabited land was started, when the local king introduced an institutional framework, which debarred the tribe from their own rights.

In addition to this, the rising population demand and pressure on the land also reflected in this region, when people from Mirzapur and adjoining districts, particularly the upper caste families, migrated to this forest area and reclaimed the land, by providing a nominal gift to the Raja of this locality. In this way, the flow of migration increased and the forest land was converted into agricultural land. In the meantime, large number of tribals who belonged to Kol tribes, agreed to work as bonded labourers for the migrant agriculturists. This added a new dimension to their life, from emancipation to subjugation. Their ownership of land had changed into a patron-client relationship.

After Independence

After independence, the region started getting the attention of the planners, basically for its large coal deposits, which could be utilised for generating power for the urban-industrial development of the country.

In conformity with this national goal, the region was opened up by a rail-road connection. Rihand Reservoir, also known as Govind Ballabh Pant Sagar, has proved to be a boon for the people, especially the farmers. The land has become fertile, particularly, on the banks of the reservoir. After the construction of the Govind Ballabh Pant Sagar in the 1960s, a number of super thermal power plants came up; some large energy-dependent heavy industrial plants were installed; and the coal mines rapidly raised their production, to meet the growing demand of these plants. Construction, of three dams in quick succession, brought a big change to these regions. First, in the mid-1950, on the River Belan, the Barundha Dam was constructed. Next, in mid-1960, Sirsi Dam was constructed on the River Sirsi, and finally in 1970, the Adva Dam was constructed on the River Adva.

By late 1980s, this region became one of the most important power-generating centres in the country, feeding the urban-industrial centres of the north, central and western India, and thus emerged as an area of strategic importance for the whole country.

But the construction of all these dams did not benefit the tribals of this region; instead, the water flowed to other areas for irrigation purpose. During the time of construction of the dam, the government acquired large patches of land; a part of whatever was left was occupied by the migrants, while the Forest Department became active to preserve the remaining land. Thus, the native inhabitants, the Kol tribe, led a helpless life as they were left without a patch of land. The very survival of these people has been in danger since then.

During mid-1970s, the issue of tribal land and its distribution through *Gram Samaj* had brought some hope for the tribals. But due to misdeed and fraud character of the functionary Revenue Department of the government, the land records provided a legitimate claim for the tribals to occupy their land – the revenue officials re-allocated the plots to persons, who provided more money (Rath *et al.*, 2009).

Even the Ceiling on Land Holding Act, 1960, provides several exemptions. The big land-owners transferred a substantial part of their land, in different names to avoid sealing, and the land remained in their possession. The tribals, who are illiterate and innocent, were never interested to go through the cumbersome procedure in the administrative system, to make a *patta; the* legal hassles were very difficult for them to understand, and so they did not go through the process to claim the land as their own.

Present Demand

Recently, Uttar Pradesh's Sonbhadra District has become the epicentre of a major land rights struggle. This struggle has been organised, under the banner of the Kaimur *Kshetra Majdoor Mahila Kisan Sangarsh Samiti* (KKMMKSS). The KKMMKSS won a land mark victory, not just for the local movement, but also for other land struggles across the country. With the strong and persistent political pressure, created by the tribes in this region, the Mayawati Government was forced to withdraw charges on activists, under the draconian National Security Act, within 10 days. In a historic decision, the State Government also agreed to the demands of the Kaimur *Samiti* for land distribution to the Dalit and Adivasi families.

For several years now, the Kaimur Region and several districts, of eastern Uttar Pradesh, have been the focus of a struggle between the Forest Department and the forest dwellers, mostly the landless Adivasis and Dalits, for the return of the land, which the local community claims as their traditional *Gram Samaj* land, had been procured by the Forest Department. The KKMMKSS, a movement led by women, Dalits and Adivasis, has been at the forefront of this struggle. Repeated protests and clashes have ensued, while the Forest Department refused to negotiate the issue or recognize the rights of local communities.

The local landowners and forest officials, in nexus with the police, have done every bit to suppress the movement, by branding the Dalits and Adivasis, involved in this peaceful struggle, as Naxalites. Roma, a woman leader of the KKMMKSS, and a steering committee member of the National Forum of Forest People and Forest Workers (NFFPFW), along with three other KKMMKSS activists, Shanta Bhattacharya, Lalita Devi and Shyamlal Paswan, were picked up by the police from Robertsgunj in Sonebhadra District, on the 3rdand 5th of August, while campaigning for the implementation of the Forests Rights Act. Whereas, all arrested were charged under IPC 144, 143, 447, 5/26 and 63 of the Indian Forest Act, Roma was also charged under 120B of the IPC and the National Security Act. This was a clear attempt to demoralize the members and activists of the movement. However, this failed to dampen the spirit of the struggling people, especially that of the women force. They vehemently opposed the police action and agitated and blocked the main highway for hours and continued the *dharna* at the District Court premises, throughout this period. The local communities, successfully controlled the 5000 acres land, which they had recaptured earlier, standing firm against an all-out attack by the police and the Forest

Department, in alliance with the local mafia. This is remarkable and it reaffirms the strength of struggle truly owned by the local people's organisation. The struggle, continued strongly, despite the fact that the police registered FIRs against 300 people, half of whom were women. The struggle made it impossible for the UP Government to ignore the demands and on 17th August, Chief Minister Mayawati herself signed orders, directing the withdrawal of charges under NSA. In the matter of other local cases assurance was given by the state to file a final report and quash all the cases.

The core issue in this struggle was the enactment of the Forest Rights Act 2006. The passing of the Act by the Parliament in December 2006, created an enthusiasm among the forest dwellers, who have been fighting for their rights for centuries. They could see the dawn of a new era, which would help them liberate themselves, from the landlordism of the Forest Department in the forest areas. At the same time, through this legislation, a strong possibility of unity of forest dwelling communities is also emerging, as Adivasis and Dalits are coming together against the local landlords and the Forest Department quite decisively. The emerging situation is definitely threatening the very basis of this unholy alliance between the Forest Department, the local landlords, contractors and the police. Even, as the struggle, for land and for withdrawal of false charges on all activists, continues in Sonebhadra, this experience and victory holds significant lessons. It underlines that, where land has not been easily given to the landless, they have to and will take possession by themselves through democratic process and sustained effort. It may take a longer time, but it has to come. There is no other shortcut.

Alternative Strategy: Indian Policy Planning at a Glance

The major setback for policy panning in India is that, only when the international bodies force them, they implement the policy. For example, the Government of India has come, with a National Policy on Resettlement and Rehabilitation (NPRR) for project affected persons in 2003 (Gazette of India, 2004). Before that for some state, they adopted a policy during 1980s. It is assumed that India formulated this policy in 2003 under pressure from the World Bank. The NPRR of 2003 was published in the Gazette of India on February 17, 2004. Much deliberation and debate had taken place after its publication. Some serious researchers and experts opined that both NPRR and Land Acquisition Act (1894) have conflicting clauses, and that this law serves the vested interests of land-acquiring bodies. Even the NPRR-2003 is criticised, because the land will be acquired from the individuals for public purpose and in return he/she would be compensated monetarily. This is again the gamble of influential people. Any how, this policy lays down the minimum norms for rehabilitation of the affected persons and broadly outlines an approach, and devises an institutional framework to achieve the objective.

Even the Land Acquisition Act has serious shortcomings, which need much attention in the present time, to revise and reformulate. The Act does not contain any specific provision dealing with resettlement, in other words, in relation to income resettlement of persons whose land is acquired for public purpose. It also does not allow for compensation (except for houses) for landless labourers, artisans, and those sharing the use of land without legal rights. Even the method of valuation of land is not a satisfactory one. The Act also computes the value of land through the sale statistic method. But NRRP (2007) has come out with a novel feature, known as Social Impact Assessment (SIA) for displacement (Mishra, 2009), in addition to skill development and preference for a project job. But despite this progressive policy, the requirements of the people, who are affected by displacement and forceful evacuation, are met. The problem is that, the national policy defines a cut-off threshold tied to the number of families that need to be displaced, for the policy to be triggered. Once the national policy is adopted, there is no guarantee that the condition of the affected family will improve. In order to give some concession, the government comes out with a plan, to provide food items at a minimum rate on showing their ration card. But the food material, which is distributed through the Public Distribution System (PDS), never reaches these people. A stringent legal action, along with community rights over government sanction scheme to these tribes, will bell them out of these crises for the time being. For achieving the long term goal, the government must listen to the people who are facing the real crisis. In such a situation, the government must empower the affected people, by giving them the political right to choose their leader and come out with a consensus, of what will be better for them. Because once land is taken away from these people, they feel helpless. So land and nature (forest), which are synonymous with tribal culture must be given due regards, so that sustainable development will be achieved along with preserving the legitimate right of the tribals over the forest land. The government must discourage mafia and other big corporation houses to maintain restraint of the forest land. In such a situation, awareness and creating an opinion, conducive to their socio-cultural setting, is indispensable, to make the affected people lead a life, full of peace and tranquillity.

Conclusion

Land has both instrumental and constitutive value for people. The tribals, who dwell in the forest, are happy with their own civilisation and culture. But the so-called growth resulting from a development policy, adopted by the government, not only brings misery to their life, but also makes them handicapped; and when they protest for their occupied land, they are beaten mercilessly by the police, the so-called coercive apparatus of government.

Hence, displacement is only merely confined to the physical removal of someone from their home; it can be a deprivation of productive land, or other income generating assets, or the displacement of collectivists, which causes an economic crisis for all or most of those affected with sudden disarticulation, and sometimes also triggers a political crisis, as it has happened in the Kaimur Region. It is a complex phenomenon, as Upendra Baxi has put it, which is not a one-time event but a series of happenings affecting human lives in myriad ways. The tribals of this region want the implementation of the Forest Act 2006, which gives community rights to the tribals, over forest land for their livelihood. And whatever welfare policy, the government provides them in each successive plan, to fulfil their bare minimum needs in the form of distribution of food, is controlled by the upper caste *pradhan*, while the food grains, which come from the government never reach the disadvantaged mass. To realise a policy which will certainly bring hope to this exploited tribals, the government, must listen to their voice and implement such policies, where they must be a part, to deal with the problem of resettlement and displacement issues, to make the development model a real success.

References

Basu, M. (1996): "Development and Discontent: Where lies the Hope?" *Mainstream*, Oct. 5.

Baxi, U. (1989): "Notes on Constitutional and Legal Aspects of Displacement and Rehabilitation", In Walter Fernandez and Enakshi Ganguly Thakral (eds.), *Development, Displacement and Rehabilitation*, pp. 164, New Delhi: Indian Social Institute.

Choudhary, K. (2000): "Development Dilemma: Resettlement of Gir Maldharis", *Economic and Political Weekly*, 35(30): 2662-2668.

Fernandes, Walter (1996): "Resettlement Studies and Specific Issues: Sharing in the benefits of Development, Key Note Address, Refugee Studies Programme", Organised by University of Oxford, 9-13, September.

Gadgil, Madhav and Ramchandra Guha (1995): *Ecology and Equity*, New Delhi: Penguin.

Government of India (2004): "National Policy on Resettlement and Rehabilitation for Project Affected Families-2003", Government of India, Ministry of Rural Development (Department of Land Resources), Published in the Gazettes of India, Extraordinary, Part-1, Section 1, No. 46, Date 17 February 2004.

Mehta, Mona (2001): "In New Tehri, People Long for their Gods", *The Times of India*, December 20.

Murickan Jose *et al.* (2003): *Development-Induced Development: Case of Kerala,* Jaipur: Rawat Publications.

Patwardhan Amrita, "Dams and Tribal Peoples in India" contributing paper prepared for thematic review, World Commission for Dams, accessed from http://www.dams.org/

Pande, G.C. (2003): *Social Sustainability and Economic Development,* New Delhi: Anamika Publisher.

Ramnathan, Usha (2002): "Common Land and Common Property Resources", in Praveen K. Jha (ed.), *Land Reforms in India: Volume 7 Issues of Equity in Rural Madhya Pradesh*, New Delhi: Sage Publications.

Sarin, Madhu (2005): "The Scheduled Tribes (Recognition of Forest Rights) Bill 2005: Undoing Historical Injustice to Tribals", *Lawyers' Collective*, 20 (6), pp. 8-15.

Shankar, K. (2006): "Land Alienation among Tribals in Uttar Pradesh", in Govinda Chandra Rath (ed.), *Tribal Development in India, The Contemporary Debate,* New Delhi: Sage Publication.

Tripathy, A. (2009): "Expolited Tribals being Forced into Revolt", *The Times of India*, September, 27.

United Nations Millennium Declaration (2000), G.A. Res. 55/2, U.N. GAOR, 55th Sess., Supp. No. 49, U.N. Doc. A/RES/55/2 available:www.un.org/millennium/declaration/ares552e.htm

Verma, M.K. (2004): *Development, Displacement and Resettlement,* Jaipur: Rawat Publication.

Vidyarthi, L.P. & Binay Kumar Rai (1985): *The Tribal Culture of India,* New Delhi: Concept Publishing House.

Yadav, A. (2007): Development-Induced Displacement,http://www.doccentre.org/docweb/development- induced-displacement.php

List of Contributors

Aparajita Mishra, Research Scholar, Department of Anthropology, University of Hyderabad, Hyderabad, Andhra Pradesh.

Bhaskar Majumder, Professor in Economics, G.B. Pant Social Science Institute, Allahabad-211019.

Chunnu Prasad, Academic Officer, National Institute of Open Schooling, Department of Education, MHRD, Government of India.

D.C. Sah, Professor and Director, MPISSR, 6, Bharatpuri Institutional Area, Ujjain - 456010.

Debendranath Jena, Professor and Head, Department of Sociology, Utkal University, Vani Vihar, Bhubaneswar, Orissa.

Falendra Kumar Sudan, Associate Professor, Department of Economics, University of Jammu, Jammu, Jammu and Kashmir-180006.

Hema Banerjee, Head, Department of Economics, J.N. Government College, P.O. Shadipur, Port Blair-744106, Andaman.

Kabita Kumari Sahu, Lecturer in Economics, North Orissa University, Baripada, Orissa.

Kamal K. Misra, Director, Indira Gandhi Rashtriya Manav Sangrahalaya, Shamla Hills, Bhopal (M.P.)

Madhusmita Kar, Senior Lecturer, Department of Humanities, Purushottam Institute of Engineering and Technology, Rourkela, Orissa.

Mrutuyanjaya Sahu, Academic Research Fellow, Centre for Public Policy, Indian Institute of Management (IIM), Bangalore.

N. Venkata Sivaiah, Research Scholar, Department of Anthropology, University of Hyderabad, Hyderabad, Andhra Pradesh.

Narendra K. Behera, Department of Economics, Larambha College, Larambha, Bargarh, Orissa-768102.

Nata Kishore Mishra, Social Activist, Centre for Integrated Rural and Tribal Development, Sundargarh, Orissa.

Nanda Kishore M.S., Consultant, Administrative Staff College of India, Bella Vista, Hyderabad, Andhra Pradesh.

Nihar Ranjan Mishra, is Assistant Professor of Sociology at National Institute of Technology, Rourkela, Odisha.

Nilakantha Panigrahi, Faculty in Anthropology, Nabakrushna Choudhury Centre for Development Studies, (ICSSR and Government. of Orissa sponsored), Bhubaneswar-751013.

Premananda Panda, Professor in Anthropology, Department of Anthropology, Sambalpur University, Sambalpur, Orissa.

R.K. Kumbhar, Assistant Professor, Department of Economics, Sambalpur University, Sambalpur, Orissa.

Raju Narayana Swamy I.A.S. Secretary to Government of Kerala, Parliamentary Affairs Department.

Rudra Prasad Sahoo, Assistant Professor and Assistant Director, Center for the Study of Social Exclusion and Inclusive Policy (CSSEIP), Babasaheb Bhim Rao Ambedkar Central University, Lucknow, Uttar Pradesh.

S.K. Biswas, Associate Professor, P.G. Dept. of Political Science, JN Government, College, P.O. Shadipur, Port Blair - 744106, Andaman.

S.N. Tripathy, Professor of Economics, Gokhale Institute of Politics and Economics, Pune-411004, Maharashtra.

Saswat Kishore Mishra, Research Scholar, Dept. of Humanities and Social Science, IIT Kharagpur.

Sujit Kumar Mishra, Assistant Professor, Council for Social Development, (Institute of ICSSR, GOI and RBI), Rajendranagar, Hyderabad, Andhra Pradesh.

Vinita Pandey, Academic Consultant, Department of Sociology, Nizam College, Osmania University, Hyderabad.

Index

N

V